Transforming
Settler States

Zimbabwe

Northern Ireland

Transforming Settler States

Communal Conflict and Internal Security in Northern Ireland and Zimbabwe

Ronald Weitzer

UNIVERSITY OF CALIFORNIA PRESS
Berkeley · Los Angeles · Oxford

University of California Press
Berkeley and Los Angeles, California

University of California Press, Ltd.
Oxford, England

© 1990 by
The Regents of the University of California

Library of Congress Cataloging-in-Publication Data

Weitzer, Ronald John.
    Transforming settler states : communal conflict and internal
security in Northern Ireland and Zimbabwe / Ronald Weitzer.
        p.   cm.
    Includes bibliographical references.
    ISBN 0-520-06490-9 (alk. paper)
        1. Internal security—Northern Ireland.   2. Northern Ireland—
Politics and government—1969–   3. Internal security—Zimbabwe.
4. Zimbabwe—Politics and government—1965–1979.   5. Zimbabwe—
Politics and government—1979–1980.   6. Zimbabwe—Politics and
government—1980–   I. Title.
HV8197.5.A2W45 1990
363.2′ 09416—dc20   89-20692
                                                                          CIP

Printed in the United States of America

1 2 3 4 5 6 7 8 9

The paper used in this publication meets the minimum requirements of
American National Standard for Information Sciences—Permanence of
Paper for Printed Library Materials, ANSI Z39.48-1984.   ∞™

Contents

Tables

Preface

Max Weber described the state as a system of "organized domination" that "claims the monopoly of the legitimate use of physical force within a given territory." That coercive structures are quintessential elements of state power the scholarly literature often seems to take for granted, but few studies systematically examine internal security systems.

This study pays special attention to the coercive dimensions of state power in two societies with histories of settler rule. Settler societies tend to be "communally divided": fractured politically and socially along racial, ethnic, or religious lines. The dominant communal bloc consists of settlers and their descendants who typically build a highly sectarian internal security apparatus to preempt or suppress threats from the indigenous population. The transformation of settler states remains deficient insofar as the security establishment of the old regime remains intact; lasting substantive democratization requires a radical overhaul of inherited security structures.

This work analyzes the rise and breakdown of settler states in Northern Ireland and Rhodesia/Zimbabwe and proposes an explanatory model for understanding the conditions of change and continuity in internal security systems after the dissolution of settler rule. In Northern Ireland and Zimbabwe settler rule was replaced in 1972 and 1980, respectively. These cases represent very different routes away from settler rule and distinct outcomes under new political orders.

In the interest of examining larger questions and themes in comparative perspective, the empirical chapters necessarily sacrifice some of the specificity and thoroughness possible in a single-case study. Although I present substantial material on each society, my overriding aim is to demonstrate the value of a particular analytic framework applicable to other cases. The model sectarian security system discussed in Chapter 1 and settler state described in Chapter 2, I argue, apply to other settler societies such as South Africa, Liberia, and Israel, to which occasional comparisons are drawn throughout the book.

The study is based on fieldwork in Northern Ireland and Zimbabwe. Unfortunately, the collection of data on matters of state security and politically sensitive issues is fraught with difficulties. Many of the best potential sources are often inaccessible: cabinet minutes, classified documents, or key elites who refuse to grant interviews. The data collected are therefore destined to be incomplete. Aware of such problems at the outset of my research, I hoped that conditions in Zimbabwe—two years after independence was declared—might yield freer research access than had been the case under the white Rhodesian regime. My expectations were only partially accurate: several data sources had been destroyed, had been removed from the country before independence, or were otherwise unavailable. Collecting material on the new regime was trickier still, given the incumbent government's acute sensitivity to any kind of scrutiny. Nevertheless, considerable information was obtained from government publications, parliamentary debates, newspapers, and the reports of official commissions of inquiry and independent human rights organizations. Identical sources were examined in Northern Ireland, where the research climate was considerably more favorable. The documentary materials were complemented with in-depth interviews in both settings. Given the subject matter, the specific findings on both societies should be treated cautiously, but I believe the data presented here are sufficient for the purposes of addressing the larger themes of the book.

Documentary research was conducted in Zimbabwe at the National Archives, the Library of Parliament, the University of Zimbabwe, and the Ministry of Information Library; in Northern Ireland at the Public Records Office, the Linenhall Library, and Queen's University; and in England at the Institute of Commonwealth Studies Library and the Public Records Office.

I carried out approximately fifty intensive semistructured interviews in both countries with former and incumbent judges, legislators, cabinet ministers, senior civil servants, police and military officials, and leaders of political parties, human rights organizations, and the media. In some cases I was successful at interviewing the most senior official in the agency under investigation; in others I spoke to less senior officials; in a few cases, requests for interviews were flatly rejected. Interviews were arranged either directly by phone or after letters of introduction that briefly described the purposes of the research. After the initial interviews, snowball sampling was used to generate names of prospective interviewees.

The interviews explored, inter alia, decision-making processes, assessments of security problems and requirements, and assessments of legal and institutional arrangements and actual or hypothetical reforms. I geared each interview to the particular respondents in their official capacities, and each informant made a different and unique contribution to the study. Every effort was made to crosscheck the interview findings with data from other interviews and documents. Gaps in documentary sources were, in turn, addressed in the course of interviewing. Some informants agreed to a second interview, and others responded in writing to specific follow-up questions that I mailed after returning to the United States.

As is common in intensive interviewing, I gathered much interview material that does not appear in the text. With a few exceptions, however, the interviews not directly cited offered important insights into larger issues, stimulated new research questions, helped test working hypotheses, and gave unique meaning to specific events and actors' constructions of reality.

Although many informants gave me permission to name them, in most cases I have preserved their anonymity; only in cases where someone's identity could not be disguised, because there was only one such person (a prime minister), have I named names. As interested parties, many of my respondents may disagree with some of the arguments and conclusions in this work, but I remain deeply grateful for their insights and hospitality. In addition to their observations and information, these informants brought the subject matter to life as no other source can.

From August 1982 through June 1983, I was a research associate at the Center for Applied Social Sciences at the University of Zimbabwe in Harare, and I am grateful to the center's director, Marshall Murphree, for his support and encouragement. In the summers of 1983 and 1984, I was a research fellow at the Institute of Irish Studies at Queen's University in Belfast. I returned in 1986 for follow-up research. Support for the initial research came from the Africa Program of the Social Science Research Council, the Institute of International Studies at the University of

California, Berkeley, the Law and Social Science Program of the National Science Foundation, and the Institute for the Study of World Politics. The faculty enrichment committee of the University of Puget Sound supported a return visit to Zimbabwe in 1987.

For their insightful suggestions on parts of this work, I wish to thank Adrian Guelke, Leon Grunberg, William Kornhauser, Norma Kriger, Carl Rosberg, Philip Selznick, Neil Smelser, Steven Tuch, Michael Watts, Laurie Wermuth, and Lois West. Michael Burawoy deserves special thanks for his enthusiastic support for the project from its inception; I deeply appreciate his penetrating criticisms and suggestions. I am also indebted to David Page for his encouragement and assistance.

I am grateful to Cambridge University Press for permission to reprint parts of my article "In Search of Regime Security: Zimbabwe since Independence," *Journal of Modern African Studies* 22, no. 4 (December 1984), in Chapters 4 and 6, and to *Comparative Politics* for permission to use revised sections of "Contested Order: The Struggle over British Security Policy in Northern Ireland," *Comparative Politics* 19, no. 3 (April 1987), in Chapter 7.

CHAPTER 1

Sectarian Security Systems

Structure and Transformation

In the past decade surprising numbers of authoritarian states have yielded to democratic experiments, primarily in Latin America and Southern Europe. The process has awakened academic interest in transitions to democracy—in the causes of regime breakdown and the dynamics of the transition. The literature has accorded much less attention to outcomes under the new order.

Of the factors affecting transitions to democracy, coercive institutions have attracted little scholarly attention.[1] Their neglect is a major theoretical deficiency: not only do most authoritarian regimes rely on highly repressive forces, but the latter often assume a critical role in the breakdown of an authoritarian order and the vitality of any new democratic experiment. Most new postauthoritarian regimes immediately face an unreconstructed security establishment whose residual power and resistance to its own reform and to meaningful political democratization are often decisive. Forces within this sector have frustrated efforts in many transitional societies to institutionalize the rule of law and standards of human rights, thus reversing the process of democratic consolidation. Thoroughgoing change of a repressive security apparatus seems to be a precondition for genuine democratization.

---

1. Exceptions are two recent works on Brazil: Maria Helena Moreira Alves, *State and Opposition in Military Brazil* (Austin: University of Texas Press, 1985); and Alfred Stepan, *Rethinking Military Politics: Brazil and the Southern Cone* (Princeton: Princeton University Press, 1988).

This book examines the pivotal role of internal security systems in building and transforming two distinctive communally divided societies, Northern Ireland and Zimbabwe. In these societies—fractured along racial, ethnic, linguistic, or religious lines—one group systematically dominates political and economic relations.[2] After outlining the key features of the sectarian security system that lies at the core of these states, I posit conditions for their liberalization in societies where a regime ostensibly committed to democratic reconstruction has assumed power. In Chapters 6 and 7 I apply this explanatory model to our two cases.

STATES AND INTERNAL SECURITY SYSTEMS

The paramount purpose of the modern state is to protect its inhabitants from internal and external threats. While the concept of "national security" is elastic and ambiguous,[3] the "primacy of national security among the responsibilities of government" is commonly considered axiomatic.[4] The security sector of a state, that cluster of organs with direct responsibility for domestic order and external defense, is a state's inner core, the locus of its ultimate power. Unfortunately, state security structures have received far less scholarly attention than they deserve—because such sensitive and secretive institutions are difficult to research or because they are often viewed instrumentally, as tools of political or economic interests rather than as dynamic forces. The neglect is particularly glaring with respect to coercive institutions in communally divided societies where, an analyst of South Africa concluded, it often seems that "so much of politics is reducible to sheer brute force and the application of state coercion."[5]

This theoretical lacuna typifies every major perspective in political sociology, including the *state-centered* paradigm.[6] An ideal point of de-

2. Milton J. Esman, "The Management of Communal Conflict," *Public Policy* 21 (Winter 1973). Intracommunal cleavages notwithstanding, the great divide is intercommunal (see Alvin Rabushka and Kenneth Shepsle, *Politics in Plural Societies* [Columbus, Ohio: Merrill, 1972]).

3. Arnold Wolfers, " 'National Security' as an Ambiguous Symbol," *Political Science Quarterly* 67, no. 4 (December 1952): 481–502; Barry Buzan, *People, States, and Fear: The National Security Problem in International Relations* (Chapel Hill: University of North Carolina Press, 1983).

4. Richard Smoke, "National Security Affairs," in *Handbook of Political Science*, ed. F. Greenstein and N. Polsby (Reading, Pa.: Addison-Wesley, 1975), 8:248.

5. Philip Frankel, *Pretoria's Praetorians: Civil-Military Relations in South Africa* (Cambridge: Cambridge University Press, 1984), p. xii.

6. Robert R. Alford and Roger Friedland, *Powers of Theory: Capitalism, the State, and Democracy* (Cambridge: Cambridge University Press, 1985).

parture for our analysis, this perspective conceptualizes the state as a network of formal organizations that claim authority over and resolve conflicts within a specific territory, exercise coercive power, and have distinctive political and institutional interests.[7] Highlighting the relative autonomy of the state from social forces, the state-centered model stresses the state's operational integrity, material objectives, and ideological goals; it holds that the state functions both as an "organization-for-itself" and as a servant of outside actors.[8] As a dynamic force in its own right, the state not only responds to social pressures with appropriate outputs but also advances certain interests, molds outside demands, fosters compliance with state policy, frees itself from societal constraints, and engages in other autonomy-enhancing strategies.[9]

Despite the state-centered paradigm's Weberian origin—which sees the monopoly of legitimate force as central in defining the modern state—the use of coercive power has attracted little theoretical attention. This study offers a fresh perspective on this vital area of state power.

An internal security sector or system refers to the cluster of organizations with direct responsibility for internal security and domestic order. Included within this inner citadel of state power are the intelligence services, the military (in its domestic duties), the police, specialized security units, and the commanding heights of decision making within the executive branch (e.g., a cabinet-level security committee, a national security council).[10]

The security sector can be understood as the core of the state because it is the locus of ultimate coercive power; it has a unique mandate and capacity to defend the nation-state from mortal threats; and the remainder of the state depends for its existence on the security sector's survival. Once the core has been captured or crippled by an enemy, the executive branch and other state organs become vulnerable to a hostile takeover. Having this vital role, security systems throughout the world feature

---

7. These include domestic order, territorial defense, legitimation, extraction of revenue, and basic ideological commitments.

8. Theda Skocpol, *States and Social Revolutions* (Cambridge: Cambridge University Press, 1979), p. 27; see also Eric Nordlinger, *On the Autonomy of the Democratic State* (Cambridge, Mass.: Harvard University Press, 1981); Stephen Skowronek, *Building a New American State: The Expansion of National Administrative Capacities 1877–1920* (Cambridge: Cambridge University Press, 1982); Peter Evans, Dietrich Rueschemeyer, and Theda Skocpol, eds., *Bringing the State Back In* (Cambridge: Cambridge University Press, 1985).

9. Nordlinger (*Autonomy*) draws special attention to these autonomy-enhancing techniques.

10. Excluded are departments that have some input into security matters but no direct responsibility for this function.

common properties: a tendency toward secrecy, autonomy from outside scrutiny and accountability, and a greater insulation from spending cuts than other state bureaucracies.[11]

Notwithstanding these commonalities, there is significant cross-national variation in the structural, ideological, and operational dimensions of security systems. Ideal types range from the liberal to the totalitarian. In the latter category—in the Soviet Union, for example— "'security' aspects are perceived to be present in virtually all aspects of Soviet life" and almost "the entire Soviet population is the target" of its security apparatus.[12] In the liberal system associated with democratic states, the opposite would obtain: threats would be narrowly defined and the targets few. Falling somewhere between these two types are the various authoritarian systems—autocracies, oligarchies, and military dictatorships. We focus on another form of authoritarianism, settler rule, and its sectarian security system. Characteristic of settler (as well as other communally divided) societies, this security system is designed to perpetuate racial, ethnic, or religious domination through the suppression of threats from the subordinate population.

A sectarian security system displays the following features:

• a concentration of power and resources within the security sector, which contributes to its *autonomous* position over other state branches;

• a tendency to pursue order and maintain relations of domination in a highly *repressive* fashion, unleavened by considerations of justice, legitimacy, and basic human rights;

• a *partisan* orientation on behalf of the dominant sector of society, instead of the collective interests of the wider population or the nation-state.

Its autonomy and repressive features also typify other authoritarian polities, but its communally partisan orientation is specific to the sectarian model. Let us examine each of these dimensions in greater depth.

11. See Nicole Ball, *Security and Economy in the Third World* (Princeton: Princeton University Press, 1988).

12. Jeffrey Richelson, *Sword and Shield: The Soviet Intelligence and Security Apparatus* (Cambridge, Mass.: Ballinger, 1986), pp. 39, 247. See also Alexander Dallin and George Breslauer, *Political Terror in Communist Systems* (Stanford: Stanford University Press, 1970); Zbigniew Brzezinski, *The Permanent Purge: Politics in Soviet Totalitarianism* (Cambridge, Mass.: Harvard University Press, 1956).

INTRASTATE AUTONOMY

The security core typically enjoys greater insulation both within the state and from civil society than other state sectors.[13] Yet the relative power and autonomy of this branch vary significantly across time and place. It may be omnipotent, so shielded from other state branches that it constitutes a formidable state-within-a-state, its agencies "independent centers of power . . . isolated from moderating social contexts and capable of resisting political authority."[14] This situation reflects either the political subordination of judicial and legislative branches or their active collusion with the security establishment.

In sectarian and other authoritarian systems, security agencies have tremendous political influence, elite status, and access to state resources.[15] Not only is the security branch privileged and autonomous in these states, it often dominates other agencies. At the extreme, it may operate above the law and be "empowered to control unilaterally other bodies of the state and the civil society."[16] South Africa, for example, has witnessed "the enthronement of the security authorities as a lawless power in the country."[17]

In liberal systems, the agencies of control have less sweeping power.[18] The legislature, judiciary, and other oversight agencies may take the initiative in exerting control over security institutions and serve as loci of incursion by outside groups seeking to influence security arrangements. Security systems in liberal democracies typically operate under greater legal and financial regulation than sectarian and authoritarian systems.[19]

There is, of course, continual tension in democratic states between security agencies' quest for autonomy and legislative and judicial efforts to

13. J. A. Tapia-Valdés, "A Typology of National Security Policies," *Yale Journal of World Public Order* 9, no. 1 (Fall 1982): 10–39; Nordlinger, *Autonomy,* pp. 39, 96.

14. Philippe Nonet and Philip Selznick, *Law and Society in Transition: Toward Responsive Law* (New York: Harper and Row, 1978), p. 33.

15. On authoritarian Brazil and Argentina, see Stepan, *Military Politics*; and Juan Corradi, "The Mode of Destruction: Terror in Argentina," *Telos,* no. 54 (Winter 1982–1983): 69–70.

16. Tapia-Valdés, "Typology," p. 27.

17. Anthony Mathews, *Freedom, State Security, and the Rule of Law: Dilemmas of Apartheid Society* (Berkeley: University of California Press, 1986), p. 267.

18. On the differentiated structure of the American national security sector, see Robert H. Trice, "The Structure of the National Security Policy System," in *National Security Affairs,* ed. B. Trout and J. Harf (New Brunswick: Transaction, 1982); see also Tapia-Valdés, "Typology," p. 18.

19. Stepan (*Military Politics*) makes an identical argument in comparing Brazil with liberal democracies.

keep them on a short leash.[20] The efforts of the United States Congress, particularly since the early 1970s, to control the FBI, CIA, and National Security Council are a case in point.[21] Congressional supervision of these agencies has been intermittent and diffused among various committees; Congress continues to give them significant latitude.[22] The degree of accountability in liberal democracies therefore should not be exaggerated, but the existence of legal and administrative checks points to qualitative differences between democratic states and those where institutional oversight is absent.

The insulation from other state branches that the security sector possesses is also evident in its autonomy from groups outside the state. During normal times, and relative to other agencies, security organs seem universally concerned to shield themselves from popular accountability and from liberalizing influences in civil society. Outside actors typically have little information about and few, if any, channels of access to these hidden corridors of power. To borrow Easton's metaphor, the security bureaucracy has perfected the art of exclusionary "gatekeeping," systematically blocking or neutralizing the demands of outside groups.[23]

Security systems actively seek to maximize their autonomy from civil society—by exaggerating the seriousness of threats to the nation and stressing their "ultra-sensitive" position, "dangerous" work, and the need for absolute secrecy in decision making. They typically brand outside criticism "unpatriotic" and elevate national security to the most hallowed position in the political universe, identifying it with the survival of the nation-state. Their defense of sacrosanct values provides an iron curtain behind which they can pursue priorities other than those relating to internal security: ensuring the incumbency of the ruling party, neutralizing dissent, aggrandizing elites, expanding the national security bureaucracy, and so forth.

20. Security agencies attempt to maximize their autonomy from one another as well as from other state organs (Morton Halperin, *Bureaucratic Politics and Foreign Policy* [Washington, D.C.: Brookings Institution, 1974], pp. 51–54. See also Max Lowenthal, *The Federal Bureau of Investigation* [New York: Harcourt Brace Jovanovich, 1950]; Victor Marchetti and John D. Marks, *The CIA and the Cult of Intelligence* [New York: Dell, 1974]; Philip Agee, *Inside the Company: CIA Diary* [New York: Stonehill, 1975]; Frank Donner, *The Age of Surveillance* [New York: Vintage, 1980]; James Bamford, *The Puzzle Palace* [Boston: Houghton Mifflin, 1982]; Nigel West, *A Matter of Trust: M.I.5* [London: Coronet, 1983]; Morton Halperin, Jerry J. Berman, Robert L. Borosage, and Christine M. Marwick, *The Lawless State* [New York: Penguin, 1976]).

21. Before the 1970s the U.S. Congress paid little attention to the activities of the CIA and FBI.

22. The imposition of administrative or legal checks on security agencies may encourage their illegal activity, whereas in nondemocratic states the lack of these checks reduces the need for illegal activity

23. David Easton, *A Systems Analysis of Political Life* (New York: Wiley, 1965), pp. 87–93.

REPRESSIVENESS

By their very nature, domestic security agencies are inclined to put a premium on order and social control. The question is, how does a state maintain order? What balance does it strike between control and individual rights? In one corner are those states that strive to maintain order and cope with outbreaks of unrest in a manner that is both firm and just; their security establishments follow the rule of law and the norm of minimum force. By contrast, *the sectarian security system is structurally predisposed to impose highly repressive controls.* Of course, communally divided societies feature significant cross-national and longitudinal variation in the magnitude, target groups, duration, geographical scope, and kinds of repression. Still, in accordance with the institutionalized mission to defend decidedly partisan interests, the threat or reality of repression is endemic.

State repression refers here to the deliberate violation by state agents of fundamental civil and political rights, as these are catalogued in the major international declarations of human rights.[24] Repression may be either systematic or haphazard and indiscriminate and can range from torture and killing to restrictions on fair trials, free press, elections, assembly, and speech. All states engage in repressive practices from time to time, but in some repression is a relatively isolated and situationally specific event; in others it is an institutionalized condition, a routinely used mechanism of state power.

The institutional sources of state repression have attracted little systematic research.[25] The relevant literature is often highly impressionistic or paints the state as a dependent variable or black box, unproblematically registering and punitively responding to societal stimuli: it fails to advance persuasive explanations or theoretical understanding.[26] Some

24. These include the United Nations Declaration of Human Rights and the European Convention on Civil and Political Rights.
25. Juan Linz, "Totalitarian and Authoritarian Regimes," in *Handbook of Political Science,* ed. F. Greenstein and N. Polsby (Reading, Pa.: Addison-Wesley, 1975), vol. 3; Amos Perlmutter, *Modern Authoritarianism* (New Haven: Yale University Press, 1981); Guillermo O'Donnell, *Modernization and Bureaucratic Authoritarianism,* 2d ed. (Berkeley: Institute of International Studies Press, 1979); David Collier, ed., *The New Authoritarianism in Latin America* (Princeton: Princeton University Press, 1979).
26. Ernest A. Duff and John F. McCamant, *Violence and Repression in Latin America* (New York: Free Press, 1976); Robert Goldstein, *Political Repression in Modern America* (Cambridge, Mass.: Schenkman, 1978); Alan Wolfe, *The Seamy Side of Democracy: Repression in America* (New York: Longman, 1978); Michael Stohl and George A. Lopez, eds., *The State as Terrorist: The Dynamics of Governmental Violence and Repression* (Westport, Conn.: Greenwood, 1984). One impressive exception discusses the authorities' competing interests in order and legitimacy that shaped repressive responses to unrest in U.S. ghettos in the 1960s (Isaac Balbus, *The Dialectics of Legal Repression: Black Rebels before the American Criminal Courts* [New Brunswick, N.J.: Transaction, 1977]).

formulations portray repression as an inevitable consequence of gross societal inequalities, deeply rooted cultural proclivities, chronic or acute economic problems, and so forth. When advanced in a mechanical fashion, these arguments ignore important variables such as the institutional sources of repressive practices and the interests and objectives of elites. An examination of these dimensions of state repression is long overdue. Our analysis of Zimbabwe and Northern Ireland will be concerned primarily with the structural factors that increase and decrease the likelihood of repressive events.

COMMUNAL BIAS

To say that security agencies are relatively autonomous organizations is not to suggest their political neutrality or ideological indifference. Security organs—even those that are infused with universalistic standards—are likely to act in ways that benefit certain groups to the detriment of others. In the ideal liberal system, however, such agencies do not target particular social strata for pacification, nor are they highly politicized. The state may at times assert control in an illiberal fashion—over social movements, labor, political extremists—but it is not dependent on the systematic immobilization or physical repression of a category of people. When these practices occur, the state violates its universalistic ideals.[27]

In communally divided societies, internal security tends to be profoundly sectarian—however much the regime strives to associate itself with the lofty goals of defending the public interest, law and order, or national survival itself. While relatively autonomous of social pressures, security agencies display a profound corporate attachment to the interests of a particular racial, ethnic, or religious constituency. The repressive system is designed to maintain communal structures, not "the shared interests of a horizontally bonded citizenry" in collective security.[28] The paramount function of the security system is to preempt or

27. Democratic states have exported repression to Third World client states by training and supplying security forces and by supporting authoritarian regimes for reasons of stability, of strategic or economic interests (Michael Klare and Cynthia Arnson, *Supplying Repression: U.S. Support for Authoritarian Regimes Abroad* [Washington, D.C.: Institute for Policy Studies, 1981]; Noam Chomsky and Edward Herman, *The Washington Connection and Third World Fascism* [Boston: South End Press, 1979]).

28. Cynthia Enloe, *Ethnic Soldiers: State Security in Divided Societies* (Athens: University of Georgia Press, 1980), p. 232.

neutralize opposition rooted in the subordinate population. By definition linked to a dominant communal group, a sectarian system is more
permeable to privileged forces in civil society than are other authoritarian and liberal systems. Communally divided societies, in short, feature
differential access to and influence over the security core, which is sensitive to dominant forces and inaccessible to subordinate interests.

This link does not mean that the demands of dominant racial, ethnic,
or religious groups are necessarily synchronized with the activities of
control organs or that the latter are convenient instruments of domination. Paramount organizational priorities, doctrines, and considerations
of resources may clash with the demands of sections of the dominant
community. The growing clamor of right-wing South African whites
and Israeli Jews for more ruthless sanctions against militant blacks and
Arabs are cases in point.

The ideal type sketched here only imperfectly fits specific cases. In particular, the premise of *functionality*—that sectarian security systems effectively maintain the position of a dominant communal group—needs
qualification. In specific cases the degree of functionality is affected by
countervailing pressures and unintended consequences. Foremost
among such factors are serious, sometimes debilitating, conflicts within
the control apparatus or between coercive agencies and other state organs;[29] limited resources and sheer overload on control facilities that
may exceed the system's capacity for effective repression; and the routine
operations of these agencies, which may damage social cohesion, the
system's legitimacy, and political stability. Unrest and insurgency are
likely to intensify these problems, as analysis of our two cases will show.

DIMENSIONS OF SYSTEMIC LIBERALIZATION

Social scientists have paid insufficient attention to the role of police, military, and intelligence organs in nation building,[30] and to the precondi-

29. Althusser's discussion of "repressive state apparatuses" wrongly assumes that they
are necessarily "unified" and that this cohesion is reproduced "easily" (Louis Althusser,
"Ideology and Ideological State Apparatuses," in *Lenin and Philosophy and Other Essays*
[New York: Monthly Review Press, 1971], pp. 142–49).

30. Enloe, *Ethnic Soldiers*; Samuel Huntington, *Political Order in Changing Societies*
(New Haven: Yale University Press, 1968); Charles Tilly, ed., *The Formation of National
States in Western Europe* (Princeton: Princeton University Press, 1975); Morris Janowitz,
The Military in the Political Development of New Nations (Chicago: University of Chi-
cago Press, 1964); David Bayley, *The Police and Political Development in India* (Princeton:
Princeton University Press, 1969); Ernest Lefever, *Spear and Scepter: Army, Police, and
Politics in Tropical Africa* (Washington, D.C.: Brookings Institution, 1970).

tions for liberalization or modernization of these institutions.[31] Drawing on the Weberian literature on political development, I suggest that liberalization consists of changes that transcend narrow, sectarian interests and reflect fidelity to ideals of neutrality, universalism, and rationalized authority, which may bridge communal cleavages and promote nation building.[32]

Our dependent variable—the structural and ideological liberalization of a security system—entails transforming the three basic dimensions of the sectarian security system outlined in the preceding section. It means reconstituting substantive goals and values and redistributing institutional power. As an ideal type, systemic *liberalization* includes the following:[33]

• a marked shift in the balance of power between the security bureaucracy and other branches of the state, which subjects security agencies to legal restraints on their jurisdiction and practices and makes them accountable to other state branches;

• an institutionalized sensitivity to considerations of legitimacy, the rule of law, civil and political rights, and the ideal of justice, which helps to restrain the use of repressive force;[34]

• a reconstituted agency culture: a universalistic ethos and a normative commitment to impartial maintenance of order replace the security branch's parochial interests and encourage restraint in security practices.

A liberalized security system is not a contradiction in terms. It does not strip the state of its institutional capacities to maintain public order, although state elites commonly plead that significant liberalization

31. I use the term *institutional modernization* as synonymous with *liberalization,* without implying agreement with modernization theory's evolutionary assumptions or the Western-oriented political development model. I have used aspects of the latter approach in my framework of institutional liberalization.

32. In this paradigm a modern polity has a highly differentiated system of government, rationalized authority, mass political participation and equality, and an expanding capacity of state institutions (see Leonard Binder et al., *Crises and Sequences of Political Development* [Princeton: Princeton University Press, 1971]; Dankwart Rustow and Robert Ward, introduction to *Political Modernization in Japan and Turkey,* ed. Robert Ward and Dankwart Rustow [Princeton: Princeton University Press, 1964], pp. 6–7).

33. Our model of liberalization draws in part on Nonet and Selznick's discussion of autonomous law, which they contrast with repressive law (*Law and Society*). See also the reforms advocated for U.S. intelligence agencies in Halperin et al., *The Lawless State,* chap. 12.

34. Mathews's analysis of South Africa emphasizes that the security system needs a radically different "framework of values," based on the rule of law and democratic accountability (*Freedom, State Security,* p. 273).

would spell state suicide.[35] In fact, by minimizing arbitrary and repressive practices that fuel popular unrest and political violence, liberalization can *enhance* order and stability and thus promote the long-term interests of the security establishment. Elites at the helm of sectarian agencies rarely see any value in liberalization, intent rather on maintaining absolute control over the subordinate population. Similarly, they rarely appear sensitive to the potentially counterproductive effects of repression. In contemporary South Africa, for example, the "authorities appear to have learnt nothing" from the fact that "disorder has increased in direct proportion to the application of harsh security measures."[36] This example underscores the paradox that security agencies may themselves unwittingly threaten state security and domestic order, just as liberalization may promote security and stability.

The thoroughgoing liberalization of a security system should be distinguished from more routine organizational adjustments, innovations, and reforms.[37] These changes ordinarily reinforce, rather than shake, the foundations of the system.[38] Likewise, the incremental repeal or amendment of repressive laws often has little impact on the underlying structure or values of a security system, which may replace its legal powers with extralegal devices or revive them later. Similarly, replacing hardline security personnel with those more moderately inclined may not change the organization's values and practices.

In a sense, liberalization in the security system may be viewed as an integral part of democratization, but for analysis it is useful to separate these processes. Changes and continuities in security and in political arrangements may, but do not necessarily, have reciprocal effects; consider three different possibilities:

1.   democratic formalism: the introduction of universal suffrage and procedures for free competitive elections, which do not necessarily undermine repressive institutions. Formal democratization may occur without a corresponding change in the security system inherited from the old order: Zimbabwe exemplifies this point.

---

35. Mathews points out that "a reduction in security powers in a situation of crisis is not necessarily harmful" (ibid., p. 279).

36. Ibid., p. 277.

37. Peter M. Blau, *The Dynamics of Bureaucracy* (Chicago: University of Chicago Press, 1963).

38. For example, Marchetti and Marks conclude that "the CIA and the intelligence community are incapable of reforming themselves" and require "intense outside pressure" to generate meaningful changes (*CIA*, pp. 12, 351).

2. liberalization of a security system *without* formal democratization. Although it may be rare, significant reform of institutions of control may occur without corresponding democratization of the polity. Northern Ireland illustrates this point.

3. liberalization of a sectarian security system as a necessary condition for genuine, not formal, political democratization. Substantive democratization cannot proceed far if security organs remain politicized, sectarian, unaccountable, and powerful enough to intervene to reverse the process of democratic consolidation. As Mathews forcefully argues, "Only those societies that have successfully grappled with the problem of the political accountability of their intelligence and security communities, can have any claim to being fully democratic." [39]

In a nutshell, the argument is that changes in the political order and in the coercive order may have *reciprocal effects* or may *vary independently,* but that *lasting, substantive democratization requires liberalization of the security system.* By removing the supports for repression within and among institutions, sweeping liberalization may help to preserve democratic gains.

CONTINUITY AND CHANGE: RIVAL MODELS

Caution is needed in specifying the conditions for democratic political development and for liberalization of a security apparatus. Some analysts insist that political transitions are highly indeterminate and that their outcomes are impossible to deduce from macrostructural factors. [40] Others take the opposite view. This section examines three general perspectives on transitions to democracy: those that focus almost exclusively on socioeconomic factors, on political factors, or on transitional contingencies.

SOCIOECONOMIC ACCOUNTS

The functionalist paradigm posits a set of social requisites of democracy. Among the factors that seem to correlate with stable democracies are

---

39. Mathews, *Freedom, State Security,* p. 290.
40. Guillermo O'Donnell, Philippe Schmitter, and Lawrence Whitehead, eds., *Transitions from Authoritarian Rule: Prospects for Democracy* (Baltimore: Johns Hopkins University Press, 1986), pp. 5, 19; Dankwart Rustow, "Transitions to Democracy: Toward a Dynamic Model," *Comparative Politics* 2, no. 3 (April 1970): 337–63.

economic development and societal complexity or modernization.[41] Critics charged that it was impossible to prove a causal relation between socioeconomic factors and democratic stability; these factors are preconditions neither for the decay of authoritarianism nor for the rise of democracy. Too many actual cases have failed to evolve in the predicted direction. Three of the most advanced societies in Latin America, for instance, were traumatized by military regimes in the 1970s: Argentina, Chile, and Uruguay. Dahl puts the matter forcefully: "The evidence simply does not sustain the hypothesis that a high level of socioeconomic development is either a necessary or a sufficient condition for competitive politics nor the converse hypothesis that competitive politics is either a necessary or a sufficient condition for a high level of socioeconomic development."[42]

Another socioeconomic approach centers on underdevelopment. One variant posits a natural affinity between economic dependency and authoritarianism and portrays repressive Third World states as servants of international capital; some accounts elevate the existence of repressive regimes to a law of dependent development. Petras flatly asserts:

> The origins and proliferation of repressive regimes are not products of internal developments, but responses to demands that originate primarily on a global level. . . . The neo-fascist [Third World] state functions essentially within and as an instrument of dependent development. . . . In this context high growth rates are an index of the high rates of exploitation and repression.[43]

Senese concurs: "In Latin America . . . national security is the security of foreign economic groups who are pillaging the country."[44]

More sophisticated economistic formulations include the bureaucratic-authoritarian model, which links the economic requirements of high levels of modernization (as in Argentina and Brazil) to the repression and political deactivation of the popular sector.[45] Other works carefully correlate levels of political repression or changes of regime with macroeconomic developments (hyperinflation, balance of

---

41. Seymour Martin Lipset, "Some Social Requisites of Democracy: Economic Development and Political Legitimacy," *American Political Science Review* 53, no. 1 (March 1959): 69–105.

42. Robert Dahl, *Polyarchy* (New Haven: Yale University Press, 1971), p. 71.

43. James F. Petras, *Class, State, and Power in the Third World* (Montclair, N.J.: Allanheld, Osman, 1981), pp. 125, 129, 133.

44. Judge Senese, "The Transformation of Juridical Structures in Latin America," in *The Repressive State*, ed. J. Weil (Toronto: Brazilian Studies/LARU, 1976), p. 87.

45. O'Donnell, *Modernization*.

payments crises, high cost or failure of economic stabilization programs). One version of this approach claims that (manifest or expected)
popular opposition to orthodox economic policies predisposes an incumbent regime toward repression and helps to explain the survival of
authoritarian rule.[46] Another version sees economic factors—both economic crises and the pressures of economic development—as causing
the erosion of authoritarianism and the restoration of civilian government.[47] As Rouquie suggests, these explanations are weakened by their
reversibility.[48]

The causal power to be attributed to macroeconomic factors in the
immediate or long-term collapse of an authoritarian regime or the rise
of a democratic state must clearly be reconsidered. Common to the
economistic formulations described above is the assumption that domestic political realities and other extraeconomic factors are epiphe-
nomenal and determined by economic forces. A more tenable position
would acknowledge the role of political variables in mediating or directly affecting outcomes and would acknowledge that economic and
political developments may vary independently. In some cases economic
problems have undoubtedly catalyzed or contributed to a regime's
breakdown or change, but they cannot be elevated to the status of necessary conditions. A body of literature offers three correctives to economically driven models: authoritarianism is not a requirement for the
survival of dependent economic relations; underdevelopment can be
found in a wide variety of political systems, some highly repressive,
some not; state elites often have interests in repression that are independent of prevailing economic pressures.[49]

46. David Pion-Berlin, "The Political Economy of State Repression in Argentina," in
The State as Terrorist, ed. Stohl and Lopez; John Sheahan, "Market-oriented Economic
Policies and Political Repression in Latin America," *Economic Development and Cultural
Change* 28, no. 2 (January 1980).

47. Gordon Richards, "Stabilization Crises and the Breakdown of Military Authoritarianism in Latin America," *Comparative Political Studies* 18, no. 4 (January 1986).

48. Alain Rouquie, "Demilitarization and the Institutionalization of Military-
Dominated Polities in Latin America," in *Transitions,* ed. O'Donnell, Schmitter, and
Whitehead, p. 125.

49. Fernando Henrique Cardoso, "On the Characterization of Authoritarian Regimes
in Latin America," pp. 51–52; Jose Serra, "Three Mistaken Theses Regarding the Connection between Industrialization and Authoritarian Regimes"; and Robert R. Kaufman, "Industrial Change and Authoritarian Rule in Latin America," pp. 247–52, all in *New
Authoritarianism,* ed. D. Collier. See also Douglas Chalmers, "The Politicized State in
Latin America," in *Authoritarianism and Corporatism in Latin America,* ed. James Malloy
(Pittsburgh: University of Pittsburgh Press, 1977), pp. 37–41.

POLITICAL ACCOUNTS

An alternative model places special emphasis on political variables, particularly intrastate factors.[50] O'Donnell and Schmitter state categorically that "there is no transition whose beginning is not the consequence—direct or indirect—of important divisions within the authoritarian regime itself, principally along the fluctuating cleavage between hardliners and soft-liners."[51] This model does not suggest that pivotal struggles within the state occur in a social vacuum but places primacy on intrastate developments. Schmitter generalizes from the Portuguese case:

> The sources of contradiction, necessary if not sufficient for the overthrow of authoritarian rule, lie within the regime itself, within the apparatuses of the state, not outside it in its relations with civil society. . . . "Objective" constraints and "subjective" opponents may create and/or articulate the persistent strains and episodic pressures that exacerbate internal cleavages, upset delicate balances between established hierarchical orders, weaken the resolve of regime supporters to act, and decrease the viability of certain preemptive and repressive policy options. However, alone, without such prior "reflexive" changes within the governing apparatus itself, they are not likely to be sufficient to threaten the regime, much less overthrow it.[52]

This model posits disturbance within the state—severe strain, contradiction, or conflict—as a necessary condition for the breakdown of authoritarian rule.[53] It does not imply that equilibrium or homeostasis is a normal condition—that the state is typically free from internal discord—but claims that at exceptional junctures the pressures intensify and reach breaking point. In Schmitter's formulation, pressures from

50. Guillermo O'Donnell and Philippe Schmitter, "Tentative Conclusions about Uncertain Democracies," in *Transitions,* ed. O'Donnell, Schmitter, and Whitehead. O'Donnell has now moved away from his earlier stress on macroeconomic factors in shaping authoritarian rule.

51. Ibid., p. 19. Related arguments are those of Adam Przeworski ("Some Problems in the Study of the Transition to Democracy," in *Transitions,* ed. O'Donnell, Schmitter, Whitehead) and of Jose Casanova ("Modernization and Democratization: Reflections on Spain's Transition to Democracy," *Social Research* 50, no. 4 [Winter 1983]: 929–73).

52. Philippe Schmitter, "Liberation by *Golpe:* Retrospective Thoughts on the Demise of Authoritarian Rule in Portugal," *Armed Forces and Society* 2, no. 1 (November 1975): 20–21.

53. Easton's systems theory emphasizes the stress of external societal pressures on the political system and neglects disturbance generated from within the state itself (*Systems Analysis*). See also Neil Smelser, *Theory of Collective Behavior* (New York: Free Press, 1962); and Chalmers Johnson, *Revolutionary Change* (Boston: Little, Brown, 1966).

civil society are not necessary to the development of intrastate frictions. The latter may be generated by a factional backlash against a new policy or an institutional reform, a changing balance of forces inside the state (e.g., from hard-liners to moderates or innovators), a crisis of confidence within the security agencies, or a sharpening of jurisdictional conflict among agencies. If the regime cannot reduce such dissonance, internal strain may further erode state cohesion and authority, activate outside social forces, and lead to a crisis of order and governance.

This state-centered perspective must be tempered, since it underplays the role of social forces in catalyzing or deepening conflicts within the state.[54] It is true that social forces rarely trigger democratic change on their own, let alone the transformation of an internal security apparatus. A necessary condition is that the "resurrection of civil society"— to use O'Donnell and Schmitter's term—coincide with important dislocations within the state. The pressures of social forces thus become salient only in conjunction with the development of serious strains within the state. This state-society nexus during crises and transitions needs further study.

TRANSITIONAL CONTINGENCIES

The parameters of a transition from authoritarian rule may be difficult to pinpoint in an empirical case, but it can be said to begin with the dissolution of the old regime and culminate in the installation of a new one, whether democratic, authoritarian, or revolutionary. The fluidity of transitions gives state elites unprecedented opportunities to change security systems, however rarely in practice they seize this moment. In the transition, security agencies may be untouched, reformed, fortified, or dismantled, but—having a survival instinct—they do not simply wither away.

The highly contingent and indeterminate character of transitions makes predictions problematic.[55] One argument is that the *type* of transition is itself an important variable shaping political outcomes. For our purposes, the most important question is whether a particular type of transition relates positively to the liberalization of a security system or,

54. A *social force* is a group of actors outside the state, with collective resources and identifiable interests, e.g., communally-based groups, labor unions, social movements, churches, interest groups, the press, extra-parliamentary parties, and insurgent organizations.
55. O'Donnell and Schmitter, "Tentative Conclusions," p. 19.

alternatively, whether variables unaffected by transitional contingencies best explain the outcome. Some authors predict that a transition initiated and controlled from above (e.g., in Spain or Brazil) will feature substantial institutional continuity, whereas a transition that follows the breakdown of an authoritarian regime (e.g., in Argentina), will display a more pronounced rupture with earlier structures.[56] However plausible, these hypotheses do not seem to fit cases such as Haiti, the Philippines, Paraguay, and even Spain.

Externally orchestrated transitions, such as the interventions that follow a military defeat (in Japan, West Germany, Italy), are perhaps the best examples of extensive liberalization. More generally, a period of foreign domination may advance rather than impede democratization. Dahl found that seventeen of the twenty-nine democratic states existing in 1970 had been inaugurated during foreign domination.[57] Chapter 7 examines how this pattern applies now to Northern Ireland under British rule, a special case of external intervention.

Transitions driven by revolutionary or guerrilla struggle seem to cluster at the other end of the continuum: they rarely yield liberalized security systems and genuinely democratic polities and instead produce new authoritarian orders.[58] Chapter 6 examines this pattern in contemporary Zimbabwe, where a new regime was installed after a decade of guerrilla war.

AN ALTERNATIVE MODEL

The perspectives I have discussed above may be faulted for their one-dimensional emphasis on societal, on state, or on transitional variables. A superior model would systematically link these variables.

Consider first the impact of the transitional period: our position is that this process shapes but does not rigidly determine important variables such as the survival and power of security institutions tied to the old regime, the actors who are likely to prevail under the new order, and the capacities of the new regime. The model presented below incorporates these transitional effects but also places considerable independent weight on what happens after the transition.

56. Eduardo Viola and Scott Mainwaring, "Transitions to Democracy: Brazil and Argentina in the 1980s," *Journal of International Affairs* 38, no. 2 (Winter 1985): 193–219.
57. Dahl, *Polyarchy*, pp. 193–98.
58. Theda Skocpol, "Social Revolutions and Mass Military Mobilization," *World Politics* 40, no. 2 (January 1988): 147–68; Samuel Huntington, "Will More Countries Become Democratic?" *Political Science Quarterly* 99, no. 2 (Summer 1984): 213.

In addition to the scope and intensity of prevailing security problems, our model highlights four interacting macrovariables that shape the prospects for a security system's liberalization after the demise of settler rule: (1) the values embedded in the political culture; (2) the independent power and proclivities of surviving security agencies; (3) the strength and interests of groups (parties, movements, insurgents) and key institutions (churches, labor unions, the media, voluntary associations) in civil society; and (4) the interests and capacities of the postsettler regime.[59] Each variable may function either to constrain or facilitate systemic liberalization, the frequency and intensity of repressive events, and the prospects for political democratization.

The four variables are interrelated. The first variable conditions the other three through its impact on political values and interests. The second and third variables interact with the fourth insofar as they determine much of the capacity of the new regime, helping to fetter or empower it. The fourth factor is the master variable, greater than the others in explanatory power. It is decisive because the postsettler regime is directly responsible for determining security policy, law, and institutional structures and practices—conditioned, of course, by the other variables. Let us consider each variable in the context of our cases.

POLITICAL CULTURE

The study of state structures in new nations must take into account both institutional and cultural factors.[60] The seeds of a democratic political culture seem necessary for the growth of liberalized structures of law and order. Yet their cultivation is chronically problematic in deeply divided societies where communal groups lack a sense of national identity or a shared cultural tradition. Persistent communal cleavages and at-

59. This model builds on arguments in O'Donnell and Schmitter ("Tentative Conclusions"), Stepan (*Military Politics*), and Larry Diamond, Seymour Martin Lipset, and Juan Linz, "Building and Sustaining Democratic Government in Developing Countries," *World Affairs* 150, no. 1 (Summer 1987): 5–19. Binnendijk comes close to our model when he argues that a transition from authoritarian rule is shaped by the contingencies of the transition itself and the interrelations among three variables: a democratic tradition or a supportive external model, the "institutional foundation" for the growth of democracy, and the orientation and capabilities of the new regime's leaders (Hans Binnendijk, "Authoritarian Regimes in Transition," *Washington Quarterly* 10, no. 2 [Spring 1987]: 159). None of these authors, however, incorporates all four dimensions of the model proposed here or gives sufficient weight to our master variable.

60. Prager demonstrates the importance of the cultural dimension in his study of Ireland after 1921 (Jeffrey Prager, *Building Democracy in Ireland* [Cambridge: Cambridge University Press, 1986]).

tachments set tight limits on institutional changes and suggest the necessity of reconstituting cultural orientations in conjunction with institutional reform. A political culture devoid of trust and compromise may not sentence societies to perpetual authoritarianism but it clearly frustrates their democratic progress and fuels instability and disorder.[61] Their cultural heritage, therefore, is an amorphous but crucial contextual variable that is resilient and resistant to change—at least in the short term. This cultural lag presents a formidable challenge to modernizing elites.

Given their settler-oriented histories (described in Chapter 2), both Northern Ireland and Zimbabwe lack traditions of democratic accommodation, tolerance of political opposition, and institutionalized support for basic human rights. Northern Ireland has a "polarized political culture" par excellence, rooted in two national identities that define compromise as betrayal of one's side.[62] The contiguity of Northern Ireland to Britain makes democratic values only slightly more salient there than in Zimbabwe. The population views the British regime as a morally bankrupt actor; hence, the British operate within a hostile cultural environment and have met with only modest local acceptance in their attempt to impose change on Ulster. In postsettler Zimbabwe, the official democratic ideology clashes with the authoritarian tendencies of the regime. In neither case, therefore, is the existing political culture conducive to democratic political development or liberalized security arrangements.

THE INHERITED SECURITY APPARATUS

A more immediate problem facing a new regime is that of grappling with the security establishment inherited from its predecessor, insofar as it survived the transition. Some bureaucratic inertia can be taken as an iron law of organizational life. Organizations have an interest in their survival (or expansion) and a commitment to entrenched doctrines and

61. The literature assumes a basic congruence between a nation's political culture and political structure. Northern Ireland illustrates one way they may diverge; Argentina, Chile, and Mexico exemplify another: the coexistence of authoritarian regimes with democratic political cultures (see John Booth and Mitchell Seligson, "The Political Culture of Authoritarianism in Mexico," *Latin American Research Review* 19, no. 1 [1984]: 106–24; and Susan Tiano, "Authoritarianism and Political Culture in Argentina and Chile in the mid-1960s," *Latin American Research Review* 21, no. 1 [1986]: 73–98).

62. Gabriel Almond and G. Bingham Powell, *Comparative Politics*, 2d ed. (Boston: Little, Brown, 1978), pp. 28–29.

traditional modi operandi.[63] They rarely undertake self-reform even under a new regime. If all else is constant, it is reasonable to predict that unreconstructed sectarian security organs will continue repressive operations in the new order.

Just as they may threaten, and often subvert, nascent democratic institutions, surviving security agencies and other protagonists of the old regime can often sabotage reforms of coercive organs. Recent history is filled with examples of new civilian regimes unable to tame, let alone overhaul, inherited coercive structures. Not only unlikely to commit suicide, the agencies often fight their broad demotion within the state, jurisdictional encroachment from other organs (e.g., courts or legislatures), cuts in material resources and personnel, and plans to punish security personnel for prior abuses of human rights.

None of this should imply that these agencies are completely averse to change; under a new executive they are likely to reflect both traditional commitments and new demands. Likewise, as events in many democratizing states have shown, a regime must often seek a balance between placating and reforming inherited security organs. An aggressive strategy toward the military, on the one hand, may render a civilian government unstable (vulnerable to military interference or a coup), as in contemporary Argentina. On the other hand, an overly accommodating posture that allows the military to keep its grip on official coercion, as in Brazil, may promote political stability but deny the civilian regime effective power, thus compromising genuine democratization.[64] In Brazil since 1985 this arrangement has contributed to widespread repression. Stepan suggests that the alternative to a negative executive (the Argentinian model) or a passive executive (the Brazilian) is a "positive executive" that actively persuades security elites to accept civilian control, increased professionalism, and a narrowing of their prominent role in domestic affairs.[65]

After the collapse of settler rule in Northern Ireland, the repressive orientation of the security apparatus was diluted: some agencies were dissolved, others reformed, and new oversight bodies created. In Zimbabwe the opposite occurred: existing agencies were fortified and mobilized for punitive action. In other words, the repressive traditions of

---

63. Grundy writes that "institutions instinctively behave in ways designed to solidify or enhance their power. The security establishment is a model example" (Kenneth Grundy, *The Militarization of South African Politics* [Bloomington: Indiana University Press, 1986], p. 109); see also Ball, *Security and Economy,* chap. 2.
64. See Stepan, *Military Politics,* chap. 7.
65. Ibid., p. 139.

settler security organs have been somewhat checked in Ulster, officially countenanced in Zimbabwe.

CIVIL SOCIETY

Centralization of power tends to weaken democracy and encourage repression, whereas dispersal of power within the state and throughout civil society may have the opposite effect.[66] The extent to which democratically oriented forces in civil society mobilize pressures can account for some cross-national variation in democratic outcomes.[67] Despite their institutional insulation, security organs do not exist in a social vacuum; influential elites and civic bodies may provide a rich source of opposition to political repression. Goldstein concludes that a lack of opposition "facilitates an expansion of repressive policies,"[68] but the presence of opposition may also generate repression. If opposition groups have at times succeeded in curbing state power, they often provide the targets for repression and unwittingly contribute to the fortification of coercive institutions.

The forces that may affect structural change in a security apparatus include civic organizations (media, churches, labor unions, intelligentsia, business groups), social movements, and opposition political parties. There is, of course, substantial cross-national variation in the organizational sophistication, availability of resources, and resultant potential leverage of these forces. In some cases the infrastructure of civil society develops through vibrant alliances among various organized forces. In others, an earlier highly charged civic order has been deactivated, yet a latent social network remains. Still others lack a tradition of civic life altogether or feature a highly fragmented civil society, incapable of effecting even minor changes in security arrangements. Many authoritarian elites are experts at atomizing and depoliticizing civil society, using cooptation, ideological control, or naked force.[69]

Societal fragmentation exists throughout postcolonial Africa.[70] Even where independence was won through a protracted struggle and popular

66. Alves, *State and Opposition*; Diamond, Lipset, and Linz, "Building and Sustaining Democratic Government."

67. This hypothesis is supported by a recent comparison of Latin America and southern Europe (Philippe Schmitter, "An Introduction to Southern European Transitions from Authoritarian Rule," in *Transitions,* ed. O'Donnell, Schmitter, and Whitehead, pp. 7–9.

68. Goldstein, *Political Repression,* pp. 572–73, 559.

69. O'Donnell and Schmitter, "Tentative Conclusions," p. 48.

70. Jean François Bayart, "Civil Society in Africa," in *Political Domination in Africa,* ed. P. Chabal (Cambridge: Cambridge University Press, 1986).

mobilization, it is possible for the new regime to deactivate countervailing sources of power in civil society. This has occurred in Zimbabwe. In Northern Ireland, by contrast, civil society is hyperactive but its achievements are uneven, largely because civil society is torn asunder by two antagonistic communities. Progressive forces have pressed for reforms, yet opposing forces—mainly those of the settler community—have also somewhat contained liberalization. This outcome suggests that a developed civil society may be a blessing or a curse for democratization and liberalization, depending on the interests and values of the actors involved. As Stepan argues, lasting democratization requires social forces to "revalorize democracy" and commit themselves to holding security agencies accountable.[71]

THE NEW REGIME

A fourth, binary variable seems to have the greatest power in accounting for security system outcomes after regime transitions: the interests and capacities of the new regime.[72]

Liberalization requires, first, that the new regime have a genuine *interest* in and commitment to building institutions that are impartial, accountable, legitimate, and informed by human rights norms. The interests of governmental leaders are shaped in part by the values embedded in the political culture and by the central goals of the regime or ruling party. The regime's ability to implement its goals depends on the legacy of the transitional period as well as new contingencies. Specifically, its *capacity* depends on its material resources, its leaders' skills, the support or resistance of its population, the posture of coercive agencies, and the magnitude of domestic unrest and security threats that may limit its room for maneuver.[73]

In sum, the new regime's independent value commitments and resources are critically important. But its capacities are also contingent on

71. Stepan, *Military Politics*.

72. Most studies of democratization have placed insufficient weight on this factor. For a recent example, see *Democracy in Developing Countries,* ed. Diamond, Linz, and Lipset.

73. Cf. Charles Tilly, *From Mobilization to Revolution* (Reading, Pa.: Addison-Wesley, 1978), chap. 7; S. N. Eisenstadt, *Revolution and the Transformation of Societies* (New York: Free Press, 1978), p. 251; Karen Remmer, "Public Policy and Regime Consolidation: The First Five Years of the Chilean Junta," *Journal of Developing Areas* 13, no. 4 (July 1979): 441–61; Juan Linz, *The Breakdown of Democratic Regimes: Crisis, Breakdown, and Reequilibration* (Baltimore: Johns Hopkins University Press, 1978), pp. 87–88.

the support it can marshal from outside social forces and other branches of the state, including the security sector. In Zimbabwe, the regime itself functions as the major constraint on liberalization; in Northern Ireland, the British government is a key proponent of reform. In the former, the regime has the capacity for but little interest in modernizing the security apparatus; in the latter, the situation is reversed.

The next chapter discusses the basic features of settler societies as a prelude to an examination of Rhodesia/Zimbabwe and Northern Ireland. These chapters examine longitudinal changes in comparative perspective: the rise of settler rule in each case, the breakdown of both settler states, and the dynamics of the new order. Chapters 6 and 7 pay special attention to developing a theoretical perspective on change and continuity in internal security structures. The explanatory model should be useful in understanding outcomes in other postsettler societies, which are likely to feature differential mapping of our variables. Contemporary Taiwan, for example, scores favorably (for liberalization) on each variable except for its security agencies; Liberia closely resembles the pattern of Zimbabwe.[74]

74. J. Gus Liebenow, *Liberia: The Quest for Democracy* (Bloomington: Indiana University Press, 1987); Lawyers Committee for Human Rights, *Liberia: A Promise Betrayed* (New York: Lawyers Committee, 1986).

CHAPTER 2

The Pillars
of Settler Rule

Settler rule is one form of political domination that is in decline around the world. Recently a number of settler regimes have either collapsed (Liberia, Rhodesia, Northern Ireland) or grown increasingly vulnerable (South Africa, Taiwan). They share in the general historical decline of colonialism, but settler states have shown more resilience because they represent permanent home to a dominant group that is prepared to resist metropolitan pressures for change and any hint of native resistance. The settlers' characteristic intransigence makes the transformation of these states considerably more difficult and complicated than the decolonization of conventional colonies, where imperial powers disengaged with the broad support of local social forces. This chapter examines the conditions of existence and characteristic social and political structures of the model settler state, setting out the framework that informs our investigation of Rhodesia and Northern Ireland.

DEFINING THE SETTLER STATE

Settler societies are founded by migrant groups who assume a superordinate position vis-à-vis native inhabitants and build self-sustaining states that are de jure or de facto independent from the mother country and organized around the settlers' political domination over the indigenous population. (Throughout, the terms *native, indigenous,* and *indigene* are used interchangeably to identify the inhabitants of the territory prior to the arrival of the settlers: blacks in Rhodesia, Catholics in Ireland.) In some cases (Rhodesia, South Africa, Liberia), economic interests (exploitation of natives and prosperity of settlers) provide a key rationale for political domination; in others (Northern Ireland, Israel, Taiwan), economic considerations have been secondary to other imperatives: maintaining a specific religious or cultural order (Northern Ireland, Israel), a refuge or homeland (Taiwan, Israel).

To constitute a settler state, the descendants of settlers must remain politically dominant over natives, who present at least a latent threat to the settlers' supremacy. The period during which the foundations of settler domination were laid is therefore not the distinguishing feature; settler states were established in the seventeenth century in South Africa, the nineteenth century in Rhodesia and Liberia, the 1920s in Northern Ireland, and as late as the 1940s in Taiwan.

In certain cases, original divisions between settlers and natives no longer shape the sociopolitical order. Societies that assimilated or annihilated the indigenes would fall outside the category of settler states. A number of former settlement colonies imposed final solutions on their "native problems." In the United States and Australia, the indigenous population was forcibly displaced and largely eliminated, and quasi-European societies were established. Conversely, in Latin America racial and ethnic assimilation was fairly common but rarely complete, as lingering conflicts in Brazil and elsewhere attest.

Settler states should also be distinguished from conventional colonial states, which were organized around imperial economic and geopolitical objectives, such as acquiring territory from other European competitors, establishing military outposts, monopolizing trade, opening markets, and exploiting natural resources. To maintain imperial advantages, extensive occupation and administration were usually unnecessary. Variations among colonies notwithstanding, their infrastructures were often reduced to bare essentials, with a skeletal coercive structure and small contingents of colonial administrators—a "thin white line" throughout Africa.[1] As the satellite of a metropole, a colonial state apparatus was superimposed on civil society, not rooted in it (even under indirect rule, where traditional native elites exercised administrative duties in the

---

1. To control native populations, small colonial administrations made use of native collaborators and the selective application of coercion. See A. H. M. Kirk-Greene, "The Thin White Line: The Size of the British Colonial Service in Africa," *African Affairs,* no. 314 (January 1980): 25–44; David Killingray, "The Maintenance of Law and Order in British Colonial Africa," *African Affairs,* no. 340 (July 1986): 411–37; D. K. Fieldhouse, *Colonialism: 1870–1945* (New York: St. Martin's, 1981).

countryside). Given these distinguishing features, a conventional colony was critically vulnerable to shifting imperial interests.

Settler states developed much more elaborate political and economic infrastructures, encouraged more intensive European settlement, and achieved de facto or de jure political independence from the metropole.[2] Settlers considered the territory their permanent home; this paramount interest shaped all social, economic, and political relations with the indigenous population. Compared to the minimalist coercive apparatus of the classic colonial state, a settler state is institutionally strong: the security core of the state has at its disposal substantial resources (finances, personnel, weaponry), and the exercise of repression is determined by settlers' assessments of security, not metropolitan approval.[3] Independent control over state coercion empowers settler regimes to resist domestic threats and foreign machinations; thus attempts to transform them have been more problematic than those to decolonize conventional colonies.

The first imperative of stable settler rule, therefore, is *to achieve autonomy from the metropole in the exercise of political authority and coercive power.* The greater the degree of autonomy, the greater the settlers' room for maneuver in molding economic, social, and political structures. Under de jure independence (e.g., in Liberia, South Africa, Israel), the metropole relinquishes its juridical authority to interfere in issues such as native political rights, land expropriation and labor exploitation, and the fundamental constitutional status of the territory. This freedom from imperial intervention does little, however, to shield a settler society from internal conflicts and international pressures, as the recent history of Israel, Liberia, and South Africa attests. Under de facto autonomy (e.g., in Rhodesia, Northern Ireland, Taiwan), the imperial power loses control over political and coercive institutions but continues to claim sovereignty over the territory. It may assert this residual authority against the wishes of the settlers, with or without success, as our analysis of Rhodesia and Northern Ireland will show. Both cases illustrate, first, how concerted and protracted defiance by settlers may expose the limits of metropolitan leverage over a settler state and, second,

---

2. Leo Kuper, "Political Change in White Settler Societies," in *Pluralism in Africa,* ed. Leo Kuper and M. G. Smith (Berkeley: University of California Press, 1969).

3. On ethnic control over security in divided societies, see Cynthia Enloe, *Ethnic Soldiers: State Security in Divided Societies* (Athens: University of Georgia Press, 1980), pp. 18–23.

how precarious de facto state autonomy can be in keeping the metropole at bay during crises.

The second condition of stable settler rule is *to consolidate control over the indigenous population.* Effective control is necessary to prevent or contain natives' political mobilization, unrest, and threats to the system's stability and also to discourage metropolitan interference on their behalf. Of course, the scope, intensity, and substance of control vary over time and place. Controls may be extensive and intensive in political, economic, and social spheres—as in South Africa—or less comprehensive—as in Israel and Northern Ireland. Variation is also evident in the relative importance of ideological, coercive, administrative, and cooptative mechanisms.

The system of control may be so successful in disorganizing political mobilization, restricting physical mobility, and ensuring economic dependence of the subordinate group that overt physical repression is rarely necessary to maintain stability. Kuper's argument that "white settler societies are notoriously repressive and undemocratic" and Biermann and Kössler's claim that "direct brutal force is thus a constant and necessary element of settler rule" therefore deserve some qualification.[4] Naked force alone is rarely sufficient or desirable to maintain social cohesion; selective use of the carrot may offer stabilizing dividends. Settler states vary significantly in the degree to which they accommodate indigenous populations; conciliation has been more evident in latter-day Liberia and Taiwan, for instance, than in Rhodesia, Ulster, and South Africa. In Israel proper (excluding the West Bank and Gaza), an elaborate system of segmentation, dependence, and cooptation has maintained control over Israeli Arabs; until recently, writes Lustick, this system was effective "at very low cost to the regime in terms of resources expended, overt violent repression, and unfavorable international publicity."[5] Notwithstanding these examples where a measure of accommodation and soft control has been present, the imperatives of settler supremacy militate against substantial advancement of the subordinate caste that might encroach on the settlers' political power.[6]

4. Kuper, "Political Change," p. 170; Werner Biermann and Reinhart Kössler, "The Settler Mode of Production: The Rhodesian Case," *Review of African Political Economy* 18 (May–August 1980): 112.

5. Ian Lustick, *Arabs in the Jewish State* (Austin: University of Texas Press, 1980), p. 26.

6. According to Good, settler rule is distinguished by "political rigidity" (Kenneth Good, "Settler Colonialism: Economic Development and Class Formation," *Journal of Modern African Studies* 14, no. 4 [December 1976]: 597–620).

The third pillar of settler supremacy is *to maintain the settlers' caste solidarity and the state's cohesion*. Although the great divide is that between settlers and the indigenous population, settler unity is never a foregone conclusion. Internal conflicts within the state and dominant community—along class, ethnic, political, or cultural lines—can be dangerous insofar as they compromise the state's capacity to deliver repression or if cracks in the settler monolith present an opportunity for natives to mobilize. Ideological glue and material incentives promote cohesion. In their ideologies regimes often dramatize communal differences by marshaling the folk wisdom of native "paganism," "barbarism," "animalism," "untrustworthiness," and "subversiveness." As material incentives, they commonly dispense privileges to the lower echelons of the settler caste—where they exist in significant numbers—to avert the growth of class alliances with natives. Hence, the emergence of "labor aristocracies" of Protestant workers in Northern Ireland and white workers in South Africa and Rhodesia.

A single- or dominant-party political system may also lessen friction among settlers. It is no accident that a single party ruled Northern Ireland for 50 consecutive years (the Unionist party), Taiwan for over 40 years (the Kuomintang), South Africa for over 40 years (the National party), and Liberia for 103 years (the True Whig party). During the decades of one-party rule in these cases, opposition parties within the settler population were either discouraged, marginalized, or banned outright. Liberia's ruling minority endured a chronic danger:

> the possibility of dissension within the ranks of the Americo-Liberian [settler] community weakening it during a moment of crisis. Thus, means had to be found to control...the tendency toward factionalism that has characterized Americo-Liberian society. The ultimate solution to this problem was the emergence of a single dominant party which has maintained the solidarity of the settler community in the face of both internal and external threats for almost a century.[7]

Never monolithic politically or socially, settler populations nevertheless must maintain some threshold level of cohesion in the face of the common enemy—the subordinate population and, in some cases, the metropole. In Israel and South Africa, moderate and hard-line factions have repeatedly tested this threshold. Yet tensions between them have not yet become unmanageable, in the sense of threatening critical settler

---

7. J. Gus Liebenow, *Liberia: The Evolution of Privilege* (Ithaca: Cornell University Press, 1969), pp. 59–60.

unity on the fundamental native question or leading influential settler elites to break ranks to ally with native interests. In Northern Ireland and Rhodesia, the basic commitment to settler domination tended to overshadow intrasettler cleavages on more secondary matters for most of the life of each state. When serious internal divisions did surface in Rhodesia in 1962, they were resolved by a purist regime that replaced the reformists and succeeded in rebuilding settler solidarity. Ulster Protestants were not so fortunate. The erosion of Unionist cohesion from 1969 to 1972 was a process that could not be reversed; it culminated in the breakdown of the settler state and its replacement with direct British rule.

It should be clear that the three conditions of stable settler rule identified above may be met in varying degrees, but stability is likely to be enhanced if all three are satisfied to a high degree. The greater the autonomy from the metropole, control over the indigenous population, and settler solidarity, the greater the likelihood that settler rule will be maintained. The weakening of one condition does not necessarily jeopardize settler rule in the short run, but it may gradually increase its vulnerability. In Rhodesia during the 1970s white solidarity and autonomy from the Crown remained intact, while black radicalization and insurgency intensified and shook the foundations of the state. The failure of only one condition in this case helps to explain why the inevitable collapse of the settler order was delayed for a decade. In short, Rhodesia in the 1970s exemplified unstable settler rule. In contemporary South Africa two pillars of settler stability are increasingly problematic: white cohesion and control over the black population. In Northern Ireland in the late 1960s all three conditions quickly deteriorated, thus expediting the demise of settler rule.

SETTLER SOCIETIES AS CASTE SOCIETIES

Settler rule is a particularly resilient form of authoritarian domination. Viewing the country as their permanent abode, settlers typically regard the political system as their private preserve, and the socioeconomic order as the vehicle for their exclusive prosperity. They often expropriate the richest land, lay claim to prime natural resources, introduce social segregation, and exploit native labor (under minority rule) or marginalize it (under majority rule).

Settler societies are extreme examples of "plural" or "communally divided" societies.[8] Unlike societies integrated along universalistic lines, a *plural society* is characterized by persistent and mutually reinforcing cleavages—typically ethnic, racial, or religious—between two or more sections of the population. By virtue of their cultural diversity, communal interests, and ascriptive socioeconomic inequality, the separate communities are differentially incorporated in the social order.

The concept of a communally divided society should not suggest that communal groups live in worlds apart, that social relations are filled with tension and hostility, or that political polarization between them is necessarily intense. Common institutions and shared interests are not altogether absent, and divisions may not pervade the entire social order. Some cooperation and interdependence (e.g., in economic relations) are evident even in the most rigidly stratified and segregated societies. Yet these bonds are insufficient to neutralize social divisions. On the most vital issues facing the society, the norm is a basic intracommunal consensus and intercommunal estrangement, with intracommunal discord and intercommunal harmony the exceptions to the rule.[9]

The model settler society is typically structured along *caste* lines: that is, a hierarchical structure of endogamous, hereditary groups, with pronounced social distance in intergroup relations, differential socialization, and a caste etiquette governing contacts between dominant and subordinate groups:[10]

- Intermarriage is discouraged across the caste line, but sexual unions often obey a double standard—that of sexual apartheid for native

8. See Kuper and Smith, eds., *Pluralism in Africa*; Ian Lustick, "Stability in Deeply Divided Societies: Consociationalism versus Control," *World Politics* 31, no. 3 (April 1979): 325–44; Sammy Smooha, "Control of Minorities in Israel and Northern Ireland," *Comparative Studies in Society and History* 22, no. 2 (April 1980): 256–80; Hermann Giliomee, "The Elusive Search for Peace: South Africa, Ulster, Israel," *Optima* 36, no. 3 (1988): 126–35 (Smooha's and Giliomee's comparative analyses are deeply flawed).

9. Alvin Rabushka and Kenneth Shepsle, *Politics in Plural Societies* (Columbia: Merrill, 1972), pp. 67–68.

10. The concept of caste has been applied to communally divided societies, including the American South, Liberia, Israel, Northern Ireland, and South Africa (see W. Lloyd Warner, "American Caste and Class," *American Journal of Sociology* 42, no. 2 [September 1936]: pp. 234–37; John Dollard, *Caste and Class in a Southern Town* [Garden City: Doubleday, 1949]; Allison Davis, Burleigh Gardner, and Mary Gardner, *Deep South: A Social Anthropological Study of Caste and Class* [Chicago: University of Chicago Press, 1941]; Gerald Berreman, "Caste in India and the United States," *American Journal of Sociology* 66, no. 2 [September 1960]: 120–27; Sammy Smooha, *Israel: Pluralism and Conflict* [Berkeley: University of California Press, 1978]; Liebenow, *Liberia: Evolution*).

men and settler women but not for settler men and native women (the pattern in Rhodesia and South Africa).[11]

• Social distance is relatively high in the areas of friendships, leisure activities, and work.

• Intercommunal interaction in everyday life may be superficially cordial, as members of each caste keep their prescribed places. Caste etiquette requires deferential conduct toward superiors, expressed in speech, body movement, and general demeanor—behavior that reaffirms dominant or subordinate status, reduces friction, and defuses dominant members' fears of the subordinate group.

• Such patterned interpersonal relations are reinforced by economic and political inequality and by the dominant value system. In Rhodesia, South Africa, Israel, Liberia, and (to a lesser extent) Northern Ireland, dominant stereotypes portray the subordinate population as backward, primitive, subhuman, childlike, irrational, lazy, and immoral;[12] these attributions help to justify the privileges of the dominant caste and work against social assimilation and political incorporation of the "uncivilized" caste.

There is naturally some variation in the degree to which actual cases approximate these caste patterns. Variation may be found in other areas as well: (1) racial, ethnic, or religious similitude between the castes; (2) the ratio of settlers to natives and whether the dominant group is a minority or majority (see Table 1); (3) the degree of assimilation and miscegenation allowed; (4) settlers' and natives' attitudes toward one another; and (5) the balance between coercive and other forms of social control. Although these variations are often significant in the settlers' and the natives' lives, the universal sine qua non remains the preservation of settler power and privilege.

The first two variables deserve more extensive discussion here. In some cases, racial or ethnic similarity between settlers and natives may soften the harsh features of settler domination. Common racial background between Chinese settlers and natives in Taiwan is associated

11. For Israel, see David Shipler, *Arab and Jew* (New York: Penguin, 1986), chaps. 10, 17. For Rhodesia, see Cyril Rogers and Charles Frantz, *Racial Themes in Southern Rhodesia* (New Haven: Yale University Press, 1962). On sexual norms in the American South, see Dollard, *Caste and Class*.
12. Dollard, *Caste and Class*; Smooha, *Israel*; Rogers and Frantz, *Racial Themes*; Shipler, *Arab and Jew*; Sammy Smooha, "Jewish and Arab Ethnocentrism in Israel," *Ethnic and Racial Studies* 10, no. 1 (January 1987): 1–26; Sally Belfrage, *Living with War: A Belfast Year* (New York: Penguin, 1987).

TABLE 1   SELECTED SOCIETIES WITH SETTLER POPULATIONS

Type of State	Percentage of Settlers in Population[a]
Settler state: de jure independent	
Israel (1948–present)	86[b]
Liberia (1847–1980)	3
South Africa (1910–present)	15
Settler state: de facto independent	
Northern Ireland (1921–1972)	63
Rhodesia (1923–1980)	5
Taiwan (1949–present)	14
Colonial state: dependent	
Algeria (until 1962)	12
Kenya (until 1963)	1
Namibia (until 1990)	7
New Caledonia	37
Zambia (until 1964)	3
Zanzibar (until 1964)	17

[a]Population figures are for 1987, except for Algeria (1954), Kenya (1960), Rhodesia (1979), and Zanzibar (1948).
[b]The figure for Israel excludes the occupied territories of the West Bank and Gaza.

with significant assimilation and low social distance. In Northern Ireland and Liberia, however, racial similarity could not neutralize profound ethnic and cultural differences. When former American slaves settled in Liberia in the 1820s,

> their views of Africa and Africans were essentially those of nineteenth-century whites in the United States. The bonds of culture were stronger than the bonds of race, and the settlers clung tenaciously to the subtle differences that set them apart from the tribal "savages" in their midst.[13]

Generally, the core characteristics of the settler model seem to be little affected by racial or ethnic factors.

Whether a minority or a majority, the settler caste monopolizes state power and excludes the native caste from meaningful political participation. Yet the respective mechanisms of political domination differ. Dominant majorities can afford to extend formal political rights to

13. J. Gus Liebenow, *Liberia: The Quest for Democracy* (Bloomington: Indiana University Press, 1987), p. 23.

subordinate populations—as in Northern Ireland and Israel.[14] By contrast, dominant minorities universalize the franchise only at their peril, driven by the "overriding fear. . .that they stand to be overwhelmed by a vastly larger majority."[15] The settlers must protect their island of privilege by de jure political exclusion of natives, limitations on natives' civil rights, and reliance on draconian measures of control (e.g., in Rhodesia, South Africa, and Liberia). Minority settler rule is normally associated with a "Herrenvolk" or master-caste democracy, in which the settlers practice internal democracy while the indigenes experience authoritarian rule.[16] This contradictory combination—democratic principles for settlers and dictatorship over natives—suggests that the "Herrenvolk democracies contained the ideological seeds of their own destruction";[17] but rigid and comprehensive mechanisms of domination may long postpone their collapse.

A dominant majority—however politically secure because of its numerical advantage—may attempt to manipulate the democratic rules of the game through elaborate voting qualifications, gerrymandering, and other devices. These mechanisms serve two purposes. First, they help to exclude the minority from the political arena and seem particularly desirable where the majority considers the minority to be innately inferior (in the American South) or politically subversive (in Northern Ireland) or both (in Israel). Second, political concessions may create rising expectations or a domino effect, giving minority groups the impression that they deserve equal opportunities in economic and social life. Their socioeconomic advancement, in turn, may appear to the majority as a challenge to its own privileges, prosperity, and expectations of deferential treatment.

For these reasons, a settler majority may be just as wary as a settler minority of granting concessions to the subordinate group. Under both majority and minority rule, attempts to introduce reforms by "enlightened" settlers may be rejected as premature or self-destructive. Because of their deviations in this regard, reformist premiers in Rhodesia in 1962 and Northern Ireland in 1969 were replaced by hard-liners. In most cases where modernizing elites have gained power, the concessions

14. The exception is Israel's occupied territories, where Arabs lack all political rights under military rule.
15. Rabushka and Shepsle, *Politics in Plural Societies,* p. 158.
16. Pierre van den Berghe, *Race and Racism* (New York: Wiley, 1967), p. 18; Kenneth Vickery, "Herrenvolk Democracy and Egalitarianism in South Africa and the U.S. South," *Comparative Studies in Society and History* 16, no. 3 (June 1974): 309–28.
17. Van den Berghe, *Race and Racism,* p. 216.

granted are usually too little and too late. This "failure of reformism"—
to quote Kuper—is rooted in the settlers' continuing refusal to relinquish
state power and in the subordinate community's resulting radicalization.[18] Faced with the futility of reform, the subordinate population typically abandons peaceful opposition in favor of armed struggle.[19]

Few contemporary settler regimes have attempted to open the polity
to the extent of threatening continued settler supremacy. Taiwan may
prove to be a deviant case.[20] Since 1987 the regime has lifted martial law
(which had been in effect for thirty-nine years), tolerated the formation
of opposition parties, eased press restrictions, and freed political prisoners. A native Taiwanese has become president (after the sudden death
of Chiang Ching-Kuo). Despite these significant reforms, repressive
emergency laws remain in effect; mainland settlers (14 percent of the
population) are vastly overrepresented in the three legislative bodies
(more than 80 percent); and powerful military elites and ruling party
stalwarts remain opposed to further democratization and liberalization.
According to one observer, the bottom line is that the ruling party (the
Kuomintang) will not allow itself to be dislodged from power, and the
softening of authoritarian rule should not be confused with genuine democratization.[21] It remains to be seen if a reformist solution will indeed
make Taiwan unique among settler states.

The case of Taiwan notwithstanding, settlers are generally more
likely than other authoritarian elites to perceive genuine democratization as a threat to their vested (caste) interests. For European settlers in
Africa, the ideals of the Enlightenment—liberty, equality, and democracy—were stripped of their universalistic value and reserved for the settlers alone; the natives were simply too primitive to qualify. Though the
great seal of Liberia proclaimed, The Love of Liberty Brought Us Here,
it had a terribly hollow ring for the indigenous population and reflected
the paradox of a formerly enslaved group (having fled America to escape
oppression) systematically denying liberty to African natives. Rhodesian
whites saw themselves as embodying "Western Christian civilization,"

18. Kuper elevates this "failure of reformism" to a "law" of minority racial and ethnic
domination (Leo Kuper, *The Pity of It All: Polarization of Racial and Ethnic Relations*
[Minneapolis: University of Minnesota Press, 1977], pp. 270–71).
19. Kuper considers inevitable the violent overthrow of such systems (ibid).
20. Edwin Winckler, "Institutionalization and Participation on Taiwan: From Hard to
Soft Authoritarianism," *China Quarterly*, no. 99 (September 1984): 481–99; Yangsun
Chou and Andrew Nathan, "Democratizing Transition in Taiwan," *Asian Quarterly* 27,
no. 3 (March 1987): 277–99.
21. Marc J. Cohen, *Taiwan at the Crossroads* (Washington, D.C.: Asia Resource Center, 1988), p. 65.

but it was never clear if or when they would allow blacks to advance. Where the natives had undeniably evolved, elites marshaled other arguments to maintain the sectarian order—such as "majority rule" or the defense of a unique religious or cultural tradition in Northern Ireland and Israel.

Some of the preconditions for a flourishing democracy (discussed in Chapter 1) are typically lacking in settler political systems. Absent is a unitary political culture—based on accommodation, agreement on constitutional principles, or a shared national identity. Rather, settler systems commonly counterpose a supremacist political culture to the native subculture and assert their ideological hegemony over it. A second deficiency is that of dynamic civic institutions to serve as a brake on repressive policies and promote democratic change; most settler societies have a poor record in this regard. Rhodesia's settler state depended on the thoroughgoing pacification of all countervailing institutions, particularly those of the native community. South Africa's more developed civic order has had a relatively minor impact on the regime's policies. In Ulster and Israel, Catholics and Arabs have their own media, churches, schools, political parties, and voluntary associations. Yet Arab institutions have little leverage over the Israeli state; Jewish civic organizations have registered much more success in containing state power. In Northern Ireland in the late 1960s, widespread Catholic protests and British pressures profoundly influenced the settler regime. Prior to that, Catholic forces were as powerless as their Israeli Arab counterparts.

FAILURES IN STATE BUILDING

Before turning to Northern Ireland and Rhodesia, let us examine a few cases where settlers were unsuccessful at state building, primarily because they failed to capture coercive institutions and free themselves from metropolitan interference. In several African colonies with white populations, the metropole supported settler domination—politically, economically, and militarily. Settler systems offered unique advantages to the metropole. It could maintain them at low cost, yet they served its geopolitical and economic interests. The metropole could assert its claim to territory against other colonial predators, and the territory supplied it with food and raw materials as well as an export market.

Nevertheless, the imperial government and the settlers often became partners in conflict; their interests and visions regarding critical issues (the pace and scope of territorial expansion, the treatment of natives, the territory's constitutional status) in many cases led the two parties into protracted struggles.[22] Although the British colonial administration often acted inconsistently, it was formally committed to protecting native interests—under the doctrine of "trusteeship"—which had enough reality to arouse settlers' insecurity and anxiety about their future in Africa. Rotberg writes of central Africa:

> In the period between the two world wars, white settlers north of the Zambezi had but one major political preoccupation: they tried desperately to free themselves from overseas-imposed restrictions in order to secure their own way of life for the future, and in order to prevent Africans from ever challenging that way of life.[23]

Tensions became particularly acute in settler domains during the twilight of colonialism in Africa. Emmanuel argues that such conflict was inevitable and that it ultimately drove the settlers and the home country in opposite directions: independence under settler rule versus independence under native majority rule. The settler community, writes Emmanuel, "could only be saved by secession from the metropolis and by setting up an independent 'white' state." The rather abrupt granting of independence to some colonies reflected "the home countries' need at a certain moment to steal a march on their own settlers who were threatening nearly everywhere to secede and form White States."[24]

The metropole prevailed in Kenya, where white settlers never managed to persuade London to support their quest for full autonomy.[25] Exercising great influence over the local Colonial Office administration in most territorial affairs and receiving repeated assurances from London of its support, the settlers never managed to make lasting alliances with local security agencies or, better, to capture the state in its entirety. This failure sealed their fate. Kenya's whites were unable "to maintain political and military dominance without expensive support from the metro-

22. See George Fredrickson, *White Supremacy: A Comparative Study of American and South African History* (Oxford: Oxford University Press, 1981); Louis Hartz, ed., *The Founding of New Societies* (New York: Harcourt, Brace and World, 1964).

23. Robert Rotberg, *The Rise of Nationalism in Central Africa* (Cambridge, Mass.: Harvard University Press, 1965), p. 93.

24. Arghiri Emmanuel, "White-Settler Colonialism and the Myth of Investment Imperialism," *New Left Review,* no. 73 (May–June 1972): 39, 43; see also K. Good, "Settler Colonialism."

25. George Bennett, "British Settlers North of the Zambezi, 1920 to 1960," in *Colonialism in Africa,* ed. L. Gann and P. Duignan (London: Cambridge University Press, 1970), p. 61.

pole." [26] That these settlers required British military force to put down the Mau Mau rebellion was a measure of their weakness. The metropole that had crushed black resistance in the 1950s then did a volte-face and granted independence to the colony in 1963, in the midst of stiff but unsuccessful settler resistance.

After failed attempts to win home rule in Northern Rhodesia (now Zambia) and Nyasaland (now Malawi) after World War II, white settlers struggled to convince the British Colonial Office to devolve another form of minority rule on these colonies through a merger with Southern Rhodesia, which already enjoyed self-government. The goal of such an alliance was to insulate Northern Rhodesia and Nyasaland from British interference—"to negate the comparatively benevolent, and therefore, to [the settlers], distasteful British regard for African rights" [27]—and prevent the feared granting of independence to the black majority. The campaign resulted in the formation in 1953 of the Central African Federation. After the federation disintegrated in 1963, the settlers of Northern Rhodesia and Nyasaland once again found themselves at London's mercy. The imperial government abruptly granted independence to the two colonies one year later. The experience of a decade in the federation under Southern Rhodesia's protective umbrella did nothing to enhance the leverage of these two settler enclaves in imperial decisions affecting the status of the colonies.

The same fate awaited Arab settlers in Zanzibar. During most of the period when Zanzibar was a British protectorate (1890–1963), British officials consistently endorsed the Arabs' political and economic domination over the African majority. Arabs received preference for top governmental positions; a minority of the population (17 percent) dominated the Legislative Council and had a disproportionate influence over public policy. Yet Arab ruling elites enjoyed only a precarious dominance. Their power was conditioned by the British Colonial Office's control of the core of state power: the police and the ministries of defense, finance, and internal security. The Arabs' failure to gain control of these vital organs underscored the fragility of settler rule in Zanzibar, which collapsed in the 1964 revolution. [28]

26. Gary Wasserman, *Politics of Decolonization: Kenya Europeans and the Land Issue* (Cambridge: Cambridge University Press, 1976), p. 21.

27. Rotberg, *Nationalism,* p. 93.

28. See Michael Lofchie, *Zanzibar: Background to Revolution* (Princeton: Princeton University Press, 1965); Michael Lofchie, "The Plural Society of Zanzibar," in *Pluralism in Africa,* ed. Kuper and Smith.

Britain's devolution of powers for law and order to American, Canadian, and Australian settlers was not the pattern in its African colonies. The British pattern in Africa was evident also in the French and Portuguese colonies. To their shock and dismay, Algeria's colons and Mozambique's settlers found themselves ultimately sacrificed by Paris and Lisbon after the colonies became political, military, and economic liabilities. Their abandonment particularly perplexed settlers who had benefited from the metropole's commitment of military forces to crush native revolts. Much like Kenya, Mozambique is a textbook example of this pattern. Unlike their Rhodesian neighbors, Portuguese settlers in Mozambique depended on the metropole for protection against organized native resistance. When a guerrilla war broke out in the 1960s, these settlers were at the mercy of the Portuguese military. Increasingly frustrated as the war wore on, the occupying troops and the settler community experienced a rift that developed into "the worst relations between a colonial army and a white community on record." [29] After the military coup in Lisbon in April 1974, the interests of Mozambique's settlers were jettisoned and state power transferred to a new black regime.

In Algeria an arrangement of dual power existed, whereby settlers controlled the bureaucracy and much of the civil government while internal security (policy making, military, police) remained in the hands of the metropole. [30] Algerian colons managed to win the sympathy of the local French administration and military, giving added force to settlers' resistance to the metropole's efforts at decolonization. But these alliances were no substitute for independent control of all instruments of state power; the settlers' interests were ultimately sacrificed on the altar of national independence. [31]

In each case and precisely because settlers had failed to capture the core of state power, they proved unable to maintain their advantages in the face of natives' political mobilization and metropolitan pressure. Dependency on the mother country was initially a blessing, later a curse. It was a blessing because the metropole's military defense of the settlers against native attacks was often decisive in ensuring the settlers' survival. But this protection also left the settlers critically vulnerable to the shifting calculations of the metropole. The best way to ensure the long-

29. Douglas Porch, *The Portuguese Armed Forces and the Revolution* (London: 1977), p. 32.

30. Ian Lustick, *State-Building Failure in British Ireland and French Algeria* (Berkeley: Institute of International Studies, 1985).

31. Miles Kahler, *Decolonization in Britain and France* (Princeton: Princeton University Press, 1984), chap. 5.

term survival of the settler community was not through dependency on the metropole, as Lustick believes, but rather through the building of a fully independent state, complete with coercive machinery.[32] Namibia's whites (7 percent of the population) recently suffered the same fate, at the hands of another settler state cum colonial power, South Africa, which controlled the military and police in Namibia until independence in 1989.[33] The prediction that "a truly independent Namibia would also remain heavily dependent on the South African-trained security forces and civil service" is a contradiction in terms.[34] Any nation "heavily dependent" on an outside life-support system is only nominally independent.

In some cases the ascendancy of the settler community came only after protracted or violent struggles with the imperial government had escalated into full-scale wars of independence. The British Mandate in Palestine, for example, was fraught with tensions between Jewish settlers and the colonial government. After World War II, guerrilla forces (Irgun, Stern Gang) fought British troops until they won independence for the new state of Israel in 1948. In South Africa, Afrikaner settlers took up arms against the British Government's attempts to enforce its native policy in the midnineteenth century. When direct confrontation could not force London to accept their claims for self-government and unfettered control over native affairs, Afrikaners embarked on their Great Trek away from the Cape Colony (ten thousand settlers did so from 1836 to 1846). Only by renouncing and physically escaping British jurisdiction could these settlers fully institutionalize their racial supremacy. The struggle between London and the Afrikaners continued well into the twentieth century, but by then Afrikaner ascendancy could not be arrested; a republic was declared in 1961.

Liberia may be unique in that settlers fairly smoothly achieved independence from the home country, the United States. With the help of the private efforts of the American Colonization Society (ACS), emanci-

---

32. Lustick, *State-Building Failure,* pp. 8, 61. A settler population's size appears to correlate with the extent of its material interests in the country (Kuper, "Political Change," pp. 171–72) and its capacity to resist metropolitan initiatives (Kahler, *Decolonization,* p. 317). There are exceptions, however: Zanzibar's Arab settlers were 17 percent of the population yet remained subordinate to London; Rhodesia's and Liberia's more powerful settlers, by contrast, totaled only 5 percent of their populations. Sheer size mattered less than autonomy with domestic power.

33. Tensions between Namibia's settlers and the South African authorities intensified as Namibia approached independence in November 1989.

34. John Battersby, "Namibia Challenge for South Africa," *New York Times,* 29 June 1987.

pated American blacks began to settle in Liberia in 1822. Only twenty-five years later they declared themselves independent of the ACS; in 1862 the United States government extended diplomatic recognition to the new state. Since the quasi metropole had never claimed imperial rights over and responsibilities for this territory, it could easily turn a blind eye to oppression of the natives. There was, in short, little juridical basis for conflict between these settlers and the mother country.

COMPARING RHODESIA AND NORTHERN IRELAND

The study of a single case is of limited value if the aim is to account for macrostructural continuities as well as changes. Only through careful comparative analysis can scholars begin to explain important continuities and changes in coercive structures and effectively address larger theoretical issues. Several basic similarities in the creation of settler states in Rhodesia and Northern Ireland and in their political institutions provide common ground for our analysis of key differences in the breakdown of settler rule and the rise of two rather different postsettler orders.

At first glance, these seemingly disparate cases appear to offer little basis for comparison. One was settled in the early seventeenth century, the other in the late nineteenth.[35] One is located in western Europe, the other in southern Africa. Northern Ireland is the site of a long-standing national identity crisis; as in Israel and Taiwan, survival as a distinct political entity has been chronically problematic. Northern Ireland shares a border with a state, the Republic of Ireland, whose constitution lays claim to Ulster; at the same time, it is officially an integral part of the United Kingdom. Unlike Scotland and Wales, however, it is only a conditional member: detachable once the majority so decides. By contrast, the fundamental conflict in Rhodesia (and South Africa) centered on internal structures and practices rather than the integrity of the nation-state.

Other differences can be mentioned. Some of the features of caste societies are muted in Northern Ireland but rather pronounced in Rhodesia: Catholics suffered less extensive economic, political, and social

---

35. In 1609, King James I established the plantation of Ulster, which attracted Scottish settlers. Pioneers first came to Rhodesia from South Africa in the 1880s. One treatment of the two, short on direct comparisons, is Barry Schutz and Douglas Scott, "Patterns of Political Change in Fragment Regimes: Northern Ireland and Rhodesia," in *The Politics of Race,* ed. I. Crewe (London: Croom Helm, 1975).

subordination than Rhodesian blacks; they were not expected to show routine deference toward Protestants; they were not subjected to the intense labor exploitation suffered by Rhodesian blacks. Also unlike white Rhodesians, Ulster's settlers constituted the majority of the population and built a majoritarian political order.

Despite these important differences, the cases reveal broad and striking similarities. Formally subordinate to Britain, these settler states enjoyed practical autonomy from the metropole in internal affairs, including control over key political and coercive institutions. The security sectors were a settler preserve, with sectarian orientation and modus operandi. As plural societies, both featured important divisions along cultural, political, and economic lines. Although the degree of subordination was by no means similar, both Catholics and blacks were disproportionately underprivileged, politically powerless, and socially segregated.

After almost a decade of guerrilla war, white Rhodesian rule succumbed in 1980 to black majority rule. After three years of sectarian political violence and unrest, Protestant rule in Ulster was replaced in 1972 by direct British rule. In both cases, the new governments proclaimed their intentions to modernize the state apparatus, dismantle repressive institutions, and create a radically different political order—one that would no longer privilege settlers and ignore native interests. Since the transfer of power, each government has confronted persisting low-intensity insurgency (from Catholic and Protestant militants in Northern Ireland and rural guerrillas in Zimbabwe) and traditional communal rivalries: Protestant-Catholic in Ulster, Shona-Ndebele in Zimbabwe.

The demise of imperial jurisdiction and white settler domination in Zimbabwe has not contributed to the liberalization of the internal security system; basic features of the inherited system remain intact and continue to foster repression. This case demonstrates that the collapse of settler rule is not necessarily associated with the dismantling of the state apparatus supporting it. By contrast, the reimposition of British colonial rule in Ulster has helped to modernize certain features of the security system. Contrary to the conventional wisdom on Northern Ireland, significant—but by no means complete—changes have taken place in the security system's structure and normative order.

The next chapter analyzes the rise and consolidation of settler states in Northern Ireland and Rhodesia; subsequent chapters examine their breakdown and distinctive outcomes under a new order.

CHAPTER 3

Building Settler States

*Foundations in Rhodesia and
Northern Ireland*

The development of stable settler states depends on three conditions:
the settlers must secure political and military autonomy from the metropole; they must build an effective system of control to preempt or
crush native resistance; finally, they must cultivate internal solidarity on
vital issues facing the settler community and minimize conflicts along
class, generational, or political lines that weaken their control over the
subordinate population. The shattering of one pillar of settler rule can
rock the entire house, although it may take some time to crumble—as in
Rhodesia in the 1970s. The decay of all three is likely to hasten the collapse of the system—as occurred in Ulster from 1969 to 1972.

SECURING INDEPENDENCE FROM LONDON

In 1889 London granted Cecil Rhodes and his British South African
Company (BSAC) a charter to occupy, exploit, and govern what became
Southern Rhodesia. The settlement of the area was part of a British
strategy to establish a territorial counterbalance to the regional claims of
Germany, Portugal, and South Africa. In this instance, rather than direct
involvement Britain preferred absentee expansion through its BSAC
proxy, because it simultaneously extended Britain's sphere of influence
in Africa and avoided the expense of formal colonization.[1]

---

1. Claire Palley, *The Constitutional History and Law of Southern Rhodesia* (Oxford:
Clarendon Press, 1966), pp. 24–26.

Britain retained nominal jurisdiction over the territory, including the power to revoke the company's charter; behind this facade, the BSAC exercised de facto control over the territory. London was prepared to assert itself only "if Company action was likely either to result in diplomatic difficulties, to involve Britain with powerful chiefs, to involve exploitation of the British name, or to occasion adverse parliamentary or press comment." [2] In practice, intervention was rare and the company enjoyed extraordinary quasi-state autonomy and latitude from 1890 to 1896. [3]

Conflicts over land and labor provided the initial source of hostilities between settlers and natives. For the blacks (or "Africans"), company rule meant summary land expropriation, forced labor, and physical abuse. [4] In reaction to this mistreatment a massive African revolt broke out in 1896–1897. The rebellion was of such magnitude—10 percent of the settler population died—that London could no longer turn a blind eye to the colony's race relations. A Legislative Council was introduced wherein power was divided between representatives of the company, the settler community, and a British commissioner.

Britain's slightly increased involvement after the rebellion was designed to mitigate the oppressiveness of BSAC rule; yet the metropole avoided drastic steps such as abolishing the company's charter, because it was unwilling to assume the financial burden that such action would require. [5]

Although the British South Africa Company retained control over internal affairs, its position was eroding as British involvement rose and the settler community grew bolder in asserting its interests against BSAC power. [6] Discontent mounted over disputed mining claims and over the company's expropriation of unalienated land, and the settlers began to press for the replacement of the charter with devolved government. The center of political gravity shifted from the company to the settlers in 1922, when settlers voted in a referendum for devolved government rather than incorporation into the Union of South Africa. [7] Southern

2. Ibid., pp. 42–43.
3. Lewis Gann, *A History of Southern Rhodesia: Early Days to 1934* (London: Chatto and Windus, 1965), p. 208; Palley, *Constitutional History,* p. 100; Robin Palmer, *Land and Racial Domination in Rhodesia* (Berkeley: University of California Press, 1977), p. 25.
4. Charles van Onselen, *Chibaro: African Mine Labour in Southern Rhodesia, 1900–1933* (London: Pluto Press, 1976).
5. Palley, *Constitutional History,* p. 129.
6. Terence Ranger, *Revolt in Southern Rhodesia: 1896–1897* (Evanston: Northwestern University Press, 1967), p. 336.
7. Because of franchise limitations, the African voice was not heard in this election. Only 60 of the 18,810 voters were African (James Mutambirwa, *The Rise of Settler Power in Southern Rhodesia, 1898–1923* [Cranbury, N.J.: Associated University Presses, 1980], p. 217).

Rhodesia officially became a "self-governing colony" in 1923. (Hereafter, references to *Rhodesia* and *Southern Rhodesia* are interchangeable; Northern Rhodesia, which became independent Zambia in 1964, was a separate colony.)

London retained sovereign authority over the territory, but Rhodesia enjoyed virtual dominion status.[8] Britain retained "reserved powers" over native affairs and foreign relations but almost never vetoed legislation passed by Rhodesia's all-white Legislative Assembly.[9] Prime Minister Godfrey Huggins boasted in July 1951 that "the British Government know that in practice the reservations are not worth the paper they are written on."[10] Unlike other British colonies—including those with sizable settler populations like Kenya, Zanzibar, and Northern Rhodesia— Rhodesia was not subject to the administrative or military authority of the British Colonial Office (a resident governor performed largely ceremonial duties). By 1923 the settlers had at their disposal both the political and coercive levers of state power. In achieving de facto autonomy from Britain, Rhodesia mastered the first imperative of a settler state.

Northern Ireland is often depicted as the scene of a deep-rooted, if archaic, religious conflict. But religion is only part of the problem. Civil strife tends to occur along religious lines, but the essence of the conflict lies in the distribution of political power, disputes over national identity, and the constitutional status of the territory. Northern Ireland contains "two nations" with diametrically opposed national identities, Irish and British, which render the survival and integrity of the state problematic. In this it is like Israel and Taiwan but unlike Rhodesia and South Africa. In both Israel and Northern Ireland, religious cleavages are secondary to, but clearly exacerbate, conflicts on fundamental constitutional and existential questions.

Unlike its Rhodesian counterpart, the Northern Ireland state was forged in the heat of a meltdown of order and authority that accompanied the partition of Ireland in 1920. The Anglo-Irish War of 1919–1921 was followed by a civil war in the south in 1922; in the north continuing political violence by the Irish Republican Army was coupled with sectarian attacks between rival groups of Catholics and Protestants. Between

---

8. The dominions of Canada, New Zealand, and Australia formally recognized the British monarch as head of state but enjoyed full self-government.

9. Larry Bowman, *Politics in Rhodesia: White Power in an African State* (Cambridge, Mass.: Harvard University Press, 1973), pp. 6–8.

10. Huggins, quoted in C. Leys and C. Pratt, eds., *A New Deal in Central Africa* (London: Heinemann, 1960), p. 28. Throughout the text I follow British usage in capitalizing Government when I refer to the executive.

June 1920 and June 1922 in Ulster, 428 people were killed and 1,766 wounded.[11]

After decades of frustration in dealing with unrest and violence in Ireland, Westminster not surprisingly became the prime mover in founding this settler state, whereas in other cases the settlers often took the initiative. Since London wished to extricate itself from its exhausting entanglements in Ireland, it rejected the alternative of direct rule over Ulster.

Before partition, British efforts to grant home rule to all of Ireland (in 1886, 1893, and 1912–1914) were fiercely resisted by Protestants, who feared that home rule would mean "Rome rule"—that is, that Catholic doctrines would become state policy and that the Protestant minority would lose its political and economic privileges. Unlike settlers elsewhere, they campaigned against devolved power, convinced that their paramount interest in remaining outside a Catholic Ireland was best protected under the mantle of full incorporation in the United Kingdom.

Faced with stiff Protestant opposition to home rule, British political elites sought a compromise. In an effort to placate both northern Protestants and southern Catholics, Britain granted home rule or dominion status to the south (the Irish Free State) and devolved separate power to six of the nine northern counties of the province of Ulster (which remained within the United Kingdom). Decades later Britain would find that partition had been a colossal mistake. But before 1921 it seemed the best solution for northern Protestants and southern Catholics alike, just as it promised to free the Crown from its "Irish problem" once and for all. In order to ensure that Protestant preferences would prevail in Northern Ireland, Britain deliberately drew the boundaries in a way that guaranteed a Protestant majority enclave.

After power was devolved on the new northern state in 1921, the Unionists quickly discovered distinct advantages in reducing their vulnerability to the vicissitudes of metropolitan policy shifts. A candid 1936 report by the Ulster Unionist Council revealed its primary fear:

> Had we refused to accept a Parliament for Northern Ireland and remained at Westminster, there can be little doubt that now we would either be inside the [Irish] Free State or fighting desperately against incorporation. Northern Ireland without a Parliament of her own would be a standing temptation to cer-

11. Patrick Buckland, *A History of Northern Ireland* (Dublin: Gill and Macmillan, 1981), p. 46.

tain British politicians to make another bid for a final settlement with the Irish Republic.[12]

The Government of Ireland Act of 1920 established the constitutional relation between Britain and Northern Ireland whereby Westminster remained the supreme authority. Matters concerning the United Kingdom as a whole—including foreign relations, defense, revenue and taxation, and external trade—were excluded from the powers of the new Ulster parliament. All other matters became the concern of the settler state. The Protestant government had control over the civil service and internal security forces. Under the constitution, defense of the border was a metropolitan responsibility and a small contingent of the British army was garrisoned in the province for this purpose. But the principal instruments of law and order were answerable to the settler regime alone: the Royal Ulster Constabulary (RUC), the Ulster Special Constabulary (USC), and the Ministry of Home Affairs. Unlike Britain's conventional unarmed police, Ulster's forces were armed and militarized, almost totally Protestant, and fierce champions of Protestant supremacy. Control over the forces of order put the settlers in much better stead than their counterparts in conventional colonies, where metropolitan-controlled forces handled both internal and external security. London initially armed and financed the Protestant security forces.[13] The Unionist Government was aware that the British might prove unreliable allies and took steps to ensure that it would not have to depend on them or face London's interference in the future. (Settler groups elsewhere were much slower to take such steps.)

Overt Catholic resistance to the new order was crushed in the early 1920s; thereafter, the minority became rather passive. Yet Catholics, like Israeli Arabs after 1948, remained opposed to the new state and dismissed it as an artificial creation designed to perpetuate domination by a factitious majority. To the respective settlers, therefore, Ulster's Catholics and Israel's Arabs seemed to constitute an "enemy-affiliated minority." Catholic alienation from the northern state,[14] coupled with the

12. Report quoted in R. J. Lawrence, *The Government of Northern Ireland: Public Finance and Public Services, 1921–1964* (London: Oxford University Press, 1965), p. 75.

13. Michael Farrell, *Arming the Protestants: The Formation of the Ulster Special Constabulary and the Royal Ulster Constabulary, 1920–1927* (London: Pluto, 1983), p. 280.

14. Catholic political parties consistently demanded the dissolution of the northern state and unification of Ireland; Catholics' alienation was widely perceived by Protestant civilians and state officials and is generally accepted by scholars. Unfortunately, there is no representative attitudinal data on perceptions of Catholic "disloyalty" from 1921 to 1972; on attitudes toward Arab "disloyalty" in Israel, see Sammy Smooha, "Jewish and Arab Ethnocentrism in Israel," *Ethnic and Racial Studies* 10, no. 1 (January 1987): 1–26.

perceived threat from southern Ireland, perpetuated a siege mentality in Unionist quarters and helped justify sectarian discrimination against the minority.[15] A two-thirds majority in Ulster, the Protestants are a minority in Ireland as a whole (one-fourth of the population) that remains important in light of the Republic of Ireland's constitutional claim of sovereignty over Ulster.[16] Driven by chronic insecurity, the Protestant regime organized to arrest minority political mobilization, cement the border against an irredentist neighbor, and consolidate settler supremacy in the province. It was not so much a question of whether Catholics were actually plotting or engaged in subversive activity but instead what they might do if given the opportunity, that is, if controls were relaxed. Rather than seek accommodation with the disaffected Catholic community in the wake of the early disturbances, successive Unionist regimes took steps that exacerbated communal divisions and thus reinforced Protestants' sense of insecurity.[17] The logic was clear: since Catholics were beyond the pale as incorrigible fifth-columnists, any official accommodation would be suicidal for the state.

Catholic opposition to partition and disloyalty to the settler state had unique advantages for the Protestants. MacDonald argues that the continuation of Protestant domination required, and thus encouraged, Catholic disloyalty in order to legitimate settler privileges, amplify the salience of Protestant "loyalty" to Britain, and reproduce class solidarity among Protestants.[18] Catholic legitimation of the new state might have shattered the arguments justifying the Protestant monopoly of power: that Protestants alone could be trusted by London to maintain order and the union.

Public order and political stability were from the beginning and remain today London's overriding concerns in Northern Ireland. The integrity of the political system and the extent to which Ulster's political culture deviated from British standards were not—until the late 1960s—

15. The terms *Unionist* and *Loyalist* refer generally to the Protestant population, and are often used interchangeably. Unionists sought to maintain the union of Northern Ireland with the rest of the United Kingdom. Yet their "loyalty" to the British Crown has been contingent on the metropole's perceived defense of Protestant interests; as a 1978 survey found, 85 percent of Protestants stated that a "loyalist is loyal to Ulster before the British government" (Edward Moxon-Browne, *Nation, Class, and Creed in Northern Ireland* [Aldershot: Gower, 1983], p. 86).

16. Article 2 of the Constitution of the Republic of Ireland reads: "The national territory consists of the whole island of Ireland."

17. David Miller, *Queen's Rebels: Ulster Loyalism in Historical Perspective* (Dublin: Gill and Macmillan, 1978), p. 139.

18. Michael MacDonald, *Children of Wrath: Political Violence in Northern Ireland* (New York: Basil Blackwell, 1986), pp. 22, 24.

serious concerns in the metropole. During the formative years of the new state, Britain did attempt to temper the Unionist Government's largely confrontational approach toward Catholics, but once order had been restored in the early 1920s, metropolitan interest receded. In May 1923 Westminster adopted a convention that Ulster's domestic affairs were not to be discussed in the House of Commons and turned a blind eye to the province's political and internal security arrangements. In this same year Britain devolved political power to the Rhodesian settlers.

Over the next several decades, "the policy . . . was to minimise British involvement politically and militarily. Action was taken only where the alternative appeared ultimately to entail a greater degree of involvement." [19] Britain retained the power to suspend or abolish devolved government in the province, but this ultimate sanction also posed the greatest risk of a backlash and would have required the very involvement that London was concerned to avoid.

Members of Parliament in Westminster showed no interest in the affairs of the new settler state. As in Rhodesia, the resident governor almost never exercised his veto power over legislation. Similarly, the premier agency responsible for Anglo-Ulster relations, the Home Office in London, played a minimal role in the province. [20] Its skeleton staff for Northern Ireland affairs operated under the (incorrect) assumption that "questions of law and order are entirely for the Government of Northern Ireland." [21] As one Home Secretary admitted, "I had no occasion to seek more work or to go out and look at the problems of Northern Ireland, unless they forced themselves upon me." [22] With respect to internal affairs, the metropolitan government in effect treated Ulster and Rhodesia as if they were independent states.

Finally, the fact that the Unionist regime was based on majority rule gave it a measure of moral capital that settler minorities elsewhere could never claim. That this majority status depended on an artificially created Protestant enclave was beside the point. The contested origins and problematic existence of the Ulster state were irrelevant to metropolitan elites as long as political stability and the trappings of democracy were visible. Majority rule was at that time identified with democratic gov-

19. Paul Bew, Peter Gibbon, and Henry Patterson, *The State in Northern Ireland: 1921–1972* (Manchester: Manchester University Press, 1979), pp. 185–86.

20. Bew, Gibbon, and Patterson, *The State,* p. 177.

21. Frank Newsam, Permanent Under-Secretary of State at the Home Office, quoted in ibid.

22. James Callaghan, *A House Divided: The Dilemma of Northern Ireland* (London: Collins, 1973), p. 4.

ernment in the United Kingdom. No alternative political system—such as power sharing—seemed acceptable in the Ulster context. London assumed that majority rule would operate satisfactorily and the 1920 act contained no special protections for the Catholic minority or inducements for their political participation.[23] In practice, majority rule in Ulster was a recipe for permanent settler rule and "majority dictatorship."[24]

SETTLER UNITY AND NATIVE SUBORDINATION

In the absence of serious pressure from the metropole, Northern Ireland and Rhodesian settlers had little incentive to incorporate the Catholics and blacks into the polity, elicit their consent, or nurture relations that would bridge the ethnic or racial divide. Indigenes fared somewhat better where the presence of imperial authorities diluted the settlers' power, such as Zanzibar and Kenya. De facto or de jure independence in Rhodesia, Northern Ireland, Liberia, and South Africa in effect allowed the settlers to construct the political, social, and economic arrangements best suited to consolidating their supremacy.

For all the differences between Rhodesia and Northern Ireland (e.g., minority vs. majority domination; geographical relation to the metropole; racial vs. ethnic and religious divisions), settler rule rested on similar foundations. Common to both was a commitment to build and sustain one caste's solidarity and institutionalize the other's subordination.

Fissures within a settler population can prove disastrous in two ways: they may provide an opening for native mobilization and they may undermine the state's capacity to defend settler rule. Settler cohesion is not inevitable considering the potential for class, generational, and political differences within most settler populations. There is always the possibility that enlightened segments within the settler enclave might decide to champion the rights or forge political alliances with leaders of the subordinate population—either from genuine humanistic concerns or a conviction that political and economic concessions would advance, not hinder, the long-term survival of settler supremacy. (This belief motivated moderate settlers in Liberia and Zanzibar to seek the political incorporation of indigenous blacks.) When modernizing elites in Rhodesia in the late 1950s and Ulster in the late 1960s made such initia-

23. Buckland, *History,* p. 23.
24. Arend Lijphart, "Review Article: The Northern Ireland Problem," *British Journal of Political Science 5*, no. 1 (January 1975): 94.

tives, they were promptly thrown out of office by traditionalists. Hard-line settlers in both cases were convinced that even minor concessions—although posing no immediate threat—would precipitate a revolution of rising expectations that would ultimately endanger settler power and privilege. Both political systems displayed a "built-in tendency towards illiberalism" that doomed all experiments with reform.[25]

It is also possible that working-class settlers will enter into alliances with workers in the subordinate population, based on their common class affinities. In settler societies, however, class interests are often neutralized by caste interests. Working-class settlers, typically feeling the most threatened by competition and advancement of individuals from the subordinate caste (because of their socioeconomic proximity to its top echelon), often become the fiercest champions of unadulterated settler supremacy. This pattern is evident in Rhodesia, Northern Ireland, Algeria, and South Africa.

In our two cases, both material incentives and symbolic threats reinforced the dominant caste identity of working-class settlers. Materially, they enjoyed the privileges of a labor aristocracy: formal or informal mechanisms prevented natives from competing with working-class settlers for particular jobs. Symbolically, the settlers' cultural "superiority" was counterposed against the "primitive" ways of the indigenes, which reinforced their conviction that settler supremacy was morally justified. Caste unity was presented as vital to avoid the dire consequences of capitulation to native interests. Protestant elites in Northern Ireland routinely insisted that any concessions to Catholics would ultimately lead to "Rome rule" and "papist domination" in a reunited Ireland; white elites in Rhodesia pointed to the specter of "black barbarism" and a host of other evils associated with premature African advancement. In both cases, working-class settlers not only accepted these claims as articles of faith but became their most committed exponents.

This ideological glue was reinforced with political cement. A strong one-party or dominant-party state, for example, may help to unify a settler community, as it did for the True Whig party in Liberia; its full century in office helped contain factionalism. The dominant-party systems of Ulster and Rhodesia similarly minimized intrasettler conflicts. How did the settler power structures contribute to control over natives?

---

25. Colin Leys, *European Politics in Southern Rhodesia* (Oxford: Clarendon Press, 1959), pp. 293, 175.

The fact that state power was based on majority rule in Ulster and minority rule in Rhodesia accounts for some of the variation in the organization of politics in general and of the franchise in particular. As a small minority of the population, Rhodesian settlers (like those in South Africa and Liberia) depended on rigid, de jure political exclusion of the majority. Natives were denied voting rights and their political parties were harassed or proscribed. Having the strength of numbers, Ulster Protestants (like Israeli Jews) had little need to disenfranchise the minority population. They could maintain settler domination through ostensibly democratic institutions.

Nevertheless, Ulster's electoral and parliamentary order was de facto exclusive. The political culture allowed little democratic accommodation of those whose loyalty to the state was deemed suspect. Thus, Catholics were excluded from top executive positions—a pattern of exclusion that, according to Rose, was "matched nowhere else in the Western world."[26] Ulster's uniqueness is dimmed, however, once it is placed in proper comparative company with other settler states.

The national franchise was formally open, but circumstances made Catholic representation hollow and reinforced a "tyranny of the majority." Party representation in the Stormont Parliament did not fluctuate markedly over time (there were few floating voters);[27] the Catholic vote was systematically underrepresented after the plurality system replaced proportional representation in 1929; property and other qualifications in local elections served to reduce the votes of the disproportionately disadvantaged Catholics (about one-fourth of those eligible to vote in Westminster elections were ineligible in local elections).[28] These devices helped ensure that Catholics would not win control of Londonderry or the three border counties—where they constituted the majority—in local or parliamentary elections. Finally, political parties did not circulate in and out of power. The Unionist party's grip on power lasted for the state's entire fifty-year life; in England no party has remained in power for more than twenty consecutive years since the early nineteenth century.

In the first election to the Stormont Parliament in May 1921 the Unionists won forty seats and the Catholic parties won twelve, underrepre-

26. Richard Rose, *Governing Without Consensus: An Irish Perspective* (Boston: Beacon, 1971), p. 443.

27. Roughly 5 percent of Catholic voters voted for the Unionist party and 1 percent of the Protestants voted for the Nationalist party.

28. Rose, *Governing,* p. 441.

senting the Catholic population. Expressing the minority's general reluctance to cooperate with the new regime, Catholic MPs refused to take their seats. For Protestants, this action was proof positive of Catholic disloyalty to the state and justified the state's reluctance to aggregate Catholic interests. In later decades, Catholic representatives vacillated between participation and abstention at Stormont.

The Rhodesian and Ulster Parliaments had some of the trappings of British parliamentary democracy but little of the substance. Neither parliament was a genuine center of power, aggregator of interests, or arena for political struggle over law and order. Members were typically either uninterested in or incapable of challenging security legislation and policy. In this most vital area of state power, these parliaments gave the executive carte blanche, delegating to Cabinet much broader powers than is customary under the Westminster system. In Britain, the political culture permits freer debate and encourages opposition parties to take an active role in reviewing proposed legislation. Ulster and Rhodesian legislatures functioned primarily to endorse executive policy.[29]

The judiciary in settler Rhodesia and Northern Ireland was an equally ineffective constraint on executive power, for several reasons: judges identified strongly with the basic precepts of settler domination and were demonstrably inclined to favor the claims of settlers over natives (some judges were directly affiliated with the ruling party); and the narrow scope of judicial authority in the security field reduced opportunities to issue decisions against the executive. In divided societies, a vigorous tradition of judicial review can be a particularly valuable, if partial, corrective to abuses of state power.[30]

The exclusivist character and settler orientation of the Ulster and Rhodesian states were predictably most pronounced in the Cabinet and the upper reaches of the civil service. The state bureaucracy was a settler citadel, despite the presence of a few Catholic or black officials at lower levels.

The branches of the state tended to act in concert on security matters because of the executive's dominance over other agencies and the shared institutional commitment to uphold settler rule. In Northern Ireland and Rhodesia, divisions within the state and within the ruling party

29. See Patrick Buckland, *The Factory of Grievances: Devolved Government in Northern Ireland, 1921–1938* (New York: Barnes and Noble, 1979), pp. 27, 35.

30. This is evidenced to some extent in contemporary South Africa (Hugh Corder, "The Supreme Court: Arena of Struggle?" in *The State of Apartheid*, ed. W. James [Boulder, Colo.: Lynne Rienner, 1987]).

were generally secondary to and overshadowed by the great divide between settlers and natives. This remarkable intrastate cohesion was shaken only during crises, that is, periods of metropolitan intervention or native mobilization (examined below and in Chapters 4 and 5).

States lacking the active consent of the governed are not necessarily precarious; they may survive for long periods. An effective apparatus of control may produce sufficient popular acquiescence for relative stability. Regimes in Rhodesia and Northern Ireland placed the consent of the subordinate population secondary to the premium of maintaining the regime's legitimacy among the settler population—a value that concessions to Ulster Catholics or Rhodesian blacks would vitiate.[31] The confidence of the settler population could not long survive attempts to win the support of the native population through serious reform of the system; conversely, natives were hardly likely to support a regime steadfastly committed to undiluted settler supremacy. Although this formula of sectarian legitimacy cannot be elevated to a general law of settler domination—since some regimes have attempted to strike a balance between native and settler consent—it applies to them more than to some other forms of authoritarian rule, which place a somewhat greater emphasis on securing popular or corporatist legitimacy.[32]

If building native consent was not high on the agenda in our two cases, how then did they maintain order? Control over Catholics was achieved in part through the enforcement of security laws, electoral gerrymandering, police harassment, and periodic intimidation by Protestant vigilante groups. These controls helped perpetuate Catholics' acquiescence and served to discourage organized resistance.

Coercive and administrative controls were less severe and extensive in Ulster than in Rhodesia, because as a minority the Catholics were easier to handle, and highly repressive control in a province of the United Kingdom risked unwanted attention from London. Compared with

31. Race relations in Rhodesia had a measure of white paternalism like the romanticized American Southern version, which viewed white domination as beneficial, contributing to gradual black advancement. In 1938, Prime Minister Godfrey Huggins outlined Rhodesia's "two pyramid" or "parallel development" policy:

the country should be divided into separate areas for black and white. In the Native area the black man must be allowed to rise to any position to which he is capable of climbing. . . . In the European area the black man will be welcomed, when, tempted by wages, he offers his services as a laborer, but it will be on the understanding that he shall merely assist, and not compete with, the white man. (Quoted in Bowman, *Politics in Rhodesia,* p. 15)

32. See Maria Alves, *State and Opposition in Military Brazil* (Austin: University of Texas Press, 1985).

Rhodesian and South African blacks, Ulster's Catholics were less dependent economically on the dominant group (having an independent economic base), had more autonomous institutions (parties, churches,
media, schools), and were not subjected to formal apartheid restrictions
(though informal segregation existed in housing, jobs, and education).
The fact that in Rhodesia, as in South Africa, the difference between
settlers and natives was racial and that the settlers were a tiny minority
made an elaborate and rigid infrastructure of control necessary to inhibit black mobilization. From the beginning, extralegal coercion—
exercised by white farmers and mining companies to acquire and exploit
cheap black labor—coexisted with discriminatory legal instruments. At
least twenty-four statutes applied solely to blacks and many others
aimed primarily at control of natives.[33] Most important were the 1930
Land Apportionment Act and the 1934 Industrial Conciliation Act. The
first act legalized the extant system of land inequality (by 1930, the
white population controlled 51.7 percent of the country's land, the Africans 29.7 percent; by contrast, settlers owned 7 percent of the land in
colonial Kenya, 14 percent in Algeria, and 87 percent in South Africa).
The second act legalized an industrial color bar that segmented black
and white laborers into different reward structures and disallowed competition between them and mobility across this racial chasm. (Among
whites unemployment was almost nonexistent; for blacks joblessness
and underemployment were facts of life.)

In addition to being denied rights of political participation and equal
economic opportunities, Africans were caught in a web of "petty apartheid" restrictions in Rhodesia as in South Africa. Caste norms prevented
interracial marriages, discouraged interracial friendships and recreational activities, and exacted deferential behavior from blacks. Pass laws
existed from the beginning of the state. A 1902 statute required that
blacks carry a registration certificate at all times, and the Native Registration Act of 1936 stipulated that urban Africans carry additional identity papers. Racial segregation was instituted in housing, education,
health care, public transportation, and other public facilities; government spending in these areas systematically discriminated in favor of
whites. As they did in South Africa, whites varied somewhat in their attitudes toward specific caste restrictions, as Rogers and Frantz found in a
1958 survey (responses ranged from relatively tolerant to rigidly con-

33. L. H. Gann and Peter Duignan, "Changing Patterns of a White Elite: Rhodesian
and Other Settlers," in *Colonialism in Africa*, ed. L. H. Gann and Peter Duignan, vol. 2
(London: Cambridge University Press, 1970).

servative).[34] But subsequent events (discussed below) showed that the majority of the white population was not prepared to endorse reforms of the caste system.

This comprehensive structure of inequality and social control fragmented the African population and ensured that any resistance would be sporadic and ineffective.[35] For the first half of the twentieth century, Africans were "politically inert, passive, and virtually powerless," and were "acted upon rather than acting to a degree unusual even in a colonial situation." [36] The effectiveness of the extensive system of control meant that the authorities rarely needed to resort to arms and that internal security laws were few—until the late 1950s, when black political ferment began in Rhodesia as the winds of decolonization swept the continent. Only then did blacks' "resigned acceptance of white rule" begin to erode, which made innovations in the system of law and order seem necessary.[37]

ULSTER'S SYSTEM OF LAW AND ORDER

Rhodesia's internal security system evolved gradually after 1923 to preempt the rise of African opposition but was galvanized as nationalist opposition intensified after 1958 (discussed below); Northern Ireland laid the institutional foundations of its security system in the settler regime's first year, at the height of political violence. Both cases lend support to Alves's argument that "the character of the national security state can only be understood in relation to its interaction with . . . opposition movements in civil society." [38] Alves's argument exaggerates, however, the role of opposition movements in two respects. First, the development of a repressive internal security enterprise does not logically require manifest opposition but may be designed to prevent its growth. Second, in a nation where civil society is undeveloped, the impact of opposition forces is understandably much less salient than in nations (such as Bra-

---

34. Cyril Rogers and Charles Frantz, *Racial Themes in Southern Rhodesia* (New Haven: Yale University Press, 1962), pp. 90–94.

35. On the role of the mining compound system in subduing African workers, see Duncan Clarke, "African Mine Labourers and Conditions of Labour in the Mining Industry in Rhodesia, 1940–1974," *Rhodesian Journal of Economics* 9 (December 1975): 177–218, and van Onselen, *Chibaro.*

36. Richard Gray, *The Two Nations* (London: Oxford University Press, 1960), p. 167; Terence Ranger, *Crisis in Southern Rhodesia* (London: Fabian Commonwealth Bureau, 1960), p. 12.

37. Bowman, *Politics in Rhodesia,* p. 16.

38. Alves, *State and Opposition,* p. 9.

zil, the Philippines, or South Korea) where civic institutions provide a rich source of resistance to repressive policies.

Northern Ireland's internal security institutions were from the beginning blatantly sectarian in outlook and operation: security powers were vigorously applied to Catholics, whose slightest protest was defined as "treachery," while Protestant political crime was treated leniently or with impunity, under the rubric of "Loyalist activity." [39] According to Farrell, "The Unionists did not accept the basic assumption of British democracy—that the public administration and the security forces should be neutral between the contending parties in the state." [40] "Between 1920 and 1968," writes O'Dowd, "Unionist 'law and order' remained inviolate from the modernization of repressive apparatuses in Britain." [41] Had the regime taken steps to reduce the security system's sectarian orientation, it might have signed its own death warrant, for such action would have violated the raison d'être of the settler state: namely, the defense of specifically Protestant interests. As in Rhodesia, the hegemonic forces within the dominant caste never accepted that their long-term interests might best be served by some accommodation with the subordinate community; they conceived power as a zero-sum matter, ruling out concessions. In this deeply divided society, the settler community would almost certainly have defined universalistic enforcement of law and order as betrayal and resisted it—precisely what has occurred since 1972 under the more modernized security system imported into Northern Ireland by the metropole, as Chapter 7 shows.

During the formative years of the new state, grass-roots Protestant pressure was an important catalyst in the creation of a political and security system that would tolerate no opposition from the Catholic minority. [42] Protestant supremacist forces were particularly influential in the passage of the draconian 1922 Special Powers Act and the creation and preservation of the sectarian, paramilitary Ulster Special Constabulary. Popular Protestant demands were generally consistent with the Government's interests in the development of repressive security policies and institutions: the Unionist regime sought to maximize its control over the minority, nurture Protestant solidarity, perpetuate the party's incum-

39. Buckland, *Factory of Grievances,* pp. 200, 206.
40. Farrell, *Arming,* p. 278.
41. Liam O'Dowd, "Shaping and Reshaping the Orange State," in L. O'Dowd, B. Rolston, and M. Tomlinson, *Northern Ireland: Between Civil Rights and Civil War* (London: CSE Books, 1980), p. 21.
42. This is amply documented in Farrell, *Arming.*

bency, and achieve the level of stability required to keep the British Government at bay.[43]

These interests shaped the development of the core executive organizations, ranging from the Cabinet to the various security agencies. Former British Prime Minister James Callaghan once wrote that he "found it difficult to take seriously the idea that the Northern Ireland Cabinet and Prime Minister bore any resemblance to what we in Britain understood by those offices."[44] Like Unionist MPs, almost all Cabinet ministers were members of the bitterly anti-Catholic Orange Order and they were sometimes unabashed in expressing their sectarian, anti-Catholic views.[45] The first prime minister, James Craig (1921–1940), proclaimed: "All I boast is that we have a Protestant parliament and a Protestant state."[46] The third premier, Basil Brooke (1943–1963), cautioned against employing Catholics and declared, "Ninety-seven per cent of Roman Catholics are disloyal and disruptive."[47] Such views colored the thinking of the Cabinet and other state elites at least until the late 1960s.[48] Generally, the more moderate Cabinet members were eclipsed by hard-liners, but the moderates sometimes tempered extreme policies that might have invited problems with the British Government.[49]

The Ministry of Home Affairs was the center of gravity within the security establishment. In league with top police officials, it was instrumental in shaping a sectarian security policy, targeted almost entirely against Catholics.[50] In addition to policing, the ministry had responsibility for the controversial areas of local government, electoral affairs, and general law and order. Those in charge of Home Affairs were strident defenders of Protestant and Unionist interests. The first Permanent Sec-

43. Bew, Gibbon, and Patterson, *The State*, pp. 131ff.

44. Callaghan, *House Divided*, p. 77.

45. From 1921 to 1969, 138 out of 149 MPs were Orangemen (Edmund A. Aunger, *In Search of Political Stability: A Comparative Study of New Brunswick and Northern Ireland* [Montreal: McGill-Queens University Press, 1981], p. 123).

46. Quoted in Michael Farrell, *Northern Ireland: The Orange State* (London: Pluto, 1976), p. 92.

47. Quoted in Geoffrey Bell, *The Protestants of Ulster* (London: Pluto, 1976), p. 40.

48. "Councils of moderation and conciliation for their own sake were almost unknown among the Unionist leaders and, without strong and persistent outside pressure, the pragmatic elements had no incentive to urge conciliatory policies" (Farrell, *Arming*, p. 280). See also Buckland, *Factory of Grievances*, p. 22; Derek Birrell and Alan Murie, *Policy and Government in Northern Ireland: Lessons of Devolution* (Dublin: Gill and Macmillan, 1980), p. 142; C. E. B. Brett, "The Lessons of Devolution in Northern Ireland," *Political Quarterly* 41, no. 3 (July 1970); Patrick Shea, *Voices and the Sound of Drums* (Belfast: Blackstaff, 1981). In 1972, approximately 85 to 95 percent of the civil servants above the level of deputy-principal were still Protestant.

49. Bew, Gibbon, and Patterson, *The State*, pp. 131ff.

50. Buckland, *Factory of Grievances*, p. 206.

retary, Samuel Watt, doubted in 1921 whether "it was ever contemplated that these extraordinary powers [in the existing emergency legislation] should be used against those who are loyal to the Crown [i.e., Protestants]."[51] He suggested that the ordinary criminal law be used against Loyalists. Dawson Bates, minister from 1921 to 1943, regarded all Catholics as fifth columnists, and kept them out of his ministry. All in all, Home Affairs displayed what one historian calls a "contemptuous" attitude and a "hostile spirit" in its dealings with Catholics.[52]

The top levels of the police were closely linked to the Unionist establishment, and the rank and file fervent defenders of the Protestant state. It is thus not surprising that the Royal Ulster Constabulary and the Ulster Special Constabulary developed a reputation for sectarian law enforcement. Not only did the forces of order operate with bias, but there were no independent mechanisms of accountability.[53] Completely lacking was a body—representative of the entire community and detached from the Home Affairs ministry—with a mandate to scrutinize contentious police matters and hear public grievances, an entity that seems vital in communally divided societies.

In the event of the slightest hint of unrest, the police were prepared for paramilitary action.[54] Indeed, the general lack of disorder during the half-century of Unionist rule was in part a function of the fact that "Catholics did not wish to challenge a police force and a para-military service that were ready to die or kill to maintain their constitution."[55] Members of the Ulster Special Constabulary, in particular, had a reputation among Catholics as state-sponsored Protestant vigilantes. One former Chief Constable told me of the USC's serious problems: "They were not trained in normal policing, were not subject to discipline, and tended to be a law unto themselves."[56]

One of the first pieces of legislation passed by the new Parliament was the 1922 Special Powers Act (SPA). Its harsh features were officially justified as a welcome departure from Britain's previous "inept" and "vacil-

51. Watt, quoted in ibid., p. 193.
52. Ibid., pp. 204, 205.
53. [Hunt Committee] *Report of the Advisory Committee on Police in Northern Ireland,* Cmnd. 535 (Belfast: HMSO, October 1969), Lord Hunt, Chair.
54. Buckland, *History,* p. 64.
55. Richard Rose, *Northern Ireland: A Time of Choice* (London: Macmillan, 1976), p. 16.
56. Interview with author, 2 August 1984. The USC staffed road blocks, patrolled, guarded public utilities, and assisted in riot control.

lating" security policy in Ireland.[57] The act's provisions probably went further than necessary even in the midst of the serious unrest and violence of 1922.[58] It prescribed punishments of whipping and death for the possession or use of explosives or weapons, and the Minister of Home Affairs was given power to issue regulations of wide latitude that were exempt from parliamentary scrutiny and judicial review: to "take all steps . . . as may be necessary for preserving the peace and maintaining order." In due course, a host of executive regulations were promulgated. These included, inter alia, police powers of arrest and search without a warrant, the proscription of clubs and organizations, censorship of publications, imposition of curfews, and seizure of property. One sweeping regulation criminalized "doing or attempting any act calculated or likely to cause . . . disaffection among the civilian population or to impede, delay or restrict any work necessary for the preservation of peace or maintenance of order."

To cover any unforeseen activities, a blanket provision was included in section 2(4) of the act:

> If any person does any act of such nature as to be calculated to be prejudicial to the preservation of the peace or maintenance of order in Northern Ireland and *not specifically provided for in the regulations,* he shall be deemed to be guilty of an offence against the regulations (emphasis added).

This provision clearly violates the principle of *nulla poena sine lege* (no crime without violation of a specific law).

During the formative years of the state, the measure was used frequently against suspected Catholic rebels, political opponents, and "innocent and law-abiding people"—but rarely to suppress Protestants' sectarian crimes against Catholics.[59] The SPA was used to ban Republican publications, proscribe meetings and marches, crush labor protests in the 1930s, intern suspects, and facilitate general police harassment of the Catholic minority.[60] From 1938 to 1945 and from 1956 to 1961, the

---

57. Parliamentary Secretary of Home Affairs, Robert Megaw, Northern Ireland House of Commons, *Debates,* vol. 2, 21 March 1922, col. 87 (hereafter, Commons *Debates*).

58. Harry Calvert, *Constitutional Law in Northern Ireland* (London and Belfast: Stevens, 1968), p. 385.

59. [Cameron Commission] *Disturbances in Northern Ireland,* Cmnd. 532 (Belfast: HMSO, 1969); Buckland, *History,* p. 66; Kevin Boyle, Tom Hadden, and Paddy Hillyard, *Law and State: The Case of Northern Ireland* (Amherst: University of Massachusetts Press, 1975), p. 7.

60. Farrell, *Orange State,* p. 94.

act was used for internment without trial. During periods when its use was more restrained, it continued as a general deterrent to organized opposition.

By assenting to the SPA, Stormont in effect surrendered its power to make and revoke security legislation and authorized rule by executive fiat. Although the act was designed as a temporary measure, it was made permanent in 1933, when—paradoxically—serious unrest in the province had long abated. According to Buckland, the timing of its legal entrenchment was an attempt to preempt parliamentary debate over renewal of the act at a moment when Catholic opposition MPs had decided to take their seats at Stormont.[61] But the official reasoning highlighted the act's effectiveness: the statute was responsible for the peaceful conditions that prevailed and the "slightest relaxation of the law" would enable sinister forces to "plunge this Province into a welter of bloodshed."[62] A 1936 inquiry by Britain's National Council for Civil Liberties (NCCL) disagreed: "Despite occasional disorders it cannot be said that the special circumstances alleged to have existed when the Act was passed in 1922 prevail today."[63] By the 1930s, the Irish Republican Army had become a spent force and the external threat from southern Ireland had essentially vanished.

But the act had proven a convenient and effective instrument for disorganizing opposition political forces. The NCCL concluded that "the Northern Irish Government has used Special Powers towards securing the domination of one particular political faction and . . . towards curtailing the lawful activities of its opponents." The act had become the keystone of "a permanent machine of dictatorship" in the province.[64]

If manifest disorder had ceased in the early 1920s, the Government could readily define deep Catholic disaffection from the Protestant state and southern Ireland's irredentist claims to Ulster as latent security threats. Yet those "threats . . . had no *independent* significance" in explaining the character of the political system and the sectarian structure of law and order.[65] These latent threats interacted with abiding settler interests in upholding Protestant supremacy in the province. Catholic dis-

---

61. Buckland, *Factory of Grievances,* p. 219; Buckland, *History,* p. 65.

62. Minister of Home Affairs, Commons *Debates,* vol. 9, 15 May 1928, col. 1688. The Parliamentary Secretary of Home Affairs made the same argument in 1933 (Commons *Debates,* vol. 15, 14 March 1933, col. 848).

63. National Council for Civil Liberties, *Report of a Commission of Inquiry Appointed to Examine the Purpose and Effect of the Civil Authorities (Special Powers) Acts (Northern Ireland) 1922 and 1933* (London: NCCL, 1936), p. 24.

64. Ibid., pp. 39, 40.

65. Bew, Gibbon, and Patterson, *The State,* p. 216.

loyalty served Protestant interests insofar as it could be used to remind London of the imperative of "Loyalist" rule in Ulster. MacDonald stresses the functional consequences of Catholic alienation from the state:

> Protestants had a vested interest in sustaining the Catholic disloyalty that, first, legitimated Protestant privileges; secondly, accentuated the salience of Protestant loyalty to Britain; and thirdly, provided the threat that maintained Protestant solidarity.[66]

The exceptional outbreak of disorder that punctuated the half-century of settler rule—such as the abortive IRA insurgency from 1956 to 1962—suggests that the Catholic minority did not threaten security to the extent the Protestant population imagined. In order to end British occupation and to reunify Ireland, the IRA in 1956 launched a campaign of sporadic sabotage and armed attacks. Ultimately the campaign lost momentum for two reasons: it encountered swift police action and it failed to generate support within the Catholic enclave. Catholics were simply not willing to endorse a violent frontal assault on the state. When the IRA called off its campaign in February 1962, it lamented this very lack of popular support: "Foremost among the factors motivating this course of action has been the attitude of the general public whose minds have been deliberately distracted from the supreme issue facing the Irish people—unity and freedom of Ireland."[67]

The central features of this politico-security system developed in a context of deep communal and political cleavages. The system of majoritarian democracy facilitated the political subordination of the minority—a majority dictatorship under the veneer of British parliamentary democracy. The security sector was well insulated from potential checks both inside and outside the state. And it displayed a patently sectarian slant in defense of the narrow interests of the Protestant community.

The state and its security wing had not only clear sectarian commitments but also the objective capacity to institutionalize them. The first decade of the new state's existence was a history of its successful efforts to secure autonomy from British interference, win the support of the various Protestant classes, extract financial resources from Britain, and

---

66. MacDonald, *Children of Wrath*, p. 24.
67. Quoted in J. Bowyer Bell, *The Secret Army: The IRA* (Dublin: Academy Press, 1979), p. 334.

liquidate pockets of violent opposition to the state. Over the next decades, the Unionists were in a good position to maintain Protestant dominant-party rule, cement partition, disorganize both overt Catholic nationalist mobilization and perceived subterranean threats, and satisfy the Protestant electorate. These were simultaneously ends in themselves and means to guarantee a paramount interest: that of the state's very survival. Without autonomy from Britain, an inviolable border, the pacification of Catholic opposition, and broad-based Protestant support, the pillars of the settler power structure would have cracked. In the late 1960s they cracked irreparably, as Chapter 5 shows.

RHODESIA'S SYSTEM OF LAW AND ORDER

Like that of Northern Ireland, the core of the Rhodesian state was essentially immune from oversight by the judiciary, legislature, and other agencies; the state displayed little concern for the consent or the human rights of its subordinate population and organized law and order around the narrow interests of the settler minority. A resourceful and intransigent settler bloc created an apparatus of control that was considerably more elaborate than in conventional colonies as well as some settler societies such as Northern Ireland and Liberia.

During most of Rhodesian history, the leading internal security institutions were the national police force and the Native Affairs Department. Until the late 1960s, the country maintained only a rudimentary territorial army. The proportion of public revenue earmarked for defense was small, and the army played a small role in domestic order and external defense until the outbreak of guerrilla war in the 1970s. Rhodesia's British South African Police (BSAP) was the de facto defense force. Formed in 1896, it performed both conventional policing and paramilitary tasks. The Ministry of Justice had (until 1962) responsibility for policing, as well as prosecution, the courts, and law-and-order policy.

The largest and most powerful branch of the state was the Native Affairs Department (NAD), which operated with considerable resources and autonomy and had broad geographical and functional jurisdiction. As a state within a state, the department successfully resisted interference from other agencies well into the 1970s. NAD officers in the countryside were the principal agents of social control and intelligence, largely free from interference by other state sectors. They governed rural blacks with a mixture of paternalism and coercion—formally embracing the doctrine of Africans' gradual "advancement" in their "separate areas," but skeptical that Africans could ever proceed very far. The legal and institutional changes introduced in Rhodesia during the watershed years of 1959 through 1962 provided the cornerstone upon which the internal security enterprise would be further refined over the next twenty-five years. (As Chapter 6 shows, the essence of this system survives in independent Zimbabwe.) The post-1959 period analyzed here is not one of unmediated African resistance as portrayed in much of the literature on Rhodesia, in which African opposition appears to be the sole cause of repressive state responses and systemic innovations. Our analysis presents a more balanced, multicausal account by linking pressures from the African community to intra-white politics and the distinctive interests of the settler regime.

THE 1959 STATE OF EMERGENCY

In a dawn swoop on 26 February 1959, the Rhodesian Government staged a surprise arrest of five hundred members of the African National Congress (ANC) and proclaimed a state of emergency. It labeled those arrested "agitators," "fanatics," and "extremists" bent on defying authority and causing pandemonium in the country. The official justification for the state of emergency was contained in a pamphlet written by the Chief Native Commissioner and Secretary of Native Affairs, Stanley Morris, and distributed to Africans and the press:

> It is clear that these self-appointed leaders of Congresses in Southern Rhodesia, who come from the towns, are working to get rid of the tribal authorities, so that they can take control and force everyone to accept their power. These rabble-rousers. . . could not even manage a business. . . yet they seek to govern the people and recklessly disregard the harm they would bring to everyone in the country. . . . Abuse, threats and intimidation have crept into their words. Defiance and insolence have become their claim to leadership. . . . The people of certain districts have been called to meetings by these Congress leaders and exhorted to break the laws of the country and to ignore their Native Commissioners and Chiefs. . . . Government has decided to remove these agitators and trouble-makers—to remove from them the power to play with hot words, to make it impossible for them to collect more money from you, and if necessary to keep them in a place of detention until they mend their thoughts. . . . Now you can continue your peaceful lives in the Reserves and your work in the towns and on farms and on mines, secure in the knowledge that Government intends to preserve law and order, and to support the Chiefs in their status and their authority. . . . Settle down conscientiously to your work, you have nothing to fear. Use the proper channels for

addressing any grievances or requests that you may have to Government. . .
and not to a group of noisy boys who are not out to help you really, but are
looking only to their personal aggrandizement and power at your expense.[68]

The pamphlet suggested that the African detainees were guilty not of violent conduct or specific criminal acts but rather of "hot words," intimidation, and defiance and disobedience—driven by a lust for "aggrandizement and power." In classic fashion, the regime branded political
opposition subversive.[69]

Visible public support for African nationalist organizations challenged the regime's definition of the situation. Urban rallies were beginning to draw unprecedented crowds: five thousand at an ANC rally in
December 1958, three thousand in January 1959.[70] While privately
alarmed at the size of these meetings, the Rhodesian authorities (like the
Pretoria regime today) publicly dismissed them as the result of "intimidation" by the few on the lunatic fringe. To have done otherwise would
have been to accept that the ANC was generating broad support. The
preamble to the 1959 Unlawful Organizations Act reflected the official
construction of African nationalists' actions:

> [they have] assembled meetings or gatherings of ignorant and unwary per-
> sons, whereat in violent and threatening language, the speakers have wilfully
> misrepresented facts, sown seeds of discord and racial hostility, excited disaf-
> fection towards established authority, urged civil disobedience and passive re-
> sistance to the law.

A former senior official in the Native Affairs Department reflected that
blacks "were happy and content, otherwise they would have risen up
long before they did. They were roused by agitators who told them the
story that the whites had taken the best land." [71] But many were far from
"content";[72] one official commission concluded that the government had

68. Reprinted in *African Daily News* (Salisbury), 26 February 1959.
69. See Eshmael Mlambo, *Rhodesia: The Struggle for a Birthright* (London: Hurst,
1972), p. 128; *Dissent* (Salisbury), 26 March 1959. Before the Mau Mau disturbances in
Kenya, rural administrators similarly equated opposition with subversion (see Bruce Berman, "Bureaucracy and Incumbent Violence: Colonial Administration and the Origins of
the 'Mau Mau' Emergency in Kenya," *British Journal of Political Science* 6 [April 1976]:
166).
70. Mlambo, *Rhodesia*, p. 127.
71. Interview with author, 8 June 1983. A survey in 1965 found that whites believed
the nationalists lacked widespread support (Stephen Hintz, "The Political Transformation
of Rhodesia, 1958–1965," *African Studies Review* 15 (1972): 182).
72. J. Van Velsen, "Trends in African Nationalism in Southern Rhodesia," *Kroniek
van Afrika* 4 (June 1964): 149.

"generally underestimated" African "political consciousness and aware-ness of human rights." [73]

If in 1959 the prevailing tendency within the executive was to deny the existence of black discontent, a minority reformist faction held op-posing views, which gradually won support in Cabinet (including that of the prime minister, Sir Edgar Whitehead). Moderates included the Minister of Labour, who reflected on his position:

> In agreeing to the principle of the declaration of emergency and security leg-islation I made it very clear that my belief was that this could not provide a solution for the real grievances and disabilities of Africans. It could never substitute for or avoid necessary reforms. There were real grievances which had to be remedied in the quickest possible time. [74]

After 1959 the Government of the United Federal party (UFP) embraced the idea of granting minor concessions to moderate Africans—removing the so-called pinpricks of petty discrimination. [75]

The African National Congress sought more substantial changes, but less sweeping than the Government believed. Its platform advocated ra-cial cooperation, the right of all to "permanent citizenship" in the coun-try, and "equality of opportunity in every sphere," but it stopped far short of demanding land redistribution, majority rule, or independence from Britain.

Black discontent had been growing in the rural areas largely because of the disruptive impact of the 1951 Land Husbandry Act. It was de-signed to improve the rural economy in the African reserves, which ex-perienced the pressure of a growing population within fixed areas, but its provisions violated traditional practices. [76] Rather than expand the size of the reserves, the act limited cattle grazing in specified areas and provided for the de-stocking of African herds; it allowed officials to dic-tate patterns of cultivation and crop growing and to fix dwelling sites on

73. [Robinson Commission] Government of Southern Rhodesia, *Report of the Com-mission Appointed to Inquire into and Report on Administrative and Judicial Functions in the Native Affairs and District Courts Departments,* C.S.R. 22–1961, Salisbury, 20 May 1961, V. L. Robinson, Chair, p. 30.

74. Correspondence with author, 30 January 1984.

75. To channel African opinion, NAD pamphlets labeled extremists as "liable to drag people down, to bring trouble to them, even death or injury," but moderates were calm, constructive, and able to "reason things out intelligently, within the framework of consti-tutional law and regulations." Rhodesia was "full of moderates" who had achieved pro-gress, honor, and respect (NADFORM Broadsheet no. 4, Native Affairs Department, February 1959).

76. William Barber, "The Political Economy of Central Africa's Experiment with Inter-Racial Partnership," *Canadian Journal of Economics and Political Science* 25, no. 3 (August 1959): 324–35.

farm land; it prohibited cultivating or grazing without a permit and imposed compulsory labor on unemployed rural Africans. Implementation of the act meant the depletion of highly valued herds, reduction of the land under cultivation, and the forced uprooting of families and entire villages.

George Nyandoro of the ANC called the act "the best recruiter Congress ever had,"[77] and the ANC capitalized on peasants' grievances over the measure. Tasked with implementing the act, the Native Affairs Department was acutely aware of blacks' resentment and the erosion of its authority, which two 1961 commissions of inquiry documented.[78] The prime minister understood the seriousness of the problem and feared "the development of the Land Husbandry Act and indeed the whole administration of the native areas would break down."[79]

Discontent with socioeconomic conditions was growing among urban Africans as well. A recession in 1957–1958 hit blacks hard; rising unemployment and inadequate township housing contributed to their sense of deprivation and provided ready-made issues for ANC organizers.

The existence of African grievances and nascent politicization in the late 1950s—however unnerving to the authorities—posed no serious threat to public order or national security. Even the Director of African Administration for Bulawayo, E. H. Ashton, challenged the Government's line, "The Bulawayo detainees were generally responsible people, who did not fall into the category of 'rabble rousers' described by the Secretary for Native Affairs."[80] Another authority remarked, "What has happened is simply that African nationalism has become a lot more noisy . . . but it is still not backed by anything more substantial than po-

77. Quoted in Patrick O'Meara, *Rhodesia: Racial Conflict or Coexistence?* (Ithaca: Cornell University Press, 1975), p. 100.

78. The Robinson Commission underscored the "extreme opposition and bitter resentment centred on the Native Department, which has come to be regarded as the author of, and instrument for, all oppressive legislation" (p. 30). The Brown Commission (also of 1961) found that the Native Commissioner "tends to become regarded as the local symbol of a restrictive if not 'oppressive' White Government, and therefore unavoidably the target of mounting resentment" ([Brown Commission] Government of Southern Rhodesia, *Report of the Mangwende Reserve Commission of Inquiry*, 1961, James S. Brown, Chairman, para. 107). A 1968 survey found that most Africans obeyed district commissioners only "reluctantly" and out of "fear" (A. K. H. Weinrich, *Black and White Elites in Rural Rhodesia* [Manchester: Manchester University Press, 1973], pp. 54, 58).

79. Southern Rhodesia, Assembly *Debates,* vol. 42, 26 February 1959, col. 2018 (hereafter, Assembly *Debates*).

80. City of Bulawayo, *Report of the Director of African Administration for 1958–1959* (Bulawayo: Rhodesian Printers, 1959), p. 72.

litical aspirations alone. . . . Why let it frighten us?"[81] Organized political violence was not imminent, and most ANC members were hardly subversives.[82] The ANC had rather modest goals, few resources, and a rudimentary organization. Although black grievances were intensifying during this period, official controls prevented the movement from developing into a force to be reckoned with. Thus, as predicted by the resource mobilization school of social movements, African resistance remained a fledgling movement.[83]

The security panic of 1959—the official overreaction to perceived threats—is best explained within a framework that centers on the overriding concerns and interests of the ruling United Federal party. It was under pressure from several sectors of white society, including its own MPs and party loyalists, a press that had been clamoring for months for harsh action against "subversives," and the politically important white farming community.

Most disturbing to the UFP Government was the possible loss of support among a white electorate fairly evenly split in its support for the ruling party and the opposition Dominion party (DP). The white supremacist DP had been attacking the Government for nine months before the crackdown.[84] While supporting the emergency, the DP faulted the Government for not acting sooner or going further to quash African nationalism, and for having created the problem in the first place through appeasement of Africans. To DP supporters, like their counterparts in contemporary South Africa, reforms that might result in even limited African advancement were anathema. The opposition's clamor for an iron fist policy helped convince the regime to declare the emergency; as the general election of 1962 neared, this pressure became increasingly salient.

The concerns of the white electorate were abundantly expressed in local newspaper reports and letters to the editor from 1958 to 1960 that I examined. Their views were also reflected in a 1958 survey of five hundred whites that documented their mistrust of African nationalism, be-

81. Sir Roy Welensky, prime minister of the Central African Federation (of which Rhodesia was a member), *Rhodesia Herald,* 27 January 1959.

82. Clyde Sanger, *Central African Emergency* (London: Heinemann, 1960), p. 256; Philip Mason, *Year of Decision: Rhodesia and Nyasaland in 1960* (London: Oxford University Press, 1960), p. 218; Guy Clutton-Brock, "The 1959 'Emergency' in Southern Rhodesia," in *New Deal,* ed. Leys and Pratt, p. 161.

83. John McCarthy and Mayer Zald, "Resource Mobilization and Social Movements," *American Journal of Sociology* 82, no. 6 (May 1977): 1212–41; Tilly, *Mobilization.*

84. Assembly *Debates,* vol. 43, 14 August 1959, col. 1559.

lief that African political mobilization was inspired by outside agitators rather than a natural outgrowth of internal conditions, view of the ANC as a real security threat, concern that whites should have firearms, and support for tight police surveillance over African meetings.[85]

One pivotal constituency was that of white farmers. Terrified that they might lose their land, commercial farmers criticized the regime's "reluctance" to take firm action against unruly blacks who were "troubling" African farm workers. Drawing lessons from Kenya's Mau Mau disorders, they warned that "it is the farming and whole rural community which always has in Africa received the first shock of violence." [86]

Continental events provided a backdrop for the stirrings of Rhodesian blacks. In the late 1950s, nationalist movements were sweeping through other African colonies; in many, independence seemed imminent. Lurid press coverage of outbreaks of black violence elsewhere in Africa superimposed external developments on the Rhodesian situation.[87] Grisly descriptions of events contributed to fears in white circles that Rhodesian blacks would be encouraged to rebel. Such a demonstration effect was anticipated during the Mau Mau rebellion in Kenya and signs of that country's impending independence, the civil war in Algeria, and the violence against whites in the Belgian Congo and French Congo in early 1959.[88] The effect of sensationalized reports of these events was to deepen white Rhodesians' fears of murder, rape, and expulsion in the event of a black revolt or the transfer of power to the black majority.[89] In this larger context, the future of white supremacy in Rhodesia seemed to depend on the imposition of much tighter controls on the black population.

Closer to home, violence had broken out in Nyasaland, and tensions were rising in Northern Rhodesia as blacks demanded independence. (Northern Rhodesia, Nyasaland, and Southern Rhodesia had formed

85. Rogers and Frantz, *Racial Themes,* pp. 259–63.
86. Editorial, *Rhodesian Farmer,* 6 December 1957; ibid., 13 December 1957.
87. Similar panic stories in the South African press are examined in Pierre Hugo, "Towards Darkness and Death: Racial Demonology in South Africa," *Journal of Modern African Studies* 26, no. 4 (December 1988).
88. In 1960, one indignant opposition MP painted all Africans with the same brush: "The African . . . is interested in exterminating the European and it is no good anybody getting up and saying that the Southern Rhodesian native is different. . . . The Southern Rhodesian native, the Congo native, the Mau Mau terrorists of Kenya, the massacre plot African of Nyasaland, the petrol burning types of Northern Rhodesia and the ritual murderers of Basutoland, they are all the same" (Wynn Starling, Assembly *Debates,* vol. 45, 19 July 1960, col. 359).
89. The Rhodesian prime minister stated, "We had the moral of the Mau Mau trouble very much in mind" (*Sunday Mail* (Salisbury), 22 March 1959).

the Central African Federation in 1953.) Southern Rhodesian security forces had been sent into Nyasaland in February to help quell disturbances. In the regime's view, this external operation required the tightening of screws at home. Lord Malvern (former prime minister of Rhodesia and the federation) stated, "It was decided that the Southern Rhodesian African Congress must be put behind wire so that they could not create a diversion and prevent the sending of necessary police to Nyasaland."[90]

Disturbances within the federation thus precipitated the introduction of emergency rule in Rhodesia. The prime minister admitted that "*there is a real emergency not in Southern Rhodesia at the moment, but in the Federation.*"[91] The security crackdown in Rhodesia was largely a pre-emptive strike against further nationalist organizing of blacks and against potential African unrest.[92] Disorder seemed likely because of the sinister construction authorities placed on both continental pressures and domestic black politics. Such linkage of external and internal threats is common in deeply divided societies.[93]

The embryonic challenge from Rhodesian blacks was only one factor contributing to the declaration of the state of emergency. The Whitehead regime's political interests also played a role: it attempted to gain political capital among the white electorate, steal the thunder of the opposition party, and thus secure its incumbency. The Government sought in one stroke to undermine the ANC to the left, curry favor with DP loyalists to the right, and retain the support of its own constituents in the middle. Already evident in 1959, these interests grew increasingly salient as the 1962 election approached.

NORMALIZING EMERGENCY RULE

The emergency episode proved counterproductive in several respects. It ruined the prospects for genuine racial partnership, made heroes out of the detainees, and alienated moderate Africans from the Government.[94] To deflate the crisis atmosphere of the state of emergency and yet pre-

90. Great Britain, House of Lords, *Debates,* 24 March 1959, col. 258.
91. Assembly *Debates,* vol. 42, 26 February 1959, col. 2049; emphasis added.
92. Berman's state-centered analysis of the Mau Mau emergency in Kenya similarly notes, "The Emergency, in reality, was a pre-emptive attack carried out by the incumbent colonial authorities against a significant segment of the African political leadership of Kenya and its supporters" ("Bureaucracy," p. 170).
93. David Brown, "Crisis and Ethnicity: Legitimacy in Plural Societies," *Third World Quarterly* 7, no. 4 (October 1985): 989.
94. Mlambo, *Rhodesia,* p. 133; Ranger, *Crisis,* p. 34.

serve its sweeping powers as insurance against the future, the regime sought to normalize the exceptional measures by incorporating them in statute law.[95] Thus institutionalized, the official emergency came to an end.

The 1959 Unlawful Organizations Act (UOA) was novel in that it outlawed certain organizations. The act proscribed the African National Congress and provided for the banning of additional organizations if their activities were deemed "likely" to disturb public order, "prejudice" the tranquility of the nation, endanger "constitutional government," or "promote feelings of ill will or hostility" between the races. Furthermore, the UOA outlawed any organization that was "controlled by or affiliated to or participates in the activities or promotes the objects or propagates the opinions of *any organization* outside the colony" (emphasis added). The executive's banning of an organization was "not open to question in any court of law," and the burden of proving that one was not a member of a banned organization fell on the accused. Attendance at a meeting or possession of books, writings, accounts, documents, banners, or insignia "relating to an unlawful organization" were prima facie evidence of membership "until the contrary is proved." Prosecution of such offenses could be held in camera. Finally, the act provided for the complete indemnification of police and civil servants for actions connected with enforcing the measure. Between 1960 and 1965, 1,610 Africans were prosecuted and 1,002 convicted under this law.[96]

The Preventive Detention Act (PDA) was introduced to continue the detention of ANC members who had been arrested and held without charge during the state of emergency.[97] During parliamentary debate on the bill, the prime minister argued that the nationalist detainees had made a "mockery" of the law, had stirred up rural discontent, and had established connections with those outside the country who were intent on "bringing about a complete change" in Africa. He admitted that these activities were not "in any way contrary to the old laws" unless violence could be proved—hence the need for the PDA.[98]

The act authorized the detention of persons "concerned," "associated," or "supporting" "any of the activities of any organization which

95. Codification of emergency powers after a crisis is fairly common among authoritarian regimes (see Anthony Mathews and R. C. Albino, "The Permanence of the Temporary," *South African Law Journal* 83 [1966]: 16–43).

96. Bowman, *Politics in Rhodesia,* p. 60.

97. Minister of Justice and Internal Affairs, Assembly *Debates,* vol. 42, 20 March 1959, col. 2687.

98. Assembly *Debates,* vol. 42, 20 March 1959, cols. 2738–44.

led to the present state of emergency" and persons considered "potentially dangerous to public safety or public order." The decision as to whether individuals were "potentially dangerous" was left to the governor, which in practice meant the Minister of Justice and Internal Affairs. Lest the act give the appearance of completely unchecked executive power, it established a Review Tribunal—composed of a judge, a magistrate, and a Native Commissioner—to review annually the case of each detainee and recommend release or continued detention. Tribunal proceedings were held in camera; deliberations depended heavily on the evidence of the police Special Branch; and the minister was not obliged to follow the tribunal's recommendations. The tribunal rarely advised the release of detainees, and its lack of objectivity was reflected in its general report on the emergency and detention exercise of 1959, which completely whitewashed the regime's actions.[99]

A third measure, the Native Affairs Amendment Act, was introduced in 1959 to prohibit any "native" from making statements or acting in a way "likely to undermine the authority" of, or bring into "disrepute," governmental officials, chiefs, or headmen. The act abolished meetings of twelve or more "natives" without the permission of the Native Commissioner. Hence, the rural areas became much less accessible to black nationalist organizers.

In January 1960 the National Democratic party (NDP) emerged out of the ruins of the ANC. Its goals included universal adult suffrage, higher wages, improvements in African housing and education, and abolition of the Land Apportionment Act and the Land Husbandry Act. Like the ANC, the NDP had a rudimentary organization, limited resources, and no access to the press; many of its would-be leaders remained behind bars. Given the far-reaching security restrictions passed in 1959, the party's activities were bound within tight parameters. Organizing in rural areas was virtually impossible. In urban areas, however, it was attracting up to ten thousand people to its rallies, and by mid-1961 it had over two hundred fifty thousand dues-paying members.[100]

Intended to paralyze black opposition and prevent political violence, the state of emergency proved a self-fulfilling prophecy. State repression deepened black alienation from the regime and suggested to some that

99. Review Tribunal, *Preventive Detention (Temporary Provisions) Act 1959, General Report,* Presented to the Legislative Assembly, C.S.R. 27 (Salisbury, Rhodesia, 1959), T. Beadle, President.
100. Mlambo, *Rhodesia,* p. 140; Davis M'Gabe, "Rhodesia's African Majority," *African Report* (February 1967): 19.

peaceful political organizing was a dead end. With the black leadership in detention, the political vacuum was filled by the more militantly inclined. As in Kenya during Mau Mau, violence in Rhodesia "derived from the conditions of the Emergency itself." [101] In July and October 1960 large-scale demonstrations and rioting broke out in black townships. During one riot, the police killed eleven Africans. The rioters were selective: they "destroyed everything that had anything to do with the central or local government." [102]

In reaction to the disorders and to the outcry of a shocked settler community, the Government introduced more comprehensive legislation: the 1960 Law and Order (Maintenance) Act (LOMA) and the Emergency Powers Act (EPA). LOMA banned publications; criminalized "subversive statements" and "intimidation," which it defined broadly; restricted persons without trial to designated areas; empowered police to search and arrest without a warrant; and summarily prohibited meetings. It outlawed the publishing of "false news," boycotting, creating "disaffection" in the police force, and using or encouraging violence, sabotage, and terrorism.

The Emergency Powers Act enabled the Minister of Justice to make "necessary or expedient" regulations for public order, safety, peace, and the maintenance of any "essential service." It provided regulations for summary arrest, detention, and restriction. It also gave the executive power to suspend or modify "any law" to make way for emergency regulations.

Although couched in race-neutral language, LOMA and EPA were applied almost entirely to Africans. Very few whites were sympathetic to the nationalist cause, and the rights and liberties of the white population were largely unaffected. Blacks were arrested, detained, or restricted; political meetings on Sundays and holidays were proscribed (in 1961, 1,028 Africans were arrested for violations of LOMA, and 1,084 in 1962). [103] The NDP was banned in December 1961 and its successor, the Zimbabwe African People's Union (ZAPU), was outlawed in September 1962. By these actions the regime hoped to curry favor among the white electorate as a national election approached. [104]

---

101. Carl Rosberg and John Nottingham, *The Myth of Mau Mau* (New York: Praeger, 1966), p. 277.
102. Francis Nehwati, "The Social and Communal Background to 'Zhii': The African Riots in Bulawayo, Southern Rhodesia in 1960," *African Affairs* 69 (July 1970): 252.
103. Bowman, *Politics in Rhodesia*, p. 60.
104. Chengetai Zvobgo, "Southern Rhodesia under Edgar Whitehead: 1958–1962," *Journal of Southern African Affairs* 2, no. 4 (October 1977): 489.

The events of 1959 through 1962 helped to fortify the institutional power of Rhodesia's internal security agencies. The new security legislation greatly expanded the arbitrary powers of officials in the Native Affairs Department, the Ministry of Justice and Internal Affairs, and the police force; just as their manpower and financial resources were substantially enhanced.[105] New police stations were erected in black townships; the Special Branch of the police was established in December 1960 to provide intelligence on nationalists at home and on "sinister" forces elsewhere in Africa.[106] In late 1962, a powerful Ministry of Law and Order was created, with responsibility for the police. This new department specifically concerned with law and order was designed both to expand control over blacks and, once again, to give an alarmed white electorate a sense that the Government was being firm.[107]

As in contemporary South Africa, officials described repressive measures in Rhodesia as necessary to establish a bedrock of stability upon which a superstructure of reform could be built. The UFP regime gradually came to the view that it ought to balance repression with a package of concessions to Africans—a shock-absorber effect. It aimed concessions mainly at the moderate African "majority" and repression at the extremist "fringe," in order to drive a wedge between the two groups and weaken their potential for broad based political resistance. Improvements took place in African education, wages, and amenities; plans were made to dispense with some "petty apartheid" regulations the regime considered superfluous to maintaining white supremacy. The repeal of certain kinds of racial discrimination stopped far short of forced integration, as Whitehead made clear in 1959: "We will not legislate to force people to integrate who do not want to and we will not force people to meet socially if they do not want to."[108]

The use of both the carrot and stick reflected growing disagreement at the commanding heights of the security sector, some of whose elites called almost exclusively for reforms, some for undiluted repression, and others for a mixture of the two. Police chiefs and the Secretary of Native Affairs pushed strongly within Cabinet for repressive solutions, while others like the Ministers of Justice and Labour took a more "en-

105. Government of Southern Rhodesia, *Estimates of Expenditure* (Salisbury: Government Printer, 1959–1962).
106. "The Special Branch," *Fighting Forces of Rhodesia*, no. 2 (August 1975): 13.
107. Author's interview with former minister, 26 May 1983; correspondence between former Minister of Labour and the author, 30 January 1984.
108. Assembly *Debates*, 2 October 1959, col. 1457.

lightened" view.[109] As one minister in the Whitehead Cabinet later confided, conflict within the Cabinet and the ruling party over the balance between reform and repression "was a split which became deeper as the years went by. The greater the attempt to reform, the greater the reaction." [110] Despite the increased legal powers given to the police, Justice, and Native Affairs, hard-line factions within these agencies remained frustrated by the Cabinet's apparent weakness in curbing unrest. A significant number of state personnel were covert supporters of the Dominion party and its hard-line program. The 1959–1962 period was significant, therefore, not only for the growing black unrest but also for the unprecedented discord within the state over both security policy and reform of the racial order.

BREAKDOWN AND RESTORATION OF SETTLER COHESION

The increasing strain within the state over specific forms of repression and reform and over the proper mixture of the two coincided with a backlash within the dominant caste and heightened protest among the black majority. Reforms fueled white anxiety and opposition; repression further alienated African opinion. Of most consequence for the future of the Whitehead regime was its diminishing credibility within a settler population that had never given its leaders a mandate to open, even slightly, the window of social and political opportunity to Africans.

Serious electoral competition among settler parties was rare in Rhodesia. The only period in Rhodesian history when a white opposition party had any appreciable impact on security legislation was that of 1958 through 1962. During those years the United Federal party held a slim majority in Parliament and precarious support among the electorate. Unlike contests both earlier and later, the struggles over security policy from 1958 through 1962 were significant precisely because the Dominion party presented a serious challenge to the UFP's incumbency. The DP, not the African nationalists, had the capacity to bring the ruling party down. Champion of undiluted white domination and the fierce repression of African opposition, the DP sought to make political capital out of the UFP's "weakness" by stirring the pot of white fears. According to a minister in the Whitehead Cabinet, in the field of law and order, the Dominion party "influenced the UFP quite a bit." [111]

109. Former Minister of Labour, correspondence with author, 30 January 1984.
110. Correspondence with author, 28 May 1984.
111. Interview, 26 May 1983.

In 1959 Prime Minister Whitehead boasted that 99 percent of the whites and 85 percent of the blacks supported his administration[112]—a gross exaggeration at the time, and the UFP's legitimacy in both quarters had all but collapsed by 1962.

The Government's new security measures did not assuage the white electorate, disturbed both by the regime's inadequate use of the iron fist and its experiment with conciliation and gradual African advancement. Staunch advocates of settler supremacy considered Whitehead's reforms treasonous: for example, plans to extend the franchise, appoint African Cabinet ministers and increase the number of African MPs, remove petty apartheid restrictions, and repeal the cornerstone Land Apportionment Act.[113] In October 1962 the prime minister made the mistake of telling the United Nations' Trusteeship Committee that Africans "will have a majority [in Parliament] within fifteen years." Although the premier did not mean majority *rule,* his prediction was too much for the settler community to bear.[114] A 1958 survey revealed that whites believed the franchise was already too generous toward Africans, and 86.5 percent opposed repeal of the Land Apportionment Act.[115]

One barometer of white morale, migration rates, registered the falling confidence in the Government: in 1956 the country had eleven thousand immigrants; in 1961, it had two thousand emigrants. But the extent of white concern was most clearly evidenced in the December 1962 election when the DP's heir, the white supremacist Rhodesian Front (RF), won a surprise victory over the UFP.

The 1962 election was the first in which a white ruling party sought to broaden its base by enlisting African support. It failed. Of the 10,632 registered African voters (a fraction of voting-age blacks), only 2,577 voted.[116] In a context of increasing racial polarization, Africans withheld support from a Government that had arrested their leaders, banned three of their political parties, and attempted to break their spirits. The use of the stick had canceled out the desired effect of the carrot. Similarly, the white electorate was not prepared to endorse a Government

112. Assembly *Debates,* vol. 42, 24 March 1959, col. 3167.

113. See "Southern Rhodesia Polarized: Fall of the United Federal Party," *Round Table* 53, no. 210 (March 1963): 137–66; and Samuel Speck, "The Gap Widens in Southern Rhodesia," *Africa Report* 8, no. 1 (January 1963): 10–13.

114. Bowman, *Politics in Rhodesia,* p. 35.

115. Rogers and Frantz, *Racial Themes.*

116. In elections from 1962 to 1977, less than 0.3 percent of Africans of voting age were able to vote because of qualifications on property, income, and education (Anthony Lemon, "Electoral Machinery and Voting Patterns in Rhodesia, 1962–1977," *African Affairs* 77 [October 1978]: 511–30).

that seemed ready to capitulate to black pressures. In the election, the African boycott combined with a shift of white voters to the RF to defeat the UFP. The Rhodesian Front won 56.5 percent of the total vote and 35 seats; the United Federal party received 26.

Whitehead's predecessor, Garfield Todd, was removed in a Cabinet revolt in 1958 for his own slightly reformist gestures, which his colleagues considered altogether premature. But Whitehead's Cabinet could not bring itself to do its own housecleaning when he embarked on a more serious reform program than anything Todd had contemplated. It was thus left to the settler electorate to purge this deviating regime. The result of the 1962 election was convincing proof that a ruling party could attempt to reform this settler state only at its peril. A majority of white Rhodesians was simply not prepared to allow political leaders to modernize state institutions and promote serious racial conciliation. The year 1962 can thus be regarded as a "point of no return" in Rhodesia, one that soundly rejected an accommodationist solution and sharpened racial polarization.[117] The RF victory signaled a dramatic return to the traditional Rhodesian pattern, in which "power tends to gravitate towards those who are least ready for change."[118]

The coming to power of the Rhodesian Front under Premier Winston Field had a salutary effect on settler unity and state cohesion, which had so troubled the Whitehead Government. In Rhodesia, the transfer of power to an ultrarightist settler Government helped to ease strains within the state well into the 1970s. (It did not have this effect in Northern Ireland, discussed in Chapter 5.) Reunified, the Rhodesian state was better able to defend the cause of settler domination, which increased the whites' confidence in the country. The balance of power within the state shifted in favor of the hawks; moderate elites from the old regime were purged, converted, or ignored—much as occurred in South Africa after the National party's victory over the United party in 1948. In both cases the former ruling party lost all influence on security policy, ceased to offer a viable political alternative, and gradually faded from the scene.

It took time for the new regime to subdue African unrest. In August 1963 several leading nationalists broke with the banned ZAPU to form a new organization, the Zimbabwe African National Union (ZANU). Between August 1963 and August 1964, widespread violence between

117. Kuper, *The Pity*.
118. Leys, *European Politics*, p. 36.

ZAPU and ZANU supporters occurred in African townships. By 1965 this internecine rivalry had abated within the country (but continued between the exiled wings of each party), and domestic political violence had declined.

In line with the new regime's break with multiracialism, it made little attempt to cushion repression through reforms. The Government made full use of the inherited repressive machinery and introduced amendments to make the legislation even more severe; it also created an important new security agency in 1963, the Central Intelligence Organization (CIO). CIO became responsible for gathering external intelligence (and the police Special Branch then focused on domestic matters). The need for a special intelligence agency was growing with the possibility that the regime might soon unilaterally declare independence from Britain, and the international fallout that this might create.[119]

UNILATERAL INDEPENDENCE

The Central African Federation came to an end in 1963, after a decade of life. The federation had been an attempt to shield Northern Rhodesia and Nyasaland from British interference by incorporating them under Southern Rhodesia's protective umbrella, but it left open the possibility that London would unilaterally grant independence to the black majority in all three territories. The end of the federation meant that Rhodesia had successfully shed one more layer of London's formal authority over the colony. Regarding Britain with suspicion after its "sell-out" of Kenya's settlers, Rhodesia's whites realized that without full independence from the home country they would have no guarantee against a similar fate. Although British officials had seemed rather indifferent to the cycle of unrest and repression in Rhodesia after 1959, the lingering possibility that the metropole might intervene against the interests of the settlers caused tremendous anxiety within the white community. Consider this candid communiqué from Prime Minister Field to a British Secretary of State:

> so long as the last remaining links remain and the impression persists that the United Kingdom has the right to interfere in our internal affairs there is the danger of a series of serious incidents of disorder [among blacks] being en-

119. Author's interview with former CIO official, 30 May 1983; the Federal Intelligence Security Bureau operated in the Central African Federation, under British auspices.

couraged from outside in order to compel such intervention by the British Government.[120]

Field's Cabinet colleagues, however, judged him too weak to give Britain an ultimatum on independence. He resigned in April 1964 and was succeeded by Ian Smith, an ardent advocate of unconditional independence. In the 1965 election, Smith received his mandate to pursue independence vigorously and if necessary illegally and unilaterally. The Rhodesian Front swept 79.3 percent of the vote (up from 56.5 percent in 1962), and its victory confirmed that the old UFP—now the Rhodesia party—was a spent force.

Refusing to grant Rhodesia unconditional independence, the British Government stipulated six preconditions: (1) unimpeded progress toward majority rule; (2) guarantees against retrogressive amendment of the 1961 constitution; (3) immediate improvement in Africans' political status; (4) progress toward ending racial discrimination; (5) evidence that independence was acceptable to the entire Rhodesian population; and (6) formal prohibitions against racial oppression either by the minority or the majority. The settlers responded to these conditions with a litany of noes. They were most prepared to resist the first principle: majority rule was to them a euphemism for a "racialist black dictatorship," which would be suicidal for white power and prosperity and would erode "civilized standards" in the country.

The impasse between the two governments had lasted more than a year when Smith announced his country's Unilateral Declaration of Independence in November 1965. British Prime Minister Harold Wilson immediately denounced UDI as an "act of rebellion against the Crown" and predicted that the illegal action would be short-lived. British officials took quite some time to realize that Rhodesia was no longer within their sphere of influence and that the Crown's authority over Rhodesia was, in large measure, a constitutional fiction. The home country had no military or civil service personnel in the country, only an impotent governor; it was in no position to intervene with force.[121] Whitehall eventually convinced the international community to apply economic sanc-

120. Winston Field, letter to R. A. Butler, British Secretary of State, 29 March 1963, reprinted in Central African Office, *Correspondence Between Her Majesty's Government and the Government of Southern Rhodesia,* Cmnd. 2000 (London: HMSO, April 1963).

121. The use of force against Rhodesia was unpopular at home (where the Labour Government had a bare majority of one in the Commons); it went against the policy of "consensual decolonization," presented logistical difficulties, was opposed by Britain's military chiefs, and would have violated the "kith and kin" ties between the two countries (see Robert C. Good's excellent discussion, *U.D.I.: The International Politics of the Rhodesian Rebellion* [London: Faber and Faber, 1973], pp. 55–64).

tions and diplomatic isolation to bring Rhodesia to its senses. When this failed, Britain made several attempts at a negotiated solution. Yet, as neither party would compromise on basic principles, the discussions came to naught. It became increasingly clear that the Rhodesian settler state was immune to metropolitan leverage.

One week prior to UDI, the Rhodesian Front regime declared a state of emergency: it has been in effect ever since. The timing of the declaration clearly anticipated the constitutional crisis between Britain and Rhodesia and the possibility that blacks might launch an insurrection against the regime. They did not, but already in 1964 ZANU and ZAPU resolved to pursue an armed struggle against the regime from exile in Zambia. Rhodesia's security forces swiftly crushed their first attempts at guerrilla infiltration in 1966, and the campaign remained ineffective until 1972.

Although the country was peaceful in the later 1960s, Rhodesia retained the state of emergency and used the security arsenal to harass and subdue black political opponents, not simply those few involved in crime and violence. Almost all the principal nationalist leaders of the early 1960s languished in detention, restriction, or exile for several years.[122] The lack of leaders, organization, and resources to challenge the regime made this a time of disarray and frustration in the nationalist movement.

The settlers were in a different mood altogether. The rebellion against Britain and resultant international isolation cemented the settlers' political and ideological unity. The whites stood solidly behind the Government and its commitment to resist social and political change. In the general elections of 1970 and 1977, the Rhodesian Front won 77.8 percent and 86.4 percent of the vote. Settlers also broadly accepted the need for severe security powers. In one small 1971 survey, 88 percent of the whites questioned approved of the regime's handling of security; only 3 percent disapproved.[123]

CONCLUSION

The pillars of settler rule had weathered several storms. Britain and the international community had failed to affect the Rhodesian situation;

---

122. The new orders for detention and restriction declined steadily—from 650 and 1,670 respectively in 1964 to 0 and 14 by November 1969.
123. Morris Hirsch, *A Decade of Crisis: Ten Years of Rhodesian Front Rule* (Salisbury: Peter Dearlove, 1973), p. 151.

settler solidarity had been restored; peaceful black opposition had been quieted and armed struggle seemed futile.

When a maverick regime tampered with absolutist settler rule, it succumbed to a backlash consistent with the prediction that state power would "gravitate towards those who [were] least ready for change." [124] Hard-line settlers saw the most modest concessions to the natives as threatening the sacred pillars of settler rule.

Not all settler castes have displayed the political intransigence of the Rhodesians. The Arab elite in Zanzibar tried another strategy in the 1950s:

> to preserve its position by gaining the acceptance and political support of the African majority. This method was fundamentally different from the usual technique of dominant racial minorities which have attempted to retain power by coercive means elsewhere in Africa. . . . The Arab oligarchy of Zanzibar actively sought to bring about the introduction of a representative parliamentary system based on universal suffrage, and tied its political future to the idea of gaining sufficient [African] electoral support to win a majority of constituencies. [125]

But Zanzibar's experiment with gradual native incorporation was motivated by the same underlying concern as Rhodesia's UDI: to preempt a British move to grant independence to the black majority.

When Clapham wrote that "Liberia is not a sort of black Rhodesia," he had in mind the Liberian regime's efforts during the final decades of settler rule to win the compliance of the indigenous African population through partial social assimilation and political incorporation. [126] In the late 1960s and 1970s Liberia extended the franchise to Africans, relaxed coercive sanctions, and set in motion a "Unification Policy." [127] These genuine efforts at accommodation went further than anything Rhodesia contemplated, but they were nevertheless designed to streamline, not dissolve, settler rule. Liebenow notes that "the more the central bastions of settler privilege were threatened, the tighter the restrictions imposed upon significant entry of tribal persons into the upper echelons" of the

124. Leys, *European Politics,* p. 36.
125. Michael Lofchie, "The Plural Society of Zanzibar," in *Pluralism in Africa,* ed. L. Kuper and M. Smith (Berkeley: University of California Press, 1971), p. 309 and Michael Lofchie, *Zanzibar: Background to Revolution* (Princeton: Princeton University Press, 1965).
126. Christopher Clapham, "Liberia," in *West African States,* ed. J. Dunn (Cambridge: Cambridge University Press, 1978), p. 122.
127. J. Gus Liebenow, *Liberia: The Evolution of Privilege* (Ithaca: Cornell University Press, 1969).

state and economic order.[128] At the time of the coup d'état in 1980, settlers still dominated the Cabinet; the True Whig party, under tight settler control, had held power for a full century; and the native majority still had little influence on state policy.

That settler rule came to an abrupt and violent end in Zanzibar in 1964 and Liberia in 1980 illustrates the difficulties inherent in a reformist solution to settler domination. Contemporary Taiwan may prove that incremental democratization and liberalization is indeed an alternative to protracted settler rule. But most settler populations will not endorse the kinds of changes that would satisfy native interests, just as natives are normally unwilling to rest content with the modest concessions offered. Unwilling to reform themselves out of power, enlightened modernizing regimes often walk a tightrope between irreconcilable settler and native demands. This delicate balancing act is currently occupying South Africa.

Northern Ireland and Rhodesian settlers held steadfast to their power and privilege as communal divisions deepened and instability grew in the 1960s and 1970s. In those decades, they mobilized the full force of their respective security systems to defend settler supremacy. Ultimately, the repressive apparatus proved unequal to the task, as the next two chapters show.

128. J. Gus Liebenow, *Liberia: The Quest for Democracy* (Bloomington: Indiana University Press, 1987), p. 6.

CHAPTER 4

Rhodesia

Guerrilla War and
Political Settlement, 1972–1980

During the 1960s, Rhodesia's black nationalist leaders failed to build a movement capable of challenging settler rule. The sporadic armed incursions that punctuated the latter half of the 1960s also proved futile: insurgents engaged vastly superior security forces but were poorly trained and organized; they made little effort to create a base of support among rural peasants and suffered infiltration by Rhodesian intelligence operatives.

The picture changed dramatically in the 1970s. By 1973 successful guerrilla attacks had begun to shake the foundations of settler rule. The repressive system that had smothered black mobilization in the 1960s was mobilizing to defend the settler state and social order. Rhodesia experienced in the 1970s what South Africa fears today: a "total onslaught," including international political and economic sanctions and full-scale domestic insurgency. Yet for several years the white regime weathered international pressures and the costs of the escalating guerrilla war.

This chapter examines several developments in the Rhodesian state and society during the turbulent 1970s. First, protracted unrest and armed insurgency had an empowering effect on the security establishment. As threats to the state mounted, the security sector grew into a Leviathan branch; its agencies were galvanized with infusions of material resources, personnel, and legal and extralegal powers; security forces were relieved of all semblance of accountability. Second, the metropole remained, until the end of the decade, a spectator without leverage over this settler state—despite its occasional attempts to broker a political settlement. Third, under the most trying circumstances, the besieged white settler community showed remarkable solidarity in support of the Rhodesian Front regime—notwithstanding chronic conflicts within the state itself. Despite the regime's success in maintaining settler cohesion and keeping the metropole at bay, it was ultimately unable to defeat the guerrilla armies. By the end of the decade, the war's growing costs led the Government to search for a political solution that culminated in the transfer of power to a popularly elected black regime in 1980.

The Rhodesian case shows that all three conditions for stable settler rule are vital. Two conditions—settler solidarity and the country's insulation from metropolitan interference—continued to be satisfied, but the third—effective control over the native population—could not be. In shattering this pillar, black insurgency made the state's breakdown inevitable. Yet for several years the other two pillars remained sufficiently strong to maintain *unstable* settler rule. Settler rule collapsed much more rapidly in Northern Ireland (1969 to 1972) as a result of the simultaneous crumbling of all three pillars.

INSURGENCY AFTER 1972

The occasional guerrilla incursions of the late 1960s were launched from Zambia, across the Zambezi River, which was flanked by inhospitable terrain. By 1972 developments inside Mozambique created further opportunities for Rhodesia's guerrillas. The Front for the Liberation of Mozambique (FRELIMO) had forced the Portuguese to withdraw from Tete province, which borders northeastern Rhodesia. FRELIMO agreed to allow ZANU's military wing, ZANLA (Zimbabwe African National Liberation Army), to operate within Tete and eventually to open up a second front for the war in Rhodesia. In December 1972, the first incursions from Tete resulted in the killing of white farmers; by mid-1973 ZANLA had established itself in northeastern Rhodesia.

In 1974 the fortunes of the ZANLA guerrillas brightened: a military coup in Portugal in April 1974 precipitated its complete withdrawal from Mozambique in 1975. Almost immediately, guerrilla sanctuaries appeared along the vast eastern border—a frontier impossible for the Rhodesians to secure. By January 1976, several thousand ZANLA guerrillas were encamped in Mozambique, from which they made increasingly frequent sorties into Rhodesia.

The war intensified dramatically after 1976, as official statistics reflected. Between 1972 and 1976, 215 members of the security forces and 1,917 insurgents died; in 1977 alone, the casualties were 197 security personnel and 1,774 rebels. (Official figures tended to underreport casualties of the security forces and inflate those of the insurgents.) The number of guerrillas operating inside the country was another gauge of the temperature of the war. The official (conservative) estimate of 700 in early 1976 grew to 10,000 by early 1979—the majority were members of ZANLA (the wartime role of ZIPRA, the Zimbabwe People's Revolutionary Army, was much less substantial).[1] The exodus of whites is another index: in 1971 the country had 9,403 white immigrants; in 1976, 7,072 residents left, and in 1978, 13,709. White flight affected the morale of the remaining settlers and drained scarce human and financial resources from the war effort.

Learning from one of their previous mistakes, the rebels attempted to politicize and convert rural people to the cause. They solicited the active support of village chiefs, headmen, and spirit mediums along the eastern border; with villagers, they aimed at undermining the authority of the regime and capitalizing on peasants' grievances over land. But the twin goals of raising consciousness and cultivating popular support were hard to realize without fully liberated zones, where insurgent forces could operate unabated (as had occurred in Mozambique and Guinea-Bissau).[2] The Rhodesian war machine had a long reach, and the white farming strongholds were distributed throughout the countryside, scattering insurgent operations and preventing rebels from gaining a secure foothold in particular areas.

Though extensive, Rhodesia's military capacities were never as formidable as Pretoria's, and its terrain permitted greater clandestine activity than the South African. The Rhodesian insurgents thus had opportunities for their guerrilla campaign that the African National Congress of South Africa lacks. Yet Rhodesia's insurgents had two weaknesses: they were fragmented into ZANLA and ZIPRA, often antagonistic guerrilla

1. ZIPRA's forces (which were linked to ZAPU) remained in Zambia for much of the war but fought more on the western front in the late 1970s.

2. Martin Gregory, "Zimbabwe 1980: Politicisation through Armed Struggle and Electoral Mobilisation," *Journal of Commonwealth and Comparative Politics* 19, no. 1 (March 1981): 63–94; Lewis Gann and Thomas H. Henriksen, *The Struggle for Zimbabwe* (New York: Praeger, 1981), pp. 66, 119; Paul L. Moorcraft and Peter McLaughlin, *Chimurenga: The War in Rhodesia* (Marshalltown, South Africa: Sigma and Collins, 1982), p. 90; Thomas Henriksen, "People's War in Angola, Mozambique, and Guinea-Bissau," *Journal of Modern African Studies* 14, no. 3 (September 1976): 377–99.

armies, and had few links to urban movements or underground cells, unlike the ANC.[3]

The linchpin of a successful rural insurgency is often said to be the cultivation of civilian support, through persuasion and politicization. As one observer maintains, civilian support "cannot be obtained at gunpoint."[4] Yet the use of naked force to achieve civilians' compliance is not uncommon—varying, of course, across time and place, in severity, and in effects.[5]

The small body of literature on the Rhodesian insurrection disagrees on the extent to which the guerrilla armies used coercion. Some analysts say little about the dark side of the insurgents' campaign and present a romanticized view of the liberation forces, describing their support among rural blacks as voluntary, natural, and unproblematic.[6] Ranger, for instance, leaves the impression that ZANLA cadres rather easily capitalized on and intensified peasants' discontent over loss of land: the peasants' nationalist consciousness "was highly conducive to mobilization for guerrilla war."[7] Rarely do these works address guerrilla violence, and it seems to have had no effect on peasant support: "Even if particular guerrilla bands behaved brutally...peasants continued to back guerrilla war in principle."[8]

Other accounts center on the difficulties of winning popular support and the rebels' use of force to elicit compliance from uncooperative peasants. Sithole states, "The commandist nature of mobilization and politicization under clandestine circumstances gave rise to the politics of intimidation and fear."[9] Kriger draws conclusions from fieldwork in one district in Zimbabwe:

3. ZANU and ZAPU, the political wings of ZANLA and ZIPRA, respectively, merged in 1976 into the Patriotic Front, a tenuous alliance.

4. Eqbal Ahmad, "Revolutionary Warfare and Counterinsurgency," in *National Liberation,* ed. N. Miller and R. Aya (New York: Free Press, 1971), p. 159.

5. Ted Robert Gurr, *Why Men Rebel* (Princeton: Princeton University Press, 1970), chap. 8; Nathan Leites and Charles Wolf, *Rebellion and Authority: An Analytic Essay on Insurgent Conflicts* (Santa Monica: RAND, 1969).

6. Terence Ranger, *Peasant Consciousness and Guerrilla War in Zimbabwe* (Berkeley: University of California Press, 1985); David Martin and Phyllis Johnson, *The Struggle for Zimbabwe* (London: Faber and Faber, 1981); Julie Frederikse, *None But Ourselves: Masses vs. Media in the Making of Zimbabwe* (Harare: Zimbabwe Publishing House, 1982).

7. Ranger, *Peasant Consciousness,* p. 24.

8. Terence Ranger, "Bandits and Guerrillas: The Case of Zimbabwe," in *Banditry, Rebellion, and Social Protest in Africa,* ed. D. Crummey (London, 1986), p. 386.

9. Masipula Sithole, "Zimbabwe: In Search of a Stable Democracy," in *Democracy in Developing Countries,* vol. 2, *Africa,* ed. Diamond, Linz, and Lipset (Boulder, Colo.: Lynne Rienner, 1988), 248.

The ZANU-PF organizations set up by the guerrillas required guerrilla violence and force to function. Consequently, I reject the concept of sustained popular support or voluntary cooperation between guerrillas and peasants or local elites. [The] guerrilla inability to establish "liberated zones" made it inevitable that mobilization would require ongoing violence. . . . Peasants were unlikely to be enthusiastic supporters over an extended period.[10]

This stark coercion thesis simply inverts that of persuasion. Drawing on the empirical findings from both approaches, we may conclude that neither coercion nor persuasion was "inevitable" in mobilizing peasants' cooperation in specific instances or their sustained support for armed struggle. There is no logical reason why the absence of liberated zones made violence necessary; it simply made the insurgents' task of cultivating peasants' support more challenging. Likewise, there is no logical reason why peasants' support for the guerrilla cause should be automatic; it had to be won and maintained. A more balanced account seems appropriate.

At first, Rhodesia's guerrillas attempted to gain the political sympathies of rural civilians. When this failed, they, like rebels elsewhere, were not averse to meting out rough justice. For villagers suspected of selling out to the Rhodesian authorities or those who refused aid to guerrilla units from fear of reprisal by the security forces, insurgents resorted to intimidation and violence (threats, beating, rape, mutilation, and killing). In short, as in other rural insurgencies, the guerrillas used a variety of tactics to gain villagers' cooperation, and the balance between coercion and persuasion varied over time and place.

COUNTERINSURGENCY AFTER 1972

In the early 1970s Rhodesia's intelligence service grew increasingly concerned about guerrilla advances in neighboring Mozambique and alerted the Cabinet to the dire consequences of a Portuguese defeat next door. A top official at the CIO lamented that these warnings went unheeded:

The Portuguese experience in Guinea, Angola, and Mozambique was very closely studied and I believe all the appropriate lessons were passed to Cabinet whose members suffered from a "Portuguese blind spot," which took nearly eight years to clear up—and was then too late for clear vision. Why? I suppose because Ian Smith's Government was getting a much more encourag-

10. Norma Kriger, "The Zimbabwean War of Liberation: Struggles within the Struggle," *Journal of Southern African Studies* 14, no. 2 (January 1988): 306, 313.

ing account out of its emissaries to Lisbon and elsewhere, and there were too many politicians inside Rhodesia . . . who believed that just as the Portuguese had been in Africa for four centuries, so would it continue. In consequence, CIO warnings on this subject probably cut less ice than on any other.[11]

In the fall of Mozambique and Angola in 1974–1975 some white Rhodesians saw handwriting on the wall and believed the Government should strike a political deal with the black majority while whites were still ahead. Prime Minister Ian Smith was prepared to do nothing of the sort. He revealed his view in a broadcast to the nation in 1976:

> We shall be urged by some people to heed the lessons of Mozambique and Angola and to surrender now in order to avoid chaos and strife . . . I say to these people that if we were to surrender the reins of Government nothing would be more certain than the inevitability of civil war between blacks and whites in Rhodesia. . . . The fundamental difference [between Rhodesia and the Portuguese colonies] is that in Rhodesia there is no metropolitan government to surrender on our behalf. We made certain of that when we assumed our independence ten years ago.[12]

In addition to its autonomy from the metropole, Rhodesia had military forces far superior to the insurgents'. The regime had about forty-five thousand security forces, of which it could field twenty-five thousand at any time without seriously disrupting the economy and administration.[13] The security system received increasingly generous allocations, an index of both the intensification of the conflict and the steady ascendancy of the security apparatus within the settler state. From 1971–1972 to 1976–1977 the budget for the Ministry of Internal Affairs (previously the Department of Native Affairs) skyrocketed from (Rhodesian) R$9.7 million to R$42 million; that for the Ministry of Law and Order (including police) jumped from R$17.5 million to R$50 million; and expenditure for the Ministry of Defense grew from R$20 million to R$98.7 million.[14] In 1976, defense expenditure consumed 25 percent of the total budget; by 1979, it was 47 percent. Vital to the Rhodesian war economy were massive infusions of South African aid, which

---

11. Correspondence with author, 2 May 1984.

12. Transcript of broadcast, Department of Information press statement, Salisbury, 6 February 1976.

13. Gann and Henriksen, *Struggle*, p. 65. The Rhodesian security forces were no thin white line; blacks were 40 percent of the 15,000 army personnel and 60 percent of the BSAP; they also worked in the Department of Internal Affairs. Few blacks deserted or were disloyal to the white regime; they (like their South African counterparts) enlisted primarily for economic reasons.

14. Government of Southern Rhodesia, *Estimates of Expenditure* (Salisbury: Government Printer, 1971–1972 and 1976–1977).

accounted for roughly 50 percent of Rhodesia's defense costs after 1976.[15]

As the war grew more regionalized, Rhodesia resorted to frequent cross-border air strikes against enemy targets and against the infrastructures of Mozambique and Zambia as well. Roads, bridges, communication lines, and development projects were pulverized, costing the host nations dearly. Rhodesia also engaged in covert action in other countries, including assassination of nationalist leaders in Zambia, Mozambique, and Botswana.[16]

Cross-border attacks occurred in part because white citizens and military officers pressed for external operations. Such attacks also demonstrated the regime's refusal to recognize that the conflict had domestic roots, just as political elites in the 1960s denied that African nationalism had internal sources. The standard official line, that black discontent and political violence were caused by outside "agitators," was consistent with the policy of cross-border military strikes and also explained the regime's reluctance to consider domestic reforms. Privately, some elites—including Rhodesia's intelligence services—contested official dogma, to no avail. A senior CIO officer described the situation:

> The military increased its external raids into Mozambique. But the CIO believed... we must win the war inside the country.... Counterinsurgency was 80 percent political and 20 percent military. But for that you need a government that will act politically and our Government got beyond this.[17]

Preferring a military victory, the Rhodesian Front Government steadfastly refused to attend to the political causes of the war:

> The military, supported by the politicians, believed more and more that the anti-terrorist war could be won by striking at terrorist bases as far outside the country as possible; and CIO/Police believed that the war would be lost unless we could stop recruiting within the country, and towards the end being able to prove that we were not winning if 1,000 "terrorists" (mostly untrained recruits) were killed each month beyond our borders, when the recruiting rate was 2,000–3,000 a month, and each month there were more armed terrorists within the country. But we had to concede the impossibility of convincing politicians, and some others, that recruiting was proceeding at the rate de-

15. Anthony R. Wilkinson, "The Impact of the War," *Journal of Commonwealth and Comparative Politics* 18, no. 1 (March 1980): 115; Martin Gregory, "Rhodesia: From Lusaka to Lancaster House," *The World Today* 36, no. 1 (January 1980): 17–18. During the 1970s South Africa became increasingly a de facto metropole, giving Rhodesia critical material support and, toward the end, putting decisive political pressure on the Smith regime.

16. Ron Reid Daly, *Selous Scouts: Top Secret War* (Alberton, South Africa: Galago, 1982).

17. Interview with author, 30 May 1983.

scribed, because this signified that their political policies had failed—when, of course, they had.[18]

Several observers have commented on the "ingenuity," "flexibility," "efficiency," and "tactical brilliance" of the Rhodesian security forces;[19] others have noted their success in producing guerrilla casualties while keeping military casualties "low."[20] Evans claims that "while the Rhodesian security forces had won every battle, the Rhodesian politicians had lost the war."[21] This claim neglects the military's own role in undermining the war effort. Although the official line was that winning black hearts and minds was absolutely vital to overall success, military practices routinely contradicted that objective; lower-level commanders and soldiers preferred insurgent casualties to civilian support.[22] And some elites candidly admitted that a hearts-and-minds approach was eventually forsaken.[23] The Ministry of Internal Affairs insisted that blacks were too primitive to appreciate such appeals and only "respected force." In practice, therefore, a military solution remained the hallmark of Rhodesia's counterinsurgency strategy throughout the war.[24]

If this was the favored approach, there were those inside the executive who appealed for sensitivity to Africans' hearts and minds. Some senior military officers favored this strategy, as did certain intelligence elites who argued for a policy to address black grievances, minimize ruthless and counterproductive military practices, and begin political negotiations with black leaders. According to one ranking Special Branch officer, the branch was "advocating dialogue with the nationalists, versus a

---

18. CIO officer, correspondence with author, 2 May 1984. Ken Flower supports and elaborates these points (*Serving Secretly: An Intelligence Chief on Record, Rhodesia into Zimbabwe: 1964 to 1981* [London: John Murray, 1987]). Recruits (some abducted or press-ganged), came from Rhodesian villages, from urban areas with high African unemployment (exacerbated by the world recession of 1973–1974), and from refugee camps in Zambia and Mozambique.

19. James Bruton, "Counterinsurgency in Rhodesia," *Military Review* 59, no. 3 (March 1979): 27–39; Mike Evans, *Fighting Against Chimurenga: An Analysis of Counterinsurgency in Rhodesia* (Salisbury: Historical Association of Zimbabwe, 1981).

20. Gann and Henriksen, *Struggle*, p. 66.

21. Evans, *Fighting*, p. 24.

22. J. K. Cilliers, *Counter-Insurgency in Rhodesia* (London: Croom Helm, 1985), pp. 146, 148.

23. Minister of Combined Operations, Assembly *Debates*, vol. 98, 11 August 1978, col. 1724. By the time martial law was instituted, another noted, "hearts and minds had less adherence in Cabinet" (former official in Ministry of Law and Order, interview with author, 3 June 1983).

24. Ian Beckett, "The Rhodesian Army: Counter-Insurgency 1972–1979," in *Armed Forces and Counter-Insurgency,* ed. I. Beckett and J. Pimlott (New York: St. Martins, 1985); J. K. Cilliers, *Counter-Insurgency in Rhodesia* (London: Croom Helm, 1985).

purely military approach, as far back as 1963." [25] Sensitized to the lessons of failed counterinsurgency efforts in Mozambique, Angola, and elsewhere, the CIO consistently pressed for a political settlement in its reports to Cabinet. The intelligence director insisted that by the mid-1970s Rhodesia was neither winning the war nor containing the threat, and that the security situation was increasingly desperate. The Quarterly Threat Assessment of July 1977 is a case in point:

> No successful result can be attained by purely military means. It is now more vital than ever to arrive at an early political settlement before the point of no return beyond which it will be impossible to achieve any viable political or military/political solution. [26]

By 1978 the CIO held that Rhodesia had reached the point of no return. But its advice had little impact on a ruling party determined at any cost to maintain its grip on state power, and whose white constituency adamantly opposed black majority rule.

The Rhodesian state did not rely on coercion alone to preserve settler domination. It waged a multifaceted propaganda war with pamphlets, films, newspaper stories, and posters, directed at both whites and blacks. [27] My analysis of a sample of this material showed that its messages concentrated on the atrocities committed by the rebels (including the killing of missionaries and the mutilating of peasants), the specter of communism, and the inevitable "degeneration" of independent black African nations—all of which stood as an object lesson in stark contrast to the achievements of white rule and the security forces' glorified defense of the state against the enemies of Western Christian civilization in southern Africa.

The regime's propaganda and censorship paid high dividends among the white electorate inasmuch as they systematically distorted the political roots of the conflict and deprived whites of information on atrocities by the military. Exploiting whites' anxieties and resonating with their supremacist orientation, official thought control reinforced settler cohesion, minimized protest by white civic institutions, and prevented the growth of a progressive white alternative to the incumbent regime.

The propaganda machine registered much less success within the black population, as officials involved later admitted. [28] Grossly out of touch with peasants' concerns, the propaganda disseminated by Psycho-

25. Interview with author, 24 June 1983.
26. Quarterly Threat Assessment, reproduced in Flower, *Serving Secretly,* p. 310.
27. Frederikse, *None But Ourselves.*
28. Ibid.

logical Operations units made light of the grievances of the black community and often contradicted their experiences; it proffered a crude caricature of the guerrillas and a benevolent picture of the security forces that military brutality routinely undermined. A typical article appeared in the Government Information Services paper, the *African Times,* after an early rebel attack: "Let us thank the spirits of our ancestors who watch over us that a good, strong Rhodesian Government made sure that such bloated, cruel, and greedy liars never came to power, and never will." [29] Such exhortation did nothing to shore up the legitimacy of white rule among the majority of black Rhodesians. One classified army assessment revealed that in some rural areas "the civilian population is totally alienated against the Government." [30]

Given the abiding interest of the regime in preserving minority rule and whites' control of the best agricultural land, it is questionable whether any hearts-and-minds program could have registered success. The propaganda failed to take black grievances seriously, driven as it was by the official insistence that genuine grievances did not exist but were instead manufactured by outside agitators. Blacks' discontent over unequal land distribution, racial discrimination, the lack of opportunities for economic advancement, and undiluted settler rule was not accepted as genuine. Instead whites took pride in the racial harmony prevailing in the country. As Ian Smith told me, "We had the happiest blacks in the world here in Rhodesia, which was based on the fact that we weren't a UK colony. This was our home, and we were concerned to ensure good race relations." Blacks who participated in the liberation war were duped by "Communist Russian exploitation of grievances; it had nothing to do with race relations." [31]

Only in the late 1970s did the regime begin to dilute settler rule by incorporating moderate Africans into the state and by removing some forms of "unnecessary discrimination." Yet, like the Pretoria regime today, it failed to win popular approval through its belated reformist efforts. They were widely perceived as too little and too late; and the concern with reforms was altogether secondary to repression. Tellingly, the Minister of Information, who was responsible for overseeing propaganda, stated after the war, "I wanted to step up the use of the bayonet. That's the most effective propaganda—the bayonet." [32] The regime was

---

29. *African Times* (Salisbury), 30 November 1966.
30. Quoted in Cilliers, *Counter-Insurgency,* p. 99.
31. Interview with author, 29 June 1983.
32. Quoted in Frederikse, *None But Ourselves,* p. 126.

obsessed with "kill rates," and its ideological campaign did little to build peasant support for counterinsurgency. Force, to quote Gramsci, was "predominating excessively over consent," and this imbalance sent legions of blacks over to the guerrilla side.[33]

INNOVATIONS IN REPRESSION

The reliance on military repression and neglect of civilians' hearts and minds was most pronounced in the eastern countryside, the principal theater of the war. Both sides judged that control over the rural population was vital and, as usual in a guerrilla war, the civilians suffered most. Torture, beatings, mass arrest, rape, and execution were commonplace in the war zone. State elites repeatedly justified harshness in extinguishing rural support for the insurgents and persuading villagers to assist the security forces; civilian neutrality was unacceptable: "It is no good for people to close their eyes and say to themselves—this is between the terrorists and the Government."[34] One minister went a step further: "When somebody deliberately refrains from reporting terrorists, or indeed assists a terrorist in any way, then he or she is in fact a terrorist."[35]

The legal powers available to security agencies grew dramatically during the war. The Law and Order (Maintenance) Act was amended in 1973 to provide the penalty of death for aiding guerrillas or failing to report their presence, for undergoing, recruiting, or encouraging others to undergo guerrilla training, and for acts of "terrorism or sabotage." "Assisting" or "failing to report" rebel units became a crime on a par with guerrilla activity itself; in court cases, intimidation and fear of reprisals were flatly rejected as extenuating circumstances.[36] In April 1975, the Government issued an edict that executions for such offenses would be carried out in secret, and that relatives would be informed only if they inquired after the fact.

Regulations issued under the Emergency Powers Act in January 1973 empowered provincial commissioners to impose collective fines (of cash, livestock, property) upon entire villages suspected of assisting guerrillas;

33. Antonio Gramsci, *Selections from the Prison Notebooks* (New York: International, 1971), p. 80n.
34. Minister of Law and Order, *Rhodesia Herald* (Salisbury), 28 July 1973.
35. Minister of Combined Operations, Assembly *Debates,* vol. 98, 11 August 1978, col. 1720.
36. See Geoff Feltoe, "Hearts and Minds: A Policy of Counter-Intimidation," *Rhodesian Law Journal* 16 (April 1976): 47–63.

the villagers in question had no benefit of trial or appeal. Collective fines (usually the seizure of precious cattle) were destined to punish innocent people, as the Minister of Internal Affairs stated: "The imposition of collective fines must necessarily involve people who might . . . be innocent, but . . . they are all living in a communal society and must bear the responsibility for the lack of co-operation in the [counter-]terrorist exercise." [37] Officials claimed that collective punishment was consistent with African tradition, which deemphasized individual culpability. One Secretary of Internal Affairs refuted this view: "I said I disagreed with collective fines totally, since they would punish the innocent. . . . It was a fallacious argument that collective punishment was rooted in African tradition." [38] In February 1974, new emergency regulations gave local officials authority to confiscate or destroy crops, stock, and property of possible use to guerrillas; to compel residents of an area to build and maintain bridges, roads, dams, and fences; and to resettle villagers en masse into "protected villages" (PVs).

By the end of the war, over seven hundred thousand peasants had been forcibly uprooted and relocated into several hundred PVs. A Rhodesian Army idea, PVs were designed to drive a wedge between peasants and insurgents, thus isolating the latter from their supportive social base in the countryside. A governmental newspaper attempted to convince blacks that protected villages were "havens of peace, where work, study, and play can be carried on in an atmosphere of tranquility and order." [39] Yet most PVs evidenced miserable living conditions and tyrannical control by members of the Guard Force. Not surprisingly, villagers came to look on the guerrillas as their liberators from these prison camps. [40] An internal report by the Catholic Commission for Justice and Peace found that conditions in the PVs produced "a great intensification of political awareness" and "resistance" among the affected villagers. [41] In addition to deepening popular alienation from the state, the resettlement program failed to stem the tide of insurgency, much as the *aldeamento* resettlement programs failed in Angola and Mozambique. [42] Some top

37. Assembly *Debates,* vol. 83, 30 March 1973, col. 1173.
38. Interview with author, 7 June 1983.
39. *African Times,* 9 August 1978.
40. A. K. H. Weinrich, "Strategic Resettlement in Rhodesia," *Journal of Southern African Studies* 3, no. 2 (April 1977): 221.
41. Catholic Commission for Justice and Peace, "Report on Chiweshe T.T.L." [Tribal Trust Land], Salisbury, 26 August 1974, p. 14.
42. Gerald Bender, "The Limits of Counterinsurgency: An African Case," *Comparative Politics* 4, no. 3 (April 1972): 331–60; Brendan Jundanian, "Resettlement Programs: Counterinsurgency in Mozambique," *Comparative Politics* 6, no. 4 (July 1974): 540.

officials at CIO and Internal Affairs had been opposed to PVs because of the expected counterproductive impact. One Secretary of Internal Affairs explained after the war, "PVs were definitely forced on Internal Affairs. The Army had a stonewall case for this (Malaya) and Internal Affairs couldn't refute the military's arguments." [43] Rhodesia, unlike Malaya, never coupled its program with a serious effort to win popular support from resettled villagers or addressed their socioeconomic needs.

In addition, curfews were imposed, minefields created, and "free-fire" or "no go" areas declared along the border with Mozambique in an attempt to forge a *cordon sanitaire* in areas vulnerable to insurgent penetration. Any person violating curfews or caught inside "no go" zones was fair game to the security forces. When questioned about the shooting of curfew violators, the Minister of Defense, P. K. van der Byl, replied, "As far as I am concerned, the more curfew breakers that are shot the better, and the sooner it is realized everywhere the better." [44] Between December 1972 and 31 July 1978, official figures listed 322 African curfew violators killed by security forces. The curfews and the cordon failed, however, to prevent infiltration.

An additional 263 African dead were officially listed as persons "caught in the crossfire," and another 645 dead were labeled "collaborators" with the guerrillas. [45] According to the former CIO director, these categories were frequently used to cover up the extralegal murder of villagers. [46] Generally, the authorities took a callous stance toward civilian casualties, which they considered "a normal operational hazard." [47] The use of lethal force against civilians was one means whereby the regime believed it could strike fear into the rural population and thus deny succor to insurgents. As the authorities and white civilians continually insisted—not only in Rhodesia but throughout colonial Africa— "Africans respect force." One ranking security official noted that "Africans responded to the threat of violence; it was either us or the terrorists' threats." [48]

As the temperature of the war rose, the beleaguered regime found it increasingly important to remove all legal strictures on the security forces' operations. Prosecution of members of the security forces for abuses might be embarrassing to the government and demoralizing for

43. Interview, 7 June 1983; Flower, *Serving Secretly,* pp. 122–23.
44. Assembly *Debates,* vol. 90, 31 July 1975, col. 1706.
45. Department of Information, *Terrorist Casualties,* Salisbury, 1 August 1978.
46. Flower, *Serving Secretly,* p. 205.
47. Ministry of Defense spokesman, *Rhodesia Herald,* 15 June 1974.
48. Author's interview with former Ministry of Law and Order official, 3 June 1983.

security personnel. Using language identical to South Africa's Defense Act, Rhodesia's 1975 Indemnity and Compensation Act exonerated the security forces for acts done "in good faith for the suppression of terrorism." "Terrorism" and "good faith" were elastic conditions, whose satisfaction the minister determined case by case.[49] In practice, the act permitted carte blanche. Wanton killing, burning of huts and fields, beating, collective punishment, and destruction of livestock became commonplace as the war escalated. Police and soldiers routinely used torture, including electric shock and immersion in water.

On those relatively rare occasions when the behavior of the security forces was criticized in public, the authorities promptly attempted to discredit the accusers. Typical was the case of a black MP who presented a motion in the Assembly in March 1974, requesting a commission of inquiry into alleged incidents of beating, property destruction, and killing by the military. An outraged Minister of Law and Order castigated the MP for his insidious attempt to spread "alarm and despondency" (which was a crime under the security law) and noted that it was part of the "communist code" to "derogate the forces of law and order." He demanded that the author of the motion apologize for insulting the integrity of the security forces.[50] The Minister of Defense described such criticism as "vulgar and obscene," an "abuse of the privileges" of Parliament, and added that the army commander would "shudder" to think of an inquiry into military abuses.[51] Given the incidence of military brutality, one can understand why army chiefs might shudder if atrocities were brought to light.

One organization attempted to do just that. Beginning in 1973, the Catholic Commission for Justice and Peace made a series of fruitless representations to the prime minister, the Minister of Law and Order, and the Minister of Internal Affairs over the security forces' brutality. When it called for an impartial inquiry in April 1974, it was pilloried and accused of trying to advance the guerrilla cause and of provoking a confrontation between church and state.[52] In the next few years the commission published a series of reports documenting state repression, including "deliberate use of illegal and inhumane" interrogation procedures, "gross disregard for the life and property" of rural Africans,

49. See Geoff Feltoe, "Legalizing Illegalities," *Rhodesian Law Journal* 15, no. 2 (October 1975): 167–76.

50. Assembly *Debates,* vol. 86, 27 March 1974, cols. 367–71.

51. Ibid., cols. 448–53.

52. Ian Linden, *The Catholic Church and the Struggle for Zimbabwe* (London: Longman, 1980).

and assaults "which no appeal to military urgency or national interest could justify."[53] Denounced for "spreading alarm and despondency," each commission report was promptly banned by the authorities.

As atrocities by the security forces mounted, the Catholic Commission for Justice and Peace stepped up its protests. Its public opposition only made the authorities more belligerent and recalcitrant. The commission's offices were bugged and periodically raided; some of its leaders were detained or deported. The Minister of Law and Order labeled the commission a "subversive organization," but never banned it as such.[54] The Rhodesian Front's identification of dissent with treachery was consistent with the approach of previous ruling parties and, as Chapter 6 shows, remains integral to the political culture of independent Zimbabwe.

For all its efforts to neutralize political dissent and check the advance of the guerrilla forces, the regime was operating under growing duress by 1978. The arsenal of military firepower and legal repression was proving inadequate. For years, sections of the white community had seen martial law as a panacea, yet the Government and the security chiefs were not eager to declare it. The police believed it would strengthen the military at the expense of the police.[55] The military already enjoyed carte blanche in the war zone and did not relish the added civil responsibilities of martial law, which included administering martial courts. The Cabinet also was reluctant to introduce martial law, since it would concede that Rhodesia was in dire straits and might boost the morale of the enemy.

Why, then, was martial law announced in September 1978? The Rhodesian Front's frustration with the deteriorating security situation interacted with the white community's growing outcry to make more drastic measures seem attractive. A senior official at CIO underscored these factors:

> The implementation of martial law was opposed consistently by all commanders. No one believed this was necessary, since the emergency legislation was all powerful. But martial law suited the politicians, to make them appear determined to people. Martial law wasn't going to achieve the objective of winning the war, but how can you explain this to a public that doesn't understand?[56]

53. Catholic Commission for Justice and Peace, *The Man in the Middle: Torture, Resettlement and Eviction* (Salisbury: CCJP, 1975), pp. 3, 16; Catholic Commission for Justice and Peace, *Civil War in Rhodesia* (London: Catholic Institute for International Relations, 1976).

54. Assembly *Debates,* vol. 97, 5 October 1977, col. 686.

55. Author's interview with former Ministry of Law and Order official, 6 May 1983.

56. Interview with author, 30 May 1983.

A former Minister of Law and Order highlighted the concerns of the besieged white farming community:

> Martial law was a morale-boosting move. The military [chiefs] constantly said, "We don't need martial law because we have enough powers."... At every single meeting with farmers which we went to—and they were frequent—the farmers strongly wanted martial law introduced, and they didn't like the military's excuses for not invoking it. Farmers thought we were pussy-footing around. It was really that pressure from farmers which led to it.... The courts weren't really interfering with the security forces prior to martial law, but the average soldier felt inhibited by the possibility of court scrutiny. So martial law did allow the security forces to act more freely without any interference.[57]

Martial law—or martial license—relieved the security forces of all semblance of accountability. But its net effect—coupled with the protected villages, the summary shooting of curfew breakers, collective fines, indemnification of security personnel, and the "free-fire" practice in "no go" areas—was counterproductive in the long term. These measures were destined to deepen the gulf between peasants and the state and widen the stream of recruits enlisting with the insurgents.

SETTLER SOLIDARITY AND MILITARY ASCENDANCY

An essential condition for stable settler rule is the cohesion of the settler community. Between 1963 and 1978, the Rhodesian Front Government enjoyed ever-growing support among the white electorate. It won 77.8 percent of the vote in the 1970 election and 86.4 percent in 1977. Political parties to the left of the RF remained marginal and offered the settlers no real political alternative. The few pockets of white liberalism that existed in the early 1960s (the press, legal and academic communities, moderate political parties) grew silent during the 1970s.[58] Only church leaders consistently fought draconian security measures and publicized military atrocities; their protests grew as the war proceeded but had no appreciable impact on security policy.

The regime's failure to win the war generated pressure from the far right for the use of greater force against the country's foes. As in contemporary South Africa, hard-line whites in Rhodesia (e.g., the Rhodesian Action party, white commercial farmers) fought what they per-

---

57. Interview with author, 6 May 1983.
58. See Ian Hancock, *White Liberals, Moderates, and Radicals in Rhodesia, 1953–1980* (New York: St. Martins, 1984).

ceived as "watering down" of Rhodesian Front principles (those of undiluted white political power and rigid segregation) and "pussy-footing" in the war effort, even demanding that the government resign and transfer power to the military. The minority on the far right, however, was in no position to replay the 1962 electoral coup. Although increasingly concerned over the deteriorating security situation, the white electorate did not desert the RF. The "relatively monolithic character of white Rhodesia" thus contrasts with the South African scene, where the settlers are considerably more fragmented and where parties on the far right have diminished the electoral base of the ruling National party.[59]

The RF's steadfast white support was largely a function of the "laager effect" of protracted threats (economic sanctions, guerrilla attacks, diplomatic isolation) on the small white community. Georg Simmel observed that it is rather common for group solidarity to increase in the face of external attacks, but it is not inevitable.[60] Whereas in Rhodesia in the 1970s the growing threats unified the dominant caste, in Ulster (see Chapter 5) the increasing disorder of 1969 to 1972 irreparably fractured the settler bloc and led Britain to terminate settler rule.

Contemporary South Africa, like Israel, presents a different pattern: South Africa is free of metropolitan interference but troubled by deepening cleavages between English and Afrikaner settlers and, of greater political significance, within Afrikaner ranks. The "laager" model therefore applies better to Rhodesia than to South Africa. Not only is South Africa's settler community split ethnically and politically, but civil society also provides significant debate and dissent. Despite governmental restrictions, democratic opposition from the churches, trade unions, universities, voluntary associations, and the media is stronger and more sustained than it ever was in Rhodesia (although it has as yet exerted little leverage on the Pretoria regime). Reflecting both the impressive solidarity of whites and the disorganization of urban blacks, Rhodesia's civic institutions remained rather dormant throughout the 1970s.

Settler solidarity and autonomy from the metropole facilitated the steady fortification of the Rhodesian security apparatus. Unlike other settler populations containing sizable factions at odds with the regime—in Ulster, South Africa, and Israel—Rhodesian settlers saw little disjunction during the war between their own political and security interests

---

59. Kenneth Good, "Settler Colonialism in Rhodesia," *African Affairs* 73 (January 1974): 22.
60. Georg Simmel, *Conflict and the Web of Group-Affiliations* (Glencoe, Ill.: Free Press, 1955).

and those of the Government.[61] Moreover, independent of the metropole, the Rhodesian Front regime could ignore British calls for reforms
and a political settlement. During the crisis of 1969 to 1972 in Northern
Ireland, Britain clashed with the settler regime as it attempted to rebuild
security organs. Such conflict gave the impression of a Unionist regime
weak and too susceptible to British demands for reform—which accelerated splits within the settler caste.

The tolerance of repressive measures within Rhodesian society accompanied the steady erosion of checks and balances within the state.
Stripped of most of their powers over the security system, the Assembly
and Senate ritually endorsed the proposals of the Cabinet. The justification of "national interest" alone was sufficient to convince most MPs.
One former president of the Senate explained the logic to me in 1984:
"It must be remembered that the country was at war and to open 'National Interest' to debate could possibly not be in the 'National Interest'!"[62] When asked about Parliament's role in scrutinizing security
measures during the war, a former Speaker of the Assembly responded
candidly: "The Rhodesian Parliament of the day was a pretty tame affair. I could never have dreamed of taking any action to curb the Executive and would certainly have rubber-stamped the proposals of the
PM."[63] Parliamentary debate on security policy, legislation, and practices was strictly circumscribed by the Speaker, whose rulings disallowed
any discussion of the pros and cons of specific emergency regulations,
the underlying causes and necessity of the state of emergency, and allegations of atrocities by the military.[64] My examination of the relevant
parliamentary debates found that anyone who questioned such measures or actions of the security forces was ridiculed by ministers and
other MPs and accused of supporting the insurgent cause.[65]

With one exception, Parliament grew increasingly marginal to decision making on security matters. This exception was the Senate Legal
Committee, formed in 1970 to review specific legislation that contra-
vened Rhodesia's Declaration of Rights. The full Senate routinely over-
rode its adverse reports on specific security measures because the

61. Morris Hirsch, *A Decade of Crisis: Ten Years of Rhodesian Front Rule* (Salisbury:
Dearlove, 1973).
62. Correspondence with author, 26 March 1984.
63. Correspondence with author, 12 March 1984.
64. Assembly *Debates*, vol. 67, 25 April 1967, col. 145.
65. See, for instance, the comments of the Minister of Law and Order, Assembly *Debates*, vol. 84, 21 June 1973, col. 222 and Assembly *Debates*, vol. 87, 20 June 1974,
cols. 151–52.

"national interest" demanded it. At best, the Senate Legal Committee functioned to delay but not withhold legislative endorsement of far-reaching measures.

The marginalization of Parliament coincided with that of the judiciary. During the 1970s, Rhodesian courts became increasingly subservient to the executive.[66] Apparently unsure that judges would consistently rule in the desired manner, the Government sought to expunge judicial authority over security matters. The 1969 constitution removed the courts' jurisdiction over legislation in violation of the Declaration of Rights, after the Whaley Commission reported that it was "inadvisable to involve the judiciary in political controversy" by giving it powers to review legislation and "better to place reliance upon the self-restraint of the legislature."[67] In addition, the regime frequently used its power of preventive detention in cases it could not hope to prove in court.[68] Security-related cases that did go to court often carried minimum or mandatory sentences, bypassing the traditional discretion of the judges. Even under these circumstances the judges might have done more to defend individual liberties, as their exceptional decisions in favor of individuals' rights suggest.

The judicial process was beset by chronic delay and overload of cases as the war intensified. To speed decisions and reduce the burden on the ordinary courts, Special Courts were created in May 1976 to process captured insurgents and villagers implicated in security offenses. Hearings in Special Courts were held at short notice and concluded quickly.

Even more reminiscent of the Star Chamber were the Special Courts Martial established under martial law in 1978. Run by the security forces and held in camera, they permitted neither legal representation nor appeal to ordinary courts and could impose sentences of greater severity than the civilian courts.

The progressive concentration of state authority in the executive branch coincided with changes inside that branch: the most important was a shift from civilian to military preeminence. As in many other nations facing security threats, the political influence, authority, and

66. Amnesty International, *Rhodesia/Zimbabwe* (London: Amnesty International, 1976), p. 5.
67. Government of Rhodesia, *Report of the Constitutional Commission* (Salisbury: Government Printer, April 1968), W. R. Whaley, Chair, pp. 131, 133.
68. The Detainees' Review Tribunal survived, to rubber-stamp executive decisions; from 1971 to 1972, for instance, the tribunal reviewed 255 cases but recommended release in only two cases. Throughout the 1970s its meager annual budget was under R$5,000 (*Estimates of Expenditure*).

resources of the Rhodesian military grew tremendously. It gained ascendancy over the police in counterinsurgency and over civilian agencies (e.g., Internal Affairs) that were involved in security affairs.

The center of decision making on security matters shifted in 1976 from the Security Council to a War Council and in March 1977 to a new coordinating organ: the Ministry of Combined Operations (Com-Ops).[69] Headed by a civilian minister, Com-Ops was run by its military commander, General Peter Walls, who became the de facto supremo in the security system. The steady militarization of decision making reached its peak in 1978–1979 during the brief premiership of Bishop Abel Muzorewa (discussed at greater length below). Muzorewa and his black ministers were excluded from control over the security core of the state. The country was "essentially run by a military regime over which there is no political control";[70] "the Rhodesian military had begun to act as a state within a state."[71]

The ascendancy of the military did not, however, completely eclipse civilian departments or eliminate jurisdictional struggles between agencies. Com-Ops was set up to coordinate the civilian and military dimensions of the war effort, but it was preoccupied with immediate and routine matters rather than interorganizational coordination and long-term strategic planning.[72] Thus rivalries remained endemic to relations between the CIO, Internal Affairs, police, Law and Order, Foreign Affairs, Special Branch, and the various military forces.

Despite a shared commitment to winning the war and maintaining white settler supremacy, "each ministry took a different view both of the threat itself and any countermeasures to be taken."[73] Government ministers repeatedly defined the threats in terms of "black barbarism" versus "white civilization" in southern Africa and the specter of the "Red peril," much as Pretoria's officials now warn of the Communist threat to South Africa. A contrary view was held by Rhodesia's intelligence agencies, expressed by the CIO director:

> For many years now the consensus of opinion in CIO and Special Branch had been that it was more important to accommodate African nationalism than to over-concern ourselves with the communist threat. . . . [Yet] the politicians

69. Evans, *Fighting,* pp. 9, 11; Martin and Johnson, *Struggle,* p. 289.

70. Anti-Apartheid Movement, *Fire-Force Exposed: The Rhodesian Security Forces and Their Role in Defending White Supremacy* (London: Anti-Apartheid Movement, 1979), p. 3.

71. Moorcraft and McLaughlin, *Chimurenga,* p. 232.

72. Beckett, "Rhodesian Army," p. 171.

73. Cilliers, *Counter-Insurgency,* p. 66; Flower, *Serving Secretly.*

were still promoting the belief that communism was the greatest threat, whereas the [Intelligence] professionals maintained . . . that communist countries were no more likely to interfere in the Rhodesian issue than Britain or other Western countries.[74]

Needless to say, the accommodationist arguments of the intelligence chiefs fell on deaf Cabinet ears.

Bitter jurisdictional struggles also hampered intelligence gathering. CIO, Army Intelligence, the Selous Scouts, Internal Affairs, and the Special Branch each considered the intelligence collected by other agencies to be inferior to its own and insisted that competing agencies were imperiling its informers and undermining sources.[75] A former Secretary of Internal Affairs recounted such friction to me:

> I told District Commissioners not to provide the police with any information on who our informants were, because the police would blow it. Due to the police, our good informers were knocked off as sell-outs. The police were angry about not getting names. . . . The Government suppressed intelligence coming from the field and believed the top intelligence advisors. . . . I conflicted with [CIO Director] Flower. He often used to say that I was interfering with his prerogative and his field [and] encroaching on his turf. I said I couldn't care less. Internal intelligence was part of my job.[76]

The Special Branch and CIO held a diametrically opposed view. Consider the remarks of a senior Special Branch officer:

> The task of the Special Branch was to gather intelligence, but the shortage of manpower led to a reliance on Internal Affairs. The quality of intelligence coming from Internal Affairs was very poor. The subordinate African staff—responsible for sending intelligence to the District Commissioner—tended to report what was required by District Commissioners. DCs wouldn't listen to advice from the Special Branch, because it was their own territory. . . . Internal Affairs would say we were telling them lies, and they wanted to operate in their own areas. DCs wouldn't believe that Africans had guns until real contacts occurred. They didn't know how to run informers. They would blow our sources.[77]

In fact, no agency appeared ideally suited to conduct intelligence gathering in war-torn Rhodesia. The Special Branch, CIO, and Internal Affairs

---

74. Flower, *Serving Secretly,* pp. 213, 138.
75. See Reid Daly, *Selous Scouts*; Flower, *Serving Secretly,* p. 219; and my "Continuities in the Politics of State Security in Zimbabwe," in *The Political Economy of Zimbabwe,* ed. M. Schatzberg (New York: Praeger, 1984), pp. 111–12.
76. Interview, 7 June 1983.
77. Interview, 24 June 1983.

were organized to collect intelligence under peacetime conditions, and the military had chronic and serious problems in this field.[78]

The Rhodesian armed forces remained loyal and reliable; the guerrillas never captured a city or established liberated zones inside the country. Yet the intensifying conflict raised the material costs of maintaining white rule and fueled dissension within the state; personal animosities, substantive disagreements over policy and its implementation, and organizational turf battles interfered with the state's capacity to win the war. These tensions nevertheless took place within a context of broad agreement on basic goals, eclipsing the position of those few elites who favored accommodation with the black majority. Intrastate friction was therefore not of sufficient magnitude seriously to undermine the survival of white settler rule. Escalating rural insurgency played the decisive role, ultimately forcing the regime to accept a negotiated settlement in 1979.

TRANSITION TO MAJORITY RULE

In 1966 the United Nations Security Council passed mandatory economic sanctions against the Rhodesian regime, treated it to diplomatic isolation, and announced that the international community would endorse only a settlement that provided for majority rule. To rid itself of its Rhodesian albatross, London also attempted several diplomatic initiatives guided by the principle that legal independence required free elections and majority rule. Rhodesian settlers were prepared to concede nothing of the sort, and Britain had no leverage against this intransigence.

As the guerrilla war gathered steam in the mid-1970s, London's search for a peaceful solution grew. Western nations feared that the war would spread—perhaps involving Cuban or Soviet intervention on the side of the guerrillas and increased South African involvement on behalf of Rhodesia. (The guerrilla forces were already receiving material aid and training from the Soviet Union, Eastern Europe, China, and North Korea.) A negotiated solution might preempt any further internationalization and radicalization of the struggle. As British Foreign Secretary Anthony Crosland warned in a speech to NATO ministers: "If the issue were settled on the battlefield it would seriously lessen the chances of bringing about a moderate regime in Rhodesia and would open the way for more radical solutions and external intervention on the part of oth-

78. Cilliers, *Counter-Insurgency,* pp. 220ff.; Reid Daly, *Selous Scouts,* p. 588.

ers."[79] Nevertheless, some British officials advised against becoming stuck in the Rhodesian quagmire. According to one account, "In 1976 the Cabinet's instinct was [to] stay well clear of Rhodesia, which several Ministers regarded as another potentially debilitating Northern Ireland crisis for Britain."[80] Yet the Crown continued to make occasional overtures toward a negotiated resolution of the problem.

Our analysis of the transitional period centers on Rhodesia's security apparatus. How did the contestants for power view repressive laws and institutions? Were reforms of these structures ever on the agenda during negotiations on the future of the country?

The position of the Smith Government during successive negotiations was that settler control over the security system was inviolate. In a meeting between Smith, South African Premier John Vorster, and United States Secretary of State Henry Kissinger in Pretoria on 19 September 1976, Smith finally agreed to accept the principle of eventual majority rule. But he was adamant that the Cabinet portfolios of Law and Order and of Defense remain in white hands and that the white commanders of the security forces retain their posts. According to the notes on this meeting recorded by the CIO director, Kissinger agreed that the two security ministers should be white.[81]

For years, black leaders had been calling for changes in the internal security apparatus, and the leaders of ZANU and ZAPU had frequently branded Rhodesia's security apparatus "despotic" and "fascist." As early as 1963, ZANU's policy platform declared: "ZANU shall repeal the Unlawful Organizations Act, the Law and Order Maintenance Act. . . and all other repressive laws enacted by the white minority Settler-Governments."[82] In 1976 Bishop Abel Muzorewa, the leader of the reconstituted African National Congress, condemned the "crude and brutal methods" of the Rhodesian police, adding: "The people of Zimbabwe would be scared to death if these methods continued after their liberation. Police reform is high among our priorities."[83] Proposals for sweeping liberalization also came from international sources. The summit of Commonwealth leaders in June 1977 adopted a resolution calling for "not only the removal of the illegal Smith regime but also the dismantling of its apparatus of repression in order to pave the way for the

79. *Times* (London), 10 December 1976.
80. Martin and Johnson, *Struggle,* p. 256.
81. Notes on meeting reprinted in Flower, *Serving Secretly,* p. 303.
82. Zimbabwe African National Union, "Declaration of Policy," 21 August 1963.
83. *U.S. News and World Report,* 6 December 1976, p. 35.

creation of police and armed forces which would be responsible to the needs of the people of Zimbabwe."[84]

As the spiraling costs of the war approached untenable levels, the Smith regime entered into an Internal Settlement in March 1978 with black leaders unattached to the guerrilla forces. The new transitional Government consisted of an uneasy coalition of Smith and three black moderates, Bishop Abel Muzorewa, Ndabaningi Sithole, and Chief Jeremiah Chirau, in an Executive Council. A new constitution was drafted by Rhodesian Front officials and approved by the white electorate in a referendum. Under the constitution, twenty-eight seats in the hundred-member Assembly were reserved for whites for at least ten years, which gave them veto power over changes in the constitution. White personnel would also remain in control of the police, military, civil service, and judiciary for a decade; and white-owned land would not be expropriated.[85] Clearly, this power-sharing arrangement meant only that Smith had conceded an end to exclusive settler rule and retained white control over the state's core. Tellingly, Smith privately referred to the Executive Council as a "facade" obscuring the reality of white political power.[86] Muzorewa and the other black ministers exercised nominal authority; they were excluded from the War Council and from any role in military decision making.[87] Far from being a model of settler-native accommodation, the Executive Council was racked by mutual distrust, conflicts, and secret plotting of white members against black.[88]

As a departure from rigid Rhodesian Front rule, the new regime tried to win African support by dispensing concessions. In February 1979 it enacted legislation repealing petty apartheid discrimination in education, housing, health, and public facilities; it also rescinded the contentious Land Tenure Act. Elections were held under the new constitution in April 1979, ostensibly to affirm that the new order was based on majority rule. Only those parties that had accepted Smith's constitutional plan were allowed on the ballot; ZANU and ZAPU remained banned. Muzorewa's United African National Council (UANC) won fifty-one of

84. Quoted in Martin and Johnson, *Struggle,* p. 269.
85. The constitution created commissions of public service, judicial service, police service, and defense forces service; qualifications for commission membership effectively sealed white control (Robert J. Alperin, "The Distribution of Power and the (June 1979) Zimbabwe Rhodesia Constitution," *Journal of Southern African Affairs* 5, no. 1 [January 1980]: 41–54).
86. Flower, *Serving Secretly,* p. 211.
87. Cilliers, *Counter-Insurgency,* p. 72.
88. Flower, *Serving Secretly,* pp. 207, 212.

the seventy-two seats reserved for Africans and on 31 May 1979, he became the prime minister of Zimbabwe-Rhodesia.

Marking no radical departure from the past, the new regime was unable to win international or domestic legitimacy. The insurgents saw in the settlement both a ruse to perpetuate settler domination and a sign of the regime's increasing desperation. Far from creating the conditions for peace, the internal settlement galvanized the guerrilla campaign. Despite Muzorewa's earlier criticism of the security apparatus, his Government continued its predecessor's bloody campaign against civilians, putting the repressive legislation and security agencies to maximum use. New areas of the country fell under martial law, and security expenditure mushroomed. Defense spending alone absorbed 47 percent of the total budget in 1978–1979.

By 1979, the Government's position had deteriorated and the guerrillas penetrated further into the country. Of those killed during the war, one-third died in 1979 alone. By the end of the year, nearly all the country was under martial law; rural administration had broken down in many areas; the economy was bankrupt; and the war had reached a stalemate. The regime was not on the verge of collapse but was neither defeating nor containing the insurgents. Still, the balance of forces did not augur well for a decisive military victory by either side.

Finally the time seemed propitious for a lasting settlement. South Africa, which put pressure on the Rhodesians, supported a negotiated solution, as did Mozambique and Zambia, which put pressure on the insurgents (partly to end the Rhodesian military attacks they were experiencing). The new Conservative Government of Margaret Thatcher (elected on 3 May 1979) desperately wanted to recognize the Zimbabwe-Rhodesia Government but found this action politically impossible in the face of international opposition. Thatcher reluctantly announced an all-party conference at Lancaster House in London in September 1979 to address three central issues: a cease-fire, free elections, and a new constitution. Representatives of ZANU and ZAPU, the Government of Zimbabwe-Rhodesia, and the British Government attended the conference. With all of the principals involved, this conference seemed to present a unique opportunity for a political solution that might perhaps include plans to reform the country's coercive order. Even at this late date, however, the Muzorewa-Smith regime believed it could maintain settler control over the security agencies. Present at the conference to protect their organizational interests were the country's highest security officials: the Police Commissioner, Commander of the Army, Secretary for Law and Order, Air Vice-Marshall, and the Director of the Central Intelligence Organization. The Muzorewa-Smith delegation insisted that Rhodesian security forces and other state agencies remain fully intact until independence.

At Lancaster House, the Patriotic Front of ZANU and ZAPU called for reforms of internal security agencies but not basic structural changes.[89] One ZANU official claimed that the ZANU and ZAPU representatives at Lancaster House in 1979 "were all opposed to entrusting any future Government of Zimbabwe with the kind of dictatorial powers which their former oppressors had wielded."[90] Yet the paramount concern of the Patriotic Front was not the statutory and institutional foundations of the repressive order, but the question of who would control the security forces during the election of a new government.[91] The overriding fear in Rhodesia, as more recently in Namibia, was that the security forces would subvert free and fair elections. Structural change in the security sector would be left to the new regime.

The Lancaster accord did not touch the most vital branch of the Rhodesian state: "The pre-independence period should not be concerned with the remodelling of the institutions of government."[92] Existing laws would also be left intact: "It will be for the Parliament to be chosen in free elections to decide which laws shall be continued and which shall be changed."[93] Lord Soames, the interim governor of Rhodesia, praised "the humanity and efficiency which resides in the system of government of which Zimbabwe is the heir" (referring apparently to the Westminster model), a system based on "law, order, justice and impartial administration."[94]

The status quo was to remain in other areas vital to settler interests: the new constitution (1) provided for disproportionate white representa-

89. Martin and Johnson, *Struggle*, p. 273. See also the earlier Anglo-American proposals, *Rhodesia: Proposals for a Settlement*, Cmnd. 6919 (London: HMSO, September 1977).

90. Simbi Mubako, address to the National Affairs Association of Zimbabwe, reprinted as a governmental press statement, 23 May 1980.

91. See the Patriotic Front's submissions to the conference: Lancaster House Conference Papers, "Patriotic Front Proposals," CC(79)16, 18 September 1979, and "Patriotic Front Response to British Proposals for Zimbabwe," CC(79)23, 8 October 1979.

92. Government of Southern Rhodesia, *Report of the Constitutional Conference, Lancaster House, September–December 1979*, Cmnd. 7802 (London: HMSO, 1980), para. 2.

93. Ibid., para. 15. The tripartite agreement on southwestern Africa between Angola, Cuba, and South Africa, signed 22 December 1988, gives an elected constituent assembly in Namibia power to draft a new constitution.

94. Lord Soames, "From Rhodesia to Zimbabwe," *International Affairs* 56 (Summer 1980): 418.

tion in Parliament for seven years after independence (4 percent of the population, whites received 20 percent of Assembly seats and 25 percent of Senate seats); (2) included a declaration of rights that in effect institutionalized a multiparty system for ten years; and (3) stipulated that land could be purchased only when the property owner agreed. Whites were thus greatly overrepresented in Parliament and their land was protected against expropriation. An additional assurance to the settlers was the amnesty declared by the interim British governor in December 1979, which prohibited legal proceedings against anyone previously involved in the war.[95] Those guilty of atrocities on either side were thus absolved.

Indicative of Britain's dominant role in the negotiated transition, the final draft of the accepted constitution was essentially a carbon copy of the original Foreign Office proposals.[96] In sharp contrast to the reformist initiatives made during the Ulster crisis of 1969–1972, the British Government's actions at Lancaster House had a decidedly conservative effect on existing security structures. During the months preceding the March 1980 election, some Commonwealth nations and Amnesty International called on the governor to repeal the security laws and release all persons detained under emergency powers; but British officials held steadfast to their commitment not to tamper with existing security arrangements. London's principal aims were to prevent the conflict from becoming internationalized, to restore stability in southern Africa, to reopen Zimbabwe's economic lines to the West, to install a moderate government based on majority rule, and then to disengage from the country as quickly as possible.[97] The particulars of the accord were of much less concern. Britain's priorities help to explain the reluctance to tackle reforms, a task that could be left to the coming majoritarian government—as the Lancaster agreement stated. When London assumed control over the state in Ulster in 1972, no such alternative government was waiting; hence the British themselves had to begin the task of institutional reform.

Other practical considerations militated against the metropole's involvement in modernizing Rhodesia's repressive order. The Foreign Office was convinced that the settler delegation at Lancaster would reject

95. Amnesty Ordinance 1979 (3/79).
96. See Lancaster House Conference Papers, "Independence Constitution," CC(79)4, 12 September 1979 and "British Government Proposals for Independence Constitution," CC(79)19, 3 October 1979.
97. Gregory, "Rhodesia," p. 84. These aims were almost identical to Britain's objectives twenty years earlier during the Lancaster House conference on Kenya.

any plan for the sweeping transformation of state institutions. The three-month interval between the signing of the agreement and the elections for the new government also seemed to disallow any restructuring of security agencies, although legislation might have been repealed. In addition, premature tampering with security arrangements might undermine law and order during the unstable transitional period.[98] And the Crown was averse to becoming involved in another experiment with state building; Northern Ireland was enough of a problem. The British delegation, therefore, had adequate reasons to tread lightly on the statutory and institutional terrain.[99]

What about the other delegations? Both ZANU and ZAPU were confident that they would win the proposed election and, as noted above, did not insist on changes in security structures at the conference. The Muzorewa-Smith coalition believed that the incumbent regime would retain power, that existing security agencies would remain intact, and that white control over these agencies would continue for the foreseeable future.[100] For their part, the settlers in Rhodesia hoped that the Lancaster accord would end the devastating war and international economic sanctions and preserve the old order as much as possible. They expected that a victory by Muzorewa's UANC would make continued, albeit diluted, white supremacy more palatable to the black population.

The Lancaster talks were successful in part because each delegation—the incumbent regime, ZANU, and ZAPU—was convinced that its party would win the proposed election. Had there been real doubt in the ranks of one of the delegations, the entire settlement would have been doomed. This expectation also helps to explain the lack of concern with existing security legislation and institutions. Believing that it alone would inherit the political kingdom, no domestic party had an incentive to demand change. In addition, each contender expected that the losing parties would have difficulty accepting electoral defeat; in this scenario, after the transfer of power the repressive machinery might prove essen-

98. Only 850 soldiers of the Commonwealth Monitoring Force were stationed in Zimbabwe before the election, to oversee the return of guerrillas and defuse tensions (see the article by the force's deputy commander, J. H. Learmont, "Reflections from Rhodesia," *Royal United Services Institute Journal* 125, no. 4 [December 1980]: 47–55).

99. See my article comparing decolonization in Zimbabwe and Mozambique ("In Search of Regime Security: Zimbabwe since Independence," *Journal of Modern African Studies* 22, no. 4 [December 1984]). On Namibia and Zimbabwe see David Gordon ("Conflict Resolution in Southern Africa: Why Namibia Is Not Another Zimbabwe," *Issue* 12, no. 3–4 [Fall–Winter 1982]: 37–45).

100. Jeffrey Davidow, *A Peace in Southern Africa: The Lancaster House Conference on Rhodesia* (Boulder, Colo.: Westview, 1984), p. 70.

tial to subdue political foes, consolidate the new government's position, and maintain order.

Taking almost everyone by complete surprise, ZANU won a decisive victory in the March election—62.9 percent of the vote and fifty-seven of the eighty black seats in the new Assembly. The election results sent shock waves through the white community but no violent backlash like the rampage of Portuguese settlers in Mozambique at independence in 1975. Zimbabwe's independence was finally proclaimed on 18 April 1980 and a new ZANU regime installed.

This particular transition away from settler rule conditioned the new order in several respects. First, the legacy of the war shaped the new state elite's political culture and regard for opponents. The authoritarian and commandist practices of the guerrilla forces did not wither away once ZANU assumed state power, and the experience of fighting a long, bitter war made the new elite highly suspicious of enemies. Second, the new regime inherited the repressive apparatus of the settler state—its agencies, legal powers, and many of its personnel. Third, ZANU's electoral victory left politically marginal two black political parties, ZAPU and UANC, that had been key actors during the transition. They entered the new order decidedly disgruntled over the electoral outcome. Fourth, Rhodesian settlers were able to put their stamp on the new constitution, including reserved white seats in Parliament, a multiparty system, and land security.

But unlike many other transitions away from authoritarian rule—including that in Northern Ireland—in Zimbabwe the power structure of the old elite rapidly became a relic of the past: the settler community has little political role in the new order. This fact is particularly remarkable since the white community retains its economic dominance, which does not translate into leverage on extraeconomic matters.

The literature on transitions to democracy suggests that the displacement of a former authoritarian elite is a precondition for genuine democratization. This may be necessary, but by no means sufficient, for liberalization of structures of law and order, as exemplified in postsettler Zimbabwe. Other key variables remain to be examined in Chapter 6.

CHAPTER 5

Northern Ireland

Breakdown of Settler Rule, 1969–1972

From 1921 until the late 1960s, the British metropole took little interest in Northern Ireland's internal affairs, much as the American federal government earlier turned a blind eye to racial domination in the American South. In Ulster as in the American South during the 1960s, it took widespread disorder and violence to convince the metropolitan government to reconsider its comfortable isolationism and assert its authority over the dominant regional caste, in support of the minority.

Already in the mid-1960s the British curtain of silence regarding Northern Ireland was beginning to lift. Questions were being raised by Labour MPs who

> were concerned with the very great increase in financial assistance from the Westminster Exchequer to Ulster, and without constitutional reform and more liberal policies it was becoming more difficult to justify to MPs, and to some members of our Cabinet, the large sums we were being asked to vote.[1]

(Westminster subsidized the Ulster budget—$240 million in 1968—to improve social services.)

Labour politicians previously had been as hesitant as the Conservatives to question arrangements in Ulster, but the 1964 British election brought in a number of progressive Labour and Liberal MPs who were ready to open debate on Northern Ireland. In April 1965 they formed the Campaign for Democracy in Ulster, to investigate allegations of dis-

---

1. Harold Wilson, *The Labour Government: 1964–1970* (London: Weidenfeld and Nicolson, and Michael Joseph, 1971), p. 270.

crimination, propose changes in Ulster's electoral laws to conform with those in Britain, and extend the Race Relations Bill to Northern Ireland.[2] Attempting to initiate debate on these issues in the House of Commons, these MPs were repeatedly ruled out of order on the grounds that such matters were the proper concern of Stormont alone. Unsuccessful in Parliament, the campaign nevertheless drew the attention of British elites to communal inequalities in Ulster. By the late 1960s the Labour Government itself began to press for reforms.

Earlier in the decade, a rare change occurred at the top of the Ulster Government. In 1963 Terence O'Neill became the fourth prime minister of the province. Like his predecessors, he was a member of the Orange Order and shared the standard Protestant prejudices against Catholic "Fenians" and "papists." But he was also the first moderate premier, prepared to consider limited reforms in the settler order that were partly driven by an awareness of the country's economic exigencies. Only through greater economic planning and infusions of foreign capital could the decaying industrial structure be modernized and the economic decline of the late 1950s reversed. Economic modernization was linked, he believed, to reforms in the treatment of the Catholic minority.[3] He cultivated contacts with moderates among Catholics—visiting Catholic schools, meeting with priests—and displayed less tolerance for Protestant extremism. O'Neill was also more amenable than his predecessors to détente with Ulster's irredentist southern neighbor; in 1965 he held an unprecedented meeting with the prime minister of the Republic of Ireland, Sean Lemass.

Largely cosmetic, O'Neill's initial gestures affected neither the socioeconomic position of Catholics nor Ulster's sectarian security system.[4] But his early years in office were important because he embodied the promise of meaningful reform, without delivering. Like the efforts of Whitehead in Rhodesia and Botha in South Africa, O'Neill's reform efforts mobilized and radicalized the subordinate population and precipi-

2. Vincent E. Feeney, "Westminster and the Early Civil Rights Struggle in Northern Ireland," *Eire-Ireland* 11, no. 4 (1976): 3–40. The property qualification for voting in municipal elections was abolished on the mainland in 1947 but remained in effect in Ulster, where about one-quarter of those eligible to vote in Westminster elections were ineligible to vote in local elections (Richard Rose, *Governing Without Consensus: An Irish Perspective* [Boston: Beacon, 1971], p. 441).

3. Kevin Kelley, *The Longest War: Northern Ireland and the IRA* (Westport, Conn.: Lawrence Hill, 1982), p. 79. O'Neill was successful in attracting several multinational corporations to Ulster (Michael Farrell, *Northern Ireland: The Orange State* [London: Pluto, 1976], p. 229).

4. See Paul Bew and Henry Patterson, *The British State and the Ulster Crisis: From Wilson to Thatcher* (London: Verso, 1985), pp. 15, 17.

tated bitter opposition within the ranks of the dominant caste to the prime minister's "deviations."

Ever since the 1920s the Catholic minority had been politically inactive and acquiescent to the status quo. While harboring grievances, it was not ready to support armed struggle against the state. The failed revolt of the Irish Republican Army (IRA) from 1956 to 1962 was the exception that proved the rule, since it could not attract Catholic support. In the mid-1960s, however, Catholics began to push for the redress of grievances. Dissatisfied with the poor record of Catholic political parties (the Nationalist party and the Northern Ireland Labour party) in securing minority rights, Catholics began to build new organizations as O'Neill catalyzed their rising expectations. The Campaign for Social Justice, formed in 1964, and the Northern Ireland Civil Rights Association, in 1967, launched a civil rights movement inspired in part by its American counterpart.[5]

These were moderate, middle-class organizations seeking equal rights and social integration. The Campaign for Social Justice focused on socioeconomic discrimination. The Northern Ireland Civil Rights Association disputed gerrymandered electoral boundaries and property qualifications in local governmental elections; it called for antidiscrimination legislation, a mechanism to handle citizens' complaints against governmental departments, impartial allocation of public housing, disbanding of the Ulster Special Constabulary, and repeal of the Special Powers Act. Significant as they were, these demands hardly challenged fundamental political and constitutional structures. Missing from the original agenda were some of the most divisive issues: the constitutional status of the province, the Unionist monopoly of power, the existence of the border, and British claims of sovereignty over the province. Only later did militant groups enter the civil rights movement with more radical, nationalist aims (such as abolishing the border); the IRA resurfaced in December 1969 to defend Catholics against Protestant assailants but did not engage in killing until 1971.[6]

Initially, the civil rights movement had greater impact in antagonizing the Protestant community than at extracting reforms from Stormont or Westminster. Loyalists defined the civil rights groups as a front for the

---

5. For a comparison of the American South and Ulster, see Richard Rose, "On the Priorities of Citizenship in the Deep South and Northern Ireland," *Journal of Politics* 38, no. 2 (May 1976): 247–91.

6. Stephen W. Beach, "Social Movement Radicalization: The Case of the People's Democracy in Northern Ireland," *Sociological Quarterly* 18 (Summer 1977): 305–18.

IRA and their protest marches as an affront to Protestant supremacy.[7] At the same time, Catholic protests added fuel to popular Protestant outrage over "O'Neillism," or official appeasement. Protestants branded O'Neill and the reformist wing of his Government as "the enemy within" and the apparent drift of executive policy as a threat to undiluted settler supremacy and the existence of the Protestant state.[8] The threats were not just political: reforms in the socioeconomic order were anathema to working-class Protestants, who feared competition from Catholics for jobs and housing. Protestants surveyed in 1966–1967 rejected the legitimacy of Catholic grievances; only 18 percent thought Catholics were "treated unfairly." In contrast, 74 percent of Catholics believed the minority had suffered unfair treatment and 55 percent supported protests against discrimination. Since the settlers did not perceive that the minority was treated unfairly, they saw no need to endorse mechanisms to ensure fairness. Only 23 percent of Protestants felt the government should pass a law making it illegal to refuse a job or housing to Catholics because of their religion.[9] Rather paternalistically, O'Neill lamented this failure to appreciate the benefits of socioeconomic concessions:

> It is frightfully hard to explain to Protestants that if you give Roman Catholics a good job and a good house they will live like Protestants. . . . But if a Roman Catholic is jobless and lives in the most ghastly hovel, he will rear eighteen children on National Assistance.[10]

Catholic mobilization and the regime's perceived kid-gloves response enraged Protestant extremists, who (like their white counterparts in the American South and South Africa) launched a countermovement to block all concessions to the minority. Civil rights demonstrations and marches met Protestant counterdemonstrations and ended in several violent clashes and savage police attacks. The first bloody encounter in Londonderry on 5 October 1968 convinced London to press for immediate reforms. The second major incident occurred on 4 January 1969 at

7. Patrick Bishop and Eamonn Mallie, *The Provisional IRA* (London: Heinemann, 1987), p. 52. The Scarman Tribunal found that the IRA had not planned or organized the 1969 disturbances and that its involvement was "slight" ([Scarman Tribunal] *Violence and Civil Disturbances in 1969: Report of a Tribunal of Inquiry,* Cmnd. 566 [Belfast: HMSO, 1972], p. 16).

8. Kelley, *Longest War,* p. 94.

9. Rose, *Governing,* pp. 481, 484, 497. Strikingly similar, a survey of Israeli Jews noted that 75.2 percent were reserved about or opposed a law that would punish discrimination against Arabs in jobs and housing (Sammy Smooha, "Jewish and Arab Ethnocentrism in Israel," *Ethnic and Racial Studies* 10, no. 1 [January 1987]: 14).

10. Quoted in Farrell, *Orange State,* p. 256.

Burntollet bridge, when civil rights marchers were ambushed by a group of Loyalists, including off-duty members of the Ulster Special Constabulary. Later that day, the police stormed the Catholic Bogside district in Londonderry and went on a rampage. On subsequent occasions Loyalist mobs, with police support, invaded Catholic enclaves in Belfast and engaged in arson and shooting. Catholic rioting broke out later in 1969, rioting that seemed to the Government altogether sinister; a new premier claimed that the rioters sought "to overthrow a Government democratically elected by a large majority."[11] The Scarman Tribunal's investigation of the riots in the summer of 1969 flatly refuted this contention: "There was no plot to overthrow the Government or to mount an armed insurrection."[12] The tribunal found the Royal Ulster Constabulary seriously at fault during six major incidents.

The backlash among Protestant citizens had sympathizers within Stormont and the Cabinet. O'Neill encountered stiff opposition to reforms from a number of hard-line Protestant politicians, and the Unionist back bench at Stormont staged several abortive revolts against him. The most strident hard-liner in the Cabinet was the chief of the security system, Minister of Home Affairs William Craig. Craig described the civil rights movement as a "bogus" front for violence and subversion and argued that reforms were a serious mistake. (The Cameron Commission, examining the causes of the violence of 1968–1969, concluded otherwise: the movement's grievances had a "substantial foundation in fact.")[13] Craig appeared to condone violence by Loyalists and (along Rhodesian lines) publicly floated the idea of a unilateral declaration of independence from Britain; for this he was dismissed by O'Neill.

When Harold Wilson remarked to O'Neill that "Northern Ireland is rather like Rhodesia," O'Neill responded, "Maybe it is, but I do not intend to be the Garfield Todd of Northern Ireland."[14] (Todd had succumbed to a Cabinet revolt against his reformist moves in 1958.) Ironically, O'Neill suffered the same fate. In Ulster as in Rhodesia,

---

11. James Chichester-Clark, quoted by the Scarman Tribunal, p. 10.

12. Scarman Tribunal, p. 10.

13. The Cameron Commission identified causes of the violence of 1968–1969; they mirrored the grievances of the civil rights movement (housing discrimination, electoral gerrymandering, the USC, the Special Powers Act) and included Protestant fears of threats to Unionists' control of the state ([Cameron Commission] *Disturbances in Northern Ireland,* Cmnd. 532 [Belfast: HMSO, September 1969], Lord Cameron, Chair).

14. Terence O'Neill, *The Autobiography of Terence O'Neill* (London: Rupert Hart-Davis, 1972), p. 83.

power tended "to gravitate towards those who [were] least ready for change."[15]

O'Neill's resignation in April 1969 was but the most striking symptom of the rapidly eroding Unionist cohesion. The fragmentation of the state and the corresponding divisions within the Protestant community were at least as serious as the mobilization within Catholic circles at the time. The debates in Cabinet and Parliament revolved around the direction the regime should take: toward limited concessions and institutional reform, or back to traditional sectarianism. In both scenarios the vital interests of the settler community would stand; nothing would alter the status of the border or the Unionist-dominated state. The debate centered on how best to safeguard these interests. As in Rhodesia in the early 1960s, the enlightened Unionist faction could not prevail over the absolutists: the arguments for renovated settler rule were lost on a caste convinced that the minority would exploit any concessions as a stepping stone to a united Ireland. In turn, Loyalist intransigence suggested to Catholic forces that the settler state was beyond redemption: powerful Protestant forces seemed ready to fight any hint of political modernization under the traditional battle cry, No Surrender!

Rose argues that a "minority cannot fragment its opponents by its own efforts."[16] The civil rights movement did not by itself precipitate Unionist fragmentation, as is commonly assumed.[17] Only after the Unionist monolith had begun to show cracks did the mobilization of subordinate forces gather impetus. O'Neill's modernist innovations and the brief eclipse of traditional hard-line policy raised Catholic expectations and provoked a right-wing Protestant backlash inside and outside the state. Unionist divisions opened space for Catholic protest and gave their demands increasing salience.

In contrast to Rhodesia where the Rhodesian Front's victory over the Whitehead Government in 1962 eased frictions within the state, reunified the settler community, and stifled black unrest, the replacement of O'Neill accelerated both state fragmentation and the mobilization of Protestant and Catholic militants. These contrasting outcomes can be explained in part by the differential role of the metropole. In Rhodesia, as we have seen, the lack of sustained pressure from Britain frustrated

15. Colin Leys, *European Politics in Southern Rhodesia* (Oxford: Clarendon Press, 1959), p. 36.
16. Rose, "Priorities," p. 266.
17. Michael MacDonald, *Children of Wrath: Political Violence in Northern Ireland* (New York: Blackwell, 1986), pp. 76–77.

black expectations and removed one potential source of settler fragmentation. Britain's involvement in Ulster helped to crystallize grievances, raise expectations, and spark protests among Catholics. It showed that the settler state's authority in Ulster was not absolute. And it outraged a hard-line section of the Protestant community, already horrified at the specter of Catholic mobilization and the Unionist regime's apparent surrender to British and Catholic demands. The changing balance of forces produced a full-scale crisis of authority and order that led to British rule in 1972.

LABOUR'S ABORTIVE REFORMS

Despite Northern Ireland's growing unrest, the metropole's policy of least interference was paramount. Although in 1969 Harold Wilson had condemned the "nearly fifty years of. . . unimaginative inertia and repression of successive, unchallenged and. . . unchallengeable Ulster Unionist Governments," the Labour Government was reluctant to intervene.[18] The Home Secretary, James Callaghan, revealed: "The advice that came to me from all sides was on no account to get sucked into the Irish bog."[19] Another minister, Roy Jenkins, told the Cabinet: "If there is one thing I have learnt, it is that the English cannot run Ireland."[20] Callaghan's Conservative successor as Home Secretary, Reginald Maudling, took an even more pessimistic view: "I realized the virtual hopelessness of any attempt by reason to bring peace and reconciliation to this suffering and tortured people."[21]

Labour policy from 1968 to 1970 centered on encouraging the Unionist Government to accept a reform program without replacing established political institutions. Callaghan was quite explicit:

> As no reliable alternative instrument of government existed, it seemed to me to be better to win the agreement of the Ulster Unionists to what was necessary than to use the power of Parliament to dismiss them. I had no confidence that if the Ulster Unionist Government were replaced British intervention would make the situation better in the long run. These are quicksands for the British.[22]

18. Wilson, *Labour,* p. 692.
19. James Callaghan, *A House Divided: The Dilemma of Northern Ireland* (London: Collins, 1973), p. 15.
20. Quoted in Sunday Times Insight Team [hereafter Insight], *Northern Ireland: A Report on the Conflict* (New York: Vintage, 1972), p. 105.
21. Reginald Maudling, *Memoirs* (London: Sidgwick and Jackson, 1978), p. 180.
22. Callaghan, *House Divided,* pp. 24–25.

In Cabinet, Callaghan and Denis Healey expressed the view that "our whole interest is to work through the Protestant government. The Protestants are the majority and we can't afford to alienate them."[23] London believed that Stormont could become a beacon of reform—despite its past record—and that Westminster would not need to suspend the regime or legislate over its head. For Wilson, "Only speedy reform could avert irresistible pressures for legislation at Westminster...intervening in Irish affairs; none of us wanted that."[24] The Cabinet's desire to avoid legislative intervention in Ulster was critical, since there was no mechanism for metropolitan judicial intervention like that of the American federal courts during the civil rights movement.

London's overriding concern was to avoid taking direct political control of the province. British policy, one minister noted, "amounted to doing anything which would avoid direct rule."[25] Accordingly, the Labour Government simultaneously urged reforms on the Unionist Government and reassured it. The aims were to salvage Stormont's credibility as the legitimate center of authority, restore "a sense of self-confidence in the Ulster Unionist Cabinet," and fortify the coercive capacities of the regime (e.g., with the British army in 1969).[26]

This faith in, and practical reliance on, the Unionist regime was itself at the heart of the problem. Already in September 1969, the Cameron Commission's report, *Disturbances in Northern Ireland*, had linked unrest to the Unionist party's permanent monopoly of state power, which had made it "insensitive" to criticism and pressures for reform.[27] Had the British Government itself been more sensitive to the political climate in Northern Ireland and the strength of Unionist resolve to defend the existing order, it might have shown less optimism about the possibilities for funneling reforms through established political institutions. This strategy was destined to backfire in a context where ascendant supremacist forces defined reforms as unwarranted and deserving of fierce resistance.[28]

This did not mean that nothing changed in Ulster. Even limited British intervention was a sharp departure from the past and Stormont-

23. Former British Minister Richard Crossman, quoted in Geoffrey Bell, *Troublesome Business: The Labour Party and the Irish Question* (London: Pluto, 1982), p. 108.

24. Wilson, *Labour*, p. 672.

25. Quoted in Insight, p. 103.

26. Callaghan, *House Divided*, p. 70.

27. Cameron Commission, p. 12.

28. Mary Holland, "Lessons of Direct Rule," *New Statesman* (London), 23 March 1973, p. 401.

Westminster relations altered significantly. In London a new Northern Ireland department in the Home Office was formed, which gave the province a higher profile. Joint Ulster-English working bodies were created to sort out various problems. Commissions of inquiry were established to make recommendations on controversial issues. A Ministry of Community Relations was created to foster intercommunal harmony. And universal adult suffrage was introduced in local council elections. By 1971 all the original demands of the civil rights movement had been met, except repeal of the Special Powers Act.

Security arrangements were also affected by metropolitan intervention. Between 1969 and 1972, responsibility for internal security in Northern Ireland was shared between the Unionist and British Governments. In 1971, a Joint Security Committee (JSC) was created to coordinate security, with representatives from both states: the British army commander, the Chief Constable, the Unionist premier and two other ministers, and a British Government representative. Committee members had different outlooks and motivating interests but shared a commitment to restabilizing the province.[29]

The new British voice in security decision making did not guarantee structural innovations; liberalization depended on a complex set of considerations:

- desired changes in security institutions would be balanced against Britain's foremost interest in maintaining political stability and combating violence;

- reforms were most likely to materialize if they could be channeled through the Unionist Government, not unilaterally imposed by the metropole;

- reforms would be postponed if they appeared to raise the already troubling level of right-wing political opposition (from Cabinet members, the Unionist back bench, Loyalist extremists outside the party, and the regime's own "atavistic grassroots supporters")[30] and undermine the incumbent moderate Unionist leaders.

29. The prime minister and his Cabinet colleagues needed to assuage Protestant constituents and dissident Unionist MPs; the Chief Constable struggled with police morale, Catholic distrust of the force, and the sensibilities of the Protestant community; the British army commander needed sufficient military resources to suppress disorders but also sought to return security duties to the police and reduce the army's presence in the province; the British representative sought to ensure reforms of security structures with minimum British involvement (Rose, *Governing*, pp. 172–74).

30. The quoted phrase is Harold Wilson's (*Labour*, p. 270).

More thoroughgoing change in political and security arrangements would have required more direct British control over the state machinery. London was loath to take this on.[31]

The Labour Government was also reluctant to commit troops to active duty in Northern Ireland.[32] Callaghan predicted that protracted deployment of soldiers would make political intervention "inevitable" and that the army would become tainted by its association with the Unionist Government.[33] But in August 1969, as order broke down and Protestants attacked Catholic sections of Belfast and Londonderry, British troops were sent in. London hoped that military intervention would quickly restore order and obviate direct political control of the province.[34]

The problem of impartially maintaining order often arises in the course of third-party military interventions in societies troubled by communal conflicts. A recent case in point involves the peace-keeping force of Indian troops in Sri Lanka: intended to protect the Tamil minority from the Sinhalese majority and from local security forces, it rapidly degenerated into a brutal occupation force for Tamil civilians and insurgents (the Tigers).[35]

British troops in Northern Ireland initially assumed a peace-keeping role, mediating between the two local antagonists. Catholics welcomed the soldiers, who brought relief from the attacks of Loyalist mobs and whose presence seemed to confirm the Unionist political system's utter bankruptcy. The honeymoon lasted several months. But the army's official "duties in aid of the civil power" (i.e., the Unionist Government) and its routine operations gradually earned it a reputation of bias in favor of the Protestant community. Increasingly thrust into highly charged confrontations with Catholics and having little grasp of legal niceties, British soldiers acted with the same insensitivity toward civilians that had discredited the Unionist police forces: indiscriminate raids on Catholic premises, ruthless responses to demonstrations and public disturbances, and daily street harassment. The cumulative effect of these

31. In 1968 Callaghan had drawn up contingency plans to take over the Northern Ireland Government (*House Divided,* p. 23).
32. Three thousand British troops were already garrisoned in Ulster on standing military duties.
33. Callaghan, *House Divided,* pp. 21, 27.
34. Bew and Patterson, *The British State,* p. 21.
35. Over seven thousand Sri Lankan civilians have died in the fighting since 1983. Like Ulster's Catholics, the Tamils have experienced discrimination (in education, employment, and land settlement) under Sinhalese domination since independence in 1948; a majority of Tamils support the Tiger guerrillas (see William McGowan, "India's Quagmire in Sri Lanka," *The Nation,* 25 June 1988, pp. 896–99).

practices was to further radicalize and alienate Catholics from the Ulster and British governments alike and deepen communal hostilities. The commitment of British troops relieved the intense pressures on the police and opened an opportunity for reforms. The Royal Ulster Constabulary's gross mishandling of its responsibilities for public order and riot control led to unprecedented scrutiny from the metropole and condemnation or calls for dismantling the force from Catholics. A 1969 inquiry by British officers Robert Mark and Douglas Osmond criticized the poor leadership in the RUC, the excessive autonomy of the Inspector General, the outdated police intelligence system, the fortress appearance of RUC stations (forbidding and inaccessible to the public), the lack of a system for complaints and a public relations branch, and the RUC's obsession with the IRA to the exclusion of Protestant militants.[36] (The RUC claimed that the Protestant paramilitary Ulster Volunteer Force did not exist and that the police had "no records on loyalists.")[37]

Later in 1969 the Hunt Committee's investigation of the police recommended, inter alia: dismantling the Ulster Special Constabulary (or B-Specials); greatly increasing RUC personnel; disarming and demilitarizing the police; setting up a Police Authority to which the Inspector General would be accountable; introducing a system for public complaints; enlisting Catholics; improving training in riot control; repealing much of the Special Powers Act; and removing criminal prosecution from police jurisdiction.[38]

That the British Government officially accepted these proposals did not mean that the authorities put them immediately into practice.[39] Many of the Hunt Committee's recommendations were delayed, diluted, or later reversed. Catholics continued to form a small fraction of police recruits; a separate system of prosecution was delayed until 1972; and the SPA was repealed only in 1973. Sensitive to Protestant concerns and considerations of police morale, the Government balanced the committee's liberalizing recommendations by an immediate infusion of personnel and material resources into the RUC.[40]

36. Callaghan, *House Divided,* pp. 54ff.
37. John McGuffin, *Internment* (Tralee, Ireland: Anvil, 1973), p. 84.
38. [Hunt Committee] *Report of the Advisory Committee on Police in Northern Ireland,* Cmnd. 535 (Belfast: HMSO, October, 1969), Lord Hunt, Chair.
39. Callaghan was hesitant to take control of the RUC, fearing its reaction. If it refused to serve, Britain had insufficient U.K. police available to replace it, and the British Police Federation objected to its members' serving under the Unionist Minister of Home Affairs and enforcing the Special Powers Act (Callaghan, *House Divided,* pp. 19, 22).
40. Gill Boehringer, "Beyond Hunt: A Police Policy for Northern Ireland of the Future," *Social Studies* 2, no. 3 (1973): 404.

The Hunt report nevertheless challenged the sectarian style of policing. Its key recommendations were received bitterly in the Protestant community, whose antimodernist orientation to law and order held firmly that reforms were dangerous to Protestant security and tantamount to appeasement of Catholics. Unionist officials were predictably shocked by the report. The Cabinet agreed to abolish the USC only when Callaghan threatened that Westminster would legislate over its head.[41]

Protestants viewed the proposed abolition of the USC and reform of the RUC as part of a sell-out by British officials, whom they considered gullible to Catholic propaganda about the forces of order. The publication of Hunt's plan for dismantling the USC was greeted with two days of Protestant rioting during which sixteen soldiers were wounded and one police officer killed. This was just one occasion when Protestant lawlessness in the defense of settler law and order warned the British Cabinet not to push its reforms in the security sphere too far.

In order to reduce Protestant furor over the loss of the USC, two new security forces were created, the Ulster Defense Regiment (UDR) and the RUC Reserve (RUCR). Formed in 1970, the UDR was to bear no resemblance to the sectarian USC and to operate instead as a normal regiment responsible to the British army commander. The composition of the regiment undermined this goal.[42] The British Minister of Defense for Administration, Roy Hattersley, had stated in 1969 that the USC was "composed of a majority of men who have given good and honourable service to Northern Ireland and they will be welcome into the [UDR]."[43] Because of their experience and knowledge of local conditions (and a lack of alternative recruits), former USC officers were urged to apply to the new force. Some 50 percent of initial recruits were USC men who continued to embrace decidedly Unionist visions of order; the army's screening procedures were loose enough to allow fiercely anti-Catholic elements into the UDR. Over the years, a number of UDR men have been linked to illegal paramilitary organizations, and others have been convicted of crimes, including sectarian murders.

The Hunt Committee recommended that the police be relieved of paramilitary duties, since "any police force, military in appearance and

41. Arthur Hezlet, *The "B" Specials: A History of the Ulster Special Constabulary* (London: Tom Stacey, 1972), p. 223.

42. See Derek Brown, "In Defense of Ulster," *Fortnight*, 6 February 1976; Ed Moloney, "The UDR: Nine Years of Killings and Controversies," *Hibernia* (Dublin), 29 March 1979; Barry White, "The UDR," *Belfast Telegraph*, 1 April 1980.

43. *Irish News* (Belfast), 13 November 1969.

equipment, is less acceptable to minority and moderate opinion than if it is clearly civilian in character."[44] Inside the Royal Ulster Constabulary there was sentiment in favor of demilitarization and disarming: in 1969 the Central Representative Body of the RUC had sent a memorandum to the Hunt Committee expressing a "desire to abandon all military aspects of our present duties."[45] RUC constables were split on the question of arms: a 1970 poll found that 1,196 opposed and 1,085 favored retaining arms.[46] Chief Constables Young and Shillington felt that the army should be the sole armed force and that disarming the police might indeed have positive effects. The policy was put into effect briefly in 1970–1971; the Chief Constable's report for 1970 stated, "Relieving the Police of their former paramilitary duties has to some extent reduced the tension and hostility which existed in some areas."[47]

British plans to enhance the accountability of the RUC met with only partial success. Following Hunt's recommendation, a Police Authority was created in June 1970 to improve accountability and the handling of complaints alleging indiscipline and brutality. Yet the authority spent most of its time on recruitment, budgetary matters, and equipment and buildings; it deferred the larger policy issues and the question of accountability.[48] The RUC and the Ministry of Home Affairs encouraged the authority's reluctance to take an active role in major police matters. One report on the police pointed to "the obduracy and determination of the senior officials in the Ministry of Home Affairs, to manipulate the Police Authority and render it futile. . . . The Police Authority was simply another department of the Ministry of Home Affairs."[49] The 1970 Police Act stipulated that the authority's members should represent the community as a whole, yet most of its initial senior staff came directly from the Ministry of Home Affairs and failed to reflect minority interests.

The Chief Constable retained full control of operational matters—such as deployment and handling of specific disturbances—although politicians did not always respect these boundaries. As the Chief Constable later revealed, "My biggest difficulty was to try to convince politi-

44. Hunt Committee, p. 21.
45. "Ulster's Police Force Speaks Out," *The Newsletter* (Belfast), 6 September 1969.
46. Poll by the Representative Body of the RUC, cited in Rose (*Governing,* p. 147).
47. Chief Constable, *Chief Constable's Annual Report* (Belfast: Police Authority, 1970), p. 1.
48. Police Authority for Northern Ireland, *The First Three Years* (Belfast: Police Authority, 1973).
49. Central Citizens Defense Committee, *Northern Ireland: The Black Paper: The Story of the Police* (Belfast: CCDC, 1973), pp. 23, 24.

cians at Stormont and from Britain that they had no authority to interfere with police operations. It was often very difficult to convince the Unionist politicians of this."[50]

Internal organizational changes were made to rationalize and expand police capacities. In 1970 a Community Relations Branch was formed and the Press Office enlarged to improve public relations; an Operations Department was set up to coordinate and oversee the policing of public disorders, with a Security Branch specializing in security duties and prevention of sabotage.

Little progress occurred in policing during this period. The RUC continued to act in a visibly partisan manner;[51] constables were rearmed in 1971; overwhelmingly Protestant, it enforced the controversial security laws of the Unionist Government with little accountability. There are various explanations for the lack of more fundamental reforms, beyond organizational resistance to change: London's desire to bolster the incumbent Unionist regime; official fear of a Protestant backlash against sweeping reforms; and political violence, particularly from the IRA.

These considerations conditioned the possibilities for other security-related reforms. Repeal of the Special Powers Act was one that the civil rights movement demanded and the Hunt report recommended except for a "few essential provisions."[52] Anticipating British pressure to eliminate all special powers, Attorney General Basil Kelly proposed repeal of most of the SPA (retaining internment powers). But the British Home Secretary refused: the increasing street violence and the overwhelming Loyalist support for the act militated against repeal.[53]

Not only did the Northern Ireland Government retain the SPA, it passed additional security legislation: the Public Order (Amendment) Act, which restricted processions and served to prohibit civil rights marches while Protestant parades continued unabated; the Prevention of Incitement to Hatred Act, which outlawed acts designed to stir up hatred or arouse fear in a section of the public; and new regulations under the SPA.

Although many reforms proposed for the security system were limited or postponed indefinitely, they shook popular Protestant confidence in the incumbent regime—which the settlers resented for accepting Lon-

50. Interview with author, 2 August 1984.
51. Andrew Boyd, *Brian Faulkner and the Crisis of Ulster Unionism* (Tralee: Anvil, 1972), p. 73.
52. Hunt Committee, p. 35.
53. Peter Kellner and Christopher Hitchens, *Callaghan: The Road to Number Ten* (London: Cassell, 1976), p. 107; Insight, p. 200.

don's demands—and fractured the ruling party. While O'Neill's initial concessions and Britain's efforts at reform divided the Unionist Government from its Protestant supporters, they ignited Catholic demands for broader changes. This untenable situation was alleviated by the 1970 Conservative electoral victory in Britain, which marked a more favorable metropolitan posture toward the Unionists.

TORY LAISSEZ-FAIRE

Both Labour (1966–1970) and Conservative (1970–1974) administrations backtracked on the original reform program in their efforts to prevent extremists from toppling moderate Unionist regimes.[54] Common to both Labour and the Tories was a fear that Ulster might install an extreme right-wing regime or that a popular Protestant uprising might erupt, thus making Britain's posture of reform by remote control untenable. Home Secretary Callaghan wrote that the "principal achievement" of Labour's intervention was to extend "Westminster influence" without provoking a "crisis" such as a revolt by the Northern Ireland Cabinet.[55] Labour's goals had necessarily affected its critical decisions. As a case in point, Harold Wilson wanted to ban a march by the Protestant Apprentice Boys in August 1969 but granted permission for fear that an "Orange backlash" would sweep away the "insecure" Government.[56] The march resulted in two days of serious rioting in Londonderry. By Wilson's admission, the existence of "extremist right-wing pressure" remained of "acute concern" to the Labour Cabinet right through the election of 1970 when the Tories came to power.[57] The concern was not limited to the possibility of a right-wing takeover of the Government but included that of a massive Protestant rebellion in the streets. Tory Home Secretary Maudling was speaking for Labour and Conservative ministers alike when he declared that "a Protestant backlash was the great danger we all feared."[58] As Chapter 7 shows, the threat of a massive Protestant revolt remains a powerful constraint on British policy in Ulster.

Both Labourites and Conservatives, therefore, entered into a marriage of convenience with Unionist regimes, and the principal determinants of

---

54. The Unionist party was becoming "difficult to handle" and prone to rebellion against the leadership (Brian Faulkner, *Memoirs of a Statesman* [London: Weidenfeld and Nicolson, 1978], p. 87).
55. Callaghan, *House Divided*, p. 99.
56. Wilson, *Labour*, p. 692.
57. Ibid., p. 771.
58. Maudling, *Memoirs*, p. 184.

British policy outlined above characterized both administrations. But the Conservative victory in 1970 did signal a more detached metropolitan posture and a more sympathetic approach to the Unionists. Two special factors conditioned the Conservative approach. First, the traditional alliance between the Unionists and Conservatives at Westminster encouraged the Conservatives to yield to Unionist demands; the constructive engagement of Labour gave way to a more isolationist orientation on the part of the Tories. As O'Neill's successor, James Chichester-Clark (1969–1971), remarked to this writer, "The Tories liked to distance themselves from us," and as a result interstate relations became "more relaxed."[59] The essence of the change was captured by former British Minister Hattersley:

> It is not surprising that Stormont prejudices and opinions now fill the vacuum left by Whitehall's negative response to the events of the past year. The balance of power has shifted in Belfast. . . . Stormont runs Northern Ireland virtually alone.[60]

Former Prime Minister Harold Wilson concurred: "One element in a gravely deteriorating situation is the growing appearance of a British Government departing from its position of neutrality and accepting a state of alliance with a single Ulster faction."[61]

Although Hattersley and Wilson may have had partisan motives for their critiques, their conclusions appear justified in light of the Heath Government's actions. Heath displayed little concern with the Ulster crisis;[62] and Home Secretary Reginald Maudling "was continually counseling against the need for any action at all."[63] Both Heath and Maudling exercised less guidance than their Labour predecessors over the British officials stationed in Northern Ireland and over the local Unionist administration. By default, imperial inertia from 1970 to 1972 allowed power to revert to the settler elite. Northern Ireland Cabinet members did not hesitate to seize this opportunity to "reassert their independence," especially under the premiership of Brian Faulkner (1971–1972).[64]

59. Interview with author, 14 August 1984. Chichester-Clark is now Lord Moyola.
60. Roy Hattersley, "Does Maudling Dance to Faulkner's Tune?" *Guardian,* 25 August 1971, p. 10.
61. "Wilson Warns Heath," *New York Times,* 5 September 1971.
62. Margaret Laing, *Edward Heath: Prime Minister* (London: Sidgwick and Jackson, 1972), pp. 221, 224.
63. Henry Kelly, *How Stormont Fell* (Dublin: Gill and Macmillan, 1972), p. 132.
64. Callaghan, *House Divided,* pp. 177, 96.

Favoring "a more *laissez-faire* approach to security matters," the Heath Government yielded to Unionist demands and thereby helped to decelerate Labour's reform program.[65] The growing influence of Northern Ireland officials over security policy was reflected in the balance of power inside the Joint Security Committee.[66] Friction between British and Ulster members continued;[67] but the committee became, as Faulkner stated in February 1972, increasingly an arena within which "the vital interests of the Unionists must be acknowledged."[68]

A second factor conditioning the Conservative approach to the crisis was the intensifying political violence in 1971. The number of deaths increased seven times from 1970 to 1971 (climbing from 25 to 174) and the number of reported incidents of shooting and bombing soared (from 383 to 3,271). This violence fueled Loyalist demands that the USC be revived (the UDR was not enough); that more British troops be deployed; that they make more liberal use of their weapons; and that they occupy Catholic enclaves to root out insurgents.[69] Demands to unleash the army coincided with the first deaths of soldiers in 1971: 43 were killed. Whitehall eventually gave in to the Loyalist pressure; during the Conservative administration the RUC was rearmed, the army invaded Catholic ghettoes, a massive internment exercise began (see below), and the military presence increased to an unprecedented 22,000 troops. The partial British control over the army under the Labour Government (from the Ministry of Defense and army generals) clearly relaxed under the Tories. It was not much of an exaggeration to claim, as former minister Hattersley did, that under the Tories the army became an "instrument of the Unionist hegemony."[70] Although the settlers no longer monopolized the machinery of state coercion and certainly did not get every initiative they wanted from London, repressive power was increasingly mobilized on their behalf.

Former Prime Minister Wilson had taken the view that reform was necessary as a shock absorber for repression: "There is no future in a policy based on the repression of violence alone unless that is accompa-

---

65. Derek Birrell and Alan Murie, *Policy and Government in Northern Ireland: Lessons of Devolution* (Dublin: Gill and Macmillan, 1980), p. 68.
66. Callaghan, *House Divided,* p. 144; Hattersley, "Faulkner's Tune?"; Birrell and Murie, *Devolution,* p. 68.
67. Former Chief Constable, interview with author, 2 August 1984.
68. Quoted in Boyd, *Faulkner,* p. 74.
69. See John Whale, "Ulster: The Slide toward Direct Rule," *Sunday Times,* 21 March 1971.
70. Hattersley, "Faulkner's Tune?"

nied by an active or intensified search for a political solution."[71] Although Labourites had held that reforms would help defuse Catholic unrest and thus allow Whitehall to minimize direct British intervention, Tories favored greater repression as a means to the same end. The Conservative party wanted Catholic militants and the IRA suppressed at all costs; it strongly opposed the use of concessions to mitigate the problem.[72] Insisting that "concessions. . . merely result in claims for more," Home Secretary Maudling cautioned that "a Protestant backlash. . . could so easily be sparked off by the argument that the more concessions you made to the Catholics, the less result you got for them."[73]

These views seemed to contradict Maudling's claim that Tory policy was "a difficult balancing act" between the demands of the minority and majority communities.[74] In fact, policy making and implementation were sharply skewed in favor of the Protestant side between 1970–1972. Maudling described the logic behind the Conservative Cabinet's thinking:

> If. . . vigorous actions were not taken and, in particular, if it were alleged that the Security Forces would like to do these things but were being held back by the politicians, then there was always the danger of a violent Protestant reaction, and. . . the Protestants could be just as violent as the Catholics, and they were far more numerous.[75]

A violent and massive Protestant rebellion was dreaded not simply for the domestic damage that would result but also because it would force greater metropolitan military or political intervention, both of which Whitehall still hoped to limit. Indeed, "the necessity of avoiding a confrontation with the Protestants, with its implication of greater military involvement, appears to have become by 1970 the major influence upon government policy."[76] In order to minimize its involvement in the province and placate the Protestants, the Conservative Government was decidedly more willing than Labour to approve various forms of repression.

The most spectacular act of mass repression was the internment operation that began on 9 August 1971. (Internment without trial allowed

71. "Wilson Warns Heath."
72. Laing, *Heath,* p. 220.
73. Maudling, *Memoirs,* pp. 183, 184.
74. Ibid., p. 182.
75. Ibid.
76. Paul Bew, Peter Gibbon, and Henry Patterson, *The State in Northern Ireland: 1921–1972* (Manchester: Manchester University Press, 1979), p. 183; Rose, *Governing,* p. 109.

the detention of suspects on suspicion alone where evidence of wrong-doing was lacking.) In the initial sweep 342 individuals were arrested, only a fraction of whom had any connection to the IRA. In the first six months of internment, 2,357 people were arrested, two-thirds of whom were, according to McGuffin, "completely innocent men" who were released after interrogation.[77] The Chief Constable later reflected on this embarrassing failure rate: "One reason internment went wrong was that our information on who should be interned wasn't up to date."[78] Ironically, one important by-product of the detention and interrogation exercise was to update and increase the number of intelligence dossiers on members of the minority community.

A watershed in the crisis of order and authority, internment was highly counterproductive. (1) It caused a sharp escalation of violence and intercommunal tension. (2) It radicalized and mobilized Catholics, who staged mass antiinternment marches and rallies. (3) Its implementation by the British army drove the final wedge between the Catholic community and both the British and Unionist regimes.[79] Catholics believed that the Conservative government had completely forsaken them for the settler caste. (4) It brought the IRA floods of new recruits. (5) Used into the mid-1970s against individuals suspected of involvement in the IRA, detention without charge or trial made political prisoners of these suspects. Internment thus enhanced the moral standing of the IRA.

Internment was a military operation in pursuit of political aims, introduced against the advice of the police and military chiefs.[80] Faulkner's Cabinet had convinced Heath that the operation would strengthen it against both Catholic opposition and the Unionist right wing. Faulkner indeed took advantage of internment to consolidate his power in Unionist circles but failed to shore up the regime's authority.[81]

Generally, Faulkner played a more dictatorial role in security matters than his predecessors. He rarely consulted the entire Cabinet on important security matters despite frequent requests from ministers for greater consultation.[82] His ability to dictate security decisions was evident in other areas:

77. McGuffin, *Internment,* p. 87.
78. Interview with author, 2 August 1984.
79. Kevin Boyle, Tom Hadden, and Paddy Hillyard, *Law and State: The Case of Northern Ireland* (Amherst: University of Massachusetts Press, 1975), pp. 145, 147.
80. McGuffin, *Internment,* p. 86.
81. Boyd, *Faulkner,* pp. 69, 81.
82. David Bleakley, *Faulkner: Conflict and Consent in Irish Politics* (London and Oxford: Mowbrays, 1974), pp. 83, 96–97.

From August 1971 to February 1972 Faulkner was given his head, and army, not to say Ministry of Defense, opinion was systematically overruled. This was certainly the case with respect to internment and the toleration of the UDA [the Ulster Defense Association, a Protestant vigilante group], and it seems likely also to have been behind the loosening of UDR recruiting standards and the reorganization of the force on local lines.[83]

That the Unionist Government regained much of its control over security and political affairs in 1970 did not necessarily take the steam out of Protestant protests over security policy. Support was growing for extremist leaders such as Ian Paisley, who for years had been fomenting popular outrage over official "appeasement" of Catholics; he was elected to Stormont and Westminster in 1970. The Paisleyites became a thorn in the Cabinet's flesh just as right-wing whites in South Africa troubled the Botha regime. In Northern Ireland, the right wing left its mark on security policy, as Prime Minister Chichester-Clark remarked:

> One-third of the Unionist party were head cases. They wanted the security forces sent into Catholic areas to shoot them. They applied pressure to do something crazy all the time. The extremists had a big effect; they pushed Cabinet further than we normally would have gone. The Paisleyites always were a contributing factor in each security situation. We were concerned with our electoral position; some moderates were put out by the right wing in the 1970 election.[84]

Unionist regimes simply could no longer take Protestant support for granted, even during the Faulkner regime. The most hard-line premier in years, Faulkner insisted on the military defeat of the IRA and the suspension of political initiatives; even so, his actions did not satisfy the Paisleyites.[85]

Having lost the confidence of many Protestants as well as control over the Catholics, the last three Unionist regimes fared only marginally better in satisfying the third imperative of settler rule, keeping the metropole at bay. Relieved at the less intrusive style of the Tory Government, the Unionists tried to expand their political autonomy and keep London's military support. Unionists of all stripes were anxious over the possibility that this military support might lead to direct British rule or, worse, to the doomsday scenario of a reunited Ireland. But they could

83. Bew, Gibbon, and Patterson, *The State in Northern Ireland,* p. 183.
84. Interview with author, 12 August 1984.
85. Faulkner wrote: "I argued that to attempt some constitutional innovation of a major nature while IRA violence continued would be seen as setting democracy aside to appease the IRA. . . . Political progress was simply not possible in a climate of terrorism and violence" (*Memoirs,* pp. 144, 121).

see no alternative to accepting the Crown's military aid while resisting political interference, despite the lessons they might have learned from Kenya's similar experience during the Mau Mau disturbances.

In a cruel reprise, the same dynamic that had propelled O'Neill out of office acted on his successors. Try as they might to shore up state power and reestablish order, each of the last three Unionist premiers could not strike a balance between the contradictory pressures of Protestants, Catholics, and the British Government.

CONCLUSION

The last three Unionist regimes reluctantly accepted certain reforms (but resisted others) in exchange for continued devolved power. Like most other settler states, the Unionist state proved reformable only within narrow bounds. In a society with deep communal cleavages, institutionalized settler hegemony, and a bitter history of repression and resistance, the regime could not suddenly promote egalitarian political and social changes and remake the security system. Northern Ireland's settler governments were not seriously committed to this enterprise, nor was the Unionist population prepared to allow them to pursue it.

The constraints imposed on the state by the settler community clashed with the demands of the metropole. With inadequate coercive resources, each Unionist regime needed Britain's help to maintain order but feared Britain's response to the palpably sectarian practices the Protestants demanded. It could not defend settler supremacy with the flexibility that Rhodesia had after 1965 or that fully independent settler states such as South Africa and Israel have. The previous chapter showed how a Rhodesian regime left to its own devices fortified its security system; British intervention in Ulster from 1969 to 1972 checked a similar expansionist tendency. Metropolitan involvement—however limited—signaled a decisive break with customary British-Ulster relations. The irony is that the settler regime had *invited* Britain in to restore order but, much to Protestants' chagrin, the metropole overstepped its assigned role and intruded in vital matters previously monopolized by the settlers. If the Conservative Government allowed Unionist Cabinets greater leeway from 1970 to 1972 than its Labour predecessor had, it continued to interfere in domestic affairs in a manner that ultimately proved disastrous for settler rule. Failing to safeguard its autonomy from the metropole, the Unionist state mortgaged its future.

Yet the evidence presented in this chapter points to the resilience of Northern Ireland's security apparatus as the Catholics and the British pressed for reforms. The Unionist ethos, relative autonomy, and sectarian practices of the RUC and the Home Affairs Ministry were unaffected by Britain's reforms. Criminal prosecutions remained in police hands and the Special Powers Act survived for use in repressive experiments such as internment. The British army developed a reputation as an occupation force in Catholic areas and a defender of the Unionist state. Despite some institutional innovations, the maintenance of law and order meant, as in the past, *Unionist law and Protestant order*.

We have seen that a complex array of settler and metropolitan *interests* kept the essential features of the repressive order intact. Moreover, with a Unionist regime in office and reactionary Protestant forces in civil society, Britain lacked the *capacity* to overhaul state institutions and normalize Ulster's affairs by remote control. Serious reconstruction of the security system would have meant terminating Unionist rule, something the metropole wished to avoid at all costs. Direct military and political intervention is rarely the preferred option. As Callaghan explained, "The lessons of Cyprus dominated all our minds at this time: how easy it was to get into such a situation and how difficult to get out."[86] In Ulster, reforms remained altogether secondary to Britain's primary aim: *restabilization with minimal direct involvement in the province*.

The metropole's posture was shaped by several secondary considerations as well: a commitment to the principle of self-determination reflected in the trappings of Westminster majoritarian democracy; an obligation to those who had been loyal to the Crown;[87] and the conviction that "no reliable alternative instrument of government existed."[88] Only late in the day did the British Cabinet "come to learn that the Westminster pattern of democracy, which suits us so well, is not easily exportable."[89] An alternative democratic arrangement would be required. Consequently, power sharing replaced majority rule as the cornerstone of British constitutional engineering in Ulster.

London's restrained approach to the Loyalist population was also arguably influenced by its failure to handle another settler population—

86. Callaghan, *House Divided*, p. 60.
87. The 1949 Ireland Act affirmed that the obligation would not be cut "without the consent of the Parliament of Northern Ireland"; the 1973 Northern Ireland Constitution Act reaffirmed it, granting U.K. status to Ulster until a majority vote expressed otherwise.
88. Callaghan, *House Divided*, p. 24.
89. Maudling, *Memoirs*, p. 185.

Rhodesia's whites—and fears of another unilateral declaration of independence. Protestant hard-liners were indeed threatening this course of action, which London did not dismiss as meaningless posturing. Unlike Rhodesia, a unilaterally independent Ulster would be a thorn much closer to the metropole's nerves—creating tensions between London and Belfast and with Dublin, perhaps precipitating Dublin's intervention on behalf of the Catholic minority.

The events in Northern Ireland from 1969 to 1972 demonstrate how quickly a settler political system can collapse when all three pillars crack. Metropolitan intervention—however minimalist—catalyzed settler fragmentation and minority mobilization. Each development, in turn, contributed to political instability and violence: the British army served rough justice to Catholics; militant Protestants broke from the settler bloc and engaged in sectarian violence; and Catholics reacted to both groups with defensive violence, which later turned offensive. These interacting processes undermined the authority and credibility of three successive settler governments and opened the way for direct British rule of this divided society.

Illustrating the metropole's evolution from an arbiter to a principal in the conflict, British troops fired on Catholic demonstrators, killing thirteen, on Bloody Sunday. This incident in January 1972 precipitated the announcement of direct rule in March. In acting unilaterally, the metropole consulted neither Protestant nor Catholic leaders. Unlike Zimbabwe's case, Northern Ireland's transition to postsettler rule was made chiefly from above and without, albeit with Catholic support. The peculiarities of this transition conditioned state-society and intercommunal relations under the new order. British rule since 1972 has had mixed results: its direct control of the security sector facilitates liberalization but Britain contributes—by its very presence and actions—to communal polarization and political violence that, in turn, limit the scope of liberalization. Chapter 7 examines these problems.

CHAPTER 6

Zimbabwe

One-Party State

Independence Day on 18 April 1980 promised great changes in Zimbabwe. The yoke of settler rule had finally been thrown off, Britain's colonial claims withdrawn, and international legitimacy bestowed on the nation. The popularly elected government proclaimed its commitment to create a radically new state and social order based on democracy, social justice, and racial equality.[1] Under the new regime great progress has been made in redressing the inequalities inherent in the old racial order, in universalizing health care, education, employment opportunities, and, of course, the franchise.

The new constitution institutionalized certain political forms (a multiparty system, declaration of rights, reserved white seats in Parliament) but gave the new elite opportunities to initiate changes in other state structures, such as the repressive machinery that had maintained the settler elite in power. During the 1960s and 1970s, black nationalists frequently condemned Rhodesia's security laws and institutions, and many had personally experienced the iron fist of the settler state. They had promised to dissolve this apparatus once they gained power, along with other vestiges of settler domination.

A number of competing perspectives have addressed the impact of a protracted, successful liberation struggle on state structures under the new order. One is the mobilization thesis. Following Fanon, several ana-

---

1. Some legislation specifically regulating Africans had been repealed between 1977 and 1979.

lysts have drawn a distinction between "false decolonization" and genuine liberation from colonial domination. Most French and British African colonies underwent relatively peaceful transitions to independence in the 1950s and 1960s. In many cases, the changing of the guard had little impact on the development of democratic institutions; the new state structures displayed remarkable continuity with the old colonial order. Southern Africa did not follow this model of consensual decolonization; the settler and colonial regimes there were prepared to resist the winds of change sweeping the continent and had no intention of voluntarily relinquishing their control for "a thousand years," in Ian Smith's prediction. This intransigence forced African liberation movements underground and set in motion protracted guerrilla campaigns.

Several Africanist scholars greeted the rise of armed struggle and popular mobilization in Angola, Mozambique, Namibia, and Rhodesia with claims that it would lay the basis for a truly democratic postcolonial order. The long campaigns against white rule seemed to contain the seeds of opposition to any system of institutionalized repression under majority rule. For Davidson, popular organization and the creation of an insurgent, shadow "state" in liberated zones during the struggle for independence in southern Africa means that the new rulers have "no need to take over any of the structures and institutions of colonial rule." [2] According to Chabal, "successful people's wars usher in the establishment of states the legitimacy and structure of which owe little, if anything, to their colonial predecessors." [3] The guerrillas' political bodies will replace the old state apparatus and the legacy of popular activism has a democratizing effect on the new order. Chabal suggests that mass mobilization "irrevocably determined" the character of the new order in postcolonial Guinea-Bissau. [4] The mobilization thesis, in short, assumes that the experience of popular rebellion will remain salient and significantly affect the postcolonial polity. This perspective fails to appreciate that the vitality of popular forces during an insurgency often wanes after liberation and that protracted guerrilla wars have rarely resulted in new democratic polities. [5]

2. Basil Davidson, "The Politics of Armed Struggle," in *Southern Africa: The New Politics of Revolution,* B. Davidson et al. (Harmondsworth: Penguin, 1976), p. 75.

3. Patrick Chabal, *Amilcar Cabral: Revolutionary Leadership and People's War* (Cambridge: Cambridge University Press, 1983), p. 218.

4. Chabal quotes with approval a leader of that country's liberation movement (ibid., p. 95).

5. Samuel Huntington, "Will More Countries Become Democratic?" *Political Science Quarterly* 99, no. 2 (Summer 1984): 213.

A diametrically opposed argument holds that the very process of violent anticolonial struggle so hardens guerrilla forces that they adopt an authoritarian political culture and rely on coercive tactics in eliciting civilian compliance. This insurgent culture of repression is likely to survive after the guerrillas capture state power, particularly if it meshes with the old regime's authoritarian political culture. Sithole argues in this vein:

> The liberation struggle also left a significant mark on Zimbabwe's political culture. The commandist nature of mobilization and politicization under clandestine circumstances gave rise to the politics of intimidation and fear. Opponents were viewed in warlike terms, as enemies, and therefore, illegitimate. The culture from the liberation struggle was intolerant and violent.[6]

This heritage may have conditioned the former guerrilla and nationalist leaders who now wield state power to "adopt tactics and attitudes that mirror the oppressors" whom they had fought against and replaced.[7] As Chapter 4 suggests, however, the political culture of the liberation struggle had two dimensions: commandist and democratic. Since 1980 the popular democratic aspect has been eclipsed by the authoritarian, which includes what some call an "aloofness" or "elitism" on the part of state managers.[8] Citizens are routinely exhorted to identify with the ruling party and to endorse state policies after the fact, but their preferences have little impact on the elite's decision making regarding major political and security issues. Mass "departicipation" is common in other newly independent African states but especially striking in Zimbabwe, given the extensive politicization of the populace during the war.[9] In Mozambique, by contrast, state leaders are somewhat more inclined to solicit local input to state policies, although the crippling guerrilla war hampers communication between state managers and masses.[10]

6. Masipula Sithole, "Zimbabwe: In Search of a Stable Democracy," in *Democracy in Developing Countries*, vol. 2, *Africa*, ed. L. Diamond, J. Linz, and S. Lipset (Boulder, Colo.: Lynne Rienner, 1988), p. 248.

7. David Caute, "Mugabe Moves to One-Party Rule," *The Nation*, 22 February 1986, p. 204.

8. André Astrow, *Zimbabwe: A Revolution that Lost Its Way?* (London: Zed, 1983). An editorial in *MOTO* (Gweru, Zimbabwe) in February 1983 discerned "a growing gap between the people and the people's Government."

9. Ruth Collier, *Regimes in Tropical Africa* (Berkeley: University of California Press, 1982), pp. 144–45; Nelson Kasfir, *The Shrinking Political Arena* (Berkeley: University of California Press, 1976).

10. Allen Isaacman and Barbara Isaacman, *Mozambique: From Colonialism to Revolution* (Boulder, Colo.: Westview, 1982).

A third argument appears in one version of dependency theory, which reduces the practices of the postsettler state to the imperatives of international capital. According to Mandaza, the new state in Zimbabwe is a convenient instrument or "conduit through which the imperialist forces of international finance capital can compromise and control the new state." In order to thwart the anticipated opposition of the masses to imperialism, the postsettler state, now run by a black petit bourgeoisie, "depends on the repressive apparatus which it invariably expands and strengthens." [11] The state's apparent legitimacy masks the fact that, in the final analysis, it depends on the inherited repressive apparatus to contain the popular unrest latent in imperialist economic exploitation. In this reductionist account, the interests and policies of the postsettler state follow only the logic of international capital; they ignore the special political interests of the new power elite and all other domestic factors.

Each of these perspectives portrays the legacy of a liberation war in a one-dimensional fashion. Our analysis of Zimbabwe reveals a more complex reality. The theses of mobilization, authoritarian culture, and imperialism all fail to consider key variables that shape outcomes of transitions. One factor is the strength and resiliency of surviving state institutions, which may sabotage plans for liberalization. Tilly points to the constraints imposed by state organs after a revolution:

> Most revolutionaries... seize a state apparatus without that long preparation of an organizational alternative. In those cases, the already-accrued power of the state affects the probability that fundamental structural change will issue from the revolution much more strongly than does the extent of mobilization during the revolution. [12]

A welcome corrective to societally centered models, Tilly's state-power thesis is incomplete; it does not link the inertial tendencies of inherited state organizations to the goals and interests of the new executive and to the balance of forces in civil society, which may be weighted for or against modernization of state structures. These regime and societal variables are central to any understanding of the prospects for change once settler rule has been dislodged.

11. Ibbo Mandaza, introduction to *Zimbabwe: The Political Economy of Transition,* ed. Ibbo Mandaza (Dakar: CODESRIA, 1986), pp. 14–15; see also his chapter, "The State and Politics in the Post-White Settler Colonial Situation," in ibid.
12. Charles Tilly, *From Mobilization to Revolution* (Reading: Addison-Wesley, 1978), p. 222.

The transfer of political power to a popularly elected regime in Zimbabwe did not induce legal and institutional reforms of the internal security system. Instead, core pillars of the new regime rose on the foundations of the old—a pattern many other newly independent African nations followed as they marshaled existing state capacities for authoritarian purposes.[13] Neither the longitudinal continuities between settler and postsettler rule nor the partial convergence with other African polities was inevitable, however, as this chapter shows.

After describing the institutional foundations of state power in Zimbabwe, this chapter applies an explanatory model to the inherited, unreconstructed security system. Our findings suggest that the perpetuation of this system results not simply from the objective security problems facing the country but from four additional factors: (1) the political impotence or acquiescence of groups in civil society; (2) the absence of a democratic political culture; (3) the bureaucratic inertia and repressive proclivities of the security establishment; and (4) the regime's mobilization of institutional capacities to meet special political objectives. The first two factors reflect an *absence of constraints* on repression; the latter two constitute *compelling incentives* for repressive outcomes. The findings indicate that the fourth factor has the most power in accounting for the lack of liberalization in the security sector in Zimbabwe. Chapter 7 will explain Northern Ireland's distinctive security patterns, with a different configuration of these variables.

THE INTERNAL SECURITY SYSTEM

The collapse of white settler rule was in itself a profound event in Zimbabwe. The political system opened: outlawed political parties were legalized, universal suffrage announced, procedures for free competitive elections established, and civil and political rights extended to the black majority. Yet an analysis centered on these changes may obscure important political continuities. Formal democratic structures are perhaps less central indicators of the substance of a political order than the sharpness of the state's cutting edge, its structures of coercive control. The literature on decolonization has often overlooked this point.

13. At the end of 1987, six African nations had military regimes, thirty-five had one-party systems, and ten had multi-party systems. On variations in authoritarian rule in Africa, see R. Collier, *Regimes*; Rhoda Howard, *Human Rights in Commonwealth Africa* (Totowa, N.J.: Rowman and Littlefield, 1986); Robert H. Jackson and Carl G. Rosberg, *Personal Rule in Black Africa* (Berkeley: University of California Press, 1982).

There is a basic continuity in the core of state power in Rhodesia and Zimbabwe. The essential features of Rhodesia's internal security apparatus remain: it possesses tremendous power and institutional autonomy, displays a partisan bias against opponents of the regime, and operates in a consistently repressive fashion. In short, the development of internal security structures in Zimbabwe has been a continuous process, punctuated by the transfer of power to a popularly elected government in 1980.

At the same time, the moment of independence signaled its official legitimation. The regime proclaims that the security branch has acquired a universalistic ethos, and it appears to have more extensive popular support.[14] The official doctrine of national security now cites defense of the majoritarian order as a moral basis for Zimbabwe's security institutions and emergency powers. Security of the white minority has given way to security of the majority; the police force is frequently referred to as a "people's police," committed to serving the masses; the army is presented as an "army of the majority" instead of an instrument of domination; and the state of emergency that once protected white supremacy now "comes from the people and is directed to protect their interests."[15] According to the Home Affairs minister, the "state of emergency promotes rather than diminishes our freedom and independence";[16] the oppressive violence of the Rhodesian state has been replaced with the new regime's "transformative violence" in "the service of our people."[17] In a nutshell, the Government uses the language of majoritarian democracy to justify repressive controls.[18]

Zimbabwe's political leaders take an instrumentalist view of the inherited security system. Security legislation and agencies are seen as neutral instruments that are conveniently available and amenable to the incumbent executive, which may use them to foster the "transformation into a just, egalitarian, wealthy society."[19] The contrast with official discourse—and, to some degree, practice—in postcolonial Mozambique

14. No survey of public attitudes on security laws and practices exists, but impressionistic data suggest that Zimbabwe is building legitimation. My review of the magazine of the Zimbabwe Republic Police, *Outpost*, from 1980 to 1987 found ministerial comments urging recruits to dispel public mistrust and suspicion of the police, who seem to be associated with the old British South African Police.
15. Minister of Home Affairs, Assembly *Debates*, vol. 5, 13 July 1982, col. 627.
16. Minister of Home Affairs, Assembly *Debates*, vol. 11, 16 January 1985, col. 1209.
17. Minister of Home Affairs, Assembly *Debates*, vol. 6, 19 January 1983, col. 859.
18. Alves documents a similar disparity in Brazil (Maria Alves, *State and Opposition in Military Brazil* [Austin: University of Texas Press, 1985], p. 31).
19. Minister of Home Affairs, Assembly *Debates*, vol. 7, 13 July 1983, col. 416.

is striking.[20] For example, Mozambique's former president, Samora Ma-
chel, declared, "This state, this power, these laws are not neutral techniques or instruments which can be equally well used by the enemy [the
Portuguese colonial regime] or by us. . . . We cannot serve the masses by
governing with state powers designed to oppress the masses."[21] According to this essentialist view, security institutions inherited from an authoritarian regime are structurally and ideologically inclined to act
repressively.

If the official raison d'être for Zimbabwe's security system has
changed since independence, its organization has changed little. The security apparatus remains large, powerful, and insulated. Decision making is dominated by an inner Cabinet;[22] it includes the prime minister
(now the president), Minister of State for Security, Minister of State for
Defense, and Minister of Home Affairs.[23] They, along with top security
officers, constitute the commanding heights of the security core (see Figure 1).

Since independence the ruling party, the Zimbabwe African National
Union (ZANU), has held that it is politically supreme. ZANU's 1984
congress established a Politburo and five new standing committees of a
Central Committee, whose mandate is to supervise and administer ministries and secure the authority of the party over the Government. In law
and in practice, however, ZANU is secondary to the executive branch:
the Cabinet determines whether and how party resolutions are to be implemented. President Robert Mugabe himself admitted at the 1988 congress that ZANU's supremacy over the Government "has not been
achieved."[24] Supporting evidence can be found in some of the most important policy decisions: against ZANU's wishes, the Cabinet has
moved very slowly in resettling peasants on formerly white-owned
land;[25] the Government did not abolish the reserved white seats in Parlia-

20. The pressures of the long and devastating guerrilla war in Mozambique help to ex-
plain the emergence of new forms of authoritarianism since independence (see William
Finnegan, "The Emergency: II," *The New Yorker,* 29 May 1989).
    21. Quoted in my article, "In Search of Regime Security: Zimbabwe since Indepen-
dence," *Journal of Modern African Studies* 22, no. 4 (December 1984): 555.
    22. Eric Marsden, "Mugabe in 'Super-ZAPU' Clash," *Sunday Times,* 20 March 1983.
The executive consists of a pragmatic technocratic faction and a radical populist one.
Libby notes that technocrats have tended to dominate decision making, particularly on
economic issues (Ronald T. Libby, "Developmental Strategies and Political Divisions
within the Zimbabwean State," in *The Political Economy of Zimbabwe,* ed. M. Schatzberg
[Praeger: New York, 1984]).
    23. Interview with Minister of State for Security, *Commerce,* April 1983, p. 4.
    24. Quoted in Colin Stoneman and Lionel Cliffe, *Zimbabwe: Politics, Economics,
and Society* (London: Pinter, 1988), p. 80.
    25. By 1988 only 41,000 families had been resettled, out of a target figure of 162,000.

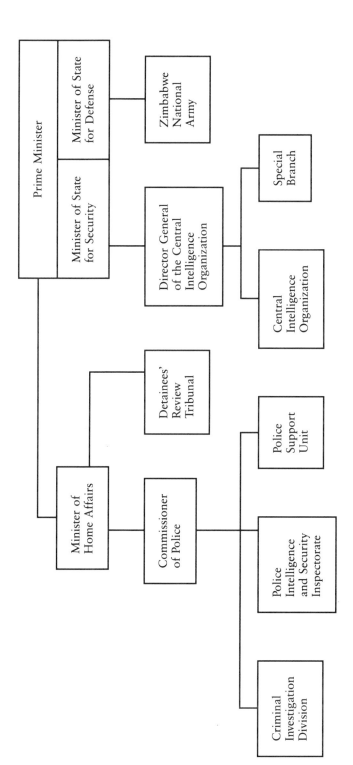

Figure 1.   Structure of the Security System (1987).

ment before the constitutionally stipulated date of 1987; the Government has postponed declaring a one-party state despite sustained party pressure since 1980. Yet relations between party and Government elites are generally harmonious, partly because ZANU's Politburo and standing committees contain prominent ministers and deputy ministers.[26] Their presence suggests that the Politburo combines both groups into a power elite; its overlapping membership helps minimize disagreement in the upper echelons. When these elites conflict with lower-level ZANU cadres over security matters, the Government usually prevails. A former Minister of Home Affairs described a typical exchange.

> There have been pressures from the party for the Government to take certain lines of security, but the Government hasn't always done so. There has been tremendous pressure to ban ZAPU [the Zimbabwe African People's Union] and have a one-party state. The Government said it wanted to follow the rules. . . . Many in the party thought Nkomo [the ZAPU leader] should be detained, but the Government didn't want to. It was a difficult position for the Government to be in.[27]

Following in the footsteps of other African nations, Zimbabwe has progressively Africanized its security system, staffing it largely with members of the Shona ethnic group, which is linked to ZANU. Since independence the number of whites in the police force, military, and intelligence agencies has dwindled to a handful. Members of the Ndebele ethnic group have little better representation. They do not receive promotion to top ranks in the police and very few serve in the intelligence service. The military is roughly one-third Ndebele, but Shona officers hold the command posts.[28]

Africanization has helped to overcome the previous racial configuration of the security branch. But this changing of the guard has had little impact on the system's structure, organizational interests and proclivities, resources, and modus operandi. In other postcolonial states, Africanization has rarely led to the liberalization of institutions of control. In Zimbabwe, two special personnel factors are relevant. The black personnel in the security sector come primarily from the ranks of ex-guerrillas who fought against the settler regime or "rehabilitated" of-

---

26. In the state's first years, the Central Committee met infrequently; there was a "tendency to determine issues in Cabinet" rather than risk debate in the party (*Africa Confidential,* 3 March 1982; Claire Palley, "What Future for Zimbabwe?" *Political Quarterly* 51, no. 3 [July 1980]: 294). The growth of greater party influence has been slow (interview with Edgar Tekere, *MOTO,* July 1984, p. 5).

27. Interview with author, 10 June 1987.

28. *Africa Confidential,* 27 March 1985, p. 4.

ficials who served that regime. It is not uncommon for state personnel to remain after a political transition; many top elites now in the CIO, the Ministry of Home Affairs, and the police are blacks who began their careers in the 1960s or 1970s. They, like the few remaining whites in these departments, apparently see themselves as professionals prepared to serve any government. But neither ex-guerrillas nor officials from the old regime tend to show special sensitivity to standards of human rights. The ex-combatants are war-hardened, and the surviving officials were trained under an authoritarian order. The Government apparently sees the new recruits differently, judging by a comment of the Home Affairs minister: "ex-combatants... are excellent recruits because they already have military knowledge and the necessary political orientation to police a dynamic and changing society." [29]

The Rhodesian Ministries of Law and Order and Internal Affairs have been dismantled, with their security functions and policing transferred to the Ministry of Home Affairs. [30] Home Affairs operates in a manner reminiscent of the Ministry of Law and Order—in part because it administers many of the same statutes. One former ranking Home Affairs official stated, "In the overall administration of law and order policy, I don't think there has been a great deal of change." [31]

Since independence, the ministry's budget allocation has grown substantially (see Table 2). Absorbing over 90 percent of the funding, the Zimbabwe Republic Police force numbers fifteen thousand, plus three thousand in the Police Support Unit. [32] The former paramilitary role of the regular police has become less prominent, but three units deal with internal security: the Police Intelligence and Security Inspectorate, the Police Support Unit, and the Criminal Investigation Division. Policing features some important continuities with the Rhodesian past, as a former ranking officer in the ministry emphasized: "The machinery of the police and their training goes on much as it did in the past. Training is very similar and police methods are much the same as they were." [33] They enforce, inter alia, the security legislation inherited from the old regime—which partly explains why the force has had difficulty over-

29. Speech delivered at senior officers' seminar, reprinted in *Outpost,* September–October 1982, p. 11.

30. "Ministry of Home Affairs," mimeo, D12/47a (c. 1984), p. 1.

31. Interview with author, 2 June 1987.

32. *The Military Balance, 1986–1987* (London: International Institute for Strategic Studies, 1986). Increases in expenditure do not necessarily indicate sinister fortification but may stem from organizational rationalization; for the police, some funding is for improved training of personnel, but the bulk is for salaries and allowances.

33. Former senior Home Affairs official, interview, 2 June 1987.

TABLE 2   SECURITY EXPENDITURES
(in Z$ millions)

	Expenditures[a]				Percentage of Total Appropriation[b]	
	Home Affairs[c]	*Police*	*CIO*[d]	*Defense*	*Home Affairs*[e]	*Defense*[f]
1978–79					12.1	17.9
1979–80					8.4	23.1
1980–81	87.9		5.7	262.2	5.5	15.8
1981–82	86.2		11.8	301.5	4.5	15.3
1982–83	104.3		12.8	349.2	3.9	13.5
1983–84	122.9	112	14.5	418.0	4.1	14.5
1984–85	145.1	131	17.0	377.1	5.3	14.7
1985–86	143.2	130	30.3	507.2	4.7	15.0
1986–87	170.2	158.3	40.9	649.5	4.6	17.5
1987–88 (est.)	187.1	173.7	36.8	720.1		

SOURCES: Government of Zimbabwe, *Estimates of Expenditure* (Harare: Government Printer, annual); Ministry of Finance, Economic Planning, and Development, *Socio-Economic Review of Zimbabwe 1980–1985* (Harare: Government Printer, 1986); *Bulawayo Chronicle*, 15 April 1987.
[a]Actual expenditures include supplementary budget, except for 1987–88, which is the original appropriation voted by Parliament.
[b]Figures for original appropriation by Parliament.
[c]The budget allocated to the Ministry of Home Affairs includes that for the police, which the table disaggregates.
[d]The budget for the Central Intelligence Organization is listed in the Government's *Estimates of Expenditure* as "Special Services" under Office of the Prime Minister.
[e]Figure for 1978–79 is for Ministry of Law and Order.
[f]Figures for 1978–79 and 1979–80 include funding for Combined Operations.

coming the public's suspicion and mistrust and disassociating itself from the old British South African Police.[34] There is evidence that some priorities of the police have been politically influenced by officials of the ruling party and that the force has become increasingly politicized and deferential to ZANU officials.[35] Party membership may not be a requirement for promotion within the force, but officers are encouraged to become members and ministers sometimes stress the proper political role of the force. One Minister of Home Affairs, for example, told police officers:

34. The police magazine, *Outpost,* often reprints official complaints about this problem.
35. Arnold Woolley, "Recruiting for Trouble," *Police Review,* 29 August 1986 and 5 September 1986.

the proposition that a police force is neutral and apolitical must be stood on its head. . . . No army, police, and judiciary are, or can be, apolitical. . . . Politicization of the police force will enhance the removal of colonial hangover [*sic*].[36]

A successor issued similar instructions: "You must make every effort to be fully informed of the government policy and above all Party policy . . . and ideology in order to. . . implement that policy."[37]

One particularly controversial arm of the police, under the direction of the Home Affairs minister, is the Police Internal Security and Intelligence Unit. It is exclusively concerned with investigating and gathering intelligence on the activities of insurgents and their civilian supporters.[38] This elite unit is known for its mistreatment of suspects in custody and harassment of ZAPU officials.[39]

The quality of policing by regular officers in Matabeleland has also been a problem. According to an Amnesty International report in 1985, "Conditions in police stations in Zimbabwe are reported to be generally poor, with severe overcrowding, poor food, lack of bedding, and no exercise. Prisoners are reported to be beaten [and tortured] both by the police and by CIO interrogators."[40] Incidents of police torture reportedly declined after the appearance of Amnesty's report, due to the circulation throughout the police of instructions forbidding torture; at the same time, however, police posts in Matabeleland were filled with strongly anti-ZAPU officers.[41]

In 1980 the Special Branch of the police was removed from police jurisdiction and fully integrated into the Central Intelligence Organization (CIO). The CIO also lost its direct access to the prime minister and is now accountable to the Minister of State for Security. Most important, the CIO's basic structure and criteria for evaluating threats and making policy recommendations were not overhauled. Initially the Government

36. Speech delivered at senior officers' seminar, reprinted in *Outpost,* September–October 1982, pp. 10–11.
37. Speech by the minister reprinted in *Outpost,* May–June 1986, p. 6.
38. Assembly *Debates,* vol. 13, 21 August 1986, cols. 1035–36.
39. *Africa Confidential,* 11 December 1985; David Caute, "Mugabe Moves to One-Party Rule," *The Nation,* 22 February 1986, p. 204.
40. Amnesty International, *Detention without Trial of Political Prisoners in Zimbabwe* (London: Amnesty International, September 1985), p. 3; see also Lawyers Committee for Human Rights, *Zimbabwe: Wages of War* (New York: Lawyers Committee, 1986), pp. 89, 109.
41. Africa Watch, *Zimbabwe: A Break with the Past?* (New York: Africa Watch, 1989), pp. 19, 41.

envisioned some change in the organization; these plans never material-
ized, as the CIO director disclosed:

> When Munangagwa [the Security minister] asked me to stay in office for at
> least the two-year period it would take to reconstruct CIO, I agreed but main-
> tained that there was little need for change. . . . Munangagwa left the profes-
> sional control of CIO to me. . . . This made for very little change in
> Intelligence functioning, and as far as the rank and file of CIO were con-
> cerned there was virtually no change in executive or administrative control.[42]

Modifications in the intelligence apparatus since independence have
not liberalized it. Previously the Special Branch would arrest and the
CIO would interrogate suspects; today CIO operatives have both powers
of arrest and interrogation and often use them with disregard for due
process of law. Since independence, the agency has been linked to scores
of incidents of torture, political kidnapping, and harsh interrogation
practices. The tremendous autonomy and freedom of action that it enjoyed under the Rhodesian state remains.

The CIO's budget climbed from Z$5.7 million in 1980–1981 to an
estimated Z$38.3 million in 1986–1987.[43] Parliament does not debate
this funding (as it does other departmental budgets); questions that MPs
have raised about its allocations have been ruled out of order by the
Speaker of the Assembly. Moreover, it is the only part of the budget exempt from auditing by the Comptroller and Auditor General.[44] The
quantum jump in the CIO's budget, its merger with the Special Branch,
and its prominent role in internal security suggest that the agency may
be even more formidable than under settler rule.[45]

What about the military? For one thing, it is larger than that of most
other African states, partly because it kept many former guerrillas in
uniform after 1980. As of 1986, the army numbered 41,000, the air
force 1,000, and paramilitary forces 38,000.[46] Changes within the army
have involved Africanizing the force; integrating previously hostile

---

42. Ken Flower, *Serving Secretly: An Intelligence Chief on Record,* London: John
Murray, 1987, p. 272. In late 1984 a commission was formed to advise the Government on
recruitment, training, and intelligence systems; its recommendations were implemented
only to a limited extent (*Africa Confidential,* 5 September 1984, p. 8; former CIO officer,
interview with author, 17 June 1987).

43. *Estimates of Expenditure* lists CIO's budget under Special Services, Prime Minister's Office.

44. Assembly *Debates,* vol. 12, 1 August 1985, col. 147.

45. Frederick Ehrenreich, "National Security," in *Zimbabwe: A Country Study,* ed.
H. Nelson (Washington, D.C.: U.S. Government Printing Office, 1983), p. 278.

46. *Military Balance, 1986–1987.* Decidedly pro-ZANU grass-roots "people's mili-
tias" (totaling twenty thousand members) have formed and been given paramilitary training to defend their communities against subversives.

armed forces and dismantling the more notorious units of the old regime (like the Selous Scouts and the Special Air Services); and retraining troops by a British advisory team.

The nominal integration of ZANLA, ZIPRA, and the Rhodesian military forces has not produced an ethnically or racially balanced defense force. The military has been Africanized and is now dominated by the Shona ethnic group and staunch ZANU loyalists. Former Rhodesian officers have resigned. Although roughly one-third of the rank and file is ex-ZIPRA, the top ranks have been purged of former ZIPRA men (some have been arrested on charges of supporting antigovernment insurgents). The celebrated integration of the three antagonistic forces has, therefore, been more apparent than real.

The retraining of troops by the British Military Advisory and Training Team (BMATT) has centered on converting a guerrilla force with an insurgent ideology and modus operandi into an apolitical, professional force with conventional capabilities. However, the Mugabe Government has moved to politicize the military and to ensure that it is run by ZANU loyalists. Top military officers are members of ZANU's Politburo and Central Committee, helping to make "the military a hidden arm of the party." [47] One of the few solid studies of Zimbabwe's military concludes that the trend toward professionalization cannot compete with that toward sectarianism: there is a "constant tension between military professionals and ethnic praetorians," with the latter acting as "a constant brake on formal professionalism." According to Evans, "comprehensive Western-style professionalization of the armed forces is unlikely to occur." [48] In short, the military has replaced one form of sectarianism with another, moving from white racial to black ethnic commitments. Communal reorientation, not liberalization, has occurred.

Defense expenditure has mushroomed under the new regime, jumping 28 percent from 1985–1986 to 1986–1987 alone. The army absorbs approximately 80 percent of this allocation, with the remainder going to the Ministry of Defense, the air force, and paramilitary forces.[49] Zimbabwe spends around 5 percent of its gross domestic product on defense (3.5 percent is the average for developing countries).[50] Defense expenditure absorbs a growing proportion of the total budget (see Table 2), and

47. Mike Evans, "Gukurahundi: The Development of the Zimbabwe Defense Forces 1980–1987," *Strategic Review for Southern Africa* 10, no. 1 (May 1988): 25.
48. Ibid., pp. 3, 30, 1.
49. *Estimates of Expenditure.*
50. *Military Balance*; *The Economist*, 21 April 1984, p. 9.

the defense proportion increasingly approaches that in 1978 and 1979, at the height of the Rhodesian war. Whereas the first budget (1980–1981) emphasized spending for development and social services, subsequent ones decreased funding for social programs and increased spending for security. Inflation and the cost of demobilizing and supporting thirty-five thousand ex-guerrillas for two years have contributed to the rising security allocations. More recently, a significant proportion of the defense budget—around 7 percent in 1987—has been maintaining from seven thousand to ten thousand troops in Mozambique to protect vital transportation lines from sabotage by guerrillas fighting the Mozambican Government.[51] The overall defense buildup since independence is officially defended in terms of ongoing security problems;[52] but critics, including some officials, contend that actual security requirements do not warrant the magnitude of spending.

One innovation in the area of law and order is the creation of Youth Brigades linked to the ruling party. Under the mantle of building national unity, the paramilitary brigades have been involved in attacks on members of opposition political parties, particularly in 1984 and 1985. Prosecutions have been rare.[53]

Like other organizations, state security agencies have a vested interest in survival, if not expansion. An internal security system inherited from a settler state is structurally conducive to repressive outcomes. Equally important may be a regime's encouragement, for political or other reasons, of these essentialist institutional tendencies. The juncture of independence in Zimbabwe provided a unique opportunity for the system's overhaul, which the new regime did not seize. Instead it fortified these agencies with material resources, personnel, and legal powers; it left them only nominally accountable; it repeatedly praised the activities of the security forces; and it assigned them missions likely to produce repressive outcomes. The following sections examine the legal, intrastate, and societal factors favoring repressive outcomes and the elective affinity between the repressive proclivities of the security sector and the new regime's political agenda.

REPRESSIVE LEGISLATION

Chapters 3 and 4 traced the development in Rhodesia of a battery of statutes, used first to preempt or curtail nationalist political opposition

51. *Washington Post,* national weekly ed., 11 January 1988.
52. Minister of Finance, Assembly *Debates,* vol. 13, 31 July 1986, col. 659.
53. Lawyers Committee, *Zimbabwe,* p. 54.

and then to combat guerrilla forces. During the struggle for independence, Rhodesia's African leaders condemned these draconian measures
and promised to repeal them once the settler state had dissolved. Since
independence, some of these measures have been removed. Martial law
and the system of Special Courts were abolished in 1980, and certain
emergency regulations (such as those permitting collective punishment
and protected villages) have been withdrawn. Yet most of Rhodesia's security legislation has been retained.[54] The availability of such sweeping
powers tends to encourage repressive solutions to political and social
problems.

The state of emergency has been in effect continuously since 1965.
One of its major provisions is executive detention. Under section 17 of
the Emergency Powers Regulations the Home Affairs minister may order
the indefinite detention of anyone if he believes it to be "expedient in the
interests of public safety or public order." Section 21 empowers the police and CIO to detain individuals for up to thirty days on the same
grounds as under section 17, and section 53 allows the police to detain
anyone for up to thirty days to facilitate an investigation. Anyone held
under section 17 is entitled to a review of the grounds for detention
within thirty days by the Detainees' Review Tribunal (discussed in the
next section). The annual number of persons in detention has not been
disclosed, but 1,334 persons were detained from January 1982 to July
1983, most for short periods; considerably fewer were detained after
1986.[55]

Under the Emergency Powers Act, the state may issue regulations that
suspend or modify "any law"; from 1980 to 1986 it amended 14 statutes
by executive decree. From 1980 to 1985, it introduced 103 new regulations.[56] Many of the regulations bear no relation to emergency requirements: for example, family planning, changes of cities' names, control
of goods, services, and prices, state revenue, and labor regulations. Reliance on such decrees is not only expedient but familiar—justified by
precedents set under settler rule, as one minister argued: "For many
years, both before and since independence, therefore, Governments have
used the Emergency Powers Act to deal with situations that do not in-

54. Some of the following discussion draws on my chapter, "Continuities in the Politics of State Security in Zimbabwe," in *The Political Economy of Zimbabwe*, ed.
M. Schatzberg (New York: Praeger, 1984), and on my article, "Regime Security." See also
Jan Raath, "The Eternal Emergency," *The Times*, 18 July 1986.
55. John Hatchard, "Emergency Powers in Zimbabwe," ms., Department of Law,
University of Zimbabwe, 1986, p. 14; see also his "Detention Without Trial and Constitutional Safeguards in Zimbabwe," *Journal of African Law* 29, no. 1 (Spring 1985): 38–58.
56. Hatchard, "Emergency Powers," p. 8.

volve public security." He added that "when this Government uses the Emergency Powers Act in similar situations, it is doing no more than following the example shown by its predecessors."[57]

The state of emergency permits nominal parliamentary control over the promulgation of executive decrees. A new regulation must be laid before the Assembly "as soon as may be" after being made, and the Assembly can annul it within twenty-eight days. This procedure means that important regulations need not be discussed in Parliament or justified by the executive; many such measures have escaped both legislative and public debate.

Since 1980, the Cabinet has been the scene of debate over continuing the state of emergency, but the consensus is that terminating it would be premature.[58] Various justifications have been advanced—domestic insurgency, needs of a socialist society, spillover from the guerrilla war in Mozambique—but a continuing threat from South Africa has been a consistent part of the official rationale. The Minister of Home Affairs underscored the latter: "Until the South African situation is resolved, the state of emergency for this country should remain."[59]

One danger of a protracted state of emergency is that it will be accepted as "normal"; another is that it will be institutionalized in statute law.[60] In the event that the EPA is repealed, legislation now exists to fill the vacuum. The Presidential Powers Act of 1986 allows the president to issue emergency decrees to deal with "situations that have arisen or are likely to arise and that require to be dealt with as a matter of urgency." (Such regulations may be amended or revoked by the Assembly.) This act, in effect, enables the incorporation of emergency regulations into the ordinary law. Tellingly, one minister noted that the act allows for a "mini state of emergency."[61]

The Law and Order (Maintenance) Act of 1960 continues to give the executive enormous powers to harass opponents and criminalize political activity. Similarly, the Unlawful Organizations Act of 1959 remains on the books, providing for the banning of organizations deemed

57. Minister of Justice, Legal and Parliamentary Affairs, Assembly *Debates,* vol. 12, 22 January 1986, col. 1476.

58. Author's interviews with top Government officials, June 1987.

59. Assembly *Debates,* 12 July 1988, col. 114.

60. Clinton Rossiter, *Constitutional Dictatorship: Crisis Government in the Modern Democracies* (New York: Harcourt, Brace and World, 1948).

61. Minister of Justice, Legal and Parliamentary Affairs, Assembly *Debates,* vol. 12, 24 January 1986, col. 1527.

"likely" to disturb public order, public safety, or defense. From time to time authorities have floated the possibility of proscribing opposition parties, but none have been banned since 1980.

Although the 1975 Indemnity and Compensation Act—which gave carte blanche to officials acting "in good faith" to suppress terrorism—was repealed in 1980, new emergency regulations revived the indemnity for the security forces in July 1982 and extended it to the CIO in late 1983. In August 1984, however, the Supreme Court ruled these regulations in contravention of the Declaration of Rights.[62] This important ruling discouraged few abuses at the time, in part because the Government "made little effort to inform rank and file officers of the decision and its implications."[63]

THE ABSENCE OF ACCOUNTABILITY

Huntington argues that "fragile African states" require a concentration of power to maintain order—that "excessive" liberty and the diffusion of power are dangerous to political stability.[64] This formulation ignores other potential consequences: the arbitrary use of concentrated power may itself be highly destabilizing and counterproductive. As Kesselman writes, "political order in developing countries is probably jeopardized more by those in positions of authority than by social mobilization from below."[65] Structures of accountability within the state are absolutely essential to prevent or redress executive abuses of power and, hence, to ensure democratic stability.

PARLIAMENT

The steady concentration of state power in the executive branch has impaired the legislature in most African states.[66] In postcolonial Kenya and Tanzania, for example, Parliament is principally a debating forum, allowing members to ventilate grievances and discuss or criticize proposed

62. *Granger v. Minister of State,* judgment no. S.C. 83/84, 17 August 1984.

63. Lawyers Committee, *Zimbabwe,* p. 101.

64. He adds, "It is in Moscow and Peking and not Washington that this lesson is to be learned" (Samuel Huntington, *Political Order in Changing Societies* [New Haven: Yale University Press, 1968], p. 137).

65. Mark Kesselman, "Order or Movement: The Literature of Political Development as Ideology," *World Politics* 26 (October 1973): 148.

66. See the excellent review by Newell Stultz, "Parliaments in Former British Black Africa," *Journal of Developing Areas* 2 (July 1968): 479–94.

legislation and existing policies. MPs react to bills but do not initiate legislation; they modify few bills during parliamentary debates and hesitate to make (or are discouraged from making) statements that embarrass the Government.[67] The net effect is that many MPs in African legislatures contribute little to debates and consistently defer to the wishes of the executive.

In Zimbabwe, the sweeping executive prerogative permitted under the security legislation and the state of emergency help to marginalize Parliament. Procedural devices curb parliamentary debate on security matters. The Speaker of the Assembly and the president of the Senate have frequently limited even the most innocuous questions and comments regarding security matters. Ministers are often unresponsive to such queries, routinely invoking the blanket notions of "national interest" and "state security" to avoid comment. Persistent questioners have had their patriotism called into question by ministers and other legislators. On the rare occasion when members of Parliament have demanded greater accountability of the executive on security matters, their motives have been similarly impugned. A 1984 motion by ZAPU and the Republican Front that Parliament establish a select committee to investigate security problems in Matabeleland was defeated on grounds that Parliament was not suited to deal with security issues and that the motion was nothing but an effort by the opposition parties to "besmirch Government."[68]

The need for the state of emergency is treated as self-evident, as the Minister of Home Affairs proclaimed:

> Clearly we are not going to defend the state of emergency. It is the state of emergency which is going to defend us. Unless we want to start changing the meaning of words, a state of emergency is something that has in itself the reasons for its existence. An emergency does not ask for discussion but for action.[69]

Taking the minister's advice, MPs have faithfully renewed the state of emergency at six-month intervals since 1980. Parliament's role in security matters has been, in short, to rubber-stamp executive policy. Its only distinction from the supine Rhodesian Parliament, and an impor-

67. Helge Kjekshus, "Parliament in a One-Party State: The Bunge of Tanzania," *Journal of Modern African Studies* 12, no. 1 (March 1974): 19–43; Newell Stultz, "Parliament in a Tutelary Democracy: A Recent Case of Kenya," *Journal of Politics* 31, no. 1 (February 1969): 95–118.

68. Minister of Justice, Legal, and Parliamentary Affairs, *Herald* (Harare, Zimbabwe), 20 July 1984.

69. Assembly *Debates,* vol. 5, 13 July 1982, col. 623.

tant one, is that it no longer reflects the interests of a tiny minority of the population.

One survival from the past is the Senate Legal Committee, which tests legislation against the Declaration of Rights in the constitution. From 1980 to 1985, the committee ruled that seven emergency regulations were in contravention of the declaration and that eight were not. After consultations with governmental legal officers, only two regulations were revoked.[70] Clearly, the committee's impact on security measures has been minimal—as it was in the Rhodesian Senate.

THE JUDICIARY

If Parliament has a marginal role in the vital area of state security, the judiciary is considerably more active in this field than in Rhodesia. The courts are independent of the executive, and judges have manifested a commitment to conduct fair trials and safeguard the rights of suspects. Much to the Government's credit, it has not attempted to pack the bench with political appointees tied to the ruling party. Individual infractions of the Declaration of Rights can now be brought before the courts. Although the continuing state of emergency has suspended important safeguards in the Declaration of Rights, in security cases the courts have ruled against the executive. Not only have they acquitted a number of prominent individuals accused of security offenses, they have reached decisions that have made slight inroads into the emergency laws. The Supreme Court's 1984 decision invalidating the indemnity regulations for the security forces is one case in point. Yet both in defending persons accused of security offenses and in ruling on the constitutionality of security measures, the judicial system presents a very limited check on executive abuses of power.[71]

Although it has secured a number of convictions on security charges, the Government has failed in several critical trials (e.g., of opposition politicians and senior military officers). These defeats have resulted from poor prosecution, denial of legal representation to the accused, insufficient evidence, spurious charges, and the discovery of forced confessions (following threats and torture). In a 1984 case, High Court Justice Tony Smith castigated the CIO for repeatedly denying the accused in se-

70. Hatchard, "Emergency Powers."
71. Zimbabwe's courts seem more vibrant than those in many other African states (see Steven Pfeiffer, "The Role of the Judiciary in the Constitutional Systems of East Africa," *Journal of Modern African Studies* 16, no. 1 [1978]: 33–66).

curity cases access to legal representation: "This court takes a very serious view of such deliberate flouting of the provisions of the Constitution by the CIO officers." [72] Other similarly critical comments have been issued by the bench.

On several occasions, the executive's irritation with judicial decisions has resulted in fierce public attacks on the loyalty and integrity of the courts. The harshest attack was issued by the Minister of Home Affairs on 13 July 1982:

> The manner in which our law courts dispense justice is gravely frustrating and undermining the work of law-enforcement agencies like the police. The security of the state is sacrificed on the altar of individual liberties. People who are engaged in activities designed to threaten the welfare and security of the state are either freed by the courts or go off very lightly. . . . It appears that the courts are sowing seeds of a revolt against the government and encouraging the sudden growth of the dissident element in Matabeleland. . . . Recalcitrant and reactionary members of the so-called Bench still remain masquerading under our hard won independence as dispensers of justice or, shall I say, injustice by handing down perverted pieces of judgment which smack of subverting the people's government. . . . Stated differently, what is the use of having good laws, good law enforcement agencies and bad law courts which could be construed as comprising a hostile Bench? [73]

Decisions in security cases unfavorable to the regime have been interpreted by some in the executive as symptomatic of a lack of concern for state security or, worse, support for armed dissidence. The judiciary has been accused of harboring a fundamental disloyalty to the "people's government," a colonial mentality, a "class bias," and using double standards.[74] More common have been complaints that the courts have released "guilty" defendants on legal "technicalities" or procedural "errors."[75] One minister summarized the problem by noting that the courts are "not in tune with the present government." [76] In reference to the wayward courts, he declared, "Until such time as we have *all the machinery of state acting in concert for the same. . . objectives*, it must be neces-

---

72. Justice Smith, quoted in John Hatchard, "The Right to Legal Representation Must Be Upheld," *MOTO,* December 1984–January 1985, p. 23.
73. Assembly *Debates,* vol. 5, 13 July 1982, cols. 630–34.
74. Minister of Home Affairs, quoted in the *Times,* 9 September 1983 and *Herald,* 16 February 1983.
75. Some less influential ministers have been staunch defenders of the independence of the judiciary (*Africa Confidential,* 17 July 1985, p. 2).
76. Minister of Home Affairs, *Christian Science Monitor,* 2 September 1983.

sary to adopt extreme measures for the preservation of the security of the state."[77] The deviations of the courts in security cases have been used to excuse executive reversals of judicial verdicts, such as the Minister of Home Affairs' immediate redetention of persons acquitted in major security cases. Under emergency regulations the courts may not challenge summary redetention, which has been justified on grounds that "Government has more facts than the Court and some facts derive from our security sources and intelligence sources."[78] The Government's poor record in security cases dealing with prominent political opponents (as distinct from insurgents) seems to have encouraged use of detention without trial.[79] Several opponents languished in detention for periods as long as four years.[80]

A Detainees' Review Tribunal (under the Home Affairs ministry) reviews detention orders every six months. This body is reminiscent in several respects of its Rhodesian counterpart created in 1959: it has meager resources, no permanent staff, operates at a slow pace, meets in camera, and is not "bound by the rules of evidence or procedure applicable to any legal proceedings."[81] Whereas the prosecution in ordinary criminal proceedings must prove a case beyond a reasonable doubt, the tribunal's test is that the detaining authority prove its case on the broader "balance of probabilities." The tribunal formulates its unique rules and procedures, which may vary according to the "peculiarities of each case."[82] It admits a wide range of evidence—information from sources that cannot be revealed, hearsay evidence—in determining whether a detainee is a threat to state security.

77. Assembly *Debates,* vol. 5, 13 July 1982, col. 633; emphasis added. Mugabe has made similar statements (*Herald,* 27 December 1983). In a speech affirming the state's desire for complete unity, the Minister of State for Political Affairs called for positions in the civil service to be "filled by zealous members of the ruling Party" so that "the Party, the Government, and the civil service would be one thing, pursuing the same objectives" (Department of Information press statement, Harare, 27 August 1984).
78. Prime Minister, Assembly *Debates,* vol. 7, 13 July 1983, col. 395.
79. See Assembly *Debates,* vol. 5, 13 July 1982, col. 631, and "Court in the Middle," *MOTO,* June 1983.
80. In December 1986, the Minister of Home Affairs stated that thirty-one persons were in detention (*Bulawayo Chronicle,* 5 December 1986).
81. Emergency Powers Regulations (Statutory Instrument 458/83), section 31(4). The tribunal's small annual budget has varied from Z$1,000 to Z$8,000 (*Estimates of Expenditure*), similar to its allocations under the Rhodesian state.
82. *Evans and Hartlebury v. Chairman of the Review Tribunal and Minister of Home Affairs,* H.C. 2562/3/84, 12 December 1984, Justice Gibson.

In most cases the tribunal has concluded that detention orders are justified. The tribunal's decisions are not binding, however, on the Minister of Home Affairs. Before 1985, the minister complied with the tribunal's recommendations, but since then he has increasingly overridden the board. Clearly this body constitutes a rather limited check on abuses of executive power.

No official, independent oversight bodies routinely monitor the security organs or have power to investigate public complaints in this area. In the courts, however, a number of security officials have appeared on charges of beating, torture, rape, or murder. Independent reports on human rights concluded that "many political killings from 1982–1985 have not been formally investigated and are unlikely to be," and that no progress has been made in locating those who disappeared during the mid-1980s.[83]

The evidence thus indicates that the wholesale absence of checks and balances on executive power that characterized the Rhodesian state also typifies the new order. Its few mechanisms of accountability are not effective.

CIVIL SOCIETY AT BAY

Pressures from social institutions and voluntary associations may reduce the scope of state power and promote civic accountability. A network of dynamic, democratically oriented groups has been instrumental in frustrating or containing authoritarianism in some African nations, like Nigeria and Ghana.[84] Among those groups are human rights organizations, the churches, the mass media, the legal community, trade unions, professional associations, student groups, and business organizations.

One writer discerns in Zimbabwe a "robustly pluralistic" civic order, which is rooted in the past: "In the event of a one-party state in Zimbabwe, other forms of pluralism would assume degrees of political importance reminiscent of intellectual, religious, and trade union opposition to white supremacy in Rhodesia."[85] Chapters 3 and 4 demonstrated that *none* of these institutions sustained active resistance to white supremacy in Rhodesia. Now their posture is "reminiscent" of

83. Department of State, *Country Reports on Human Rights Practices for 1986* and *Country Reports on Human Rights Practices for 1988* (Washington, D.C.: U.S. Government Printing Office, 1987 and 1989); Africa Watch, *Zimbabwe*.

84. See the chapters by Larry Diamond and Naomi Chazan in *Democracy in Developing Countries*, ed. Diamond, Linz, and Lipset.

85. Richard Sklar, "Reds and Rights: Zimbabwe's Experiment," *Issue* 14 (1985): 31.

Rhodesia's tradition of acquiescence. In Zimbabwe they lack the resources, the will, or the interorganizational alliances to challenge abuses
of state power.[86] The government-controlled media practice self-
censorship, have rarely taken a critical stand on security issues, and are
pro-ZANU in their news coverage and editorials;[87] labor is strictly controlled by the regime;[88] the intelligentsia has taken a low profile; the
business community and white commercial farmers have generally supported the regime's security policy; and the handful of voluntary associations with an abiding interest in human rights have had little impact.
Unlike its counterpart in Northern Ireland, Zimbabwe's settler population has become relatively marginal on issues of internal security but the
views of whites do vary. In rural areas vulnerable to insurgent attacks
white residents have supported exceptional security measures; settlers
most closely associated with the old Rhodesian Front have opposed
such measures, including the state of emergency, as unnecessary. The
views of the black population are difficult to gauge, absent public opinion surveys. The electorate's support for the ruling party in the 1985
election cannot be used to infer levels of support for particular policies.
But it does appear that public support for the regime's security policies
is considerably stronger than in white-ruled Rhodesia, insofar as the
population perceives that the security system acts in its interests.

In short, pressure groups rarely organize around issues of law and order in Zimbabwe. Neither urban elites nor grass-roots organizations
have consistently pressed for liberalization and instead tend to defer to
official interpretations of security requirements. The rare expressions of
dissent and organized protests by students, workers, and political parties
have been equated with subversion and punished.[89]

If urban groups are atomized and quiescent, what of the rural areas?
The mobilization thesis discussed at the beginning of the chapter as-

86. On other African nations, see Jean François Bayart, "Civil Society in Africa," in
Political Domination in Africa, ed. P. Chabal (Cambridge: Cambridge University Press,
1986).
87. Occasional criticisms of security practices have appeared in the *Bulawayo Chronicle,* the *Financial Gazette,* and *MOTO.*
88. See Lloyd Sachikonye, "State, Capital, and Trade Unions," in *Transition,* ed.
I. Mandaza; and Ministry of Labour, Manpower Planning, and Social Welfare, *Labour
and Economy,* report of the National Trade Unions Survey (Harare: Government Printer,
1984); see also the restrictive Labor Relations Act of 1985, no. 16.
89. In 1988 and 1989 university students protesting governmental and party corruption and authoritarianism clashed with police; the Minister of Home Affairs accused the
students and faculty of "undermining the state" and "subversion" (*Bulawayo Chronicle,*
14 October 1988). After the October 1989 confrontation the University of Zimbabwe was
closed indefinitely.

sumes that popular activism in the countryside during a successful guerrilla struggle will continue under a new regime. Zimbabwe's political
inheritance, according to Cliffe, is "a generation that has been vigorously involved in politics and organizing, has undergone extensive political education and has become used to challenging authority and to
making things happen." [90] However accurately it describes rural areas toward the end of the Rhodesian war, this statement has a decidedly hollow ring in contemporary Zimbabwe, mainly because the regime has
largely deactivated and marginalized those forces since independence. [91]
The contrast with Northern Ireland could not be greater: almost inert in
Zimbabwe, civil society is vibrant in Northern Ireland (as Chapter 7
shows).

Since independence, one human rights body has consistently opposed
repressive practices: the Catholic Commission for Justice and Peace,
which is affiliated with the Catholic Bishops' Conference. Originally
working behind the scenes in the 1970s, the commission publicized its
findings when it failed to get results through private representations to
ministers. Today the commission supports the Government and describes
its approach as private constructive engagement with the authorities.
After the commission sent a series of confidential reports on human
rights violations to the prime minister, the Government investigated and
took corrective action in some particular cases of beating, rape, torture,
and killing. [92] In defending human rights, the commission is undoubtedly
the most successful private group. Yet it takes a piecemeal approach and
has rarely pressed for changes in the agencies responsible for repression
or in the arsenal of security legislation. [93] It has had a limited impact
overall on human rights in the country.

Reinforcing the acquiescent tendencies of Zimbabwe's civil society is
the country's authoritarian political culture, anchored in ninety years of
settler rule. [94] Long schooled in intolerance, the population is inclined to
suspect opponents and to equate dissent with subversion or treason.
This cultural legacy from the old regime meshes with the intolerant side

90. Lionel Cliffe, "Zimbabwe's Political Inheritance," in *Zimbabwe's Inheritance,* ed.
C. Stoneman (New York: St. Martins, 1981), p. 31.
91. Astrow, *Lost Its Way?*
92. *Sunday Mail,* 8 June 1986.
93. One exception was its call in 1982 to repeal regulations indemnifying the security
forces (*Sunday Mail,* 25 July 1982). In 1989, it called for an end to the state of emergency
and cited increasing abuses by the police and the Minister of Home Affairs (*Financial Gazette,* 4 August 1989).
94. Neera Chandhoke, "The Prospects for Liberal Democracy in Zimbabwe," *Indian
Political Science Review* 17, no. 1 (January 1983): 52–64.

of the political culture that emerged out of the guerrilla campaign and was imported into the state by the new elite.[95] In other words, the marriage of the dominant settler cultural legacy with the insurgent subculture invites authoritarian outcomes under the new order.

Unlike contemporary Northern Ireland where the British Government has sought—albeit unsuccessfully—to nurture a more consensual political culture, Zimbabwe lacks a comparable force. It is not so surprising, therefore, that many of the democratic values and institutions enshrined in the constitution during the Lancaster House settlement have failed to thrive in the existing relatively authoritarian milieu. Instead of tolerance for opposition, disposition to compromise, support for basic political rights, and mutual trust and accommodation among various political, civic, and communal forces, ethnic distrust and intolerance of all opposition have typified the first decade under the new order.

As noted in Chapter 1, revalorizing an inherited political culture and strengthening civil society can promote the process of democratization and help check executive power and repression by the security apparatus. Yet in Zimbabwe this apparatus has been instrumental in ensuring the passivity of civic institutions since 1980. The balance of power between the state and civil society in Northern Ireland is, as we shall see, radically different.

THE MAGNITUDE OF THE SECURITY PROBLEM

Immediately after independence Zimbabwe's future was uncertain, like that of any country emerging from the ruins of a protracted guerrilla war. Managing the fifty thousand ex-guerrillas and fifteen thousand Rhodesian security forces was a delicate undertaking. Would these forces accept the new order or engage in recriminations? White and black political opponents might challenge the new regime. Would the disaffected segments of the white and black communities accept their exclusion from power?[96] Finally, Pretoria's response to ZANU's electoral victory was of concern to the fledgling state. Would South Africa intervene, directly or indirectly, to subvert the new order?

A common problem faced by governments succeeding authoritarian regimes is the residual power of former political and security elites; their

95. Sithole, "Stable Democracy," p. 248.
96. To ease the fears of minority groups, the prime minister announced a reconciliation policy, which included the appointment of white and black opposition figures to Cabinet posts.

machinations in many nations have aborted the transition to democracy. This problem might be particularly vexing in postsettler societies where settlers were long accustomed to special rights and privileges. A striking feature of independent Zimbabwe is the political eclipse of the old settler elite; the contrast with Northern Ireland could not be sharper (see Chapter 7). Like their counterparts in postcolonial Kenya, Senegal, and Zambia, Zimbabwe's whites have retained their economic privileges and a measure of economic leverage while losing their previous military and political power.[97] Most of the remaining whites seem reconciled to black majority rule and the demise of the caste system. The level of racial tension is remarkably low, although a significant number of whites disapprove of specific policies, continue to harbor prejudicial attitudes toward blacks, and talk longingly of the Lost Cause.[98] A few whites have been involved in spying and sabotage for South Africa, but generally the white community has presented no threat to Zimbabwe's Government.

Since 1980 the regime has had to contend with a variety of security problems from both domestic sources and the neighboring South African giant. The incidents include an explosion at ZANU party headquarters, the discovery of arms cached on the property of a rival party, an unsuccessful armed attack on the prime minister's residence, incursions by South African-sponsored rebels, desertions from the army by disaffected ex-ZIPRA soldiers, the destruction of aircraft at Thornhill base, and, since June 1987, attacks inside Zimbabwe by rebels fighting the Mozambican Government (who are retaliating against Zimbabwe for its military aid to the regime in Mozambique).[99]

To destabilize Zimbabwe, South Africa has used economic and military pressure, although its involvement has been minor in comparison to its devastating assaults on Angola and its destabilization of Mozam-

97. Marshall Murphree, "Whites in Black Africa," *Ethnic and Racial Studies* 1, no. 2 (April 1978): 154–74. Whites' economic power in Zimbabwe comes from their control of capital, skills, and productive land. In 1987, 60 percent of the economy remained in private, largely white hands, and 34 percent of all farmland was owned by whites (down from 42 percent at independence); only 10 percent of the country's large-scale farmers and about a dozen of the top two hundred business executives were blacks.

98. These observations are based in part on the author's field research in 1982–1983 and 1987 and articles on Zimbabwe's whites in the *Los Angeles Times,* 9 September 1985 and the *Washington Post,* national weekly ed., 7 December 1987; on the "declining significance of race" in Zimbabwe, see Marshall Murphree, "Odds On Zimbabwe," *Leadership* 5, no. 5 (1986): 24–28; cf. David Caute, *Under the Skin: The Death of White Rhodesia* (Harmondsworth: Penguin, 1983).

99. Official figures on casualties from attacks inside Zimbabwe by the Mozambique National Resistance from June 1987 to April 1989: 335 civilians killed and 280 wounded; 22 security troops killed and 44 wounded; 29 insurgents killed, 5 wounded, and 45 captured (*Washington Post,* 5 June 1989).

bique. The regional Leviathan has initiated several commando attacks on offices of the African National Congress (ANC) in Zimbabwe. But its attacks are also designed to punish the Mugabe Government for its strident criticism of apartheid and its demands for international sanctions and more generally to foment insecurity in the country.[100] Pretoria has trained and armed an unknown number of former Rhodesians at bases in the northern Transvaal and has sent some on sabotage missions into Zimbabwe.[101] The most spectacular incident was a commando raid on an office of the ANC in Harare on 19 May 1986.

Low-level insurgency troubled the western region of the country (Matabeleland) from 1982 to 1988—numerous incidents of rape, murder, torture, beating, armed robbery, kidnapping, and the destruction of schools, buses, and state property. Although the insurgents' actions often appeared random, their choice of targets seemed designed to pressure the Government at home and embarrass it abroad. Their victims included ZANU party officials and members, Government officials, white farmers, foreign tourists, and black civilians accused of supporting the regime or informing on the insurgents.[102]

Reliable figures on the extent of rebel activity are difficult to come by. The leading security official in Zimbabwe estimated that the number of insurgents operating in the country dropped from approximately three hundred in 1984 to under thirty by mid-1987.[103] Officials have presented statistics on the incidence of insurgent attacks during parliamentary debates in order to justify renewals of the state of emergency; these figures (in Table 3) should be treated cautiously, since neither the sources nor their method of compilation has been disclosed.

---

100. The ANC uses Zimbabwe as a route to infiltrate South Africa but has no military bases in Zimbabwe (Stephen Davis, *Apartheid's Rebels* [New Haven: Yale University Press, 1987]); see also Joseph Hanlon, *Beggar Your Neighbors: Apartheid Power in Southern Africa* (Bloomington: Indiana University Press, 1986).
101. Robert Davies and Dan O'Meara, "Total Strategy in Southern Africa: An Analysis of South African Regional Policy since 1978," *Journal of Southern African Studies* 11 (April 1985): 195. Zimbabwe's Security minister stated in 1984 that half of the four hundred rebels captured in the previous two years admitted to having been trained in South Africa (*Guardian*, 1 August 1984).
102. According to the Security minister, insurgents killed 101 ZANU members from 1982 through October 1985 (*Herald*, 3 November 1985).
103. Minister of State for Security, *Washington Post*, 23 June 1984; *Herald*, 14 May 1987. Insurgents inside the country during 1982–1983 were estimated to number close to one thousand (Frederick Ehrenreich, "The Zimbabwe Defense Force: Capabilities and Problems" [Paper presented at the African Studies Association meeting, New Orleans, November 1985], p. 30); an estimated eight thousand to twenty-five thousand MNR rebels have been operating in Mozambique.

TABLE 3   INCIDENCE OF INSURGENT ACTIVITY

	Killings	Rapes	Armed Robberies	Sightings[a]	Contacts[b]	Insurgents Killed	Insurgents Captured
13 July– 23 Dec. 1983	75	16	284	537	175	—	—
24 Dec. 1983– 20 June 1984	45	37	253	670	191	500 (1982–84)	—
21 June 1984– 3 Jan 1985	58	96	288	839	175	—	—
4 Jan.– 5 May 1985	29	26	139	432	61	—	—
19 July 1985– 22 Jan. 1986	103	57	263	889	96	75 (1985)	85 (1985)
23 Jan.– 15 July 1986	57	46	104	552	71	68 (1986)	15 (1986)
20 Jan.– 14 July 1987[c]	42	22	80	—	—	46 (1987)	—
15 July– 21 Dec. 1987	35	—	—	—	—	—	—
22 Dec. 1987– 12 July 1988	41	—	—	—	—	—	—
13 July 1988– 23 Jan. 1989	93	4	32	40	—	—	21
25 Jan.– 24 July 1989	80	—	22	34	14	3	17
Total	658	304	1,465	3,993	783	—	—

SOURCES: Figures on insurgent activity, sightings, and contacts (presented by the Minister of Home Affairs during biannual parliamentary debates on renewal of the state of emergency) in Assembly *Debates* (Harare: Government Printer); figures for insurgent deaths and captives for October 1982 to October 1984 provided by the Minister of State for Security in *The Herald*, 2 October 1984; for 1985 and 1986 by the police in *The Herald*, 8 January 1987; and for 1987 by the Minister of State for Security in *The Herald*, 22 December 1987.
NOTE: Empty cells reflect incomplete source data.
[a]Sighting of one or more insurgents by civilians or security forces.
[b]Direct military contact between insurgents and security forces.
[c]Figures not available for 16 July 1986 to 19 January 1987.

Any assessment of security threats must take into account the coercive capacities of the parties involved and the scope of popular support for the challengers and the authorities.[104] In the first eight years after Zimbabwe's independence, insurgents failed to penetrate throughout the country or garner widespread support; they had limited material resources, and the destruction and casualties they inflicted were minute compared to those in the final years of the Rhodesian war (when an av-

104. On the balance between regime and insurgents' capacities, see Ted Robert Gurr, *Why Men Rebel* (Princeton: Princeton University Press, 1970), chaps. 8 and 9.

erage of five hundred deaths occurred every month).[105] Zimbabwe has hardly faced a crisis "which affects the whole population and constitutes a threat to the organized life of the community," as the Home Affairs minister claimed in 1982.[106] Other officials have frequently echoed such alarmist statements, which still others have contradicted. A 1984 report by ZANU's Central Committee described insurgency as nothing more than an irritant or "military nuisance." [107] Even at the height of dissident attacks in early 1983 the Security minister dismissed them as mere "teething problems": "This country is already more stable than it was before independence...there are no problems...now which threaten state power." [108] A different impression was left two years later (when the situation had visibly improved), as the Minister of State for Defense told Parliament:

> If we were to release to the public [information about] everything that happens in all our operational areas there would be more alarm and despondency among Zimbabweans, and they would think they were living in hell. So we want to keep these things to ourselves.[109]

Government statements have therefore vacillated between assurances of stability and tranquility and attempts to arouse public awareness and vigilance regarding the nefarious elements threatening the nation. The disparity in official comments about the severity of security problems stems from the regime's twin aims of justifying repressive measures and convincing the public that the authorities are in full control.

Intellectuals, church leaders, human rights bodies, and the press have occasionally questioned the need for draconian measures but rarely as incisively as in the *Sunday Mail*'s editorial of 12 May 1985:

> There is visible peace all over the country, even in Matabeleland, despite dissidents and bandits. . . . The dissidents in this country and their insignificant number are a fleabite compared with insurgents and their activities in many other countries that deal with them by other means than a state of emergency. . . . In addition, the unpleasant irony and contradiction of a government of former freedom fighters perpetuating the very state of emergency that was contrived and used by a colonial regime to fight against them... must be brought to an end.

105. *Africa Contemporary Record,* 1982–1983, p. B 879.
106. Assembly *Debates,* vol. 5, 13 July 1982, col. 629.
107. Zimbabwe African National Union, "Central Committee Report," presented to the party's second congress, Harare, 8 August 1984, p. 10.
108. Interview, *Commerce,* April 1983, p. 5.
109. Assembly *Debates,* vol. 12, 13 August 1985, col. 434.

To this logic the Government responded in two ways: the existence and the use of exceptional powers have been responsible for bringing the insurgent problem under control; and such powers remain necessary to ensure that the insurgents "do not become as systematically organized as UNITA [in Angola] and the MNR [in Mozambique]," as Mugabe put it.[110] Reminiscent of the Rhodesian era, the executive uses both increases and decreases in the incidence of insurgent activity to justify the continuance of emergency powers: an increase is a signal to intensify the use of these powers and a decrease is "an indication" that these measures "have been effective."[111]

THE POLITICS OF SECURITY

One major theme of this chapter is that the security problems facing the country did not preordain the structure and operations of Zimbabwe's coercive machinery. In fact, without prejudicing national security, liberalization in Zimbabwe could include the following changes:

- ending the protracted state of emergency;
- redrafting security legislation;
- reorganizing the police, military, and intelligence service;
- strengthening Parliament and the judiciary and creating separate oversight bodies to monitor and ensure greater accountability of the security agencies.

Countering this argument, authorities advance a host of security imperatives that necessitate unreconstructed coercive institutions, repressive legislation, and the continued state of emergency. The dominant external imperative is defense of the country against South African aggression. Government ministers maintain that the situation in Zimbabwe will never be normal until the South African conflict is resolved and its threat to Zimbabwe removed. Tampering with the coercive order would only deepen the country's vulnerability to Pretoria. Similarly, domestic conditions serve to justify exceptional arrangements. If not for the state of emergency, a former Minister of Home Affairs told me,

110. "Interview: Robert Mugabe," *Africa Report,* January–February 1986, p. 75.
111. Minister of Home Affairs, Assembly *Debates,* vol. 11, 13 November 1984, col. 696.

"we'd be forced to act illegally." [112] Analyzing the internal situation at independence, Sithole boldly articulates the imperatives thesis:

> A premature dismantling of the coercive instruments of the former Rhodesian state was ill-advised. Such a step would have created a power vacuum deliciously attractive to the various centers of power already armed to step in. The alternative to maintaining the instruments of the former Rhodesian state was to create new ones in their place. [113]

This argument has several pitfalls. It assumes but does not demonstrate that armed groups such as ZIPRA guerrillas and Rhodesian security forces were in fact prepared to "step in" and overthrow the new regime. Even if this assertion is valid—making a "premature dismantling" of repressive institutions ill advised at the outset of ZANU rule—it does not account for the subsequent preservation and fortification of those institutions. Finally, it fails to distinguish a state's coercive requirements (for domestic order and state survival) from acts of repression designed to achieve various extrasecurity goals.

My critique raises larger analytical issues as well. Frequently proffered in nations with acute or chronic security problems, the security-imperatives thesis has intoxicating appeal. Security exigencies often appear to be an independent influence on, or the driving force of, state action. This formula is unidimensional and deterministic. First, governments facing comparable security threats may respond in markedly different ways. [114] Second, levels of repression do not necessarily correlate with the magnitude of security problems and may instead be inversely related. Cross-national data on the frequency of events of insurgency and governmental sanctions suggest that such inverse relationships are rather common. [115] In some cases the disjunction has been especially wide. In Stalinist Russia, for instance, the epidemic of terror during the Great Purge of the 1930s occurred as stability increased. [116] Some societies facing a mortal threat to national security have responded less repressively than others where the threats have been markedly less serious, as a study of twenty Latin American nations found.

---

112. Interview, 10 June 1987.
113. Sithole, "Stable Democracy," p. 240.
114. See the analysis of Israel, South Africa, and Northern Ireland in Anthony Mathews, *Freedom, State Security, and the Rule of Law: Dilemmas of Apartheid Society* (Berkeley: University of California Press, 1986), chap. 12.
115. C. Taylor and D. Jodice, eds., *World Handbook of Political and Social Indicators* (New Haven: Yale University Press, 1983).
116. Carl Friedrich and Zbigniew Brzezinski, *Totalitarian Dictatorship and Autocracy* (New York: Praeger, 1956), pp. 137ff.

Paraguay . . . was one of the least violent nations in Latin America during the fifties and sixties—but it was also the most repressive. Colombia, among the least repressive, was one of the most violent countries.[117]

This divergence suggests that authorities dealing with security problems or political challenges have various options open to them. In dealing with political opponents, elites have "a number of choices, running the gamut from genuine toleration to total suppression. The decision against toleration and the [favoring] of repressive measures are a matter of *choice*."[118]

Elites' assessments of threats and decision making often include considerations that have little to do with security requirements per se. Extra-security factors are often decisive and include the bureaucratic interests of the security agencies, the political goals of the executive, and the elites' commitment to human rights.[119] A regime may attempt to convert real or perceived threats into opportunities: it may engage in "exaggerating, dramatizing, and even inventing" problems and threats in order to enhance its authority, generate support for political initiatives, silence dissent, or legitimate the repression of opponents.[120] A graphic illustration of this dynamic is the political purge.[121]

Clearly, a regime may reap political advantages from implementing policies it ascribes to national security. The present discussion centers on the matrix of official perceptions, interests, and goals that shaped the Zimbabwe regime's reactions to actual security problems from 1980 to 1988.

Guerrilla movements are notoriously difficult for state elites to handle both effectively and sensitively. Misperception of the roots of rebellion, poor intelligence, and a blind faith in the wisdom of using the iron fist often characterize a regime's reactions. The standard response to armed challenges is brute force, denial that the insurgents have popular sup-

---

117. Ernest Duff and John McCamant, *Violence and Repression in Latin America* (New York: Free Press, 1976), p. 201.

118. Otto Kirchheimer, *Political Justice* (Princeton: Princeton University Press, 1961), p. 419.

119. See Nicole Ball, *Security and Economy in the Third World* (Princeton: Princeton University Press, 1988), chap. 2.

120. David Brown, "Sieges and Scapegoats: The Politics of Pluralism in Ghana and Togo," *Journal of Modern African Studies* 21, no. 3 (September 1983): 459.

121. See Walter D. Connor, "The Manufacture of Deviance: The Case of the Soviet Purge, 1936–1938," *American Sociological Review* 37 (August 1972): 403–13; Roy Medvedev, *Let History Judge* (New York: Vintage, 1973); Sidney Greenblatt, "Campaigns and the Manufacture of Deviance in Chinese Society," in *Deviance and Social Control in Chinese Society*, ed. A. Wilson, S. Greenblatt, and R. Wilson (New York: Praeger, 1977).

port, and dismissal of their grievances as unfounded or as cloaking ulterior motives.

Initially in Zimbabwe there was some difference of opinion in official circles over the proper response to the rebels in Matabeleland:

> A number of [Mugabe's] prominent colleagues argued strongly against using the military in a punitive way, and favoring [*sic*] continued attempts at political conciliation. . . . The Army leadership argued the case to put down the insurrection in Matabeleland by all means possible.[122]

The army prevailed, apparently with the help of pressure from ZANU radicals. This resulted, according to Hodder-Williams, in a "conscious, Central Committee approved, policy of confrontation in strength."[123] Political concessions to ZAPU were seen as unwarranted;[124] Mugabe flatly announced, "The solution in Matabeleland is a military one."[125] Some ZANU leaders did continue to favor the use of the carrot to deal with political opponents and armed insurgents, but the hard-liners overshadowed them.[126] After the coercive approach of 1982–1985 had sufficiently subdued the political opposition in Matabeleland, a more conciliatory approach was pursued, culminating in the 1987 unity accord (discussed below).

As in many societies troubled by guerrilla movements, Zimbabwe's opposition parties and their supporters—not the insurgents—suffered most from the regime's counterinsurgency campaign. At the political fringes, members of Bishop Muzorewa's United African National Council and Ian Smith's white Conservative Alliance party were detained and harassed for alleged "subversive activity."[127] Both parties were accused of fomenting dissidence and having suspicious links to South Africa. Increasingly marginalized, the UANC was disbanded in 1986 and in September 1987 Parliament voted—legally, under the constitution—to

122. *Africa Contemporary Record,* 1982–1983, p. B 886.
123. Richard Hodder-Williams, "Conflict in Zimbabwe: The Matabeleland Problem," *Conflict Studies,* no. 151 (1983): 19, 17; see also *Africa Confidential,* 11 December 1985.
124. Michael Clough, "Whither Zimbabwe?" CSIS *Africa Notes,* 15 November 1983.
125. *The Observer,* 15 April 1984; see also his remarks in Parliament (Assembly *Debates,* vol. 7, 13 July 1983, col. 393). Ironically, Ian Smith criticized the ZANU Government for "falling into the same trap" as his regime did: "The real fault which this Government is making is that they are trying to use military force to solve a political problem. . . . It did not work before when we were trying to solve our problem" (Assembly *Debates,* vol. 6, 19 January 1983, col. 872).
126. Stoneman and Cliffe, *Zimbabwe,* p. 86.
127. UANC leader Bishop Abel Muzorewa was detained without charge for ten months in 1983–1984 and released on the recommendation of the Detainees' Review Tribunal.

abolish the twenty reserved white seats. Their vote sounded the death knell of organized white opposition in the country and left only one opposition party, ZAPU.

The Zimbabwe African People's Union was ZANU's traditional rival. The longstanding bitter relations between the two parties stemmed partly from ethnic antagonisms. The ethnic cornerstone of ZANU is the Shona-speaking community; ZAPU derives its support largely from the Ndebele. After ZANU's breakaway from ZAPU in 1963, violence followed for two years and flared sporadically during the guerrilla war in the 1970s. ZAPU had difficulty accepting its defeat in the 1980 election; many within the party believed ZANU won power unfairly. Animosity was particularly acute among former guerrillas of the Zimbabwe People's Revolutionary Army (ZIPRA), linked to ZAPU.

Some analysts claim that this long history of internecine bitterness sentenced ZANU and ZAPU to a confrontation after independence.[128] Yet conflict between the two parties was not inevitable. Their political orientations were not substantially different, and their distinct ethnic bases by no means made political rapprochement impossible. Much depended on the way in which the regime and ZAPU interpreted and handled unfolding events. Immediately after independence in 1980, Mugabe moved to include ZAPU figures in his Cabinet, including the party's leader, Joshua Nkomo, who accepted the post of Minister of Home Affairs.

The initial reconciliation was shattered by a series of events that raised doubts about ZAPU's patriotism and commitment to national unity. First, armed clashes occurred in 1980 and 1981 between former guerrillas of ZIPRA and ZANLA (ZAPU's military wing, the Zimbabwe African National Liberation Army). Approximately three hundred former ZIPRA guerrillas died in one encounter in February 1981 in Bulawayo. Second, both ZANLA and ZIPRA loyalists had hidden arms as an insurance policy against the future; in February 1982 arms caches were discovered on ZAPU property. Alleging that the weapons were intended for a coup, the regime arrested former ZIPRA military officers, fired several ZAPU Cabinet ministers, and confiscated ZAPU-owned properties. According to Evans, the Government "stage-managed" this incident in order to further "ZANU's drive for supremacy" in the military: "the decapitation of the ZAPU-ZIPRA leadership in the Government and the ZNA [Army] had much more in common with the

128. Sithole, "Stable Democracy."

consolidation of Shona ethnic domination within the military, than with ZANU fear of a Ndebele coup." [129] The punitive reaction to the arms discovery led four thousand former ZIPRA men to desert from the army and set the stage for the Matabeleland conflict. Shortly after a series of guerrilla attacks in Matabeleland in 1982, ZAPU was accused of creating and commanding the armed resistance. The Minister of State for Defense had no doubts as to the rebels' sponsor: "Dissidents do not operate in a vacuum; they are ex-ZIPRA and their political allegiance is to Nkomo, and their political philosophy is ZAPU." He elaborated:

> A systematic programme was launched. . . to organize ZAPU followers into actively supporting politically motivated acts of banditry aimed at disrupting civil administration and sabotaging development projects and creating a state of armed revolt in those parts of Zimbabwe where ZAPU had significant political followers. [130]

Most official statements characterized the insurgents as politically motivated. According to the Minister of Home Affairs, "all but a few" were politically inspired and their acts were "aimed at furthering the interests of ZAPU." [131] But the dissidents were also described as antisocial, criminal malcontents. An official publication attempted to depoliticize the problem: "The acts committed are acts against humanity, not against a political enemy. The perpetrators are not political weapons— nor even soldiers. They are criminals committing criminal acts in a law-abiding and constitutionally legitimate country." [132] A revealing statement by the Security minister, however, threw all characterizations into question: "It is, of course, not possible to properly determine the motivation and loyalties of the majority" of dissidents. [133] Whether or not it viewed the insurgents as politically motivated, the Government flatly rejected the legitimacy of their grievances.

Despite considerable speculation, the origins, supply, organization, and objectives of the insurgents remain somewhat obscure. Their resources and external alliances paled by comparison with other armed movements in the region (MNR in Mozambique, UNITA in Angola,

129. Evans, "Gukurahundi," pp. 13, 14. It has been argued that the caches were made "not as a basis for a coup aimed at overthrowing the government but as an insurance policy against the future" (Hodder-Williams, "Matabeleland," p. 9).
130. *Herald,* 4 February 1983, and *Sunday Mail,* 10 March 1983.
131. Assembly *Debates,* vol. 11, 7 May 1985, col. 1939.
132. Ministry of Information, Posts, and Telecommunications, *A Chronicle of Dissidency in Zimbabwe* (Harare: Government Printer, August 1984), p. 39.
133. *Herald,* 2 February 1984.

ANC in South Africa, SWAPO in Namibia). They operated in small bands loyal to no high command and were divided over the question of accepting South African support. With no single ideological program, they were motivated by a variety of aims and grievances.[134] One writer describes the armed attacks as a "reflex reaction, not a conscious policy with considered aims."[135] The main demands must be distilled from literature these bands distributed in villages or left at the scene of attacks and from comments captured rebels made during interrogations and court trials. Among their grievances were the regime's alleged retrenchment from socialist goals; governmental favoritism of the Shona over the Ndebele; the affluence of white farmers amid landless peasants; and the regime's repression of ZAPU. Their literature declared, "Zimbabwe is still not free" and "Down with ZANU," and announced the existence of a "second liberation war." Generally the grievances revolved around political and economic problems although the insurgents also tried to mobilize and exploit ethnic resentment against the Shona. Still, these rebels made no concerted attempt to organize or politicize the civilian population, which helps to explain why they frequently used brute force to compel villagers' cooperation.

In April 1988 the Government offered insurgents an amnesty—one result of the ZANU-ZAPU unity accord—and 113 accepted the offer. Interviews with a group of 43 former rebels confirmed some of the goals and demands outlined above. In part they opposed the regime's ethnic repression in Matabeleland, as one insurgent commander declared: "We took to the bush to protest the murders and harassment of our people by the [ZANU] party army." Another stated, "Our actions came out of serious crimes committed by the Government."[136] Others demanded land and jobs, the return of confiscated ZIPRA property, an end to official corruption, a more vigorous official commitment to the liberation of South Africa, the release of captured insurgents, stronger Marxist-Leninist policies, and pensions for all former guerrillas. When 64 former dissidents threatened to resume their campaign in June 1988, it was because the Government had failed to meet their grievances: the lack of employment topped the list. One former commander insisted, "If we are not assured of our socio-economic destiny, nothing will stop us

---

134. "Bruising the Dissidents," *MOTO,* March 1983.
135. Hodder-Williams, "Matabeleland," p. 15.
136. Quoted in Andrew Meldrum, "An Amnesty for Unity," *Africa Report,* July–August 1988, p. 41, and *Times,* 1 June 1988.

from going back to the bush."[137] (Approximately 25,000 former ZIPRA and ZANLA guerrillas were unemployed as of March 1988.)[138]

Among the terms of the amnesty was a pardon to members of the security forces and to ZANU's youth wing, who had been sentenced or convicted of crimes and abuses of human rights; seventy-five security personnel and youth-wing militants were released in June 1988.[139] Government officials told Africa Watch that security forces had to be pardoned in order to defuse discontent in their ranks; but whereas the dissidents who accepted the amnesty had not been charged with offenses, most of the security force members were serving sentences for crimes, some quite serious.[140] A similar pardon was not extended to those serving sentences for dissident-related crimes.

THE PACIFICATION OF ZAPU

Having had little success against the insurgents, the Zimbabwe authorities responded as have many others confronting guerrilla campaigns. They targeted those allegedly giving succor to the rebels: the ZAPU organization, party leaders, supporters, and inhabitants of Matabeleland, the affected area. The fact that the guerrillas operated in an area where ZAPU enjoys overwhelming popular support seemed to lend credence to the view that the party was in league with the rebels.

Prime Minister Mugabe declared that ZAPU, the United African National Council, and the Conservative Alliance "yielded dissident men who have resorted to subversion in order to overthrow ZANU and its Government."[141] He accused ZAPU not simply of giving moral support to the armed insurgents but also of training and funding them. It is significant, however, that the only top ZAPU official prosecuted by the Government (for assisting dissidents and plotting a coup), MP Sydney Malunga, was acquitted in July 1986 (other top ZAPU officials arrested and detained without charge were never brought to court). Instead of prosecuting party members for crimes, the authorities chose to disrupt ZAPU's political activities and stifle dissent. This record throws into question the regime's contention that the ZAPU leadership was involved

137. *Herald,* 16 June 1988.
138. *Herald,* 21 March 1988.
139. *Times,* 1 July 1988.
140. Africa Watch, *Zimbabwe,* pp. 22, 25.
141. Robert Mugabe, speech to the ZANU Women's League conference, 15 March 1984 (*Speeches and Documents of the First ZANU(PF) Women's League Conference,* Harare, 1984).

in subversive activities. Shils's study of Asia and Africa suggests that "open opposition parties in the new states are seldom dangerous to the ruling parties, either in open electoral campaigns or in parliamentary voting or in conspiratorial activities." In suppressing opposition parties, what the regime "reacts against is more an imputed subversive intention . . . rather than a factual probability of subversion." [142]

One minister argued that the arrest of some ZAPU officers was "evidence enough to warrant banning the party";[143] other officials threatened to ban ZAPU on numerous occasions. Ministers branded ZAPU a "dissident organization" and a "subversive organization," equating it with the South African-sponsored MNR in Mozambique and UNITA in Angola.[144] Why, then, did the Government not proscribe ZAPU? A ranking CIO official stated in 1983: "ZAPU is being left free until something drastic happens. . . . Banning it now can only unite the people in Matabeleland." [145] One Cabinet minister gave me this explanation in 1987:

> The banning of any party has not been on the agenda. Banning is against the spirit of the constitution, the right of political association. Instead we took strong measures against ZAPU leaders, putting pressure on the party as a whole and picking on individuals. We had good security reasons for banning ZAPU and legally good grounds to do it, but politically it's something we didn't want to do.[146]

In addition, a formal ban would almost certainly provoke a domestic outcry and international protests and would perhaps include a suspension of foreign aid and investment in the country. That the banning of a party may be counterproductive was abundantly evidenced in the 1960s and 1970s. Short of outright proscription, the Government made every effort to undermine ZAPU's ability to function as a political party. If sufficiently crippled, ZAPU might cease its opposition and the regime would avoid the possible fallout from a formal banning.

From 1982 to 1986 the Government waged a campaign to undermine ZAPU. Official harassment took various forms and occasionally precipitated freelance violence by militant ZANU supporters, like the Youth Brigades. ZAPU MPs and city councillors were detained or mysteriously disappeared. ZAPU meetings were closed, forcing members to meet in

142. Edward Shils, "Opposition in the New States of Asia and Africa," in *Center and Periphery: Essays in Macrosociology* (Chicago: University of Chicago Press, 1975), pp. 428–29, 436.
143. Minister of Mines, *Herald,* 7 March 1983.
144. *Herald,* 19 September 1985; 27 March and 19 April 1983; 22 September 1987.
145. CIO official, interview with author, 29 June 1983.
146. Former Minister of Home Affairs, interview with author, 10 June 1987.

private. Almost every party office was at some point closed by the authorities or torched by ZANU militants. Several ZAPU-linked firms were closed and ZAPU property confiscated without compensation. ZAPU members were forced to attend ZANU rallies and purchase ZANU membership cards.

The strategy of linkage the authorities used to associate ZAPU with the insurgents parallels the "destabilization alliance" it alleged between ZAPU and the South African Government.[147] By dramatizing the alleged connection between internal and external threats, the Zimbabwean regime, like its Rhodesian predecessor and so many others, sought to justify its treatment of domestic elements. One analyst notes that "a great temptation exists for governments to invoke national security in their defense by identifying domestic political opponents with the policies of some foreign state."[148] Although a number of individuals sympathetic to ZAPU have received training, arms, or other aid from within South Africa, the degree of involvement by the Pretoria regime itself remains obscure. The Permanent Secretary of Home Affairs himself made the distinction: "I don't know whether there is a connection between the South African authorities and dissidents, but they are receiving support from within South Africa. . . . I've never seen direct proof that the South African Government is funding them."[149] Moreover, no hard evidence has been presented to prove any pact between the ZAPU hierarchy and strategists in Pretoria. The CIO conceded in 1983 that "there is no connection between ZAPU *as a party* and South Africa";[150] none has since been established. Yet ministers persisted in claiming that ZAPU, South Africa, and the insurgents had forged a sinister alliance bent on overthrowing the regime.

For its part, ZAPU repeatedly proclaimed its innocence and condemned insurgents' attacks. Although some dissidents defined themselves as ZAPU's vanguard, this did not mean that they were ZAPU's creation. One observer argues that the "dissidents were not an intrinsic part of ZAPU's organization and strategy,"[151] and another concludes, "It is plain that the dissidents were *not* operating as part of ZAPU."[152] In

147. *Herald*, 26 February 1983.
148. Barry Buzan, *People, States, and Fear: The National Security Problem in International Relations* (Chapel Hill: University of North Carolina Press, 1983), p. 59.
149. Interview with author, 8 June 1987.
150. CIO official, interview with author, 29 June 1983; emphasis added.
151. Hodder-Williams, "Matabeleland," p. 20.
152. Terence Ranger, "Matabeleland since the Amnesty," *African Affairs* 88 (April 1989): 165.

fact, guerrillas harassed, beat, and killed ZAPU supporters and local party officers.[153]

Some security officials privately conceded that they did not know whether the ZAPU hierarchy gave its blessing to the insurgents;[154] some ministers also raised questions about the ZAPU–dissident link.[155] Yet the dominant official line persisted until the unity talks between the parties in 1986. To help explain the new interparty rapprochement one minister quipped, "ZAPU now realizes that dissident activity doesn't pay."[156] After the unity talks fell apart in 1987, however, the regime once again accused ZAPU of supporting the dissidents. The alleged connection may depend less on hard evidence than on the prevailing relations between ZANU and ZAPU.

ZAPU also experienced violent attacks by ZANU militants like the Youth Brigades.[157] In the months preceding the 1985 election, a wave of mass demonstrations by ZANU loyalists took place; the protesters demanded that ZAPU and UANC be banned and Nkomo hanged, that a one-party state be declared immediately, and that all non-ZANU civil servants be dismissed. The demonstrations frequently ended in vandalism or destruction of ZAPU offices and assaults on ZAPU supporters and officers, sometimes while the police stood by.[158] ZANU zealots also forced their opponents to attend ZANU rallies, and ZAPU supporters had difficulty obtaining permits for their own rallies.

Three years of violence and harassment against ZAPU had a cumulative crippling effect on its ability to organize and campaign in the 1985 election.[159] ZAPU nevertheless won all fifteen seats in Matabeleland. Despite its own strong showing in the election, the ruling party was sur-

153. One hundred to one hundred fifty ZAPU officials had been killed by mid-1984, as well as sixty-eight ZANU officials (Frank G. Wisner, Senior Deputy Assistant Secretary for African Affairs, Department of State, testimony on 24 May 1984 before the House Subcommittee on Africa, in *Zimbabwe: Four Years of Independence* [Washington, D.C.: U.S. Government Printing Office, 1984] p. 27).

154. CIO official, interview with author, June 1983; Permanent Secretary for Home Affairs, interview with author, 8 June 1987.

155. The Minister of Information, for instance, made the surprising comment in January 1984 that "ZIPRA elements are no longer in the field as bandits. Nor are Nkomo and other ZAPU leaders involved in the second phase of terrorism" (*Sunday Mail*, 29 January 1984).

156. Former Minister of Home Affairs, interview with author, 10 June 1987.

157. Jim Cason and Mike Fleshman, "Zimbabwe: Election Campaign Turns Bloody," *Africa News*, 28 January 1985.

158. Ibid.; Michelle Faul, "Mugabe's Election Maneuvers," *Africa Report* 30, no. 1 (January–February 1985).

159. International Human Rights Law Group, *Zimbabwe: Report on the 1985 General Elections* (Washington, D.C.: IHRLG, 1986).

prised and troubled by the remaining bedrock of regional support for ZAPU. After the election both disappearances and arrests of ZAPU supporters and officials accelerated, which encouraged a flood of defections to ZANU. The combination of mob violence, police arrests, and mass defections gave ZAPU little choice but to agree to unity talks with ZANU in late 1985. After the talks broke down in April 1987, all ZAPU meetings were banned and all its offices ordered closed. Now in complete disarray, the party was forced either to accept a merger with ZANU on the latter's terms or to vanish altogether from the political scene. It opted for the former; the two parties united in December 1987.

REPRESSION IN THE COUNTRYSIDE

Matabeleland is one of the poorest regions in Zimbabwe, and economic conditions there have declined markedly since independence. The region's rate of unemployment is higher than the national rate of 23 percent; economic development schemes have been stalled; and peasants' continuing hunger for land and discontent over the regime's minimalist land-reform policies are acute.[160] These conditions, coupled with the regime's harassment of ZAPU, have alienated the region's population from the central government.

Insurgents typically depend on the local population for food, clothing, shelter, and information. In Matabeleland there was naturally variation in the degree to which Ndebele villagers cooperated with insurgents by choice or by force, and in how they defined or identified with the insurgent cause. Some civilians distinguished "good" from "bad" dissidents, but the rebels' reputation for indiscriminate brutality seems to have discredited their campaign over time.[161] Some officials flatly claimed that villagers were either potential insurgents or voluntarily aided dissidents. Other observers maintained that popular sympathy for the rebels was low, and that civilians were interested primarily in regional peace and development.[162] Even the Home Affairs minister concluded in 1987 that the majority of people in the affected areas did not

160. Sam Moyo, "The Land Question," in *Transition,* ed. Mandaza; Nick Davies, "Zimbabwe Torn Apart by Old Issue of Land," *Guardian,* 24 March 1983; Fred Barnes, "Search and Destroy," *New Statesman,* 18 March 1983; Julie Frederikse, "Blood Feud in Zimbabwe," *The Progressive,* September 1983, pp. 34–36; *Africa Confidential,* 5 September 1984.
161. Ranger, "Matabeleland since the Amnesty."
162. Barnes, "Search and Destroy," p. 15; *Financial Times,* 18 May 1982; Stoneman and Cliffe, *Zimbabwe,* p. 47.

support the guerrillas.[163] Yet the actions of the security forces were driven by their presumption of the local population's guilt, rather common in counterinsurgency campaigns.

Like many other counterinsurgency forces operating in an ethnic enclave whose support they lack, the security forces in Matabeleland from 1982 to 1986 treated the civilian population roughly. Abuses by the security forces were often difficult to verify but followed a consistent pattern; independent investigations uncovered "incontrovertible evidence" of security forces' involvement in atrocities.[164] The army and CIO used mass detention, beating and heavy-handed interrogation of civilians, the burning of villagers' houses, arbitrary killing, and rape.[165] Amnesty International reported that many detainees were held for lengthy periods without regard to legal procedures; it also found evidence of "widespread" torture of suspects (e.g., electric shock and suffocation under water) by the police, CIO, and army from 1982 to 1985.[166] In 1989, an investigation by Africa Watch pointed to a "culture of torture" within these agencies, particularly the CIO.[167]

According to the International Commission of Jurists, "over 1,000 people, mostly unarmed civilians, were killed and many more tortured and beaten by the army in January and February" of 1983.[168] Other estimates numbered civilians killed between two thousand and three thousand.[169] According to Father Hebron Wilson, "some villages...were almost completely annihilated."[170] During this period, the authorities were inundated with detailed reports of brutality by security forces from eyewitnesses, wounded victims, community leaders, medical personnel,

163. *Herald,* 14 September 1987.
164. Zimbabwe Catholic Bishops' Conference statement, *Herald,* 30 March 1983; see also the citations below.
165. One local paper condemned "the increasing incidence of rape by soldiers in uniform out on operation" (*Bulawayo Chronicle,* 29 March 1984).
166. Amnesty International, *Detention;* see also David Caute, "Mugabe Brooks No Opposition," *The Nation,* 31 August 1985, p. 140; *Africa Confidential,* 11 December 1985.
167. Africa Watch, *Zimbabwe,* pp. 13, 43–54.
168. International Commission of Jurists, "Zimbabwe," *Review of the International Commission of Jurists* 30 (July 1983): 29. The figure was based on reports from rural hospitals, missions, and schools.
169. The U.S. State Department's estimate was more conservative: "Our Embassy provides the informed opinion that between 1,000 and 1,500 people have been killed in Matabeleland over the past three years. In addition, between 4,000 and 6,000 people have been abused in one way or another. Government security forces are probably responsible for the bulk of these depredations, with the dissidents and/or bandits culpable for the remainder" (Wisner, Department of State, *Zimbabwe,* p. 20).
170. "Zimbabwe: 5 Years Later," transcript of "60 Minutes" broadcast, CBS Television, 28 April 1985.

teachers, missionaries, and other independent sources. The cumulative weight and consistency of this evidence challenged the regime's denials of culpability. The report of the Zimbabwe Catholic Bishops' Conference stated that the regime had embarked on a "reign of terror":

> Methods which should be firm and just have degenerated into brutality and atrocity. . . . Violent reaction against dissident activity has, to our certain knowledge, brought about the maiming and death of hundreds and hundreds of innocent people who were neither dissidents nor collaborators. We are convinced by incontrovertible evidence that many wanton atrocities have been, and are still being, perpetrated. . . . It seems that the indemnity regulations issued in July 1982 may have given certain units of the security forces the impression that they are above and outside the law. . . . The facts point to a reign of terror caused by wanton killings, woundings, beatings, burnings, and rapings. . . . The innocent have no recourse or redress, for fear of reprisals.[171]

The military campaign of 1982–1983 was followed by a second siege of the region from February to April 1984. Food supplies were cut off to the five hundred thousand residents of southern Matabeleland, and civilians again fell prey to military repression.[172] Despite numerous civilian casualties, one report revealed, "there have been practically no guerrillas killed." [173]

On 2 April 1984, the Catholic Bishops' Conference again sent to Mugabe a detailed report chronicling army atrocities, which commented: "Commanders gave the impression that it is the policy of the army to make all the people in the area suffer because of the dissidents." It recommended that the Government begin "serious dialogue" with ZAPU and other opposition groups.[174]

The military's "reign of terror" in Matabeleland bore striking similarities to the ruthless operations of the Rhodesian forces during the 1970s. As an investigation by the Lawyers Committee for Human Rights concluded, "the Ndebeles have been subjected to a campaign of harassment and repression that has been scarcely distinguishable from the counterinsurgency campaign waged by the old white regime." [175]

The main unit deployed in the region from 1982 to 1984 was the controversial Fifth Brigade; it was supported by the Sixth Brigade, the Police Anti-Terrorist Unit, the commando battalion, and operatives of the Cen-

171. *Herald,* 30 March 1983.
172. *Sunday Times,* 8 April 1984.
173. *Africa Confidential,* 11 April 1984, p. 2.
174. *New York Times,* 16 April 1984.
175. Lawyers Committee, *Zimbabwe,* p. 2.

tral Intelligence Organization. The Fifth Brigade was highly politicized and loyal to the Government, poorly led, and palpably anti-Ndebele. Civilians, even police officers, and regular soldiers voiced complaints about the brutal exploits of the unit. Eyewitnesses to atrocities implicated the unit in testimony that the perpetrators spoke Shona and wore the brigade's distinctive red berets.[176] Tellingly, British military instructors retrained the discredited brigade in 1984; it was withdrawn from Matabeleland, its commanders replaced, and its troops tamed.

Like many other governments around the world, the Mugabe regime consistently dismissed general criticism of the security forces and reports of specific outrages as the propaganda of disingenuous elements. The prime minister called the allegations of Amnesty International "a heap of rubbish" and labeled the human-rights body "Amnesty Lies International."[177] (Since 1986 Amnesty International has not received permission to operate in Zimbabwe.) In response to criticisms from the Catholic Bishops' Conference, the Minister of Information called the bishops' account "irresponsible, contrived and propagandistic" and the prime minister branded the bishops "sanctimonious prelates" and ZAPU agents.[178] And the Minister of State for Defense labeled as "dissidents" those accusing the army of committing atrocities.[179] These comments reflect the Government's overriding presumption of the security forces' innocence. Mugabe's statement in Parliament in 1983 is telling:

> My knowledge is that anyone who is guilty of any irregularity, be it torture or anything, is subject to correction or discipline by his commanders. . . . In circumstances in which we find ourselves, tempers rise in the police because of the long hours which they work. They find themselves acting rather over-enthusiastically. We must sympathize with them rather than begin to criticize them. . . . What the courts regard as torture now might not have been torture in the days of Ian Smith . . . but because we are more liberal, we have a democratic order, any little scratch . . . is interpreted as torture. I think we must feel for those whose duty it is to give maximum security to the nation.[180]

Top officials have responded to the issue of civilian casualties in three ways: they have denied the security forces' culpability, blaming the dissidents instead; they have minimized the problem (e.g., "some innocent civilians get some bruising");[181] or they have suggested that civilians

176. International Commission of Jurists, "Zimbabwe."
177. *Herald,* 21 November 1985.
178. *Herald,* 30 March and 6 April 1983; 16 April 1984.
179. *Herald,* 25 April 1984.
180. Assembly *Debates,* vol. 7, 13 July 1983, cols. 397–98.
181. *Herald,* 4 February 1983.

were killed in "the crossfire" between the rebels and security forces. These claims fit the lexicon that the Rhodesian state used to deny wrongdoing and mask indiscriminate shooting. Rarely, however, have officials spoken as bluntly as Mugabe did to a crowd in Matabeleland: "We have to deal with this problem ruthlessly. Don't cry if your relatives get killed in the process."[182]

Internal inquiries by officials in the security forces and Home Affairs exonerated security personnel of wrongdoing.[183] One independent Committee of Inquiry into allegations of atrocities by security forces was appointed by the Government (in June 1983) and received a considerable amount of evidence from local people.[184] It never made its findings or recommendations public and appears to have had little impact on security practices or policy.

Like the Rhodesian Front Government before it, the ZANU regime apparently gave little consideration to the counterproductive effects of military repression in driving a wedge between civilians and the state and contributing to political instability. Military operations brought an atmosphere of fear and bitterness to Matabeleland and discredited the regime throughout the region. One report found the army "extremely unpopular" and another discerned widespread popular "disenchantment" with the central government.[185] ZANU's failure to win a single seat in the region in the 1985 election may be another indicator of popular alienation from the regime.

The intensity and character of state violence in Matabeleland were by no means constant from 1982 to 1987. Instead, cycles of repression and relaxation alternated within the context of an overall decline in violations of human rights. Each year after 1983 registered a lower incidence of repression than the previous year, in part through changing levels of involvement by different security forces. The blanket military violence of 1982–1985 gave way to a more selective approach by police and intelligence operatives in 1986–1987; consequently, abuses were attributed increasingly to the police and the CIO.[186]

182. Quoted in *Africa Contemporary Record,* 1982–1983, p. B 882.

183. *Herald,* 21 May and 10 April 1984.

184. Secretary of the Committee of Inquiry, *Herald,* 29 March 1984.

185. *Africa Confidential,* 27 March 1985, p. 5. Tony Rich, "Zimbabwe: Only Teething Troubles?" *The World Today* 39, no. 12 (December 1983): 501. The military campaign had "the effect of consolidating a divided province into a sullen antagonism to the dominant party and the majority tribe associated with it" (Hodder-Williams, "Matabeleland," p. 20).

186. Department of State, *Country Reports on Human Rights for 1988.*

ENTRENCHING ONE-PARTY RULE

Several factors help to account for repressive events in Matabeleland from 1982 to 1988. Part of the explanation centers on the composition and experiences of security personnel assigned to the region. In this category are the military's infrequent direct contact with insurgents, which led to soldiers' vicarious punishment of villagers who seemed uncooperative; the deployment of poorly trained and undisciplined units; and the intense ethnic hostility between primarily Shona military regiments and Ndebele civilians. The Fifth Brigade, in particular, seemed intent on convincing Ndebele villagers of their ethnic inferiority. Later, when Enos Nkala served as Minister of Home Affairs (mid-1985 through 1987), many of the police posts in Matabeleland were assigned to "virulently anti-ZAPU" officers.[187]

Reinforcing these specific contributing conditions is the essentialist factor, documented earlier in the chapter. Inherent systemic characteristics—an illiberal ethos, traditional (Rhodesian) decision-making processes, the lack of accountability—foster repressive outcomes in Zimbabwe.

Another part of the explanation has to do with the activities and signals coming from Government ministers. These elites do not appear to have orchestrated violence per se against ZAPU supporters and civilians; the security forces and ZANU militants acted with considerable autonomy in their encounters with civilians. But the regime was intent on destroying ZAPU, as manifested in the waves of harassment visited on the party: rallies banned, offices closed, leaders arrested. In addition, ministers and top officials in the CIO, police, and army took few steps to stop the violence. Instead, Cabinet members consistently blamed ZAPU and the insurgents for casualties, praised the "sterling" work of security forces, refused to take the initiative in holding security personnel accountable, and reacted bitterly to any public accusations of officially sponsored repression. In addition, the Government consistently encouraged the security agencies to follow a hard line in dealing with political opponents. This encouragement may neither explain particular incidents and waves of state violence nor suggest that top officials were directly responsible for specific abuses of power by rank-and-file personnel, but the regime undoubtedly created a climate that seemed to condone use of the iron fist.

187. Africa Watch, *Zimbabwe*, p. 41.

The larger thesis is that law and order has been pursued since independence in a manner consistent with, albeit not reducible to (because of genuine concerns with stability and order), ZANU's central political objectives. The repressive approach to the Matabeleland problem had a purposive dimension, a "conscious...policy of confrontation in strength," whereby the Government seized on genuine security problems and transformed them into opportunities.[188] One analyst concludes that the military's "brutal actions seemed sufficiently purposeful to indicate an intention to cripple, if not destroy, ZAPU's political infrastructure in Matabeleland."[189] Much of the security program therefore can be explained by the ruling party's grand design: to dominate the political landscape by subduing the opposition. The linchpin of that grand design was the creation of a one-party ZANU state.

Unilateral imposition of one-party rule would have violated the constitutional clause guaranteeing freedom of association, including the right to form and belong to political parties. Under the constitution (sect. 51), this provision was alterable prior to 1990 only with the consent of all one hundred MPs, and the Government waited until 1987 to begin to lay the formal groundwork for the one-party system.

Beginning in October 1985 ZANU and ZAPU held a series of ten meetings, with a view toward unification. Finally on 22 December 1987 the two parties merged under the banner of ZANU. On 31 December, Mugabe became the executive president of the country and Nkomo was appointed a senior minister without portfolio. Zimbabwe became the thirty-fifth African nation to embrace the one-party model, leaving ten multiparty states remaining on the continent.

Just as multiparty systems are not necessarily democratic in practice, a one-party state is not necessarily despotic. There is cross-national variation in one-party regimes, along a continuum from dictatorial to relatively open systems. Inherently restrictive to some degree, they can be structured to allow for the representation of various interests and popular participation. Like other African nations, the Zimbabwe Government maintains that one-party rule will be an unqualified blessing: it will promote genuine democracy, accord with Zimbabwe's traditional values, foster political stability and national unity, and undermine subversive forces. The text of the unity agreement proclaims that the merger of ZANU and ZAPU will promote "national unity, political stability,

188. Hodder-Williams, "Matabeleland," p. 17.
189. Rich, "Only Teething Troubles?" p. 501.

peace, law and order, social and economic development." [190] One-party rule has generally failed to produce these benefits elsewhere in postcolonial Africa. [191] How did the ZANU Government envisage its one-party system?

An article of faith in Zimbabwe's ruling circles is that the one-party state will promote national ethnic integration rather than factionalism, which a multiparty system allegedly fosters, particularly where political parties have ethnic, racial, or tribal bases. Yet the record shows that African one-party systems have performed poorly in managing communal divisions and promoting national unity. [192]

New nations commonly define dissent as sedition and criticism of the government as an attack on the nation, rejecting the concept of loyal opposition parties as a contradiction in terms. [193] A multiparty system does give the opposition a public forum within which to challenge government policy and embarrass executive officeholders. In their quest for political unanimity, many African ruling parties are acutely sensitive to such criticism. From 1980 to 1987 the ZANU Government dealt with political opposition in two ways: belittling it as unimportant or exaggerating its dangerousness. Mugabe claimed that under a one-party state, "we would not have this useless quibbling. . . . We want to avoid that useless exercise of opposing for the sake of opposing." [194] He called interparty rivalry "anathema to democracy"; it reflects "the politics of negativism." [195] Even more troubling, it "creates room for a mixture of subversives-cum-opportunists to plan more disunity and destabilization in the vain hope that one day they will achieve power." [196] One minister stated, "ZANU . . . rules this country. Anyone who challenges that is a dissident and should be dealt with." [197] On one occasion the minister

190. Text of unity agreement, *Herald,* 23 December 1987.
191. S. E. Finer, "The One-Party Regimes in Africa," *Government and Opposition* 2, no. 4 (July–October 1967): 491–509; W. Arthur Lewis, *Politics in West Africa* (Toronto: Oxford University Press, 1965); Shils, "Opposition"; Aristide Zolberg, *Creating Political Order: The Party-States of West Africa* (Chicago: Rand McNally, 1966), p. 36. See also James Coleman and Carl Rosberg, eds., *Political Parties and National Integration in Tropical Africa* (Berkeley: University of California Press, 1964), pp. 655–80.
192. Finer, "One-Party."
193. David Apter, "Some Reflections on the Role of a Political Opposition in New Nations," *Comparative Studies in Society and History* 4, no. 2 (January 1962): 154–68. It was a feature of early United States history, especially under the Federalist government (Seymour Martin Lipset, *The First New Nation: The United States in Historical and Comparative Perspective* [New York: Basic, 1963], pp. 39, 43).
194. Interview with Robert Mugabe, *MOTO,* October 1984.
195. Mugabe, speech to Women's Conference; *Times,* 7 April 1981.
196. Mugabe, speech to Women's Conference.
197. Minister of Home Affairs, *Christian Science Monitor,* 2 October 1987.

drew an explicit connection between opposition to one-party rule and the official labeling of opponents as subversives: "The Ndebeles would benefit more by entering into unity with other tribes because they would no longer be branded dissidents."[198]

Hostility toward political opposition may inhibit a new nation's long-term stability. Responsible opposition parties may assume a positive role: they can provide vital information, represent sectional interests, formulate alternative policies, and thus serve as a unifying, not a divisive, force. These corrective functions are limited within a single-party framework.

ZANU identifies itself with "the masses" and claims that "the Party and the people have increasingly become one."[199] Mugabe's logic: "My party is in the majority, so [the electorate] wants a one-party state."[200] Yet one-party rule may have less popular support than Governmental pronouncements suggest. In the only representative opinion poll taken since independence—administered during the 1985 election—55.6 percent favored and 40 percent opposed one-party rule.[201] Among the reasons people cited for opposing the one-party state were fears that it would lead to a dictatorship (13 percent) or be undemocratic (16 percent). One major finding is that a core of opposition to one-party rule exists among the Government's own supporters. In some party strong-holds, approximately 30 percent of ZANU supporters rejected one-party rule: 31.5 percent in Mashonaland East, 29.3 percent in Mashonaland West (see Table 4). A more impressionistic 1988 account found "a great lack of enthusiasm for the one-party state" that reflected "an anxiety for the power of the state to be constrained."[202] The 1985 poll also highlighted the degree of political polarization within ZAPU's regional stronghold, Matabeleland, where ZAPU supporters overwhelmingly rejected one-party rule. One alternative—a federal arrangement whereby Government would delegate some regional power to Matabeleland—was never seriously entertained since it might undermine the power and authority of the central state.

198. *Herald,* 29 November 1985.

199. ZANU Party Congress, *Resolutions,* August 1984. As Shils comments, "in no country in the world are party and people one" ("Opposition," p. 429).

200. Mugabe, *MOTO,* October 1984.

201. 1985 Zimbabwe election survey, conducted by Masipula Sithole, Department of Political and Administrative Studies, University of Zimbabwe, 1985.

202. Terence Ranger, "Matabeleland Now," Britain-Zimbabwe Society newsletter, 5 October 1988, p. 9.

TABLE 4   PUBLIC ATTITUDES, BY PARTY AFFILIATION
(in percentages)

Question: Would you want to see Zimbabwe become a one-party state?

	ZAPU Supporters		*ZANU Supporters*	
	Yes	No	Yes	No
Matabeleland South	15.8	84.2	90.0	10.0
Matabeleland North	25.9	74.1	87.3	12.7
Mashonaland East[a]	5.9	94.1	68.5	31.5
Mashonaland West[a]	0	100	70.7	29.3

Question: Are you better off today than you were five years ago?

	ZAPU Supporters		*ZANU Supporters*	
	Yes	No	Yes	No
Matabeleland South	35.0	65.0	96.0	4.0
Matabeleland North	47.2	58.2	96.2	3.8

SOURCE: 1985 Zimbabwe election survey by Masipula Sithole, Department of Political and Administrative Studies, University of Zimbabwe; used by permission of Professor Sithole.
$N = 1,209$
[a]The very low numbers of ZAPU supporters polled in the ZANU strongholds of Mashonaland seem to have skewed these findings.

Given the regime's comfortable margin of support in the country—reflected in two national electoral victories—why did it see a one-party system as a panacea, as nothing less than ZANU's "religion"?[203] A de jure one-party state will allow the Government to monopolize political power by right, with no challengers to question ZANU's performance as a political party.

A more important consideration has to do with the question of long-term rule. Dahl argues that democracy may require a system of "mutual guarantees" to competing parties that they will not be annihilated in the event of electoral defeat.[204] Losing an election can mean a regime's final loss of power if its successor is not itself prepared to yield if it loses a competitive election. Replacement by electoral means has, in fact, rarely occurred in postcolonial Africa.

However secure, ZANU's position as ruling party was not permanent under the multiparty order. In the long run, ZANU might deplete its

203. Mugabe, Assembly *Debates,* vol. 10, 11 July 1984, col. 248.
204. Robert Dahl, *Polyarchy* (New Haven: Yale University Press, 1971).

reservoir of political capital among urban and rural constituents: if so-cioeconomic problems (such as growing unemployment, rising prices for basic commodities, discontent among the urban working class) in-tensified or if key Government pledges (e.g., for land reform and reset-tlement programs) were not redeemed, or for other reasons (elite cor-ruption, officials' detachment or unresponsiveness to popular con-cerns).[205] The dissolution of the multiparty system removes once and for all the possibility of future electoral defeat. Like other new nations and most independent African states, Zimbabwe has embraced the one-party system as a vehicle for permanent ZANU rule.[206] The security ap-paratus has been mobilized to demonstrate the futility of opposition to ZANU's monopoly on state power.

Does the integration of ZANU and ZAPU usher in a "new era" in the country? One observer answers in the affirmative, contending that the change "promises dramatic relief for the nation" and creates a "radically altered political scene" in the country.[207] Another claims that "unity and amnesty in Matabeleland have inaugurated a new era; a second 'miracle' of reconciliation to match that with the whites in 1980."[208] Such predic-tions may be premature. Whether the accord will be the basis of a fragile coalition of elites or a lasting consociational settlement, it does not present a clean break with the past as much as it reflects the logical cul-mination of political developments since independence. The formal unity of ZANU and ZAPU does not appreciably alter the previous bal-ance of power, but in removing a key challenger to ZANU it reaffirms ZANU's supremacy.

The manner in which one-party states in Africa have come into being seems to have affected their political stability. A study by Collier found one-party African states imposed by force (by banning opposition par-ties or prohibiting opponents from contesting elections) to be less stable and more susceptible to military coups than those whose one-party sys-tems were based on electoral victories or the merger of parties.[209] Other

---

205. Astrow cites similar reasons for the attractiveness of one-party rule (*Lost Its Way?* p. 182).

206. ZANU's elites seem less attached to using their positions for material advantages than is common elsewhere in Africa; in 1989, however, several prominent Cabinet minis-ters resigned in disgrace after a panel found them guilty of misusing their offices for per-sonal gain ("Corruption Inquiry Condemns Six Harare Ministers," *Times,* 14 April 1989). On the dominant African pattern of using power for personal enrichment, see Shils, "Op-position"; R. Collier, *Regimes*; Howard, *Human Rights.*

207. Jan Raath, "Unity Pact Raises Hopes for Peace in Matabeleland," *Times,* 24 De-cember 1987.

208. Ranger, "Matabeleland since the Amnesty," p. 173.

209. R. Collier, *Regimes,* pp. 100–104.

analysts maintain that elite "pacts" or "settlements" may foster stable democracies.[210] Having traveled this route with the 1987 unity accord, Zimbabwe might be expected to have a stable political future. Yet genuine elite settlements require "the consensual unification of previously disunified elites," and in Zimbabwe this consensus is precarious.[211] Before ZANU and ZAPU united, a leading minister stated: "We believe that everything is right in ZANU . . . and, therefore, we see no need for concessions, compromise, and accommodation."[212] ZANU made few concessions indeed in the final agreement. The fact that the merger resulted not from the force of argument but from the argument of force may continue to color politics under the one-party state. Much will depend on the extent of genuine democratic participation within the party and the degree to which former ZAPU leaders and supporters are satisfied with their role in the political process.[213] It is possible that the withering away of ZAPU will lessen the pressure for internal solidarity within ZANU, as Simmel would predict, and open a window of opportunity for internal democratic debate.[214]

Those refusing to join ZANU may find dissent dangerous. When asked in 1984 whether those who disagreed with the party on fundamental issues could participate in politics, Mugabe responded: "They can stand out. We don't say that everybody will be compelled or coerced into joining the ruling party." Yet he added, "Those people who stand out . . . certainly will not be friends of Zimbabwe or in keeping with the general spirit of the moment."[215] These incorrigible opponents might also find their activities curtailed by the regime. A case in point is the recently formed (May 1989) Zimbabwe Unity Movement. Critical of government corruption and repression and surprisingly popular, the new party immediately had its rallies banned; several of its members were de-

---

210. Elite settlements are "rare events in which warring national elite factions suddenly and deliberately reorganize their relations by negotiating compromises on their most basic disagreements" (Michael G. Burton and John Higley, "Elite Settlements," *American Sociological Review* 52, no. 3 [June 1987]: 295).

211. John Higley and Michael G. Burton, "The Elite Variable in Democratic Transitions and Breakdowns," *American Sociological Review* 54, no. 1 (February 1989): 29.

212. Herbert Ushewokunze, "Yes to Unity, No to Concessions," *Sunday Mail,* 19 January 1986.

213. In early 1989 the press reported "an apparent apathy" toward party integration in Matabeleland (*Herald,* 10 January 1989).

214. Georg Simmel, *Conflict and the Web of Group-Affiliations* (Glencoe, Ill.: Free Press, 1955), pp. 91–98.

215. Mugabe, *MOTO,* October 1984, p. 10.

tained without charge in 1989; and the party has repeatedly been accused of being South Africa's pawn.[216]

CONCLUSION

It is important to appreciate that since 1980 Zimbabwe has experienced significant internal and external problems. But the structure and practice of law and order in the country have a logic that is somewhat independent of actual security requirements; the latter should not be viewed as unmediated "determinants" of official policy. Equally important in explaining the fortification of the inherited security apparatus in post-settler Zimbabwe are two interacting phenomena: the *lack of constraints* on, and the presence of *compelling incentives* for, state repression. The absence of constraints is reflected in the country's lack of a deeply rooted democratic political culture and the atomization of civil society. Incentives for the use of repression include the security sector's proclivity toward repressive practices that political elites have mobilized against ZANU's rivals. The master variable in our explanatory model is the regime's interests and capacities. Much depends, therefore, on how a new regime approaches the existing political culture (does it try to revalorize the culture?); how it handles the power and organizational inclinations of the security establishment (does it attempt to curb repressive practices and overhaul structures?); and how it responds to democratic pressures within civil society (does it invite, facilitate, or suppress such activity?).

Zimbabwe's political culture offers little scope for democratic practices and reconstitution of the security apparatus. Reminiscent of the settler order, the relationship between the state and civil society in Zimbabwe has been highly asymmetrical. Civic institutions remain inert, lacking the commitment and the resources (popular support, access to the media, alliances with other elites) to influence official policies on

216. Before he formed the Zimbabwe Unity Movement in May 1989, Edgar Tekere had been secretary general of ZANU, which expelled him in October 1988 after he accused party leaders of imposing a repressive dictatorship on the country. An outspoken and popular political figure, Tekere had also criticized the "rotten leadership" in the Government and ZANU and the regime's steady centralization of power. He called one-party rule corrupt, inefficient, and nepotistic and criticized executive interference with the judiciary (*Bulawayo Chronicle*, 15 July 1988; *Guardian*, 24 October 1988; *Times*, 11 August 1988; *MOTO*, August–September 1988). In March 1989 the Government instructed the *Bulawayo Chronicle* not to publish an interview with Tekere on his intent to campaign against ZANU on a "clean administration" platform (*Times*, 18 March 1989).

law and order. Occasional public protests and dissent by workers, students, and church groups have been swiftly quashed by the authorities. A characteristic problem facing a postauthoritarian regime is that of neutralizing or containing the power of old regime protagonists. Modern Latin American history is punctuated by attempts of such loyalists to undermine democratization and plans for institutional liberalization. In Zimbabwe by contrast, the elimination of the settlers' political and military power was remarkably smooth and rapid. Consequently the whites can neither force nor resist change. Their political marginalization removes one obstacle to democratic political development but by no means guarantees it. The case of Zimbabwe thus confirms a larger argument: that the displacement of a former authoritarian elite is not a sufficient condition for genuine democratization or liberalization of a security system.

The evidence presented in this chapter indicates that the essentialist view—that Zimbabwe's security organs function according to an inner dynamic that invites repressive outcomes—should be balanced by factors of external demand. It is true that war-hardened coercive institutions often prove particularly resilient to change, and that their transformation requires determination and resourcefulness on the part of new state managers. In Zimbabwe these elites have done the opposite: they have galvanized the security sector, with legal and extralegal powers, generous material resources, and insulation from effective accountability. Convinced that the inherited system is part of the solution to political and security problems, the Zimbabwe Government has systematically fortified it. There is, in other words, an elective affinity between the institutional predispositions of the security establishment and the goals of the new regime. The two factors positively interact: the regime's plan to crush organized political opposition to ZANU constitutes the driving force behind its activation of the security apparatus inherited from the Rhodesian state.

Authoritarian and repressive practices were not inevitable in independent Zimbabwe. Had the political objectives of the ruling party been different or the determination and organization of democratic social forces stronger, the repressive practices of the security agencies might have been curbed and the process of institutional modernization begun.

Since independence, Zimbabwe has experienced uneven political development. On the one hand, the state is no longer organized around the sectarian interests of a small minority. The franchise has been universalized, procedures for free elections introduced, and civil and political rights extended to all. The new regime has formally embraced the interests of the black majority, which settler rule had ignored for ninety years. And the ZANU regime enjoys a much broader base of support than its predecessor.

On the other hand, the protection of minority rights has not had a high priority under the new order. Consequently, the growth of national identity and support for the regime among members of the Ndebele ethnic group have stalled. The coercive cutting edge of the old regime remains, and its operations have had an adverse impact on nation building, political stability, and substantive democratization.[217] In both Rhodesia and Zimbabwe, the police, military, and intelligence forces have been key actors in deepening communal cleavages—racial in Rhodesia, ethnic in Zimbabwe. Majority rule may therefore coexist with repressive security institutions—both of which minority groups may experience as contributing to a tyranny of the majority. Lijphart, for one, singles out "Zimbabwe's majoritarian system as the underlying cause of its civil strife," but our findings suggest additional factors that are central.[218]

The next chapter demonstrates the utility of our model in explaining the partial liberalization of Northern Ireland's security system under British rule.

217. David Caute, "Zimbabwe: Grim March to a Loss of Liberty," *Times*, 6 May 1986.

218. Arend Lijphart, *Power-Sharing in South Africa* (Berkeley: Institute of International Studies, 1985), p. 21.

CHAPTER 7

Northern Ireland under British Rule

By 1972 the three pillars of settler rule in Northern Ireland had collapsed. The British metropole had concluded that the Unionist Government's grip on state power and handling of matters of law and order were altogether divisive and destabilizing. The settler regime was presiding over a crisis of authority among Protestants and Catholics alike. Political violence and public disorder had risen sharply, and coercive resources were stretched to the breaking point. Unrest of this magnitude had not occurred in Northern Ireland since the stormy birth of the state in 1921.

Although London had used the threat of direct rule to temper earlier Unionist recalcitrance, it viewed this option as the last resort. Faced with a steadily deteriorating security situation and pressure from army chiefs, the British Cabinet decided on 22 March 1972 to assume full control of law and order.[1] Stormont found this action unacceptable; in Prime Minister Brian Faulkner's words, it would irreparably undermine the Government's "powers, authority and standing. . . without justification" and would give the impression that "violence *does* pay." Refusing to share power with the metropole, the Unionist Cabinet abruptly resigned and London assumed full political control over the troubled province. Direct rule was not envisaged as a final solution to the Ulster problem but as a temporary expedient awaiting a more lasting political

1. Peter Jenkins, "Ulster: A Kind of Victory," *Guardian,* 17 January 1972.

settlement. It remains in place today and a political solution to the conflict appears more elusive than ever.[2]

If Catholics initially saw direct rule as a partial victory over the Unionists, Protestants saw it as an act of betrayal and appeasement to Ulster's enemies. On March 27, Faulkner bitterly declared, "Northern Ireland is not a coconut colony";[3] the Home Affairs minister accused Britain of using double standards: "Majority rule in Rhodesia, minority rule in Ulster."[4] Even though London never entertained the notion of minority rule in Ulster, it had begun to reassess the appropriateness of Westminster-style majoritarianism to this divided society. By 1973 it considered that "the Executive itself can no longer be solely based upon any single party, if that party draws its support...virtually entirely from only one section of a divided community."[5] In a nutshell, "simple majority rule would (as in the past) leave the minority in perpetual and ineffectual opposition."[6]

The advent of direct rule seemed to offer an unprecedented opportunity to break what Harold Wilson called "fifty years of unimaginative inertia and repression" under Unionist rule; in 1972 direct rule itself signaled the most significant change in political and security structures since partition. In one sweep, London dissolved the Northern Ireland executive, suspended the Stormont Parliament, and assumed full control over security. Settler rule came to an abrupt end.

In reference to the Protestants' intractability and residual influence, an editorial in the London *Sunday Times* of 10 April 1988 observed, "The harsh fact is that Ulster is a 'settler' problem." Yet few studies have examined Northern Ireland within the settler/postsettler paradigm.[7]

In sharp contrast to Zimbabwe, postsettler Northern Ireland has featured significant but partial liberalization of the settler-created internal security apparatus. This modernization within limits can be understood

---

2. An attempt at power sharing interrupted direct rule for five months in 1974 but set off a massive strike by Protestant workers and paramilitary groups (see Robert Fisk, *The Point of No Return: The Strike Which Broke the British in Ulster* [London: Andre Deutsch, 1975]).

3. Brian Faulkner, *Memoirs of a Statesman* (London: Weidenfeld and Nicolson, 1978), p. 157.

4. *Newsletter,* 25 March 1972.

5. *Northern Ireland: Constitutional Proposals,* Cmnd. 5259 (London: HMSO, 1973), p. 13.

6. *Northern Ireland: A Framework for Devolution,* Cmnd. 8541 (London: HMSO, 1982), p. 5.

7. Another study that analyzes Northern Ireland as a settler state highlights continuities and unfortunately ignores important changes under British rule (Michael MacDonald, *Children of Wrath: Political Violence in Northern Ireland* [New York: Blackwell, 1986]).

with the help of our explanatory model, which highlights (1) the values embedded in the political culture; (2) the interests and demands of major forces in civil society; (3) the independent power and organizational predilections of security agencies; and (4) the commitments and capacities of the new regime. As in Zimbabwe, the fourth factor has the greatest power in explaining the character and degree of liberalization in Ulster, but the first and second variables are also crucial. Ulster's polarized political culture and intense communal loyalties and rivalries present major obstacles to democratic political development and the building of universalistic institutions. Throughout civil society, opposing Protestant and Catholic forces are extremely active (unlike the situation in Zimbabwe); their demands on the state often neutralize one another, maintaining the status quo and retarding political progress and communal accommodation.

This raises the issue of the basic dimensions of Ulster's divided social order. Historically deep cleavages between Protestants and Catholics are sustained today by structures of differential communal socialization and institutional insulation: high degrees of communal endogamy; residential, educational, and recreational segregation; sectarian socialization in the family and neighborhood; conflicts between communally-rooted churches and political parties; frequent provocative, triumphalist marches that celebrate ancient victories of one side over the other; and violence by Republican and Loyalist insurgents and the security forces.[8]

Although these divisions are sufficiently deep to justify the use of the term communally divided society, they should not be exaggerated or considered absolute. First, class is an important qualifying variable. Divisions are sharpest between working-class Catholics and Protestants, more muted within the middle class. Second, Northern Ireland is less thoroughly divided than societies with a history of minority domination or those where extreme economic exploitation or fidelity to a caste etiquette in interpersonal relations typifies intercommunal relations. Yet Ulster's divisions are sufficient to sustain mutually exclusive political aspirations and fears, intercommunal hostilities, and two decades of political violence. Communal cleavages mar efforts to create integrative institutions and values. (One of the few nonsectarian bodies, the Alliance party, has the support of only 5 to 10 percent of the electorate.) The uncompromising character of Ulster politics subjects Catholic and

---

8. See John Whyte, "How Is the Boundary Maintained between the Two Communities in Northern Ireland?" *Ethnic and Racial Studies* 9, no. 2 (April 1986): 219–34.

Protestant leaders who seek accommodation to excommunication from their host community.

Views on the organization and operation of Northern Ireland's security institutions are intimately connected to communally entrenched political positions and aspirations. Security, like politics, tends to be a zero-sum matter. What one side demands or supports, the other rejects; concessions to one side risk alienating the other. For most Catholics liberalization has not gone far enough to attract enthusiastic support (there are still too many incidents of repression); for most Protestants, reforms have already gone much too far (demonstrably undermining law and order). In this highly charged polity, changes in security arrangements alone are unlikely to have much positive impact on nation building.

BRITISH RULE: ENLIGHTENED COLONIALISM?

At least three alternative views have been advanced regarding the British state's overall objectives in contemporary Northern Ireland. The first portrays British rule as a classic case of imperialist domination. This is the position of the Irish Republican Army (IRA) and its political wing, Sinn Fein.

> Violence in Ireland has its roots in the conquest of Ireland by Britain. The conquest has lasted through several stages for many centuries and. . .it has used violence, coercion, sectarianism, and terrorism as its methods and has had power as its objective.[9]

This argument by the leader of Sinn Fein is taken as axiomatic in some scholarly writing as well. Farrell, for example, flatly asserts that "since Britain was and is an imperialist power it is evident that the existence of the [Northern Ireland] statelet has served the interests of imperialism."[10] The logic behind these claims is suspect; the Crown's historical political subjugation and economic exploitation of Ireland does not automatically characterize the contemporary period. Today the costs of continued British rule far outweigh any benefits to the metropole. Some four hundred British soldiers have been killed in Ulster since 1971; the prov-

9. Gerry Adams, *The Politics of Irish Freedom* (Dingle, Ireland: Brandon, 1986), p. 62.
10. Michael Farrell, "Northern Ireland: An Anti-Imperialist Struggle," in *The Socialist Register,* ed. R. Miliband and J. Saville (London: Merlin Press, 1977), p. 72; D. R. O'Connor Lysaght, "British Imperialism in Ireland," in *Ireland: Divided Nation, Divided Class,* ed. A. Morgan and B. Purdie (London: Ink Links, 1980); Alfred McClung Lee, "Imperialism, Class, and Northern Ireland's Civil War," *Crime and Social Justice,* no. 8 (Fall–Winter 1977).

ince is a political liability, an international embarrassment, and an economic drain for Britain;[11] it offers little compensation in return (e.g.,
cheap labor, a market for exports, counterinsurgency lessons).[12]

A second perspective depicts British rule as an instrument or guardian of Protestant interests, consistently favoring their constitutional
preferences, socioeconomic supremacy, and demands for sectarian control of Catholics. Northern Ireland's Social Democratic and Labour
party (SDLP) maintains that "the British government's role in Northern
Ireland is not as 'honest broker' or 'peacemaker,' but as a crutch for the
loyalist majority."[13] Sinn Fein holds a similar position.[14] Farrell argued in
1976 that Britain was "fast becoming the servant of the Ulster Loyalists."[15] Ten years later MacDonald claims that "Britain tacitly and actively backs Protestant domination. . . . For once Britain allows Protestants to block unification [with the Irish Republic] it ends up preserving Protestant hegemony."[16] This argument mistakenly equates the
maintenance of partition—the core Protestant demand—with internal
hegemony and supremacy over Catholics. MacDonald also insists that
the Protestants "manipulate" and "use Britain to uphold their domination over Catholics";[17] he presents no evidence of either manipulation or
domination. In his view, the transfer of power in 1972 simply marked a
transition from indirect to direct British support for Protestant domination: "Sixty-five years after Northern Ireland was created and 17 years
after it erupted in violence, British policy remains much the same as always: it maintains Protestant hegemony militarily, politically, and economically." The only difference is that Britain is now "actively and
directly" involved in "maintaining a status quo biased in favor of Protes-

11. Britain's 1989–1990 subvention to Ulster—the difference between public spending
and revenues raised in taxes and levies—was over £1.6 billion.

12. Anders Boserup, "Contradictions and Struggles in Northern Ireland," in *The Socialist Register*, ed. R. Miliband and J. Saville (London: Merlin Press, 1972). On counterinsurgency lessons, see Carol Ackroyd, Karen Margolis, Jonathan Rosenhead, and Tim
Shallice, *The Technology of Political Control* (London: Pluto, 1980).

13. Social Democratic and Labour Party, *"Justice" in Northern Ireland* (Belfast: SDLP,
1985), p. 9. Since the 1985 Anglo-Irish Agreement (discussed below) the SDLP has modi-
fied its views, seeing Britain as more neutral, and stated that Britain's only interest in Ireland was to see that "violence or the threat of violence shall not succeed" (quoted in "The
Nationalist Divide," *Belfast Telegraph*, 5 September 1988).

14. Adams, *Freedom*, p. 89.

15. Michael Farrell, *Northern Ireland: The Orange State* (London: Pluto Press,
1976), p. 331.

16. MacDonald, *Children of Wrath*, pp. 102, 150.

17. Ibid., pp. 121, 150.

tants." Disregarding the evidence (discussed below), MacDonald contends that the British Government has "entertained but rarely implemented reforms." [18]

A final approach sees Britain as a third party acting as a neutral umpire, arbitrating between and seeking the consent of both sides, balancing their divergent interests in the decision-making process, and impartially maintaining order. Not surprisingly, this is the official position of the British Government. One former British Secretary of State for Ulster declared that "the security forces are not there to protect some Protestant ascendancy or colonial rule, but the basic right to live in peace";[19] other ministers consistently characterize British rule as mediating between the "tribalism" of Protestant and Catholic forces. This perspective neglects three important considerations: the British Government's pivotal role in determining Ulster's constitutional status; the extent to which its specific actions and presence in Ulster fuel communal hostilities, however unwittingly; and its lack of moral authority and leverage over the principal antagonists, based partly on the public perception that official policies consistently favor one side.

None of these perspectives satisfactorily captures the reality of British intervention in contemporary Northern Ireland. The first two fall victim to the fallacy of historical continuity: the assumption that historical patterns accurately characterize contemporary arrangements, when the facts contradict this continuity. Notwithstanding the objections of the preceding paragraph, the third approach provides the best point of departure for the present investigation. Contemporary British rule in Ulster approximates an enlightened colonialism, insofar as the metropole has imposed its rule on Ulster in a rather dictatorial (colonial) fashion with the (enlightened) goal of promoting democratic political development and liberalizing the apparatus of control. Compared to postsettler Zimbabwe and Liberia, Ulster has had a significant measure of success in its modernization under British tutelage.

The argument that British rule has contributed to systemic reform as well as overall progress in human rights in Northern Ireland should not be exaggerated. First, the process has not been uniform: some agencies have only slightly improved and others appear to have regressed. Second, the coercive system has been fortified: it receives far greater re-

18. Ibid., p. 149.
19. Douglas Hurd, quoted in "Reports on NI Policy Dismissed by Hurd," *Irish Times* (Dublin), 4 April 1985.

sources and commands a more formidable technology of surveillance and control than under settler rule. Third, practice frequently departs from the ideal of neutrality. In a number of areas discussed below, the routine operations of the security and criminal justice systems violate the logic of liberalization. Finally, the maintenance of law and order is confounded by enduring societal problems: political progress and economic development have been stalled for decades and working-class people—especially Catholics—still experience high levels of socioeconomic deprivation.

COLONIAL RULE

The most significant changes in Ulster's political institutions occurred at the moment settler rule was terminated. Since 1972 the British Government has had responsibility for Northern Ireland's executive and legislative functions (except for the power-sharing executive of 1974). In practice London devolves considerable responsibility to the adjunct administration at the Northern Ireland Office (NIO) in Belfast. The NIO formulates policy under the general guidance of Westminster and Whitehall; it coordinates the state's administrative departments (some inherited, some new) and is responsible for security policy, criminal law and procedure, the judiciary, prisons, police, and public prosecutions. At the NIO, a Secretary of State for Northern Ireland and three junior ministers (all British) perform the duties of former Unionist ministers, assisted by civil servants from both Northern Ireland and Britain.[20] Although the British Foreign Office and the Ministry of Defense are involved in Ulster—and have a substantial voice in Cabinet decisions regarding the province—the NIO is the *primus inter pares*.[21]

In practice, the NIO is largely free from parliamentary scrutiny. Legislation at Westminster concerning Ulster takes the form of Orders-in-Council presented to Parliament for its approval (but not amendment).[22]

20. Approximately two-thirds of NIO civil servants come from Britain and the balance from Ulster, although some departments at NIO, like the Police Division, are entirely from Northern Ireland (NIO official, interview with author, 17 July 1986). As of January 1985, 13 percent of the civil servants at NIO were Catholic, compared to 33 percent for the Northern Ireland civil service as a whole (*Belfast Telegraph,* 22 July 1986, p. 4).

21. John S. Ditch, "Direct Rule and Northern Ireland Administration," *Administration 25*, no. 3 (Autumn 1977): 336; Edward Moxon-Browne, *Nation, Class, and Creed in Northern Ireland* (Aldershot: Gower, 1983), p. 47.

22. One Secretary of State justified Orders-in-Council on the grounds that legislation by conventional bills would place "an intolerable burden on Parliament" (Great Britain, House of Commons *Debates,* vol. 19, 5 March 1982, col. 250).

This system allows Northern Ireland MPs no effective role in the legislation affecting the province.[23]

Like Parliament, successive British Cabinets give low priority to Northern Ireland's affairs unless some crisis demands immediate attention.[24] One former Secretary of State for Ulster, Merlyn Rees, concluded: "Except in times of crisis Northern Ireland does not loom large in [Cabinet] considerations. . . . In practice, the responsibility falls almost completely to the Secretary of State allied closely with the Secretary of State for Defense."[25]

Decision making on most security matters is confined to the Secretary of State, the Chief Constable, and the army commander, who meet monthly in a Security and Policy Committee. Since the signing of the Anglo-Irish Agreement on 15 November 1985, the Government of the Republic of Ireland has had an unusual consultative role in policy discussions in the north;[26] in their Inter-Governmental Conference meetings Irish and British officials discuss matters of law and order, including policing, the courts, and cross-border cooperation on security. Although the Government is under no obligation to accept the Republic of Ireland's specific recommendations, the agreement has added an important element to the calculus on security issues.

Direct rule in effect installed a system of colonial rule—an act of recolonization unprecedented in twentieth-century settler societies.[27] The new regime in Northern Ireland, unlike that in Zimbabwe, has no roots in civil society and has precarious authority at best. As in other colonial

23. Paul Maguire, "Parliament and the Direct Rule of Northern Ireland," *Irish Jurist* 10 (Summer 1975): 88.

24. G. Bell, *Troublesome Business*, p. 106.

25. *Belfast Telegraph,* 12 March 1980.

26. Unable to secure a settlement within Ulster, the British Government sought external support for its position in the province; the Anglo-Irish Agreement appears to have lessened international pressure on Britain (Adrian Guelke, "The Political Impasse in South Africa and Northern Ireland" [Paper presented at the American Political Science Association meeting, Washington, D.C., September 1988]).

27. The British Government sees direct rule as neither colonial nor undemocratic; it defines the province as an integral part of the United Kingdom. Northern Ireland sends seventeen MPs to Westminster; the Secretary of State and his junior ministers are elected (albeit not by Ulster's citizens). Yet Northern Ireland has acquired the essential features of a colony or an "internal colony," which Hechter defines as a region politically dominated and materially exploited by the core region but having greater administrative-legal integration, formal citizenship and rights, and geographical contiguity with the core than a conventional colony (Michael Hechter, *Internal Colonialism: The Celtic Fringe in British National Development, 1536–1966* [Berkeley: University of California Press, 1975], p. 349). These criteria seem to fit Ulster, except that the core no longer exploits economically but instead materially supports the province.

states, the British administration is superimposed on society and institutionally detached from local social forces. This detachment renders the local acceptability of regime-initiated changes problematic.

Although the 1973 Northern Ireland Constitution Act and various official pronouncements affirm the principle of self-determination, the Government has narrowly construed the pledge as respecting the desire of the majority to remain within or exit the United Kingdom. In the meantime, few formal channels exist for democratic participation. A local but purely advisory Northern Ireland Assembly existed from 1982 to 1986; Northern Ireland sends 17 MPs to the British House of Commons (which has 635 members); and Ulster's citizens elect their own city councillors. Devolving control over national affairs to local actors London sees as premature and apt to degenerate into a tyranny of the Protestant majority or incessant altercations between Protestant and Catholic leaders.

Symptomatic of the domestic political vacuum, several major policy shifts have been imposed from London with little or no input from interested local forces. One such change was the "Ulsterization" of security in 1976 (discussed below), which put the police in the front line of counterinsurgency. Another is the Anglo-Irish accord, which is designed to promote the interests of both sides. In drawing up the agreement, London and Dublin consulted the Social Democratic and Labour party but neither of the Unionist parties; during three years of operation the Inter-Governmental Conference has allowed no direct involvement by local parties.

The lack of democracy is a common grievance across the spectrum of political opinion in Ulster, although there is little consensus on the preferred direction of democratic development. Protestants and Catholics equally and almost unanimously oppose the continuation of direct British rule. Both sides view the British administration as morally bankrupt; their estrangement affects the regime's efforts to build new political institutions. At the same time, the constitutional options receiving the strongest support from one side meet almost unanimous opposition from the other (see Table 5). Protestants flatly reject a united or federal Ireland and joint British-Irish sovereignty; Catholics dismiss independence, full integration into the United Kingdom, and majority rule. It is noteworthy, however, that only a small proportion of Protestants continue their allegiance to the principle of majority rule. Most Protestants realize that London would not countenance a return to this system. Even

TABLE 5 PREFERRED FORM OF GOVERNMENT
(in percentages)

	Catholics						Protestants					
	1988a	1988b	1987	1986	1982	1974	1988a	1988b	1987	1986	1982	1974
Complete integration with the U.K.	5	9	12	5.7	11	6	46	47	50	35.4	40	33
United Ireland	22	25	22	21.5	38	16	1	1	1	0.5	1	1
Direct rule	3	2	7	6.0	N/A	8	7	4	6	11.7	N/A	8
Power sharing	35	31	36	27.8	31	55	18	17	16	20.9	33	18
Joint authority, London and Dublin	11	12	N/A	16.9	N/A	N/A	1	1	N/A	1.6	N/A	N/A
Majority rule	2	1	2	2.4	1	1	13	14	14	17.7	18	33
Independence	3	4	9	5.3	2	1	4	7	8	6.2	3	2
Federal Ireland	2	7	N/A	5.0	13	7	0	1	N/A	1.0	3	1
Don't know	13	10	11	9.7	4	7	8	8	6	5.0	2	6

SOURCES: 1988a: Coopers and Lybrand poll, *Belfast Telegraph*, 5 October 1988; 1988b: Coopers and Lybrand poll, reprinted in *Fortnight*, no. 261 (April 1988); Coopers and Lybrand poll, *Ulster Television Political Opinion Poll*, May 1987; Coopers and Lybrand poll, *Belfast Telegraph*, 15 January 1986; NOP Market Research poll, *Political Attitudes in Northern Ireland* (Belfast: Ulster Television, February 1982); NOP Market Research poll, 1974, cited in Richard Rose, Ian McAllister, and Peter Mair, *Is There a Concurring Majority about Northern Ireland?*, Studies in Public Policy, no. 22 (Glasgow: University of Strathclyde, 1978), p. 19.

NOTES:

N/A = not asked.

1974 poll: first preference for "Northern Ireland's future" (N = 979).

1982 poll: the one political change respondent would "personally prefer" (N = 998, 667 Protestant, 331 Catholic).

1986 poll: "best form of government over the next five years" (N = 2,004, 57% Protestant, 39% Catholic).

1987 poll: "best form of government for Northern Ireland" (N = 1,059, 632 Protestant, 427 Catholic).

1988 polls: "best form of government for Northern Ireland" (1988a, N = 1,100).

Inconsistencies in whether Ns are provided or broken down by religion reflect discrepancies in the data sources.

the paramilitary Protestant organization, the Ulster Defense Association, recognizes that "majority rule in deeply divided societies" is "profoundly undemocratic."[28] On the Catholic side, despite the common claim that a united Ireland is a "natural" aspiration of Catholics, only about 25 percent consider it the best political scenario.

Whether there is consensus on an alternative to direct rule depends on the question posed. When asked in 1988 if they agreed in principle with the notion of power sharing between Ulster's political parties, 76 percent of Catholics and 62 percent of Protestants said yes.[29] Yet this approval is more shallow than it appears. On the issue of the "best" form of government, power sharing receives much less cross-community support, as Table 5 shows. It is still the most popular option for Catholics. For Protestants, power sharing ranks lower because they believe full integration with the United Kingdom would best protect their interests or because they see power sharing as a means whereby Catholics could subvert the state from within.

ENLIGHTENED RULE

London's central objectives in Northern Ireland are as follows.[30] Relative stability—or the containment of disorder within manageable bounds—is the chief immediate priority. Institutional transfer and cultural convergence with the metropole are more long-term goals and means whereby a permanent settlement might be reached. The end result would be a political order based on power sharing among moderate leaders of the majority and minority, impartial administration, and the growth of accommodationist values; and a system of law and order that is politically neutral, acceptable to both communities, and committed to the ideal of justice. Once these conditions have been fulfilled, Britain claims that it will leave Northern Ireland once and for all. In short, London's grand design is to remake Ulster in conformity with British political norms—to the extent that this reconstruction is possible in a divided so-

28. Ulster Defense Association, *Common Sense* (Belfast: Ulster Political Research Center, 1987), p. 1.
29. Coopers and Lybrand poll, *Belfast Telegraph,* 5 October 1988. Thirty-nine percent of Catholics and 37 percent of Protestants thought the parties involved should have the power to make laws; 23 percent of Catholics and 43 percent of Protestants thought they should only administer laws created by Westminster.
30. The aims motivating government elites' policies and actions are difficult to document but may be inferred from official pledges and programs, and from relatively consistent patterns of action.

ciety.[31] The qualification is crucial, since Ulster's divided social order is a principal impediment to political development and reform of the system of law and order.

In the meantime, the British administration attempts to govern the province without becoming tarnished by identification with either side. Hence it places a premium on state autonomy, particularly in internal security affairs: divorced from partisan interests and managing political disputes from above rather than becoming an arena of struggle between contending social forces. Like the classic Bonapartist state, the British administration stands above and even "against civil society." While attempting to elicit consent from Protestants and Catholics for its political innovations, the regime has distanced itself from those groups. This posture is both colonial and enlightened: colonial because the regime dictates policies without consulting local forces, enlightened because this detached rule helps to shield the regime from sectarian influences.

PARAMETERS OF POLITICAL VIOLENCE

Since 1976, the number of incidents and fatalities resulting from political violence has remained well below the level of 1971 through 1976 (see Table 6). Judging by these indicators, the security situation has improved considerably since the final years of settler rule and the first years of British rule. Yet political violence continues to dominate communal relations and political life in the province.

Qualitative changes in political violence are also evident. First, the sectarian attacks by Protestant or Catholic mobs in the early 1970s declined sharply after the mid-1970s, with a corresponding reduction in the proportion of civilian fatalities: from 74 percent of those killed in 1972–1977 to 59 percent in 1982–1987. Second, the IRA became more selective in its targets, attacking a greater proportion of security personnel. Between 1972 and 1976, 24 percent of all those killed were members of the security forces; between 1984 and 1988, the figure had risen to 40 percent.

Table 7 lists the deaths caused by political violence from 1969 through 1988. Republican insurgents have been responsible for 57.6 percent of all deaths, Loyalist insurgents 24.8 percent, and the security

31. Full integration with the U.K. might promote thoroughgoing modernization, but Britain opposes this solution because of its expected political costs. Acting as a neutral modernizer while pressing Ulsterization allows London to distance itself from the Ulster imbroglio.

TABLE 6   THE SECURITY SITUATION, 1969–1988

	1969	1970	1971	1972	1973	1974	1975	1976	1977	1978	1979	1980	1981	1982	1983	1984	1985	1986	1987	1988	Total
Fatalities																					
RUC	1	2	—	14	10	12	7	13	8	4	9	3	13	8	9	7	14	10	9	4	168
RUC Reserve	—	—	—	3	3	3	4	10	6	6	5	6	8	4	9	2	9	2	7	2	89
Army	—	—	43	103	58	28	14	14	15	14	38	8	10	21	5	9	2	4	3	21	410
UDR	—	—	5	26	8	7	6	15	14	7	10	9	13	7	10	10	4	8	8	12	179
Civilians[a]	12	23	115	321	171	166	216	245	69	50	51	50	57	57	44	36	25	37	66	54	1865
Total	13	25	174	467	250	216	247	297	112	81	113	76	101	97	77	64	54	61	93	93	2711
Terrorist incidents																					
Shooting	—	213	1756	10,628	5018	3206	1805	1908	1081	755	728	642	1142	547	424	334	237	392	674	537	32,027
Bombs[b]	8	170	1515	1853	1520	1113	635	1192	535	633	564	400	529	332	367	248	215	254	384	458	12,925
Incendiaries	—	—	—	—	—	270	56	239	608	115	60	2	49	36	43	10	36	21	9	8	1562
Total	8	383	3271	12,481	6538	4589	2496	3339	2224	1503	1352	1044	1720	915	834	592	488	667	1067	1003	46,514
Finds																					
Weapons	—	—	324	717	1595	1260	825	837	590	400	301	203	398	321	199	187	175	174	206	489	10,465
Explosives (tons)	—	—	0.4	2.6	31.6	23.7	9.9	16.9	2.7	3.5	0.9	0.8	3.4	2.3	1.7	3.8	3.3	2.4	5.8	4.7	147.8
Terrorists charged																					
All offenses	—	—	—	531	1414	1362	1197	1276	1308	843	670	550	918	686	613	528	522	655	468	439	13,980

SOURCE: Chief Constable, *Chief Constable's Annual Report* (Belfast: Police Authority, 1988).
[a]Includes suspected terrorists. For a breakdown of civilian and insurgent fatalities, see Table 7.
[b]Includes devices defused.

TABLE 7   DEATHS FROM POLITICAL VIOLENCE, 1969–1988

Fatalities	Agents				Total	Percentage of All Deaths
	Security Forces	Nationalist Paramilitants[a]	Loyalist Paramilitants	Others + Unidentified		
Security forces	13	823	10	4	850	31.2
Nationalist paramilitants	123	144	18	8	293	10.8
Loyalist paramilitants	12	18	36	3	69	2.5
Catholic civilians	148	170	492	73	883	32.4
Protestant civilians	25	371	107	63	566	20.8
Unknown religion	5	21	11	1	38	1.4
Prison officers	0	23	2	0	25	0.9
Total	326	1,570	676	152	2,724	100
Percentage of all deaths caused by this agency	12.0	57.6	24.8	5.6	100	
Percentage of civilian deaths caused by this agency	11.8	38.7	40.5	9.1	100	
Civilian deaths as percentage of deaths by this agency	54.6	37.3	90.5	90.1		

SOURCE: Irish Information Partnership, reprinted in *Fortnight*, no. 270 (February 1989).
[a]For paramilitants (used in the source) this study consistently uses the term insurgents.

forces 12 percent. Republicans and Loyalists have been responsible for roughly equal numbers of civilian fatalities, 38.7 percent and 40.5 percent respectively; the security forces were responsible for 11.8 percent. However, civilian casualties caused by Republican insurgents often appear accidental; members of the security forces are their main targets (52.4 percent of deaths caused by Republicans). Loyalist insurgents have more intentionally trained their sights on Catholic civilians (72.8 percent of deaths caused by Loyalists), often in revenge for Republican attacks on security personnel. According to McKeown, from 1969 to 1980 most of the civilians killed by the security forces "were at the time of death engaged in totally legitimate activities." [32] But the same verdict applies to civilians killed by Catholic and Protestant insurgents.

THE SECURITY FORCES

One of the few growth industries in Northern Ireland is that of law and order, with expenditures skyrocketing since the beginning of British rule. Net expenditure on the Royal Ulster Constabulary jumped from £15.8 million in 1971–1972 to £361 million in 1987–1988; the proportion of public spending committed to policing grew from 2.5 percent to 6.5 percent from 1971 to 1985. [33] This growth came largely from pay increases for officers, more sophisticated police equipment, and the construction and fortification of police stations. The extra cost of maintaining the British army in Ulster (above the cost of stationing it in Europe) was £14 million in 1971–1972 and £143 million in 1982–1983. [34] Between 1969 and 1982 the indirect economic and direct exchequer costs of Ulster's violence totaled £8.9 billion, including £4.2 billion in extra security costs alone. [35]

THE BRITISH ARMY

From 1969 to 1976, the British army was in the forefront of the internal security enterprise. It served as the de facto police force in Catholic

32. Michael McKeown, "Chronicles: A Register of Northern Ireland's Casualties, 1969–1980," *Crane Bag* 4, no. 2 (1980–1981): 3.

33. Expenditure figures provided by RUC Headquarters, Belfast; proportions cited in John Brewer, Adrian Guelke, Ian Hume, Edward Moxon-Browne, and Rick Wilford, *The Police, Public Order, and the State* (New York: St. Martin's, 1988), p. 58.

34. New Ireland Forum, *The Cost of Violence Arising from the Northern Ireland Crisis since 1969* (Dublin: 'Government Stationary Office, 1983), p. 10.

35. Ibid., pp. 10, 25–26. These figures do not include the cost of political administration of the province.

working-class areas, patrolling streets, searching houses, controlling demonstrations and riots, and implementing internment. The police focused primarily on the safer Protestant areas, where they investigated specific offenses and brought suspects to court. This differential deployment in the two communities produced what Boyle, Hadden, and Hillyard call a "military security" approach in Catholic areas and a "police prosecution" approach in Protestant areas.[36]

Under the British Conservative Government of 1970–1974, a military victory over Republican insurgency was assumed to be possible, and soldiers were given a relatively free hand to deal with suspected troublemakers and uncooperative citizens.[37] Soldiers' frustration with the security situation encouraged indiscriminate violence, and harassment of the civilian population became a feature of everyday life—during street checks, interrogations, raids, and general house searches. In the words of a former officer, the army did not "have hang-ups about using force of the most vicious kind whenever possible," and civilians often supplied "the excuse for a bit of physical intimidation."[38] Burton's field study of Belfast during the mid-1970s graphically illustrates the traumatic repercussions of Catholic encounters with aggressive British soldiers.[39]

Internment without trial of political suspects, which began in 1971 as mainly an army operation, was a costly mistake. It threw into question the Government's fidelity to the rule of law and was a boon to the IRA, which portrayed its detained members as political prisoners suffering summary punishment. For these reasons, the Gardiner Committee recommended in 1975 the phasing out of internment and of "special-category" privileges for convicted political offenders, as well as a fundamental reappraisal of security policy.[40] The Labour Government (1974–1979) recognized the failure of internment and abandoned the view that terrorism could be defeated by military means. It hoped instead that conspicuous reliance on the law—with its presumed "higher

36. Kevin Boyle, Tom Hadden, and Paddy Hillyard, *Law and State: The Case of Northern Ireland* (Amherst: University of Massachusetts Press, 1975), pp. 42–47.

37. Paddy Hillyard, "Law and Order," in *Northern Ireland: Background to the Conflict,* ed. J. Darby (Belfast: Blackstaff, 1983), p. 43. Other observers noted a "continual super-imposition by the security forces of 'executive justice' when decisions of the courts displeased them" (Boyle, Hadden, and Hillyard, *Law and State,* p. 135).

38. A. F. N. Clarke, *Contact* (London: Secker and Warburg, 1983), pp. 53–54.

39. Frank Burton, *The Politics of Legitimacy: Struggles in a Belfast Community* (London: Routledge and Kegan Paul, 1978), pp. 106, 87.

40. [Gardiner Committee] *Report of a Committee to Consider, in the Context of Civil Liberties and Human Rights, Measures to Deal with Terrorism in Northern Ireland,* Cmnd. 5847 (London: HMSO, January 1975), Lord Gardiner, Chair.

authority"—might succeed where military power had failed and might diminish both domestic and international criticism of British rule.[41] One minister wrote, "I am certain that in our regular dealings with the United States... to be able to say we were doing it [maintaining order] within the law was of inestimable value."[42] Later, Conservative Secretary of State Humphrey Atkins (1979–1981) affirmed: "The aim is to defeat the terrorist by use of the law. Generally it means accepting the law of civilized countries."[43]

The larger policy reorientation (after 1976) consisted of "Ulsterization" and "criminalization," whose broad objectives were to normalize and legitimize the system of control and to depoliticize Ulster's violence.[44] Under *Ulsterization*, British troops gradually disengaged while the local RUC and UDR mobilized to fill the resulting security vacuum. Replacing the army's summary internment of suspects, the police investigated greater numbers of political offenses, which the courts adjudicated. Insurgent violence was officially shorn of its political dimension and defined as strictly criminal activity. In prison convicted terrorists were treated like ordinary prisoners. (Ten men died during the hunger strike of 1981 at the Maze prison—in which Republican prisoners demanded a set of privileges in accordance with their political status. The strike extracted no concessions from the Thatcher Government but revived waning popular support for the IRA, led to rioting in response to the deaths, and produced an upsurge in casualties from political violence for the year.)

Criminalization refers to the use of the criminal law and criminal justice system to depoliticize and delegitimate insurgent activity. In Ulster, criminalization is diluted by the authorities' reliance on emergency measures to arrest and charge insurgents, who are tried in special non-jury Diplock courts as terrorists rather than ordinary suspects. Balbus's study of ghetto riots in the United States in the 1960s assumes that criminalization will be successful: it "tends to depoliticize the consciousness of the participants" and "delegitimate their claims and grievances."[45]

41. Mike Tomlinson, "Reforming Repression," in *Northern Ireland: Between Civil Rights and Civil War,* ed. L. O'Dowd, B. Rolston, and M. Tomlinson (London: CSE, 1980), p. 191.

42. William van Straubenzee, "International Law and International Terrorism," in *Ten Years of Terrorism,* ed. J. Shaw (London: Royal United Services Institute for Defense Studies, 1979), p. 157.

43. *Belfast Telegraph,* 26 September 1979.

44. See Tomlinson, "Reforming Repression."

45. Isaac Balbus, *The Dialectics of Legal Repression: Black Rebels before the American Criminal Courts* (New Brunswick, N.J.: Transaction, 1977), p. 13.

Northern Ireland does not conform to these predictions, at least not in Catholic working-class areas. And it is doubtful that strict use of ordinary criminal laws and courts—as opposed to exceptional ones—would have the predicted effect. Catholic working-class areas are not so amenable to official constructions of reality. A 1978 poll found that 34.3 percent of Catholics disagreed with the statement that the IRA is made up of "criminals and murderers"; 46.3 percent thought that the IRA consists of "patriots and idealists"; 57 percent said that the authorities should "stop treating people convicted of crimes which they claim were politically motivated, as ordinary prisoners." [46]

Ulsterization has not spelled the end of military activities but rather a progressive reduction in their scale. The strength of army forces fell from 22,000 in 1972 to 10,123 by May 1988, while the strength of locally recruited forces—UDR and RUC—rose from 15,000 to 19,237 during the same period. The remaining troops have concentrated in areas where Republican insurgents are most active or where criminal investigations are difficult (the southern border, West Belfast). Outside these hot spots the army has reverted to its conventional role of aiding the civil power and providing support to the police, as needed. At the same time the army has increased its involvement in surveillance and covert operations,[47] which include attacks by the elite Special Air Services (SAS) on suspected insurgents.[48] Between 1976 and 1988 the SAS was responsible for killing 23 Republican insurgents, some of whom were armed and on active-service missions at the time.[49]

The narrowing scope of army operations after 1976 resulted in a corresponding reduction in military violence toward civilians. Compared to the public clamor over military brutality from 1969 to 1976, criticism of the army has become more muted; as the UDR and the RUC have grown prominent in the security field, Catholic complaints have centered on these forces. Still, 34 percent of Catholics and 5 percent of Protestants in 1979 wanted the army withdrawn.[50]

46. Edward Moxon-Browne, "The Water and the Fish: Public Opinion and the Provisional IRA in Northern Ireland," *Terrorism* 5, no. 1–2 (1981): 41–72.

47. Incidents of army involvement in kidnapping, assassination, death threats, and sabotage are described by former Army Intelligence Officer Fred Holroyd in Duncan Campbell, "Victims of the Dirty War," *New Statesman,* 4, 11, and 18 May 1984.

48. The SAS was deployed in 1976 apparently to placate the Protestant community: "When the murder of a number of loyalists brought indignation to the boiling point, it was as a political device that the SAS was sent to Ulster" (Tony Geraghty, *Who Dares Wins: The Story of the SAS* [London: Fontana, 1981], p. 182).

49. *Times,* 1 September 1988. Such shoot-to-kill operations by the SAS have generated less controversy than similar actions by the RUC's Special Branch.

50. Opinion Research Centre poll, *New Society,* 6 September 1979.

THE ULSTER DEFENSE REGIMENT

This regiment now provides the first line of military support for the police in 85 percent of the province. Although the regiment's absolute
strength has declined along with that of the regular army, its proportion
of the total military presence grew from 30 percent in 1972 to 42 percent
in 1986. Each battalion serves under a regular British army commanding officer, but the force has more autonomy from central control than
other military regiments.

The UDR is over 97 percent Protestant; Catholics are dissuaded from
joining by threats from the IRA and by popular perception of the regiment as a sectarian reincarnation of the Ulster Special Constabulary.
(Approximately 50 percent of its initial recruits were former members of
the USC.) In a recent poll, 89 percent of Catholics were opposed to any
extension of the unit's role.[51] The Social Democratic and Labour party,
predominantly Catholic, considers that the UDR "has by far the worst
record for serious sectarian crimes of any Regiment presently in service
with the British Armed Forces."[52] A number of UDR personnel have engaged in free-lance violence, apparently out of frustration with legal restrictions on counterinsurgency methods or out of sectarian motives.
From 1970 to 1985, seventeen UDR soldiers were convicted of murder
or manslaughter and ninety-nine of assault; others were charged or convicted of armed robbery, weapons offenses, bombing, intimidation and
attacks on Catholics, kidnapping, and membership in the illegal Ulster
Volunteer Force (a Protestant vigilante group).[53] An unknown number
belong to the legal but sectarian Ulster Defense Association. Only a small
fraction of the 32,000 full-time and part-time soldiers who have passed
through the UDR have been involved in crimes, but the proportion appears to be higher than that for regular British troops and the RUC.[54]

The Government maintains that the regiment has been molded along
British military lines and that to paint the UDR as a sectarian force is
unfair.[55] It has rejected pressure to dismantle the force for two reasons:

51. Ulster Marketing Surveys poll, *BBC Spotlight Report: An Opinion Poll* (British
Broadcasting Corporation, May 1985).
52. Social Democratic and Labour Party, "Security," Submission to the Secretary of
State's Conference in 1980, Belfast, p. 2.
53. For a list of offenses committed by UDR personnel from 1972 through 1985, see
Irish Information Partnership, *Agenda: 1985* (London: IIP, 1986).
54. Hugo Arnold, "Crime, Ulsterization, and the Future of the UDR," *Fortnight,* no.
226 (1985).
55. "UDR Backed in Secret MoD File," *Belfast Telegraph,* 27 March 1986; Defense
White Paper, cited in "Boost for UDR," *Belfast Telegraph,* 12 May 1986.

the expected backlash from Loyalists, who see the UDR as absolutely essential to the stability of the province; and the vacuum left by the departure of several thousand UDR soldiers that regular army troops would have to fill, thus reversing this dimension of Ulsterization.

THE ROYAL ULSTER CONSTABULARY

Initially, the British army opposed Ulsterization because it would require the police to take the lead in the security field (which the military considered premature) and because it would place frustrating restraints on army operations.[56] Likewise, the police were reluctant to assume primary responsibility for security or undergo militarization. Already in 1973 the chair of the Police Federation, Basil Stanage, cited "a simmering fear expressed throughout our ranks that we are being. . . manipulated into a security force position again. I am persuaded that this should never be permitted."[57] After more than a decade of "police primacy," the federation still views police militarization and involvement in counterinsurgency operations as "distinctly unnatural."[58] In early 1986, the chair of the federation, Alan Wright, created a stir when he questioned official policy: "Fighting a guerrilla war is not a job for an ordinary police officer: it is a job of the military." Later he added, "The primacy of the police is one thing and it is something that we have done very successfully. . . . All we are saying is don't treat us like soldiers," and "The Government is being totally unrealistic in its policy of putting the emphasis of security on to the police."[59] Such comments reflect constables' frustrations with their security responsibilities, which have increased their potentially confrontational encounters with citizens and undermined legitimacy among affected sections of the public. These duties also put the police at great risk. With over 260 officers killed and 7,000 injured since 1969, the RUC suffers the highest casualty rate of any police force in the world.[60]

Even as the Police Federation complains about the RUC's security role, it presses for more extensive powers; both existing exceptional

56. Desmond Hamill, *Pig in the Middle: The Army in Northern Ireland, 1969–1984* (London: Methuen, 1985), chaps. 7, 8.

57. "Address by the Chairman to the Annual Conference," *Constabulary Gazette* (October 1973): 7.

58. Editorial, *Police Beat,* January 1981.

59. Editorial, *Police Beat,* January 1986; *Irish Times,* 5 February 1986; *Belfast Telegraph,* 24 January 1986.

60. *Belfast Telegraph,* 20 January 1983; *Irish Times,* 24 June 1985.

powers and police pressure for more extensive ones clearly militate against liberalization. But the logic in RUC circles appears to be that, until Northern Ireland becomes stable and tranquil, the police will require special measures to deal with unrest and political violence. Police forces throughout the world frequently seek broader powers; in Ulster, the use of exceptional powers deepens Catholic alienation and is readily exploitable by insurgent groups who profit by promoting a police-state image of the province.

Changes in policing since the early 1970s have been mixed—including elements of *both militarization and liberalization*—reflecting the contradictory mandates imposed on the police. Since 1976 the RUC has assumed the preeminent role in internal security, which has driven its steady militarization and technological development. Given the gradual narrowing of the army's role, this militarization has arisen more by default than by design. Today the RUC has specialized antiterrorist squads, operates a complex computer surveillance system, and uses highly advanced equipment. All members of the force receive paramilitary and riot training. Generally speaking, the response to riots has become more graduated and restrained, but incidents of gross overreaction and brutality continue to haunt the force.

Plastic bullets are frequently used to control public disturbances, and are described as safer than alternative techniques. From 1970 to 1989 approximately 110,000 plastic and rubber (now discontinued) bullets were fired by the police and army, resulting in eighteen deaths and hundreds of injuries to protesters and bystanders. This record of casualties may appear mild in contrast to that in other societies where plastic or rubber bullets are a staple of riot control. In little more than a year after the Arab insurrection in Israel's occupied territories began in December 1987, approximately fifty Palestinians had been killed by plastic bullets fired by Israeli soldiers.[61] The use of plastic bullets in Northern Ireland nevertheless sparks an outcry after each fatality and deepens public resentment of the police.

Covert operations and surveillance absorb a substantial proportion of police time and resources.[62] Mobile Support Units were formed in 1981–1982 for rapid-strike operations and surveillance. Both the Support Units and the RUC Special Branch have been involved in controversial incidents, including the summary shooting of suspected insurgents.

61. Bernard Trainor, "Israeli Troops Prove Newcomers to Riot Control," *New York Times,* 19 February 1989.
62. Hillyard, "Law and Order," p. 46.

The killing of six unarmed men by the Special Branch in separate in-cidents in 1982 was investigated by John Stalker, at the request of the Government. His findings: elite units had an "inclination" to shoot sus-pects without attempting to make arrests; evidence of official cover-ups of the circumstances surrounding such shootings; a lack of accountabil-ity in the Special Branch; dubious cross-border surveillance operations; mishandling of evidence in cases of police shooting; abuse of the Offi-cial Secrets Act to shroud cases of police perjury; and faulty monitoring of the RUC by the Inspectorate of Constabulary at the Home Office. Among more than forty recommendations, his unpublished interim re-port called for more vigorous investigation of shootings by the police, detailed guidelines for officers engaged in cross-border operations in the Irish Republic, greater control over the handling of informants, and re-consideration of the use of agents provocateurs to ensnare suspects.[63]

In February 1988 the British Attorney General stated that national se-curity considerations disallowed criminal prosecution of the officers im-plicated in Stalker's inquiry as well as publication of his report. The Police Authority announced that no disciplinary proceedings would be taken against the Chief Constable and two senior officers. Twenty ser-geants and constables were subjected to disciplinary hearings, in cam-era, for breaches of RUC regulations. After only two days of hearings in March 1989, eighteen men were reprimanded and one cautioned; one case was dismissed. (Reprimands and cautions are the least serious sanc-tions a disciplinary board can impose.)

This dark side of policing in Northern Ireland coexists with impor-tant progressive developments, which can be measured by examination of the RUC's ideology, impartiality, and accountability. As an integral part of the Unionist settler state, the old RUC was a patently sectarian force. This sectarian orientation has been reduced substantially, as re-flected in official instructions, organizational ideology, and police prac-tices. Senior officers champion a professional ethos within the force and fiercely resist political interference from outside groups, jealously guard-ing their independence from Ulster's politicians and Government offi-cials. The emphasis from above on impartial law enforcement seems to have permeated the force. The RUC rank and file, no less than the upper

63. John Stalker, *The Stalker Affair* (New York: Viking, 1988). See also "Big Changes Were Sought by Stalker," *Times,* 21 June 1986; "Stalker: 40 Men Face Charges," *Sunday Times,* 20 July 1986. After obstruction from Special Branch officers and the Chief Consta-ble throughout his inquiry, Stalker was removed from the investigation shortly before he was to finish, apparently because it was likely to embarrass the RUC as a whole and the Chief Constable in particular.

echelon, have embraced impartial and apolitical ideals. Not surprisingly, this claim to independence has been questioned by interested parties who believe that the RUC either is biased or should be more pliable. The new official mission of the police is itself a significant advance on the sectarian orientation of the old force. The official ideology, however, does not meet with unanimous approval throughout the force, nor does it automatically translate into practice. Some long-serving officers have strong Unionist sympathies, according to one governmental report.[64] Police work—particularly that involving internal security problems, public disturbances, and patrolling in neighborhoods most hostile to the police—is likely to involve some measure of bias and tacit instructions that disregard formal norms of minimum force and impartiality.

At the same time, it is clear that some larger patterns of policing practice have improved under direct rule. Both senior officers and the Police Federation have gone to great lengths to distance themselves from pressure groups and political parties, in their efforts to avoid the impression of communal favoritism. Moreover, RUC constables have demonstrated, particularly since the mid-1980s, a willingness to pursue both Catholic and Protestant political offenders.[65] A confidential report in 1986 by Her Majesty's Inspectorate of Constabulary concluded that the RUC could be counted on to deal impartially with Protestants and Catholics.[66] And the independent Kilbrandon Inquiry found that the RUC "has become a disciplined and professional force which has been increasingly even-handed in its efforts to eradicate terrorism by paramilitary forces both Republican and Loyalist." [67] The willingness to pursue Loyalist suspects is supported by figures on Republicans and Loyalists charged with murder, attempted murder, and explosives offenses; in their respective levels of insurgent activity from 1981 to 1988—much higher for Republicans than Loyalists—a significantly higher proportion

64. Report by Her Majesty's Inspectorate of Constabulary, cited in Chris Ryder, "RUC Will Toe the Line on Ulster, Says Report," *Sunday Times,* 6 April 1986, p. 2.

65. The RUC's first highly visible operation against Protestant offenders came in 1977 when it controlled a ten-day Loyalist strike against the Government's alleged "soft" treatment of the IRA; the police dismantled over 700 barricades and charged 124 persons with offenses.

66. Ryder, "RUC Will Toe the Line."

67. [Kilbrandon Inquiry] *Northern Ireland: Report of an Independent Inquiry* (London: British Irish Association, November 1984), p. 39, Lord Kilbrandon, Chair; see also my article, "Policing Northern Ireland Today," *Political Quarterly* 58, no. 1 (January–March 1987): 88–96.

of Loyalists than Republicans were charged with offenses.[68] These findings reflect in part the Protestant community's greater willingness to provide information to the police on its Loyalist offenders but also shows police determination to pursue these cases.

Increasingly impartial law enforcement—with other progressive changes in policing—has not greatly enhanced Catholics' confidence in the RUC. It is the working-class Catholic population that remains most alienated from the police because of lingering deep-rooted historical antipathy toward the force as an arm of Unionist domination; the RUC periodically engages in provocative and controversial activities; the police are tainted by their connection to other discredited agencies of the criminal justice system and the state as a whole. However impartial the enforcement of the law and treatment of suspects, they do not translate into public acceptance of the police if the law or the state lacks legitimacy. Such is the perception of a substantial section of the minority community as well as a section of the Protestant population. At the same time, many Catholics seem to have a higher opinion of the RUC than Catholic political leaders claim. In 1985, 38 percent of Catholics approved an increase in the size of the RUC; 47 percent believed the police operated in a fair or very fair manner.[69]

On the one hand, the RUC has made clear progress since the advent of British rule. Officers are better trained, more impartial and accountable, less politically driven, and more sensitive to their pivotal position in this divided society. On the other hand, further liberalization is limited by the fact that the force remains almost totally Protestant, militarized, heavily armed, and mired in the security business. Incidents of police repression are the logical result of the RUC's position on the cutting edge of the counterinsurgency effort. The tenuous combination of liberalization and militarization creates contradictory imperatives for policing in a society torn by deep communal hostilities and armed insurgency. Progress will be arrested as long as the RUC retains its militarized

---

68. From 1986 through 1988, for example, the Chief Constable reported 47 murders attributed to Loyalists and 40 Loyalists charged with murder; 172 murders were attributed to Republicans and 23 Republicans charged with murder (Chief Constable, *Chief Constable's Annual Report* [Belfast: Police Authority, 1988], pp. 60–61).

69. These findings are reported, along with Protestant views, in Tables 8 and 9 later in the chapter. In public opinion surveys in England and Ulster, 73 percent of English respondents found the police "approachable" compared to 51 percent of Ulster respondents, who were also much less likely to contact the police in hypothetical situations (British Broadcasting Corporation, "You and Yours: Attitudes towards the Police," September 1987).

style and is saddled with primary responsibility for internal security.[70] There appears to be no politically acceptable alternative to this state of affairs (e.g., a reversion to military primacy) under present circumstances.

SECURITY LEGISLATION

From 1969 to 1972 little reform of repressive law took place. In fact, the corpus of such legislation expanded. Only in 1973 was the cornerstone of settler security law, the Special Powers Act, finally abolished. Yet the act was quickly replaced with the 1973 Emergency Provisions Act (EPA) and the 1974 Prevention of Terrorism Act (PTA).[71] Passed in the wake of the worst year of political violence in the province (1972), the EPA applies solely to Northern Ireland. The abrupt enactment of the PTA in one day was precipitated by the bombing of a Birmingham pub in November 1974 that left twenty-one persons dead.

Ostensibly temporary measures, these acts have been renewed annually and biannually by Westminster, often with little debate.[72] The official rationale for the laws is their absolute necessity to protect the public; the exclusion of Ulster's insurgency from mainland Britain; and the need for an alternative to the restrictions the ordinary criminal law places on the counterinsurgency effort.[73] That the scope of the security laws might exceed the province's requirements was acknowledged by a former Secretary of State: "I know also that there is a sort of inertia about these matters. It is easier to continue to shelter behind these powers than to determine at a certain point that they are dispensable."[74]

In some respects the EPA and PTA are reminiscent of the Special Powers Act:

---

70. For an elaboration of this argument, see my article, "Policing a Divided Society: Obstacles to Normalization in Northern Ireland," *Social Problems* 33, no. 1 (October 1985).

71. The EPA was amended in 1975, 1978, and 1987; the PTA was amended in 1976 and 1984.

72. Bipartisan support for the acts finally ended in March 1983 when the Labour party voted against renewal of the PTA (which a Labour Government had introduced in 1974). Labour's 1983 election manifesto called for repeal of the PTA and reform of the Diplock courts. In July 1984 Labour voted against the EPA for the first time on the grounds that necessary amendments had not been made.

73. On the content of the relevant Commons debates, see Matthew Lippman, "The Abrogation of Domestic Human Rights: Northern Ireland and the Rule of British Law," in *Terrorism in Europe,* ed. Y. Alexander and K. Myers (London: Croom Helm, 1982).

74. Humphrey Atkins, Great Britain, House of Commons, *Debates,* vol. 995, 10 December 1980, col. 1030.

- they abolish jury trials in security cases, place the burden of proof on the accused for possession of firearms or explosives, and make bail virtually impossible to obtain;

- extend powers of warrantless search, seizure, arrest, and detention by the army (for up to four hours) and by the police (for up to seven days), and allow security forces to stop and question any individual believed to be connected with "terrorist incidents";

- proscribe organizations "connected with terrorism" and prohibit membership in, recruitment for, and support of such organizations;

- authorize the British Home Secretary and the Northern Ireland Secretary of State to exclude individuals from Britain and Ulster if they are "satisfied" that the person is or may become connected to terrorism.

Until it was amended in 1987, the EPA did not require officers to have "reasonable suspicion" that an offense had been committed to justify arrest, search, or seizure; mere suspicion was sufficient; constables and soldiers did not have to justify their decisions. As Colonel Robin Evelegh revealed, "The vast majority of those arrested by the Army in Northern Ireland were arrested without being suspected of anything except in the most general sense."[75] This carte blanche allowed authorities to detain, interrogate, and release without charge about 50,000 individuals since 1973. (The proportionate number of the United States' population would be 6.8 million.)

The RUC and army routinely use arrest and interrogation to harass suspects, gather intelligence, and develop informers.[76] Between 1978 and 1986 only 13.7 percent of those arrested under the EPA were charged with an offense (in Britain, 80 to 90 percent of persons arrested in ordinary criminal cases are charged). The other 86.3 percent were interrogated and released. A study of detentions in 1980 found that interrogators sought information about detainees' movements, political sympathies, associates, and families; only 28 percent of these individuals were questioned about a specific offense.[77] The study concludes that the powers of arrest and interrogation are used deliberately for "intelligence gathering, surveillance, and harassment": interrogation is designed to generate dossiers on individuals and to deter them from

75. Robin Evelegh, *Peace-Keeping in a Democratic Society: The Lessons of Northern Ireland* (Montreal: McGill-Queens University Press, 1978), p. 120.
76. The last purpose is cited in ibid., p. 75.
77. Dermot Walsh, *The Use and Abuse of Emergency Legislation in Northern Ireland* (London: Cobden Trust, 1983), pp. 33, 69.

supporting radical political causes.[78] The importance of detention and interrogation is evident in the RUC's growing use of the seven-day power under the PTA instead of the three-day power under the EPA.[79] The lengthier detentions "allow the police to exercise greater pressure on suspects to confess or cooperate."[80]

Northern Ireland differs from postsettler Zimbabwe and Liberia in that peaceful political opposition is not branded subversive and suppressed. Even groups with connections to insurgent organizations and thus on the borderline of violence—Sinn Fein, Ulster Defense Association—are legal, albeit frequently harassed by the authorities. Groups with an incontrovertible record of violence, however, are proscribed under the security legislation; they include the Irish Republican Army, Irish National Liberation Army, Ulster Volunteer Force, and Ulster Freedom Fighters. The EPA allows the police to arrest anyone suspected of membership or general "involvement" with proscribed organizations.[81]

Under the EPA, the cases tried in special Diplock courts are those of "scheduled offenses" connected to political crimes; one judge presides without a jury. From 1980 through March 1989, 93 percent of the 5,774 defendants tried in these courts were convicted (82 percent had entered guilty pleas, up from 56 percent in 1973). (Confessions admitted as evidence in Diplock courts need not be corroborated by other evidence.)[82] Of the cases where defendants pleaded not guilty, 39 percent were acquitted, down from 57 percent in 1973.[83] The declining acquittal rate may indicate a "hardening" of the judges involved, who hear many

78. Walsh, *Use and Abuse,* p. 39; cf. Kevin Boyle, Tom Hadden, and Paddy Hillyard, *Ten Years On in Northern Ireland: The Legal Control of Political Violence* (London: Cobden Trust, 1980).

79. The seven-day power was used in 7 percent of the arrests under the two acts in 1979, and approximately 50 percent in 1984.

80. Steven Greer, Tom Hadden, and Martin O'Hagan, "Arrest and Screening," *Fortnight,* 18 February 1985, p. 6.

81. By infringing freedom of association and expression, the banning of organizations arguably goes further than necessary to control the undesirable activities of the members of these groups (see Committee on the Administration of Justice, *Emergency Laws: Suggestions for Reform in Northern Ireland,* pamphlet no. 5 [Belfast: CAJ, September 1983], p. 10). The British Government has equivocated on the issue of proscribing organizations; in 1974 it lifted the ban on Sinn Fein and the Ulster Volunteer Force, and countenanced the view that individual offenders would be pursued instead of organizations (see the statement by Secretary of State Merlyn Rees, House of Commons, *Debates,* vol. 871, 4 April 1974, col. 1476).

82. A recent review of the EPA recommended that confessions be tape-recorded to ensure their voluntary character ([Baker Report] *Review of the Operation of the Northern Ireland (Emergency Provisions) Act 1978,* Cmnd. 9222 [London: HMSO, April 1984], Sir George Baker, Chair).

83. NIO figures, cited in *Belfast Telegraph,* 1 November 1989; 1973 figures are from Walsh, *Use and Abuse,* p. 94.

similar cases without the check of a fresh jury to evaluate each one. This arrangement increases the chances that the accused will be wrongfully convicted.

Despite the fact that Diplock courts show no systematic religious bias in the decisions rendered, they remain highly controversial among Catholics and seem to have affected the standing of the legal system as a whole (see Table 9).[84] It is widely believed that public confidence could be restored only if the Diplock courts were reformed or abolished.

A relatively recent experiment in these courts was the "supergrass" system, which relied on the uncorroborated testimony of informers to convict individuals accused of political offenses. From 1981 to 1983, 450 people were arrested and charged with terrorist-related offenses on the evidence of 18 Republican and 7 Loyalist supergrasses. The police granted immunity to about half of the supergrasses in return for their testimony, and several received generous monetary payments as well.[85] An independent investigation by Lord Gifford concluded that the use of uncorroborated evidence had led in some cases to the conviction of innocent persons.[86] The supergrass system was abandoned at the end of 1986 after the acquittal of a number of defendants on grounds of the informers' lack of credibility.

Persons arrested under the PTA have no right of habeas corpus, are not informed of the charges against them, and have no right to remain silent or to appeal decisions. Abridging the standard right to freedom of movement within one's country, exclusion orders banish suspected terrorists from one part of the United Kingdom to another (most exclusions are from mainland Britain to Ulster). In Britain from 1974 to 1986, 6,246 were detained under the PTA, of whom 4.5 percent received exclusion orders and 8.5 percent were charged with an offense. Of the 7,627 detentions in Ulster between the end of 1974 and July 1987, 31 individuals were given exclusion orders and 2,462 (32 percent) were charged with an offense.

The Shackleton Report on the PTA excused its low rate of exclusions and charges by celebrating "the preventative nature of the legislation in its widest aspects."[87] Another official justification for exclusion is that it

84. Boyle, Hadden, and Hillyard, *Ten Years On,* p. 86.
85. Secretary of State, *Irish Times,* 27 February 1985.
86. Tony Gifford, *Supergrasses: The Use of Accomplice Evidence in Northern Ireland* (London: Cobden Trust, 1984), p. 34.
87. [Shackleton Report] *Review of the Prevention of Terrorism (Temporary Provisions) Acts,* Cmnd. 7324 (London: HMSO, August 1978), Lord Shackleton, Chair.

is necessary when charges cannot be brought against those suspected of planning acts of terrorism in Britain.[88]

Some have objected to the principle of exclusion or internal exile, noting that this special treatment belies the official position that Ulster is an integral part of the United Kingdom. Others consider it simply unnecessary: the authorities issued exclusion orders (from Britain to Ulster) against only fourteen persons in 1983, two in 1984, and four in 1985, suggesting that it was "no longer of any great significance in the prevention of terrorism."[89] But the act has been used to induce information from persons with Irish backgrounds and "to severely limit the activities of legitimate groups campaigning on Irish issues in mainland Britain."[90]

The powers contained in the existing security legislation constitute some improvement—in terms of human rights and the rule of law—over the Special Powers Act of the Unionist state. The current legislation no longer defends a system of sectarian power and privilege. In marked contrast to the regime in Zimbabwe, the British Government has shown a willingness to drop certain provisions of the security law as a result of pressure from opposition parties at Westminster or of recommendations from independent review commissions. But several other provisions arguably overstep what circumstances in the province warrant. In the area of legislation, the net effect of British rule is limited liberalization. The same diagnosis applies to the system of accountability.

MECHANISMS OF ACCOUNTABILITY

Inasmuch as executive departments in Ulster are now answerable to Westminster, formal British involvement is an improvement on the old settler state. But apart from crises, the British Cabinet assigns low priority to Northern Ireland, and Westminster shows little interest in the problem: Parliament's review of the security laws has rarely been more than perfunctory.

88. Penny Smith, "Emergency Laws and the Prevention of Terrorism Acts," in *Securing the State,* ed. P. Hillyard and P. Squires, European Group for the Study of Deviance and Social Control, Working Papers in European Criminology, no. 3 (1982), p. 222. See also Catherine Scorer and Patricia Hewitt, *The Prevention of Terrorism Act: The Case for Repeal* (London: National Council for Civil Liberties, 1981).

89. *Times,* 8 December 1988.

90. Standing Advisory Commission on Human Rights, *Annual Report for 1984–1985* (Belfast: HMSO, 1985), p. 23.

One abortive experiment in local democracy and accountability was the Northern Ireland Assembly, which operated from 1982 to 1986. Although it had a narrow advisory role, the Government accepted approximately 75 percent of its recommendations.[91] In the area of security, however, despite its frequent and impassioned debates, the Assembly had little influence. A Security and Home Affairs Committee was limited to making recommendations and ventilating local concerns over security problems; it was generally disregarded by the Government, as a NIO official confided: "We regard the Committee as something that has to be quieted down rather than something that has to be taken seriously."[92] Boycotted by the SDLP and Sinn Fein and sometimes the scene of unruly Unionist theatrics over unmet demands, the Assembly was dissolved in June 1986 by the British Cabinet amid protests from the Unionist parties.

In the field of criminal prosecution, a new office of Director of Public Prosecutions (DPP) was established in 1972, following recommendations of the Hunt Committee and the report of a working party on public prosecutions. According to one former minister, the DPP's office was designed so that it would "not be open to the same allegations of bias" that were leveled at the previous system of police prosecution.[93] The DPP is responsible for the prosecution of all cases of serious crime in which the police have decided to prefer charges and determines whether complaints against police justify criminal charges. In his first and primary responsibility, the DPP has proven to be a valuable corrective in bringing about more impartial treatment of Loyalist and Republican suspects.[94]

The DPP's role in improving police accountability is less clear, since his decisions to prefer charges against officers depend mainly on prior police investigation. The DPP has prosecuted few officers accused of misconduct and has consistently refused to disclose the reasons behind his decisions. Yet the DPP's involvement does introduce a check into the old system under which police investigated themselves.

The response of the police to citizens' complaints has been a chronic problem in Northern Ireland. The difference between the number of

91. Secretary of State Tom King, Great Britain, House of Commons, *Debates,* vol. 99, 19 June 1986, col. 1202. Cf. Brigid Hadfield, "The Northern Ireland Assembly," *Public Law* (Winter 1983): 550–57, and Northern Ireland Assembly, *Local Democracy at Work* (Belfast: HMSO, 1984). Almost all the Assembly's sitting members were Unionists; fourteen SDLP and five Sinn Fein members boycotted the Assembly from its inception.

92. NIO official, Law and Order Division, interview with author, 16 August 1984.

93. Lord Windlesham, Minister of State at NIO, *Irish Times,* 2 May 1972.

94. Boyle, Hadden, and Hillyard, *Ten Years On,* p. 68; *Fortnight,* September 1983.

complaints registered and those that are substantiated by the police authorities has been high but relatively constant from 1982 through 1988.
In 1985, for example, 51 complaints were substantiated out of a total of
3,237 complaints registered (1,349 complaints were withdrawn or not
proceeded with).[95] An unknown proportion of the complaints registered
every year consists of attempts by Republicans to undermine public confidence in the force or tie up police resources, but the Bennett Committee of Inquiry found that such malicious motives "can scarcely account
for the volume of complaints" registered.[96] Changes over time in the
number of complaints registered may reflect, inter alia, fluctuations in
complaint-provoking conduct by officers, but one independent body
concluded, "No clear explanation has emerged."[97]

Attempting to build public confidence, a Police Complaints Board
was created in June 1977 to oversee complaints of disciplinary (not criminal) breaches by officers. Between 1977 and 1981, the board received a
total of 2,895 complaints. In only 21 cases (0.7 percent) did it disagree
with the decision of the Deputy Chief Constable not to prefer disciplinary charges. Continuing public dissatisfaction over the handling of
complaints led to the replacement of the Police Complaints Board in
February 1988 with an Independent Commission for Police Complaints,
which has an enhanced role in investigating cases.

A substantial number of complaints registered in the 1970s stemmed
from allegations of assault under police custody and mistreatment
during interrogations. This problem was the focus of several official investigations. The Compton Commission concluded that "physical ill-
treatment" had occurred during prolonged police questioning.[98] Hood-
ing, noise treatment, threats of violence, and forced standing for prolonged periods were among the techniques used to extract information
or confessions. From 1976 to 1979, ill treatment of suspects in police
custody was apparently tolerated by police chiefs and top government

95. Chief Constable, *Annual Report* (1985); on the complaints system, see my article,
"Accountability and Complaints against the Police in Northern Ireland," *Police Studies 9*,
no. 2 (Summer 1986): 99–109; for England, see Steven Box and Ken Russell, "The Politics
of Discreditability: Disarming Complaints against the Police," *Sociological Review* 23, no.
2 (May 1975): 315–46.
96. [Bennett Committee] *Report of the Committee of Inquiry into Police Interrogation Procedures in Northern Ireland,* Cmnd. 7497 (London: HMSO, March 1979), Judge
Bennett, Chair; p. 112.
97. Police Complaints Board, *Annual Report for 1985,* p. 3.
98. [Compton Commission] *Report of the Enquiry into Allegations against the Security Forces of Physical Brutality in Northern Ireland Arising out of Events on the 9th August 1971,* Cmnd. 4823 (London: HMSO, November 1971), Sir Edmund Compton, Chair.

officials; they had received evidence of brutality from physicians and others.[99] NIO ministers and police managers insisted that detainees' wounds were self-inflicted, and that allegations of brutality were part of the IRA's propaganda war. Independent investigations found otherwise. In 1978 the European Court of Human Rights ruled that the use of certain interrogation techniques in Ulster constituted "inhuman and degrading punishment";[100] Amnesty International concluded that "maltreatment of suspected terrorists by the RUC has taken place with sufficient frequency to warrant the establishment of a public inquiry to investigate it." [101] A subsequent investigation by the Bennett Committee confirmed that suspects had sustained non-self-inflicted injuries in police custody.[102] After the implementation of most of the committee's recommendations—including television monitoring of interrogations—allegations of mistreatment in custody diminished considerably.

In settings outside the interrogation room, however, allegations of police assault remain high. In 1980, 33.1 percent of the total complaints dealt with by the authorities alleged assault (compared to 19.6 percent in England and Wales); in 1984 the figure was 27.0 percent for Northern Ireland (19.2 percent in England and Wales).[103]

Another formal mechanism of accountability is the Police Authority (created in 1970). This body is undoubtedly an advance over the Unionist system where the Ministry of Home Affairs was responsible for policing. Its purview might be expected to include the use of undercover specialist police units, the discharge of weapons, and public complaints. But neither controversial incidents nor the causes of recurrent policing problems have been its major concern; it has focused instead on technical and organizational matters.[104] The authority has the power, which it rarely exercises, to request reports on policing issues from the Chief Constable and can even call for his resignation. On those rare occasions when it has pressed for greater powers—such as its request in 1976 to attend security meetings at the NIO—it has been refused.

99. Peter Taylor, *Beating the Terrorists* (Harmondsworth: Penguin, 1980).
100. European Court of Human Rights, Case of Ireland against the United Kingdom: Judgment, Strasbourg, January 1978, p. 82.
101. Amnesty International, *Report of an Amnesty International Mission to Northern Ireland* (London: Amnesty International, June 1978), p. 70.
102. Bennett Committee.
103. Standing Advisory Commission, *1984–1985,* p. 69.
104. On the reluctance of English police authorities to exert control over police activities, see M. Brogden, "A Police Authority: The Denial of Conflict," *Sociological Review* 25, no. 2 (May 1977): 325–49.

The authority maintains that "Northern Ireland has one of the best police forces in the world." [105] With this assessment and with its highly deferential approach to the police, the authority has understandably had difficulty convincing the public that it is an effective independent check on the performance of the RUC. [106] A body more representative of the entire community, actively devising policing policies and priorities, and working to identify and solve continuing problems might enhance the RUC's image and accountability. [107]

The Standing Advisory Commission on Human Rights (SACHR) was created in 1973 to investigate areas in which religious or political discrimination existed and recommend changes to the Secretary of State. Its consistent interest in human rights and impartial orientation have made it something of a "counterweight to sectarian forces." [108] SACHR's often critical Annual Reports have concerned, inter alia, controversial aspects of security legislation, complaints against the police, the use of firearms by security forces, procedures for police interrogation, and a proposed bill of rights. SACHR has advocated changes in legislation and institutional practices bearing on human rights and has consistently counseled against policy changes that might further erode public confidence in the administration of justice. Under no obligation to accept and implement the commission's recommendations, the Government has accepted some and rejected others over the years. Governmental refusals or long delays in redressing problems usually include explanations of inconvenient timing or competing legislative priorities—reasoning that the commission does not accept.

Other independent bodies, such as the Committee on the Administration of Justice (CAJ) and the National Council for Civil Liberties (NCCL), have issued reports critical of the security laws, the system for handling complaints, plastic bullets, and fatalities caused by the police. Judging by official practices, these reports have had at best a modest impact. Several major commissions have examined institutional practices and security laws. Their reports led to new mechanisms of accountability, but the changes have stopped short of major reforms. [109] Commis-

105. Police Authority for Northern Ireland, *Report on the Work of the Police Authority for Northern Ireland: 1970–1981* (Belfast: Police Authority, 1982), p. 6.

106. See Standing Advisory Commission, *1984–1985,* p. 29.

107. See Committee on the Administration of Justice, *Police Accountability in Northern Ireland* (Belfast: CAJ, 1988).

108. Paul Maguire, "The Standing Advisory Commission on Human Rights," *Northern Ireland Legal Quarterly* 32, no. 1 (Spring 1981): 53.

sions of inquiry have, for example, not questioned the need for emergency legislation, the Ulster Defense Regiment, and the Diplock courts.

The judiciary offers a potential check on abuses as it adjudicates cases alleging criminal conduct on the part of the security forces; but the courts' record in controlling such misconduct has been less than impressive. Of the twenty-two members of the security forces prosecuted for killings while on duty, two have been convicted; one received a suspended sentence, and the other served two years of his life sentence.

As a signatory to the European Convention on Human Rights and other covenants, the British Government accepts the principle of international judicial review of human rights. The European Court of Human Rights has heard cases regarding violations of human rights in Ulster, and its adverse decisions have generated modest improvements. London has sometimes derogated from the court's rulings. In 1988 the European Court ruled that the seven-day detention power under the EPA was excessive, but the Thatcher Government opted not to comply with the verdict.

Another international oversight body is the Inter-Governmental Conference established under the Anglo-Irish Agreement of November 1985, with the Dublin Government acting on behalf of the Catholic minority. Law and order issues have featured prominently in discussions between British and Irish representatives. Thus far, the British Government has responded favorably to some Irish proposals, for instance, Dublin's objection to reintroducing internment without trial. In contrast, suggestions to reform Diplock courts—introducing juries or replacing a single judge with three—or to disband the UDR were flatly rejected by the British authorities.

The preceding discussion has focused primarily on mechanisms of oversight within the state. The question of civic accountability— whereby state agencies respond to representatives of leading social institutions—is a separate issue. It is especially problematic in deeply divided societies: a body committed to democratic accountability might find itself torn by the conflicting demands of a divided public and thus wholly ineffective. Ideally, oversight agencies would be maximally depo-

109. See the reports of the Gardiner Committee (1975), the Bennett Committee (1979), and the Baker Commission (1984); see also Gavin Drewry, "Judges and Political Inquiries: Harnessing a Myth," *Political Studies* 23, no. 1 (March 1975): 61; Boyle, Hadden, and Hillyard, *Law and State,* pp. 126–30.

liticized and composed of responsible members of the community; but in Northern Ireland enticing such persons to serve on bodies like the Police Authority has proved difficult, either because insurgent organizations have issued threats to members or because potential members consider such agencies to be illegitimate or cosmetic.

On balance, the structure of accountability that has been built since 1972 is a clear departure from the settler era, but additional checks would enhance the overall accountability of the security sector. The courts, independent commissions, and oversight bodies have not adequately scrutinized some of the most controversial activities of the security forces. Moreover, when human rights organizations and other bodies have questioned practices such as the use of plastic bullets and the so-called shoot-to-kill tactic, corrective action by the authorities has been difficult to discern.

OBSTACLES TO FURTHER LIBERALIZATION

Britain's experience from 1969 to 1972 indicated the futility of attempting by remote control to reshape Ulster's institutions. Direct involvement since then has given the metropole greater leverage, with significant results. Northern Ireland is one of the few contemporary communally divided societies where a modernizing regime has revamped important elements of the security system. The remainder of this chapter uses our explanatory model to assess the constraints on further liberalization.

The authorities in Northern Ireland have advanced the familiar security-imperatives thesis. They insist that political instability and armed insurgency have made extraordinary security precautions a dire necessity. As one RUC spokesperson told me, "Further progress [i.e., police reform] depends on the level of violence." [110] The official view is that any further relaxation of controls would create a vacuum inviting an upsurge in political violence; every violent incident, however isolated, dramatizes and justifies the need for exceptional measures.

The existence of protracted political violence is clearly an important part of the explanation for prevailing institutional arrangements in Northern Ireland. Yet, as our analysis of postsettler Zimbabwe suggested, political violence alone is not a sufficient explanation. Other social and political variables condition Ulster's security system and

110. Interview with author, 3 August 1984.

contribute to changes as well as continuities in its structure, ethos, and operations.

A SECTARIAN POLITICAL CULTURE

At the macrolevel, democratic political development and liberalization of a security system require a congruence between a society's normative and institutional orders. Prager states the case in newly independent nations:

> the construction of new institutional structures following independence always stand[s] in relation to the prevailing cultural orientations of the society. The challenge of modernization is to establish complementarity between those orientations and modern institutional forms. Normative commitments set the limits for institutional development.[111]

British reconstruction in Ulster requires both institutional transfer and cultural convergence with the metropole. Of course, it is far easier to remodel institutions than to reconstitute a cultural order—particularly one split along communal lines. Britain has had modest success in Ulster in arranging institutional transfer and, predictably, less progress in grafting norms of universality and justice onto the sociopolitical order and nurturing transcommunal solidarity. The fact that the new regime is an adjunct of an existing liberal democracy may seem to favor liberalization (in contrast to Zimbabwe and Liberia, where the new regimes lack strong commitments to democratic norms), but much depends on the degree of societal receptivity. It often appears that this divided society is "hermetically sealed from British political life and traditions."[112] Ulster's traditional communal allegiances and cultural orientations clash with new, modern institutions; this disjunction limits the legitimation of those institutions.

Because of its settler heritage, Ulster's polarized political culture is deficient in norms of mutual trust, tolerance for opposition, willingness to compromise on key issues, and a shared sense of national identity. Extreme views flourish, mutual distrust among organized Catholic and Protestant forces is the norm, and compromise equals betrayal of one's side. Overarching bonds of solidarity are weak; a tradition of zero-sum politics is strong and parochialism is valued; the cross-sectional public

111. Jeffrey Prager, *Building Democracy in Ireland* (Cambridge: Cambridge University Press, 1986), p. 5.
112. Paul Arthur, "Rules of Disengagement," *Times,* 28 October 1988.

support necessary to sustain modern institutions is precarious. Survey data and in-depth interviews document significant levels of religious intolerance as well as political polarization.[113]

Like some other deeply divided societies, the antagonistic communities in Northern Ireland are not impressed by the regime's attempts to build a universalistic and autonomous state. Though sometimes pledging nominal support for these ideals, both sides (but particularly the Loyalists) hold more particularistic and instrumentalist views of state power. They invoke the language of democracy on behalf of their communal preferences: majoritarianism for Protestants, minority rights or majoritarianism in an all-Ireland context for Catholics. Similarly, they tend to favor security arrangements that appear to advance their partisan interests.[114]

On the Catholic side, the Social Democratic and Labour party routinely lobbies for an impartial and accountable security system, not reverse discrimination against Protestants. Yet its support for liberalization is somewhat ambiguous and conditional. First, its demands understandably address problems that inflame Catholic sensitivities but ignore Protestant concerns. Second, it has given at best muted support—and more often virulent criticism—to specific institutional reforms, which it labels cosmetic. In Catholic quarters, there are electoral risks in lending support to security and criminal justice institutions; Sinn Fein is always anxious to portray the SDLP as having sold out to the British. (Sinn Fein brands all reforms as subtle forms of repression.) Third, the

---

113. Interviews with political elites can be found in Padriag O'Malley, *The Uncivil Wars: Ireland Today* (Boston: Houghton Mifflin, 1983); see also John Conroy, *Belfast Diary* (Boston: Beacon, 1987); and Sally Belfrage, *Living with War: A Belfast Year* (New York: Penguin, 1987). In the mid-1960s only 39 percent of Protestants and Catholics thought that "most people can be trusted"; 62 percent believed that the preaching of "false" religious doctrines should not be allowed (Richard Rose, *Governing without Consensus: An Irish Perspective* [Boston: Beacon, 1971], p. 498).

114. Illustrating this point is the partial erosion of Loyalist support for the security forces after the Anglo-Irish Agreement; of the Protestants polled, 33.6 percent thought the agreement would bring a reduction of confidence in the security forces; 11.6 percent expected an increase, and 46.2 percent anticipated no effect (Coopers and Lybrand poll, *Belfast Telegraph*, 15 January 1986). Another survey found that 27 percent of Protestants believed the agreement would lower public confidence in the courts; 7 percent thought it would raise confidence; and 53 percent expected no effect (Ulster Marketing Surveys, *BBC Spotlight/Newsnight: Public Opinion of Anglo-Irish Agreement* [British Broadcasting Corporation, January 1986], p. 15). In 1988, 86 percent of Protestants (and 70 percent of Catholics) believed it had not improved the security situation; 76 percent of Protestants (and 58 percent of Catholics) saw no positive effect on the administration of justice; 55 percent of Protestants (and 34 percent of Catholics) said it had not increased cooperation between the RUC and the Irish police, or Garda (Coopers and Lybrand poll, *Belfast Telegraph*, 4 October 1988).

SDLP continues to condition support for the institutions of law and order on a political solution to the conflict. The SDLP leader, John Hume,
put it bluntly: "We will only have total unequivocal identification with
the institutions of law and order when there is agreement among the
people as a whole as to how we are governed." [115] For the SDLP, a political solution spells a united Ireland—anathema to Protestants.

Protestant political forces tend to see law and state power as instruments to advance majority interests. They are, like most settler castes,
antimodernists who oppose the elevation of coercive institutions above
communal demands. The Unionists have fought virtually every change
in the direction of liberalization—from legal reforms and judicial impartiality to police accountability. On occasion, this opposition has manifested itself in street protests that have turned into full-scale riots and
attacks on the forces of order, throwing into question the celebrated Loyalist fondness for law and order.

A great deal of criticism has centered on policing, which one Democratic Unionist party (DUP) leader questioned:

> There must come a time when the conscience of each police officer must
> overrule the brainwashing. . .that professionalism must overrule conscience
> on every occasion. At present there appears to be an attitude within the RUC
> that officers. . .must carry on their task in a professional manner.[116]

A colleague warned: "The individual policeman is going to have to
choose who he is loyal to—his paymaster [the British Government] or
the [Protestant] community which has supported him for so long." [117]

Some Protestant leaders are unabashed about their preference for security structures that discriminate against Catholic offenders. One Official Unionist party (OUP) leader, Harold McCusker, questioned the
principle of impartial law enforcement and insisted that the police
should instead distinguish between offenders "who uphold the Constitution and those who would subvert it." [118] Some have placed a sinister
construction on security policies that treat such Loyalists on a par with
Catholic political offenders. Similarly, others see a world of difference
between the annual Protestant and Catholic parades. Consider the comment of a DUP member:

115. Quoted in Conor Cruise O'Brien, letter to the editor, *Times*, 20 May 1989.
116. Alan Kane, Northern Ireland Assembly, *Debates*, vol. 19, 19 March 1986,
p. 231.
117. DUP press officer, Sammy Wilson, quoted in *Irish Times*, 16 July 1985.
118. *Belfast Telegraph*, 12 July 1985.

What is the Loyalist demonstrating? He is demonstrating his loyalty to law and order and to British rule in this country. What are Republican parades demonstrating? They are demonstrating their support for murder, terrorism, and the overthrow of the state.[119]

Uttered at a particularly traumatic time for Protestants—when the RUC was banning or rerouting Loyalist parades that traditionally traveled through Catholic neighborhoods—these particular views may not be universally popular among Protestants. But they certainly reflect a widespread antimodernist orientation to institutions of law and order. One senior member of the OUP remarked: "The fact that they are 'our police' is inscribed on the Protestant mind." [120]

Northern Ireland's political culture contains strong particularistic values, despite the formal support Protestant and Catholic leaders sometimes pledge to universalistic and democratic ideals. The cultural milieu does not preclude institutional progress—as the record of partial reconstruction attests—but it makes future change more problematic.

A POLARIZED CIVIL SOCIETY

In addition to insurgency and the partisan political culture, two other interrelated factors condition Northern Ireland's security system: the interests and capacities of Catholic and Protestant political forces and civic institutions and those of the British regime.[121] After surveying Catholic and Protestant attitudes on law and order issues and the relative power of organized forces on each side, I assess their impact on the regime.

Catholic views.   Under British rule, Catholic preferences are central to the debate over fundamental political and constitutional questions. Catholic civic bodies—the church, media, voluntary associations—and political parties actively express grievances and demands on public policies, and nowhere more intensely than on matters of law and order.

The attitudinal data presented below should be treated cautiously; the sensitivity of some of the questions may produce responses that exaggerate disapproval of illegal activities and radical organizations. But it

119. Northern Ireland Assembly, *Debates,* vol. 15, 1 May 1985, p. 252.
120. Quoted in *Fortnight,* no. 239 (19 May 1986), p. 5.
121. The following discussion extends arguments in my article, "Contested Order: The Struggle over British Security Policy in Northern Ireland," *Comparative Politics* 19, no. 3 (April 1987): 281–98.

is clear that Catholic views on security matters are less uniform than conventional accounts suggest. Surveys have found that 55.5 percent of Catholics think the authorities should take a tougher line with the IRA;[122] 41 percent say that Britain's first short-term priority should be to reduce the level of violence;[123] and 86 percent disapprove of the use of violence for political ends.[124] The critical mass of loyal IRA supporters should be distinguished from those who simply tolerate the insurgents, those who occasionally support specific actions of the IRA but condemn others, and those who have been intimidated into compliance with IRA demands.[125] Catholic support for Republican insurgency is taxed periodically by attacks that have gone awry (Republican insurgents were responsible for the deaths of 170 Catholic civilians from 1969 to 1988) and by the punishment (like kneecappings) the IRA administers to suspected informers.[126] That the state lacks legitimacy among Catholics, and that IRA blunders are often followed by controversial security force operations, help to reinforce tolerance for IRA activity.

Another picture emerges from a breakdown of attitudes along party lines. Four out of five SDLP voters reject the use of political violence, and the same proportion believe that Sinn Fein should abandon the armed struggle. By contrast, four out of five Sinn Fein voters support political violence, and two out of three support the armed struggle.[127] It is noteworthy that of the Sinn Fein supporters one out of three believes the party should terminate the armed struggle, a staple of the party's strategy. These findings document important intracommunal differences on key questions facing the Catholic population. Many Catholics harbor negative views of Sinn Fein; in a recent poll only 14 percent of Catholics expressed staunch support for Sinn Fein, 53 percent said they had never sympathized with the party, and 28 percent indicated that their views were affected by more immediate events involving the IRA.[128] Actual voting results, however, suggest that Sinn Fein enjoys the support of a sizeable minority of Catholics. In the 1983 general election, Sinn Fein

122. Moxon-Browne, *Nation, Class,* p. 58.
123. Opinion Research Centre poll, *New Society,* 6 September 1979. Thirty-two percent thought the first priority should be a political solution.
124. Market and Opinion Research International [MORI] Poll, June 1981.
125. Patrick Bishop and Eamonn Mallie, *The Provisional IRA* (London: Heinemann, 1987), pp. 227–28.
126. See Table 7 above and "An Ulster Town Mourns Woman Killed by I.R.A.," *New York Times,* 16 April 1989.
127. Cynthia Irvin and Eddie Moxon-Browne, "Not Many Floating Voters Here," *Fortnight,* no. 273 (May 1989): 7–8.
128. Coopers and Lybrand poll, *Fortnight,* no. 261 (April 1988): 8.

TABLE 8   ATTITUDES TOWARD SECURITY MEASURES, 1985
(in percentages)

	Protestants in Agreement	Catholics in Agreement
Increase size of RUC	90	38
Increase undercover intelligence operations	90	25
Extend role of UDR	76	11
Impose death penalty for terrorists convicted of murder	69	20
Reintroduce internment for terrorist suspects	51	12
Use joint RUC–Irish Police border patrols	81	61
Use shoot-to-kill policy for terrorist suspects	61	7
Continue supergrass informer system	26	6

SOURCE: Ulster Marketing Surveys poll, *BBC Spotlight Report: An Opinion Poll* (British Broadcasting Corporation, May 1985).
NOTE: "Don't know" responses ranged from 3 to 8 percent.
N = 1,008

won 43 percent and the SDLP 57 percent of the Catholic, nationalist vote; in 1987 Sinn Fein's share dropped to 35 percent. In a 1988 survey, 40 percent of Catholics said that Sinn Fein should not be allowed to field candidates in the 1989 city council elections.[129]

Catholics who disapprove of Sinn Fein/IRA and political violence do not necessarily support security policies or specific institutions. A 1982 poll found that 60 percent of Catholics disapproved of the government's general handling of security while 33 percent approved.[130] There is widespread Catholic discontent with many existing and proposed security measures (see Tables 8, 9, and 10), and a majority believes that the police and the legal system operate unfairly. These attitudes contrast sharply with Protestant views and suggest that the organs of law and order remain "institutions of discord" today.[131]

129. Coopers and Lybrand poll, *Belfast Telegraph,* 4 October 1988.
130. NOP poll, "Political Attitudes in Northern Ireland," Ulster Television, February 1982, p. 6.
131. Rose, *Governing.*

TABLE 9   ATTITUDES ON LAW AND ORDER, 1985
(in percentages)

	Protestants	Catholics
Police are fair	96	47
Police are unfair	4	53
Legal system dispenses justice fairly	89	36
Legal system dispenses justice unfairly	9	57
Security forces are politically restricted	92	39
Use of plastic bullets during riots is acceptable	86	9
Use of plastic bullets during riots is unacceptable	8	87
Death penalty for terrorist murderers is appropriate	74	21
Death penalty for terrorist murderers is inappropriate	18	71
Uncorroborated "supergrass" evidence should not be admissible in court	46	81
Uncorroborated "supergrass" evidence should be admissible in court	35	10

SOURCE: Northern Ireland Consumer Panel poll, *Belfast Telegraph,* 6 February 1985.
N = 955

The IRA, Sinn Fein, and their supporters take a predictably hostile view of Northern Ireland's legal system and security arrangements, including the reforms implemented since the advent of British rule. In their view, the existing state is "unreformable"; the creation of new institutions of law and order will be possible only after the British withdraw. In the meantime, the IRA and Sinn Fein fear genuine reforms and depend on state repression to fuel the fires of Catholic discontent and support for the Republican movement. By contrast, the SDLP and its supporters advocate immediate reforms in the security system: that the UDR be disbanded, the Diplock courts abolished, the Emergency Provisions Act and Prevention of Terrorism Act withdrawn, and the police restructured.[132]

132. The SDLP has not urged Catholics to join the RUC, has been ambivalent on cooperating with the police against political violence, and has refused to give unconditional support to the force.

TABLE 10   ATTITUDES TOWARD SECURITY MEASURES, 1988
(in percentages)

	Protestants		Catholics	
	Approve	*Disapprove*	*Approve*	*Disapprove*
Internment in Northern Ireland	67	26	10	84
Internment in both Northern Ireland and the Irish Republic	71	23	11	83
Removal of suspect's right to silence	69	26	18	70
Extradition of terrorist suspects from the Republic to Northern Ireland	97	2	49	42
Sealing of the border	68	24	11	83
End of half-remission of sentence for terrorist prisoners	75	23	31	61
Requirement that city councillors publicly renounce violence before taking office	94	5	70	23

SOURCE: Marketing Research Consultancy poll, *Belfast Telegraph*, 9 September 1988.
N = 1,000

It might be expected that moderate Catholics would be the first to support liberalizing changes. But the SDLP and its supporters have given at best qualified, conditional support to reforms—because they define the changes as insufficient, or because of perceived miscarriages of justice, or because enthusiastic support for reforms might put the SDLP at an electoral disadvantage vis-à-vis Sinn Fein. Moreover, abrasive security operations disproportionately affect Catholics, creating the impression that the entire security enterprise is one-sided. The lack of support for direct rule, coupled with the lack of political progress, also colors reforms imposed by the British state. As noted earlier, Catholic support for reforms of security and criminal justice structures is unlikely to be enthusiastic if such changes do not proceed in conjunction with progress on the political front.

In the meantime, groups representing Catholic interests (the church, SDLP) and several independent human rights organizations have lobbied for major reforms in the law, police, courts, and specific security measures. Generally, the governmental response has been unfavorable. One official at the NIO insisted that it is "farcical to suggest that our security policy is determined by the minority." [133] Still, the regime has tended to avoid introducing measures likely to prompt a widespread Catholic outcry, disorders, or international protests, as indeed occurred in the early 1970s after several misguided security experiments. One measure that would be likely to inflame the Catholic minority to violent resistance is the reintroduction of internment without trial; several British officials have opposed it on precisely these grounds.

A relatively recent innovation designed to give Catholics a formal voice in decision making through representatives from the Irish Republic is the Inter-Governmental Conference established under the Anglo-Irish accord, wherein Irish officials have pressed for several liberalizing reforms. In the first four years (1986–1989), most of Dublin's recommendations came to naught.

Protestant views.   Significant proportions of Catholics (36 percent) and Protestants (22 percent) believe that terrorism cannot be defeated in Ulster (see Table 11). Of the remainder, Catholics place greater weight on political solutions whereas Protestants favor security measures. A substantial core of Protestants (29 percent) believe that security measures alone are the answer, and many others see security as the cutting edge of a strategy supported by a political offering (e.g., power sharing). Many Protestants appreciate that reliance on force alone will not defeat the IRA. Forty-four percent of Protestants and 38 percent of Catholics thought that a combination of security and political measures was the solution. (The crucial unaddressed question is the meaning of "political measures" to each community.)

The survey data presented in the tables above show that, with few exceptions and despite intracommunal differences, the *security measures that Catholics denounce as draconian and unacceptable, Protestants overwhelmingly applaud.* As a rule Protestants favor any measure that may help to subdue the IRA and its civilian supporters. Support for drastic security measures does not, however, translate into approval of the Government's overall performance in security. One survey found that

133. NIO official, Law and Order Division, interview with author, 3 August 1984.

TABLE 11 ATTITUDES ON DEFEATING TERRORISM, 1988
(in percentages)

Question: By what measures do you believe terrorism in Northern Ireland is most likely to be defeated?

	Security Measures	Political Measures	Combination of Measures	Cannot Be Defeated	Don't Know	Total
Protestants	29	3	44	22	2	100
Catholics	4	19	38	36	3	100

SOURCE: Coopers and Lybrand poll, *Belfast Telegraph*, 4 October 1988.
N = 1,000

50 percent of Protestants disapproved of the handling of security, while 44 percent approved.[134] The main reasons for this disapproval have been articulated by Unionist leaders: they complain that an alien power takes security decisions and imposes programs without the consent of the majority in Ulster; that it does not exert security powers to the fullest extent against Catholic culprits but uses them increasingly against Protestant protesters and political offenders.

Most Protestants would question the claim that the existing security system serves their interests, which is made in one model of British rule presented at the beginning of this chapter. They believe instead that British security policy and routine practices pander to the minority population, hold the security forces on a short leash, and allow insurgents to run amok. In one poll (Table 9), 92 percent of Protestants thought that the security forces were restricted by political policies. Ian Paisley's Democratic Unionist party has gone so far as to accuse Britain of having "a vested interest in not defeating the terrorism that, if permitted to succeed, would deliver it of the Province it seeks to ditch." [135]

The two Unionist political parties have aggressively and ceaselessly campaigned for greater access to security elites, fortification of coercive agencies, more vigorous enforcement of existing laws, and a host of more repressive measures. As evidenced by the wealth of the Loyalists' unmet demands, this pressure has had little direct impact on specific security arrangements. Success is most likely when their demands coincide with a major IRA attack; even then the official response—military reinforcements, for example, or blanket search-and-seizure operations in Catholic areas—is dismissed as terribly inadequate. The Unionist leaders sometimes exaggerate their impotence, however. A former OUP General Secretary stated, "We've had no success in influencing Britain on security." [136] Ian Paisley insisted that "nothing I can do in this Parliament [Westminster] is going to bring about a security situation in Northern Ireland that will give a measure of safety to my people." [137] His party's security manifesto laments, "We must be the only country where those who are fervently pro-security forces and who often pay the ultimate price for giving such support, have their loyalty repaid by the Government distancing itself from them." [138]

---

134. NOP poll, "Political Attitudes," p. 6.
135. Democratic Unionist Party, *A War to Be Won* (Belfast: DUP, 1984), p. 26.
136. Interview with author, 8 August 1984.
137. *Newsletter,* 17 November 1981.
138. Democratic Unionist Party, *War to be Won,* p. 37.

An official at the Northern Ireland Office seemed to agree:

The Unionists have very little influence on security policy. It is politically necessary for the Secretary of State to dampen down the outrage of the Protestant community after major terrorist attacks, like sending in the Spearhead Battalion. Basically, we put up with Unionist pressures on security. Security policy is settled.[139]

In most instances, the Government has indeed simply tolerated or made cosmetic responses to Unionist clamor. Another NIO official indicated the danger of accepting the Unionist program: "The Unionist demands on security are uniquely designed to make a violent situation worse."[140]

Yet the Protestants' poor record in shaping specific security arrangements does not mean that their efforts have been fruitless; their unrelenting pressure has had a more generalized deterrent effect.[141] Of utmost concern to state officials is the Protestant community's capacity for armed revolt and street disturbances. This potential for resistance—occasionally realized—circumscribes the kinds of reforms the state might place on the agenda.[142] Changes that might lead to a violent and protracted Loyalist rebellion include dismantling the UDR, demilitarizing the RUC, or repealing the emergency legislation.

Just such a backlash followed the signing of the controversial Anglo-Irish Agreement in November 1985. Loyalists see Dublin's advisory role as a wholly unacceptable intrusion into Northern Ireland's sovereign affairs and believe it is a poorly disguised first step toward the dreaded reunification of Ireland.[143] During 1986 and 1987 Loyalists expressed their indignation in a campaign of mass defiance that included several huge demonstrations and strikes; the boycotting of local governmental bodies; violent clashes between protesters and the police; the formation of an Ulster Resistance Movement to oppose the agreement; sectarian assaults on Catholics; and attacks on RUC officers, their homes, and families for the alleged police role in upholding the agreement. (In this period, 550 attacks on police officers' homes occurred and 140 police

139. NIO official, Law and Order Division, interview with author, 3 August 1984.
140. NIO official, Political Affairs Division, interview with author, 3 August 1984.
141. Walsh argues that repressive practices continue today primarily because of "the implacable resistance of the Unionist majority to reform in this field" (*Use and Abuse,* p. 122).
142. Cf. Fisk, *No Return,* pp. 231–38. This illustrates "non-decision making," discussed in Peter Bachrach and Morton S. Baratz, *Power and Poverty* (New York: Oxford University Press, 1970).
143. In 1988, three years after the signing of the agreement, 62 percent of Protestants were "just as opposed" to it and an additional 17 percent were "less in favor" (Coopers and Lybrand poll, *Belfast Telegraph,* 4 October 1988).

families were forced to relocate.)[144] This organized resistance dissipated in late 1987, but it serves as a graphic reminder of the response the state may provoke by policy shifts unacceptable to Protestants.

In the first four years after its announcement, the Anglo-Irish Agreement only exacerbated the conflict: communal polarization and political violence increased; the gulf widened between the Protestant majority and the British regime; the Catholic minority remains alienated from the state; and the objective of political reconciliation has been stymied by Protestants' refusal to cooperate and their insistence on the termination of the agreement. Failing to achieve political progress, the Inter-Governmental Conference has by default focused on security matters—resulting in increased cooperation between London and Dublin but no material improvements in security.

BRITISH CAPACITIES

Earlier in the chapter I outlined the British Government's long-term interests in Ulster and its goals for political development and reconstruction of the security system. These interests and goals are generally favorable to democratization and liberalization. One self-imposed commitment, however, has unintended consequences that limit Britain's ability to press forward with liberalization: the 1976 decision to Ulsterize the conflict, gradually disengaging and retrenching British troops and giving local agencies prominence (RUC, UDR, the Diplock courts). By removing the military from the front line of counterinsurgency and saddling criminal justice agencies with responsibility for internal security as well as conventional crime control, British officials in effect disallowed certain kinds of reform in these agencies. Thus, Ulsterizing the conflict significantly hampers further liberalization of the police and courts. One alternative, the resumption of military primacy in internal security, would contradict the logic of Ulsterization, which has bipartisan support in British political circles.

Diametrically opposed to Ulsterization is the option of full integration of the province into the United Kingdom. This scenario might offer the best hope for liberalization, insofar as it would bring an end to constitutional uncertainty and foster provincial convergence with the metropole. But integration is unacceptable to Catholics, does not appeal to a majority of Protestants (see Table 5), and is unpopular in the United

144. *Times,* 19 September 1988.

Kingdom. Integration would entail full and permanent British involvement in the province—even allowing for some devolved power as in Scotland—which would violate the premium London places on achieving an internal settlement and disengaging from Ulster.

Important environmental constraints also hinder liberalization and democratization. Although Britain has made significant progress, its capacity to drive liberalization much further is conditioned by countervailing communal forces. One critical difference between the postsettler regime in Northern Ireland and its counterpart in Zimbabwe is that the former is an adjunct of a liberal democracy. This circumstance may seem propitious for democratic political development, but a tutelary regime must be able to marshal broad-based indigenous support— something chronically elusive in contemporary Ulster. The British Government cannot depend on the consent, let alone the active support, of the Catholic minority or the Protestant majority. The system of direct rule and many of the regime's policies alienate groups on both sides.[145] Britain's very presence in Northern Ireland is the raison d'être of the Republican movement and a major objection for Loyalists who demand devolved government.

The British Government does not make history in Ulster just as it pleases. Protestants and Catholics alike have some capacity not only to derail a political settlement but also to thwart unacceptable innovations in the security field. Labour MP Clive Soley captures this point: "Neither Unionists nor Republicans have positive power. They only have negative power, the ability to dig in, to resist, to destroy."[146] Catholics have in the past reacted to repressive measures in ways that raise the political and security costs of introducing new ones; but of greater salience is the Protestant capacity to frustrate liberalizing changes. Should security policy tip too far in any direction, it might upset the fragile balance of forces and cause a full-scale crisis. In addition to the routine pressures of political parties and civic institutions (churches, the press) associated with each side, the possibility of mass mobilization and increasing violence, occasionally manifest, helps set the outer limits on the regime's political and security policies. In Zimbabwe, as we have seen, the forces of civil society have shown no comparable power of resistance.

---

145. Richard Rose, *Northern Ireland: A Time of Choice* (London: Macmillan, 1976), pp. 28, 140.
146. Clive Soley, "Britain's Duty to Make Clear Her Intentions," *Fortnight,* June 1984, p. 9; *Irish Times,* 17 August 1984.

Neither side appears to appreciate the constraints under which the British Government rules Northern Ireland and instead assumes that the regime has the capacity to prevail against the other side or unilaterally to resolve the problem.[147] London's leverage is largely fictional in light of Catholics' and Protestants' determination to boycott any innovation they perceive to violate their political interests, aspirations, and deeply felt communal identities. This social milieu is therefore unreceptive to radical initiatives. In fact, *any* security policy, whether impartial or favoring one community, is likely to antagonize either or both groups to a greater or lesser degree.

If Protestants and Catholics have degrees of negative power, the same may be said for the state. Balanced between actual or potential Protestant and Catholic pressures and lacking credibility in both communities, British power is largely reduced to limiting the damage and maintaining a semblance of order. These are manifestations of negative power. The state's military, administrative, and economic assets do not translate into decisive political leverage over entrenched domestic forces. Northern Ireland illustrates the argument that a state may be *autonomous* from civil society but also rather *ineffective* in pursuing its long-term goals. This ineffectiveness derives largely from its very autonomy, its lack of a domestic base of support for policy initiatives.

Since the mid-1970s, British officials have taken the position that security measures alone will not end Ulster's political violence. A corollary principle is that of avoiding the temptation to overreact to spectacular incidents of political violence, in light of the possible counterproductive impact (which the Government has often underestimated in its security measures). Acknowledging the need to address the underlying political causes, officials nevertheless see a political solution as remote. Bold policy initiatives thus yield by default to political drift and containment of the security problem.[148] The paramount aim is to keep the conflict within manageable bounds in Ulster and away from mainland Britain. Successive British Cabinets have feared that Ulster's street disorders, political radicalization, and polarization might have a demonstration effect on the rest of the United Kingdom. In the words of a former army commander in Northern Ireland, the price of any relaxa-

147. Bew and Patterson, *Ulster Crisis,* p. 96.
148. Liam O'Dowd, Bill Rolston, and Mike Tomlinson, "From Labour to the Tories: The Ideology of Containment in Northern Ireland," *Capital and Class* 18 (Winter 1982): 68; [Glover Report] "Northern Ireland: Future Terrorist Trends," 15 December 1978 (in Roger Faligot, *Britain's Military Strategy in Ireland* [London: Zed, 1983], p. 226).

tion in the security effort would be nothing short of "a nasty overspill indoors," contaminating mainland Britain.[149]

The incompatible communal outlooks discussed above explain why the Government is not prepared to devolve control over security policy and institutions to domestic parties. The transfer of security powers to the majority would almost certainly mean a return to sectarian maintenance of order and Protestant domination. Shared responsibility for security among leaders of both sides is also unlikely, given their diametrically opposed visions of law and order.

In contrast, British elites paint their position as supremely enlightened. One NIO official argued that "security policy is the one element that is criticized by all sides, which shows we are not influenced by any one side."[150] Not only is the statement a non sequitur, it suggests a completely neutral approach; the Government has sometimes responded favorably to communal pressures. Also misleading is the claim that "security policy is determined by an *entirely British* perspective."[151] The implication that policy develops in a vacuum ignores the environmental constraints discussed above.

These points bear on two of the three broad perspectives on British rule discussed at the beginning of the chapter. Our findings challenge the depiction of the metropole as a guardian of Loyalist interests. Particularly on security questions, contemporary British rule is no simple prop for or instrument of Loyalist supremacy. Were the Government a servant of the Loyalists, it would not generate such unrelenting and bitter Loyalist opposition to "lenient" security measures, nor would it instruct state agencies to treat Republican and Loyalist offenders evenhandedly.

One NIO official underscored the "fundamental dispute between the Secretary of State and the Unionists over security."[152] In its *ideals* of universalistic maintenance of order and restrained use of force, the Government indeed seems worlds apart from the Unionists. And yet the security program has not had a neutral *impact* on this divided society. First, there is bound to be some institutional inertia—in this case favoring the Protestant majority—in any effort to modernize state agencies, although it has been checked more vigorously in Ulster than in Zim-

---

149. General Sir John Hackett, "Containing the Explosive Mixture," *Hibernia,* 9 August 1979.
150. NIO Political Affairs official, interview with author, 16 August 1984.
151. Ibid.; emphasis added.
152. Ibid.

babwe. Second, since the principal challenge to the state comes from Republican forces rooted in Catholic working-class areas, security operations have concentrated in those areas, where they daily disrupt social life and offend popular sensibilities—quite disproportionately to anything experienced in Protestant working-class areas.

Despite Protestants' dissatisfaction over specific security arrangements, the effects of the security enterprise are generally compatible with a core Loyalist demand. Security is pursued within a context that takes for granted the constitutional status of Northern Ireland as part of the United Kingdom as long as the majority so desires. Impartial maintenance of order is thus not inconsistent with a security policy whose net effect is to favor Loyalist over Catholic constitutional preferences.

CONCLUSION

Since 1972, the trajectory of change in law and order arrangements has been uneven: the elimination of some sectarian structures, modernization of others, and retrogression in still others. British rule in contemporary Northern Ireland has made significant departures from the record of the Unionist settler state. Abolished with the settler-dominated executive and parliament were some of the most sectarian institutions (e.g., Ministry of Home Affairs); others were partially reformed (e.g., Royal Ulster Constabulary). Moreover, metropolitan intervention has produced not only organizational improvements but also systemic changes in the relations between various agencies (including oversight bodies) and the ethos cultivated in the commanding heights of the system (Northern Ireland Office). These systemic changes have brought greater internal accountability, diffused universalistic norms, and reduced the incidence of repressive events. In 1972, the police and military killed seventy-four people; in 1988, seven.[153] In the coercive order, *the net effect of British rule is the partial liberalization of the internal security system and a relaxation of repression.*

The extent of liberalization should not be exaggerated, however. The advent of bodies responsible for ensuring accountability is a significant improvement on the Unionist system, but they could be further empowered. Innocent civilians continue to experience rough justice from the security and criminal justice agencies; the policing of marches and riots is

---

153. The years between 1972 and 1988 saw a steep decline in deaths caused by the security forces.

often ruthless and bloody. The Diplock courts, Ulster Defense Regiment, and undercover units of the SAS and the RUC Special Branch have engaged in controversial activities of sufficient magnitude to contaminate the image of the entire security enterprise.

Security agencies have been in the vanguard in frustrating progressive changes in many transitional societies. In Northern Ireland the security branch vigorously resisted the original reforms but subsequently became more compliant. The police, courts, and military continue to advocate the retention of exceptional powers, but these agencies play a relatively modest role today in blocking liberalization. Other factors have a greater impact.

Northern Ireland exemplifies the special problems confronting an external regime committed to reconstructing a settler power structure and a sectarian security system but fettered in its capacity to do so. The response of communal forces may have important effects on the transformation of state institutions. There are obstacles to structural change in a postsettler polity where the regime hovers above society with little moral authority and where antagonistic social forces can sabotage major political and security initiatives. Protestant and Catholic forces are sufficiently powerful to block the political projects of their antagonists but unable to impose their own. By default, the situation has become one of political impasse and containment of the security problem. These constraints, coupled with continuing political violence and the policy of Ulsterization, circumscribe the process of liberalization.

Finally, the partial modernization of the security enterprise has had no appreciable impact on nation building in Northern Ireland. The citizens of Northern Ireland, no less today than in the past, have no single national identity or common political culture. The territory continues to host two nations, advancing irreconcilable solutions to the problem. It seems plausible to conclude that the impact of reformed security institutions on nation building in a divided society will be limited unless liberalization proceeds in conjunction with political progress. Since politics and security are so intertwined in Northern Ireland, communal attitudes toward, and experience of, security arrangements are confounded with political fears and aspirations. The history of direct rule is testimony to the difficulties inherent in working to alleviate the political fears and to satisfy the aspirations of Protestants and Catholics alike.

As alternative routes away from settler rule, the cases of Zimbabwe and Northern Ireland illustrate larger themes. Zimbabwe demonstrates that formal democratization of a polity may proceed without an overhaul of the inherited security system. Northern Ireland shows the opposite: formal democratization is not a necessary condition for significant liberalization of security structures. These outcomes suggest other conclusions: *genuine substantive democratization* in Zimbabwe will remain tenuous until the institutions of control are rebuilt; *more extensive liberalization* of security arrangements in Ulster seems contingent on political progress and communal reconciliation. Northern Ireland illustrates both the prospects and limits of institution building in a deeply divided society governed by a regime imposed from without.

Conclusion

Transforming Settler States

Northern Ireland and Zimbabwe exemplify two ways in which settler political systems may break down, possible fates that may await settler castes after their regimes are dislodged from power, and divergent outcomes for state security structures once settler rule ends. Our explanatory model helps to account for these radically different outcomes and should apply to other postsettler societies.

THE BREAKDOWN OF SETTLER RULE

The demise of Protestant rule in Northern Ireland and of white rule in Rhodesia illustrates the importance of maintaining the settler state's autonomy from metropolitan interference, control over the native population, and settler solidarity on fundamental principles and the means to defend them.

Settlers in Rhodesia and Northern Ireland grew uneasy when incumbent regimes began to experiment with native accommodation. Prime Ministers Sir Edgar Whitehead and Terence O'Neill made unprecedented conciliatory gestures toward their respective subordinate populations. For Rhodesian blacks and Ulster Catholics, the reforms sparked a revolution of rising expectations that could not, alas, be satisfied by regimes dependent on right-wing settlers for survival in office. The majority of the Rhodesian and Ulster settlers were not prepared to countenance even a limited reformist solution, convinced that concessions would inspire more radical demands from the natives and that reforms violated their cherished values and the state's raison d'être. Each regime's experiment with reform, therefore, quickly depleted the reservoir of consent within the dominant caste. In some other settler states—Liberia before 1980, contemporary Taiwan, and even South Africa—modernizing elites have had somewhat more success in mobilizing settler support for concessions, but not without resistance from reactionary forces.

Both the O'Neill and Whitehead Governments represented relatively enlightened sections of the respective settler castes. Paradoxically, these regimes were attempting not to dismantle but to strengthen and refine settler domination by partially accommodating and hence placating the native caste. Hegemonic or ascendant settler factions, however, could see no advantages in streamlined settler rule. Each maverick government's disturbance of traditional political norms and its innovations in intercommunal relations provoked intense resistance from the ultraconservative elements of the dominant community as well as hard-line elements in the state, whose confidence in the ruling elite had irreversibly shattered. They accused both Whitehead and O'Neill of forsaking the sacrosanct principle of settler supremacy by encouraging accommodation—however limited—with blacks or Catholics. Concessions of any kind were defined as a prelude to the specter of "black domination" in Rhodesia and "Rome rule" or "Catholic domination" in a reunited Ireland. In both societies, the pendulum swung back "towards those who [were] least ready for change"; and each moderate regime succumbed to an absolutist and recalcitrant one.[1] In both, the former enlightened state managers and their supporters lacked the resources and the will to oppose the retrograde direction of the new regime. After attempting to stage electoral comebacks, the modernists grew increasingly marginalized and finally vanished from the political scene. Our two cases thus support Leo Kuper's thesis that the "failure of reformism" is a powerful tendency, if not a "law," in settler states.[2]

In Ulster, the removal of Terence O'Neill and the installation of a more conservative Unionist Government further mobilized and radicalized the subordinate population. British and Catholic pressures combined to fragment and generate a violent backlash among Protestants and a crisis for the regime. O'Neill's successor, James Chichester-Clark,

1. Colin Leys, *European Politics in Southern Rhodesia* (Oxford: Clarendon, 1959), p. 36.
2. Leo Kuper, *The Pity of It All: Polarization of Racial and Ethnic Relations* (Minneapolis: University of Minnesota Press, 1977).

lasted slightly more than a year and gave way to the more hard-line Brian Faulkner. Although the Conservative Government in London allowed the settlers greater leeway from 1970 to 1972 than had the previous Labour Government, the metropole's continued interference in domestic affairs proved disastrous for the Unionist state. The last three settler regimes had little latitude in decision making. Each had simultaneously to play to the British gallery, appease right-wing critics, and appear sensitive to the demands of the Catholic minority. The escalation of mass street protests and political violence, police and military brutality, and the disarray of three successive Unionist cabinets created a full-scale crisis of order and stability by early 1972. Realizing that Unionist rule was no longer tenable, London assumed direct control of the state machinery.

Compared to Rhodesia from 1958 through 1962, Ulster experienced more widespread mobilization of the subordinate population; the overstretched security system was less able to curtail popular protest and sectarian violence; and divisions within the settler community grew deeper and less amenable to resolution. In Rhodesia, the security system was able to suppress African nationalism in the 1960s, and a new settler government was remarkably successful in reunifying the settler caste.

Immediately after its installation in 1962, the Rhodesian Front reneged on the concessions granted by its predecessor. The intransigence of the settlers over even minor adjustments in the apartheid system crystallized in 1965 when Ian Smith defiantly announced Rhodesia's Unilateral Declaration of Independence (UDI) from Britain. The black majority saw UDI as the final nail in the coffin for their aspirations. Hitherto blacks had looked to Britain to redress their grievances, but metropolitan impotence and the settler state's sweeping legal restrictions on peaceful opposition drove their campaign underground and led to a protracted armed struggle.

Effective autonomy from the metropole is an essential condition for stable settler rule. Britain's distinctive relations to Rhodesia and Ulster helped shape the trajectory of change in each. In neither case did the Crown relish the thought of direct intervention. As a former British Home Secretary, James Callaghan, wrote with Ulster and Cyprus in mind, "how easy it was to get into such a situation and how difficult to get out."[3] The ideal scenario for the metropole—the least costly or entangling—was to orchestrate political change by remote control.

3. James Callaghan, *A House Divided: The Dilemma of Northern Ireland* (London: Collins, 1973), p. 60.

Hence it applied diplomatic and economic pressure on the rebel Rhodesian regime and persevered for three years in its efforts to wring reforms out of the Unionist regimes.

If the British Government sought to avoid direct political and military intervention in Rhodesia and Northern Ireland, its *capacity* to intervene was radically different in each setting. As part (however ambiguous) of the United Kingdom, Northern Ireland was susceptible to British intervention politically, geographically, militarily, and economically; Rhodesia was not. Rhodesia's unilateral cutting of ties to Britain in 1965 gave the settlers precisely the room for maneuver that their Ulster counterparts lacked. It took the Crown quite some time to realize that Rhodesia was a uniquely incorrigible colony over which metropolitan jurisdiction and leverage were fictions. Unlike other colonies with settler populations (Kenya, Zambia, Zanzibar), Rhodesia was almost entirely outside London's sphere of influence. That it withstood fifteen years of economic sanctions and diplomatic pressures was a measure of its insulation from other international actors as well.

It is significant that an Ulster Unionist regime itself requested metropolitan military assistance in 1969 to restore public order. The settler regime attempted to forge an alliance with these troops that, as in Algeria in the 1950s, was no substitute for absolute control over the military. Britain's military support had a high price, as Kenya's settlers learned after the Mau Mau crisis. With military and administrative personnel stationed in Ulster, Britain realized the folly of working through established institutions and the need for entirely new arrangements. (It had no such "hands-on" experience in Rhodesia before 1979.)

The juridical basis for British intervention in Northern Ireland was relatively clear (whereas in Rhodesia metropolitan authority was problematic, particularly after UDI in 1965). London's residual sovereignty over Northern Ireland (as part of the United Kingdom) meant that it required no constitutional engineering or negotiated settlement before establishing direct rule. Unlike Rhodesia in 1979, Ulster had no viable alternative government waiting in the wings. Each of the last three Unionist regimes had diminishing authority, and a domestic alternative to Unionist rule—for example, power sharing—was not yet on the agenda. The absence of an internal solution and the poor three-year record of filtering reforms through Protestant regimes suggested that transforming this settler state would require direct metropolitan engineering.

In Zimbabwe, by contrast, London had strong incentives to tread lightly on the existing political and security system. In addition to the considerations outlined above and given Britain's entanglement in Ulster, the metropole hesitated to embark on a state-building experiment in Zimbabwe, which might turn into another long-term imbroglio.[4] Britain's chief concern was to arrive at a settlement and rid itself of the Rhodesian burden; the substance of the settlement was secondary provided it include provision for free elections.

Our findings show that each pillar of settler rule is absolutely vital to state survival. When one condition fails—as in Rhodesia with the sharp rise of native insurgency during the 1970s—settler rule is doomed. However, the fact that Rhodesia continued to enjoy high levels of settler solidarity and autonomy from the metropole delayed the inevitable collapse of the settler state for the greater part of a decade. When all three pillars crack—as in Northern Ireland from 1969 to 1972—dissolution of the settler order is likely to accelerate. In Ulster, the state fell apart rather quickly under metropolitan political pressure and military intervention, the unraveling of settler unity, and the activation of the subordinate population.

EXPLAINING POSTSETTLER OUTCOMES

Regime transitions provide a rare opportunity—not often seized—for rebuilding security structures and for studying the sources of continuity and change. Focusing on the creation of formal democratic procedures (e.g., universal suffrage) or the inauguration of civilian rule, much of the literature on contemporary transitions to democracy has neglected the pivotal role of security agencies in determining the prospects for and limits of meaningful democratic development.[5] However desirable in its own right, democratic formalism is neither a necessary nor a sufficient condition for change in repressive state structures. In fact, *formal democratization may impede, invite, or have no effect on repressive outcomes.* Majoritarian democracy in communally divided societies has

4. In the mid-1970s the British Cabinet hoped to "stay well clear of Rhodesia, which several Ministers regarded as another potentially debilitating Northern Ireland crisis for Britain" (David Martin and Phyllis Johnson, *The Struggle for Zimbabwe* [London: Faber and Faber, 1981], p. 256).

5. Some recent major works on transitions from authoritarianism give inadequate weight to the security sector, e.g., Guillermo O'Donnell, Philippe Schmitter, and Lawrence Whitehead, eds., *Transitions from Authoritarian Rule* (Baltimore: Johns Hopkins University Press, 1986); Larry Diamond, Juan Linz, and Seymour Martin Lipset, eds., *Democracy in Developing Countries* (Boulder, Colo.: Lynne Rienner, 1988). Studies that pay due attention to this branch are Maria Alves, *State and Opposition in Military Brazil* (Austin: University of Texas Press, 1985); Alfred Stepan, *Rethinking Military Politics: Brazil and the Southern Cone* (Princeton: Princeton University Press, 1988).

often proven to be a euphemism for the tyranny of the majority—which gives short shrift to minority rights and denies the minority meaningful political participation. Formal democratization may therefore be associated with an *increase* in repression. Lijphart's conclusion, that in divided societies "majority rule is not only undemocratic but also dangerous," producing "majority dictatorship and civil strife," is illustrated in Northern Ireland from 1921 to 1972 and in Zimbabwe since independence, where the Westminster system has contributed to authoritarian treatment of minority communities.[6] Inversely, the *replacement* of a majoritarian order with a form of dictatorial rule may have positive effects on institutional liberalization. In Ulster since 1972, British rule has contributed to the partial remodeling of security structures and an improved observance of human rights. The security system has become more accountable, less sectarian, and more impartial in its routine operations—counter to what might have been expected from an essentially colonial system of rule.

Since independence in Zimbabwe, the state has largely confined changes in its coercive core to Africanizing personnel and instilling a doctrine that celebrates the role of the security system in upholding majority rule instead of white supremacy. This official ethos—however much it is actualized—marks a clear departure from the ideological mission of the repressive apparatus under settler rule. Yet little structural liberalization has occurred, which contributes to repressive outcomes under the new regime.

Postsettler Northern Ireland and Zimbabwe have been troubled by protracted communal unrest and political violence; these factors have had a pronounced impact on each regime's responses as well as the prospects for institutional transformation. But problems of order and security are not the only critical variables. Although the very concept of national security is ambiguous and attempts to measure security problems are problematic, cross-national variation in official assessments and responses suggests that threats alone do not independently determine or fully explain state responses.[7] Intervening between apparent

6. Arend Lijphart, *Democracies* (New Haven: Yale University Press, 1984), pp. 22, 23. In divided societies, democratic power sharing might be preferable to majority rule but difficult to institutionalize in extremely polarized cases like Northern Ireland's, where decision making might be hampered by incessant friction.

7. For cross-national longitudinal data on disjunctions between the frequency of insurgent events and governmental sanctions, see C. Taylor and D. Jodice, eds., *World Handbook of Political and Social Indicators* (New Haven: Yale University Press, 1983); Ernest Duff and John McCamant, *Violence and Repression in Latin America* (New York: Free Press, 1976).

threats and official reactions, elites' assessments and decision making may be confounded with considerations quite unrelated to national security. Among the decisive extrasecurity motives for a repressive enterprise may be purges of political rivals, drives to expand a security agency's power or jurisdiction, elites' aggrandizement, efforts to consolidate racial or ethnic domination, and programs of fundamental societal restructuring.[8] Only a perspective that gives due weight to a regime's underlying aims, immediate priorities, and interpretations of reality can fully account for its security policies and practices.

Chapters 6 and 7 demonstrated the explanatory power of a four-dimensional model of security system outcomes in Northern Ireland and Zimbabwe. First, a political culture that celebrates democratic values is likely to foster democratic practices once an authoritarian regime has been replaced, as various contemporary Latin American societies attest. Since a democratic tradition is characteristically weak or absent from the political landscape in settler systems, it is not surprising that even an incipient democratic political culture is difficult to detect in postsettler Zimbabwe and Ulster. The contiguity of Northern Ireland to the rest of the United Kingdom perhaps makes democratic values more salient—as metropolitan ideals—in Ulster than in Zimbabwe, but rarely have Ulster's polarized forces shown a genuine lasting commitment to such ideals. Instead, both sides invoke the language of democracy on behalf of their narrow communal demands: majoritarianism for Protestants, the protection of minority rights or majoritarianism in a reunited Ireland for Catholics.

The power and orientation of existing security agencies is a second important variable. The security establishment is a model example of the standard bureaucratic tendency toward survival, expansion, and resistance to externally generated reform.[9] If all else remains constant,

---

8. Supporting evidence on the role of extrasecurity factors in decisions to use repression can be found in Alves, *State and Opposition*; Cynthia Enloe, *Ethnic Soldiers: State Security in Divided Societies* (Athens: University of Georgia Press, 1980); Robert Goldstein, *Political Repression in Modern America* (Cambridge, Mass.: Schenkman, 1978); David Brown, "Sieges and Scapegoats: The Politics of Pluralism in Ghana and Togo," *Journal of Modern African Studies* 21, no. 3 (September 1983); Richard M. Freeland, *The Truman Doctrine and the Origins of McCarthyism: Foreign Policy, Domestic Politics, and Internal Security, 1946–1948* (New York: Knopf, 1972); Athan Theoharis, "The Rhetoric of Politics: Foreign Policy, Internal Security, and Domestic Politics in the Truman Era, 1945–1950," in *Politics and Policies of the Truman Administration*, ed. B. Bernstein (Chicago: Quadrangle, 1970); Barry Buzan, *People, States, and Fear: The National Security Problem in International Relations* (Chapel Hill: University of North Carolina Press, 1983).

9. Kenneth Grundy, *The Militarization of South African Politics* (Bloomington: Indiana University Press, 1986), p. 109.

security agencies with origins in a settler state will incline toward repression under postsettler rule. The decisive factor is the new regime's approach to these institutional proclivities. We have seen that the Zimbabwe Government has galvanized and mobilized inherited institutions in a way that invites rough justice. The elective affinity between the orientations of security organs and the regime's grand political design suggests a strong positive interaction between the two factors that militates against liberalization. By contrast, the British Government in Ulster has attempted to arrest or minimize the repressive potential of the security sector—by abolishing some agencies, reforming others, and establishing mechanisms of accountability. Although the police and courts continue to press for exceptional powers and procedures, the agencies involved in internal security today play a relatively minor role in frustrating the process of liberalization—contrasted to their active resistance during the final years of Unionist rule.

A third factor affecting security systems is the role of the leading forces in civil society. Civic institutions and social movements with a strong commitment to justice and democracy may successfully press for human rights and systemic changes. Others, like the old regime's loyalists, vigilantes, or death squads, may be champions of naked repression. In contemporary Zimbabwe the sectors of civil society have been rather inactive and atomized; in Northern Ireland the opposite is the case. Yet the fact that civil society in Ulster is plural—reflecting rather than transcending the interests of the antagonistic communal enclaves and containing progressive as well as antimodernist forces—means that demands on the government are uneven, both discouraging and inviting greater repression. The British Government has from time to time responded favorably to communal demands but typically rejects such pressures in favor of the status quo.

THE NEW REGIME

This study suggests that the decisive factor affecting the fate of a security system is a binary variable: the interests and capacities of the postsettler regime. To transform a sectarian security enterprise, a regime must have both abiding interest and capacity to render security organs accountable, impartial, and sensitive to ideals of justice and human rights. We have seen that the Government of Zimbabwe has the capacity to remake the inherited security system but little compelling interest in doing so. Conversely, the British Government has demonstrated an interest in further liberalizing Ulster's security system but has only limited capacity to do so.

The underlying interests and objectives of state elites may be inferred from regularities in official policies and programs and patterns of action. Needless to say, our two postsettler regimes share with others the generic interests in domestic order and national security. They also seem committed to destroying the vestiges of the invidious settler system and building a fundamentally new social order. However, there are major differences between the postsettler polities envisioned by each new regime and, hence, in the interests driving their policies. The paramount political objective of the Zimbabwe Government is to cement its power through the vehicle of a one-party state. The multiparty system bequeathed to the new nation under the Lancaster House constitution gave opposition parties an arena for political activity and held out the possibility of replacing the ZANU Government. The electoral order thus contradicted the ruling party's grand design. Viewing the inherited security system as part of the solution to its political and ethnic problems, the regime fortified this branch and used it to neutralize opposition parties and thus facilitate the installation of its one-party system. The continuity of the coercive apparatus stands out, even as its official raison d'être has shifted from the defense of settler domination to the protection of majority interests.

The grand design of the postsettler regime in Northern Ireland differs radically from the Zimbabwe model. London seeks to create in Ulster a stable political order based on the consent and participation of Catholics and Protestants alike and a demilitarized, impartial, communally representative, and accountable system of law and order. Viewing the settler security system as part of the problem, the British Government moved to reform it at the outset of direct rule. Chapter 7 showed that some progress has been made in the direction of institutional liberalization.

A regime's objectives depend for their realization on its capacities, which have two dimensions. First, the regime must have sufficient *resources* to pursue goals, including skills in leadership, financial leverage, and the allegiance of state personnel. It must be able to elicit the compliance of security agencies with internal reforms, external accountability, and perhaps with their own dismantling. The regime must be able to rearrange the relations between the core and the remainder of the state, reducing the autonomy of the security sector and empowering those branches most strongly committed to human rights. Many new regimes have clearly lacked this power altogether, but those in Northern Ireland

and Zimbabwe seem to have the requisite intrastate capacity to initiate changes. The Government in Northern Ireland has registered some success in this area, although some of its own policies—such as Ulsterization—have militated against certain kinds of reform; the Government in Zimbabwe has not exerted significant intrastate leverage to promote liberalization.

The second aspect of the regime's capacity involves environmental *incentives and constraints.* Social forces have assumed very different roles in the two countries. In Zimbabwe, as in many other independent African nations, civil society is fragmented and weak vis-à-vis the state.[10] Political parties and civic groups—the media, labor, business, intellectuals, churches—have limited resources, weak alliances, or insufficient attachment to human rights norms. Hence, they have registered little, if any, positive impact on security policy. When civic forces have mustered public protests, they have been labeled subversive and sanctioned; the very existence of groups with preferences opposed to those of the incumbent regime appears to violate the official quest for national unity and political conformity. In Zimbabwe state-society relations are therefore highly *asymmetrical in favor of the state,* which gives the regime great latitude to pursue its political agenda.

Unlike Zimbabwe's acquiescent civic order, that in Northern Ireland teems with oppositional life. If a small minority like Rhodesia's whites may come to accept the hopelessness of resistance to change, a substantial majority is much more difficult to convince. Ulster Protestants have demonstrated a capacity for resistance despite their loss of formal state power. When the Thatcher Government announced a major initiative in the Anglo-Irish Agreement of 1985, for example, it precipitated a serious sustained campaign of Protestant resistance, which abated when the accord appeared to have changed little. With the strength of numbers and the force of arms, Protestants seem prepared to fight any future relaxation in the struggle against Republican insurgents and any unwelcome political initiatives by the British authorities. For their part, the Catholics have some capacity to raise the political costs of intensified repression. The imperfect equilibrium of these countervailing pressures sustains the coercive and political status quo. Their effect on state security policy is indirect: anticipating a possible backlash from one side or

---

10. Jean François Bayart, "Civil Society in Africa," in *Political Domination in Africa,* ed. P. Chabal (Cambridge: Cambridge University Press, 1986); Diamond, Linz, and Lipset, eds., *Democracy in Developing Countries;* Nelson Kasfir, *The Shrinking Political Arena* (Berkeley: University of California Press, 1976).

the other, the regime alters little. As the regime struggles to hold Protestants and Catholics in check, so these opposed forces hold the regime in check.

Since neither a military nor political solution seems possible, successive administrations have embraced the strategy of least resistance: containment. In short, the regime exercises largely negative power, limiting the damage from mass resistance and political violence and preventing its spread to the British mainland.

The case of Ulster illustrates both the prospects and limits of change in a society where an external regime is committed to comprehensive modernization of political and security structures but is constrained in its capacity to do so by intractable and contradictory domestic forces. Like other colonial states, the British regime is at once more autonomous and weaker than the (Unionist) settler state, since it has no base of domestic support for its programs. Protestants and Catholics may have some influence over change in security structures but cannot institutionalize their preferences. The communal polarities of civil society neutralize each side's potential impact on state policy. In this context, the relationship between the state and social forces consists of a *fragile balance in favor of the status quo*.

Our perspective has important implications for studies of other settler and postsettler societies as well as those, like Haiti, the Philippines, Nicaragua, and Eastern Europe, grappling with a different authoritarian legacy. The fate of their security systems can arguably be traced to some differential configuration of our four variables.

Settler rule came to an abrupt end in Liberia in April 1980, as a result of a military coup led by Samuel Doe. The record of postsettler rule there is one of rigid authoritarianism and widespread repression. Like its Zimbabwean counterpart, the Doe Government is consolidating one-party rule with help from the inherited security apparatus. But unlike the Zimbabwean, the Liberian regime lacks broad popular support and cannot convincingly invoke the cause of majority rule to legitimate the dictatorship.[11] Though Liberian civil society appears substantially more developed and active in challenging state authoritarianism than Zimbabwe's, the impact of this opposition was at best minimal during the first decade of the Doe regime.[12]

11. J. Gus Liebenow, *Liberia: The Quest for Democracy* (Bloomington: Indiana University Press, 1987); Lawyers Committee for Human Rights, *Liberia: A Promise Betrayed* (New York: LCHR, 1986).

12. Evidence for the vibrancy of Liberian civil society can be found in monthly reports of the journal *West Africa*.

Settler control of the Namibian state machinery was conditioned by the direct military and administrative involvement of South African functionaries, which limited white settlers' leverage during the 1988 negotiated settlement. The independence agreement contains no reference to existing security laws or agencies or, for that matter, to racially discriminatory laws.[13] But a proclamation signed by the South African president on 6 June 1989 repealed several discriminatory statutes as well as three security laws.[14] Members of the counterinsurgency police force, Koevoet, while officially disbanded, continue to operate (in 1989) as a sectarian force sympathetic to white settler interests.[15] The new government will confront choices regarding the security apparatus similar to those ZANU faced in Zimbabwe after independence.

In Taiwan communal divisions have been softened by decades of assimilation; democratically oriented social institutions are active; and the regime has begun to democratize the polity—all of which augur well for future political development and perhaps for overhaul of the internal security apparatus. Nevertheless, it remains to be seen if this softening of authoritarian rule will continue unabated or if forces of resistance will be able to derail a reformist solution.[16]

Analysis of other cases—South Africa and Israel's occupied territories—will have to await the installation of a postsettler regime.

The larger significance of this study for the prospects of democratic political development in postsettler societies bears repeating. A flourishing democracy requires more than formal participatory procedures, progressive legislation, or changes in specific coercive organizations. It requires reconstituted organizational cultures and changes in the structure of relations between state sectors. Democratic gains may be fragile and reversible in the absence of *systemic liberalization,* which entails the institutionalization of norms based on rationalized authority, justice, and universalism as well as the empowerment of branches committed to these norms. This sweeping overhaul is no recipe for state suicide: inter-

---

13. United States Department of State, *Agreements for Peace in Southwestern Africa,* selected doc. no. 32, December 1988.

14. The three laws rescinded were the Internal Security Act of 1950, the Public Safety Act of 1953, and the Unlawful Organizations Act of 1960 (William Claiborne, "Amnesty Set for Namibian Guerillas," *Washington Post,* 7 June 1989).

15. William Claiborne, "Alleged Police Intimidation Threatens Namibia Election Process," *Washington Post,* 19 June 1989; Christopher Wren, "Namibia Police, Rebel Hunters, Prepare for Duller Duty with Independence," *New York Times,* 15 January 1989.

16. Edwin Winckler, "Institutionalization and Participation on Taiwan: From Hard to Soft Authoritarianism," *China Quarterly,* no. 99 (September 1984): 481–99; Marc J. Cohen, *Taiwan at the Crossroads* (Washington, D.C.: Asia Resource Center, 1988).

nal security can be maintained in a fashion that respects ideals of justice and human rights. Liberalization of a security system can, in fact, *enhance order* by reducing arbitrary and repressive outcomes that may generate popular alienation, unrest, and political violence.

Thoroughgoing transformation of a state's coercive order is rare, but changes in this direction as well as basic continuities can best be understood, I suggest, with the help of the explanatory model advanced here.

Selected Bibliography

Adams, Gerry. *The Politics of Irish Freedom.* Dingle, Ireland: Brandon, 1986.

Africa Watch. *Zimbabwe: A Break with the Past? Human Rights and Political Unity.* An Africa Watch Report. New York: Africa Watch, 1989.

Alperin, Robert J. "The Distribution of Power and the (June 1979) Zimbabwe Rhodesia Constitution." *Journal of Southern African Affairs* 5, no. 1 (January 1980): 41–54.

Alves, Maria Helena Moriera. *State and Opposition in Military Brazil.* Austin: University of Texas Press, 1985.

Amnesty International. *Detention without Trial of Political Prisoners in Zimbabwe.* London: Amnesty International, 1985.

———. *Report of an Amnesty International Mission to Northern Ireland.* London: Amnesty International, June 1978.

———. *Rhodesia/Zimbabwe.* London: Amnesty International, 1976.

Anti-Apartheid Movement. *Fire-Force Exposed: The Rhodesian Security Forces and Their Role in Defending White Supremacy.* London: Anti-Apartheid Movement, 1979.

Apter, David. "Some Reflections on the Role of a Political Opposition in New Nations." *Comparative Studies in Society and History* 4, no. 2 (January 1962): 154–68.

Astrow, André. *Zimbabwe: A Revolution that Lost Its Way?* London: Zed, 1983.

Aunger, Edmund A. *In Search of Political Stability: A Comparative Study of New Brunswick and Northern Ireland.* Montreal: McGill-Queens University Press, 1981.

[Baker Commission]. *Review of the Operation of the Northern Ireland (Emergency Provisions) Act 1978,* Cmnd. 9222, Sir George Baker, Chair. London: HMSO, April 1984.

Balbus, Isaac. *The Dialectics of Legal Repression: Black Rebels before the American Criminal Courts.* New Brunswick, N.J.: Transaction, 1977.

Ball, Nicole. *Security and Economy in the Third World.* Princeton: Princeton University Press, 1988.

Barber, William. "The Political Economy of Central Africa's Experiment with Inter-Racial Partnership." *Canadian Journal of Economics and Political Science* 25, no. 3 (August 1959): 324–25.

Bayart, Jean François. "Civil Society in Africa." In *Political Domination in Africa,* ed. P. Chabal. Cambridge: Cambridge University Press, 1986.

Beach, Stephen W. "Social Movement Radicalization: The Case of the People's Democracy in Northern Ireland." *Sociological Quarterly* 18 (Summer 1977): 305–18.

Beckett, Ian. "The Rhodesian Army: Counter–Insurgency 1972–1979." In *Armed Forces and Counter-Insurgency,* ed. I. Beckett and J. Pimlott. New York: St. Martin's, 1985.

Belfrage, Sally. *Living with War: A Belfast Year.* New York: Penguin, 1987.

Bell, Geoffrey. *Troublesome Business: The Labour Party and the Irish Question.* London: Pluto, 1982.

Bell, J. Bowyer. "The Frustration of Insurgency: The Rhodesian Example in the Sixties." *Military Affairs* 35 (February 1971): 1–5.

Bennett, George. "British Settlers North of the Zambezi, 1920 to 1960." In *Colonialism in Africa,* ed. L. Gann and P. Duignan. London: Cambridge University Press, 1970.

[Bennett Committee]. *Report of the Committee of Inquiry into Police Interrogation Procedures in Northern Ireland.* Cmnd. 7497, Judge Bennett, Chair. London: HMSO, March 1979.

Berman, Bruce. "Bureaucracy and Incumbent Violence: Colonial Administration and the Origins of the 'Mau Mau' Emergency in Kenya." *British Journal of Political Science* 6 (April 1976): 143–75.

Bew, Paul, Peter Gibbon, and Henry Patterson. *The State in Northern Ireland: 1921–1972.* Manchester: Manchester University Press, 1979.

Bew, Paul, and Henry Patterson. *The British State and the Ulster Crisis: From Wilson to Thatcher.* London: Verso, 1985.

Biermann, Werner, and Reinhart Kössler. "The Settler Mode of Production: The Rhodesian Case." *Review of African Political Economy* 18 (May–August 1980): 106–26.

Binder, Leonard, James S. Coleman, Joseph LaPalombara, Lucian W. Pye, Sidney Verba, and Myron Weiner. *Crises and Sequences of Political Development.* Princeton: Princeton University Press, 1971.

Birrell, Derek, and Alan Murie. *Policy and Government in Northern Ireland: Lessons of Devolution.* Dublin: Gill and Macmillan, 1980.

Bishop, Patrick, and Eamonn Mallie. *The Provisional IRA.* London: Heinemann, 1987.

Bleakley, David. *Faulkner: Conflict and Consent in Irish Politics.* London and Oxford: Mowbrays, 1974.

Bowman, Larry. *Politics in Rhodesia: White Power in an African State.* Cambridge, Mass.: Harvard University Press, 1973.

Boyd, Andrew. *Brian Faulkner and the Crisis of Ulster Unionism.* Tralee, Ireland: Anvil, 1972.

Boyle, Kevin, Tom Hadden, and Paddy Hillyard. *Law and State: The Case of Northern Ireland.* Amherst: University of Massachusetts Press, 1975.

———. *Ten Years On in Northern Ireland: The Legal Control of Political Violence.* London: Cobden Trust, 1980.

Brown, David. "Crisis and Ethnicity: Legitimacy in Plural Societies." *Third World Quarterly* 7, no. 4 (October 1985): 988–1008.

———. "Sieges and Scapegoats: The Politics of Pluralism in Ghana and Togo." *Journal of Modern African Studies* 21, no. 3 (September 1983): 431–60.

Buckland, Patrick. *The Factory of Grievances: Devolved Government in Northern Ireland, 1921–1938.* New York: Barnes and Noble, 1979.

———. *A History of Northern Ireland.* Dublin: Gill and Macmillan, 1981.

Burton, Frank. *The Politics of Legitimacy: Struggles in a Belfast Community.* London: Routledge and Kegan Paul, 1978.

Buzan, Barry. *People, States, and Fear: The National Security Problem in International Relations.* Chapel Hill: University of North Carolina Press, 1983.

Callaghan, James. *A House Divided: The Dilemma of Northern Ireland.* London: Collins, 1973.

Calvert, Harry. *Constitutional Law in Northern Ireland.* London and Belfast: Stevens, 1968.

[Cameron Committee]. *Disturbances in Northern Ireland.* Cmnd. 532, Lord Cameron, Chair. Belfast: HMSO, September 1969.

Casanova, Jose. "Modernization and Democratization: Reflections on Spain's Transition to Democracy." *Social Research* 50, no. 4 (Winter 1983): 929–73.

Cason, Jim, and Mike Fleshman. "Zimbabwe: Election Campaign Turns Bloody." *Africa News,* 28 January 1985.

Catholic Commission for Justice and Peace. *Civil War in Rhodesia.* London: Catholic Institute for International Relations, 1976.

———. *The Man in the Middle: Torture, Resettlement, and Eviction.* Salisbury: CCJP, 1975.

Caute, David. *Under the Skin: The Death of White Rhodesia.* Harmondsworth: Penguin, 1983.

Chabal, Patrick. *Amilcar Cabral: Revolutionary Leadership and People's War.* Cambridge: Cambridge University Press, 1983.

Chief Constable. *Chief Constable's Annual Report.* Belfast: Police Authority, 1970, 1985, 1988.

Cilliers, J. K. *Counter-Insurgency in Rhodesia.* London: Croom Helm, 1985.

Cliffe, Lionel. "Zimbabwe's Political Inheritance." In *Zimbabwe's Inheritance,* ed. C. Stoneman. New York: St. Martins, 1981.

Clough, Michael. "Whither Zimbabwe?" *CSIS Africa Notes,* 15 November 1983.

Clutton-Brock, Guy. "The 1959 'Emergency' in Southern Rhodesia." In *A New Deal in Central Africa,* ed. C. Leys and C. Pratt. London: Heinemann, 1960.

Cohen, Marc J. *Taiwan at the Crossroads.* Washington, D.C.: Asia Resource Center, 1988.

Collier, David, ed. *The New Authoritarianism in Latin America.* Princeton: Princeton University Press, 1979.

Collier, Ruth. *Regimes in Tropical Africa*. Berkeley: University of California Press, 1982.

[Compton Commission]. *Report of the Enquiry into Allegations against the Security Forces of Physical Brutality in Northern Ireland Arising out of Events on the 9th August 1971*. Cmnd. 4823, Sir Edmund Compton, Chair. London: HMSO, November 1971.

Coogan, Tim Pat. *The I.R.A.* London: Fontana, 1980.

Dahl, Robert. *Polyarchy: Participation and Opposition*. New Haven: Yale University Press, 1971.

Davidson, Basil. "The Politics of Armed Struggle." In *Southern Africa: The New Politics of Revolution,* Basil Davidson, Joe Slovo, and Anthony Wilkinson. Harmondsworth: Penguin, 1976.

Democratic Unionist Party. *A War to Be Won*. Belfast: DUP, 1984.

Department of State. *Country Reports on Human Rights for 1988*. Washington, D.C.: U.S. Government Printing Office, 1989.

Diamond, Larry, Juan Linz, and Seymour Martin Lipset, eds. *Democracy in Developing Countries*. Vol. 2, *Africa*. Boulder, Colo.: Lynne Rienner, 1988.

Diamond, Larry, Seymour Martin Lipset, and Juan Linz. "Building and Sustaining Democratic Government in Developing Countries." *World Affairs* 150, no. 1 (Summer 1987): 5–19.

Ditch, John S. "Direct Rule and Northern Ireland Administration." *Administration* 25, no. 3 (Autumn 1977): 328–37.

Dollard, John. *Caste and Class in a Southern Town*. Garden City: Doubleday, 1949.

Duff, Ernest A., and John F. McCamant. *Violence and Repression in Latin America*. New York: Free Press, 1976.

Easton, David. *A Systems Analysis of Political Life*. Chicago: University of Chicago Press, 1965.

Ehrenreich, Frederick. "National Security." In *Zimbabwe: A Country Study,* ed. H. Nelson. Washington, D.C.: U.S. Government Printing Office, 1983.

Enloe, Cynthia. *Ethnic Soldiers: State Security in Divided Societies*. Athens: University of Georgia Press, 1980.

Evans, Mike. *Fighting against Chimurenga: An Analysis of Counterinsurgency in Rhodesia*. Salisbury: Historical Association of Zimbabwe, 1981.

———. "Gukurahundi: The Development of the Zimbabwe Defense Forces 1980–1987." *Strategic Review for Southern Africa* 10, no. 1 (May 1988): 1–37.

Evelegh, Robin. *Peace-Keeping in a Democratic Society: The Lessons of Northern Ireland*. Montreal: McGill-Queens University Press, 1978.

Faligot, Roger. *Britain's Military Strategy in Ireland*. London: Zed, 1983.

Farrell, Michael. *Arming the Protestants: The Formation of the Ulster Special Constabulary and the Royal Ulster Constabulary, 1920–1927*. London: Pluto, 1983.

———. *Northern Ireland: The Orange State*. London: Pluto, 1976.

Faulkner, Brian. *Memoirs of a Statesman*. London: Weidenfeld and Nicolson, 1978.

Feeney, Vincent E. "Westminster and the Early Civil Rights Struggle in Northern Ireland." *Eire-Ireland* 11, no. 4 (1976): 3–40.

Feltoe, Geoff. "Hearts and Minds: A Policy of Counter-Intimidation." *Rhodesian Law Journal* 16 (April 1976): 47–63.

———. "Legalizing Illegalities." *Rhodesian Law Journal* 15, no. 2 (October 1975): 167–76.

Finer, S. E. "The One-Party Regimes in Africa." *Government and Opposition* 2, no. 4 (July–October 1967): 491–509.

Fisk, Robert. *The Point of No Return: The Strike Which Broke the British in Ulster.* London: Andre Deutsch, 1975.

Flower, Ken. *Serving Secretly: An Intelligence Chief on Record, Rhodesia into Zimbabwe: 1964 to 1981.* London: John Murray, 1987.

Frederikse, Julie. *None But Ourselves: Masses vs. Media in the Making of Zimbabwe.* Harare: Zimbabwe Publishing House, 1982.

Gann, Lewis. *A History of Southern Rhodesia: Early Days to 1934.* London: Chatto and Windus, 1965.

Gann, Lewis, and Thomas H. Henriksen. *The Struggle for Zimbabwe.* New York: Praeger, 1981.

[Gardiner Committee]. *Report of a Committee to Consider, in the Context of Civil Liberties and Human Rights, Measures to Deal with Terrorism in Northern Ireland.* Cmnd. 5847, Lord Gardiner, Chair. London: HMSO, January 1975.

Gifford, Tony. *Supergrasses: The Use of Accomplice Evidence in Northern Ireland.* London: Cobden Trust, 1984.

[Glover Report]. "Northern Ireland: Future Terrorist Trends," Ministry of Defense, 15 December 1978, In *Britain's Military Strategy in Ireland,* Roger Faligot. London: Zed, 1983.

Goldstein, Robert Justin. *Political Repression in Modern America.* Cambridge, Mass.: Schenkman, 1978.

Good, Kenneth. "Settler Colonialism: Economic Development and Class Formation." *Journal of Modern African Studies* 14, no. 4 (December 1976): 597–620.

Good, Robert C. *U.D.I.: The International Politics of the Rhodesian Rebellion.* London: Faber and Faber, 1973.

Government of Southern Rhodesia. *Estimates of Expenditure.* Salisbury: Government Printer, annual.

———. *Report of the Constitutional Commission.* W. R. Whaley, Chair. Salisbury: Government Printer, April 1968.

———. *Report of the Constitutional Conference, Lancaster House, September–December 1979.* Cmnd. 7802. London: HMSO, 1980.

Government of Zimbabwe. *Estimates of Expenditure.* Harare: Government Printer, annual.

Gray, Richard. *The Two Nations.* London: Oxford University Press, 1960.

Great Britain. House of Commons. *Debates.* London: HMSO.

Gregory, Martin. "Rhodesia: From Lusaka to Lancaster House." *The World Today* 36, no. 1 (January 1980): 11–18.

———. "Zimbabwe 1980: Politicization Through Armed Struggle and Electoral Mobilization." *Journal of Commonwealth and Comparative Politics* 19, no. 1 (March 1981): 63–94.

Grundy, Kenneth. *The Militarization of South African Politics.* Bloomington: Indiana University Press, 1986.

Gurr, Ted Robert. *Why Men Rebel.* Princeton: Princeton University Press, 1970.

Halperin, Morton, Jerry J. Berman, Robert L. Borosage, and Christine M. Marwick. *The Lawless State.* New York: Penguin, 1976.

Hillyard, Paddy. "Law and Order." In *Northern Ireland: Background to the Conflict,* ed. John Darby. Belfast: Blackstaff, 1983.

Hintz, Stephen. "The Political Transformation of Rhodesia, 1958–1965." *African Studies Review* 15, no. 2 (September 1972): 173–83.

Hirsch, Morris. *A Decade of Crisis: Ten Years of Rhodesian Front Rule.* Salisbury: Peter Dearlove, 1973.

Hodder-Williams, Richard. "Conflict in Zimbabwe: The Matabeleland Problem." *Conflict Studies* no. 151 (1983).

Howard, Rhoda. *Human Rights in Commonwealth Africa.* Totowa, N.J.: Rowman and Littlefield, 1986.

[Hunt Committee]. *Report of the Advisory Committee on Police in Northern Ireland.* Cmnd. 535, Lord Hunt, Chair. Belfast: HMSO, October 1969.

Huntington, Samuel. *Political Order in Changing Societies.* New Haven: Yale University Press, 1968.

———. "Will More Countries Become Democratic?" *Political Science Quarterly* 99, no. 2 (Summer 1984): 193–218.

International Commission of Jurists. "Southern Rhodesia: Human Rights and the Constitution." *Bulletin of the International Commission of Jurists* 18 (March 1964).

———. "Zimbabwe." *Review of the International Commission of Jurists* 30 (July 1983): 26–30.

International Institute for Strategic Studies. *The Military Balance, 1986–1987.* London: IISS, 1986.

Kahler, Miles. *Decolonization in Britain and France.* Princeton: Princeton University Press, 1984.

Kasfir, Nelson. *The Shrinking Political Arena.* Berkeley: University of California Press, 1976.

Kelley, Kevin. *The Longest War: Northern Ireland and the IRA.* Westport, Conn.: Lawrence Hill, 1982.

Kelly, Henry. *How Stormont Fell.* Dublin: Gill and Macmillan, 1972.

Kesselman, Mark. "Order or Movement: The Literature of Political Development as Ideology." *World Politics* 26 (October 1973).

[Kilbrandon Inquiry]. *Northern Ireland: Report of an Independent Inquiry,* Lord Kilbrandon, Chair. London: British Irish Association, November 1984.

Kuper, Leo. *The Pity of It All: Polarization of Racial and Ethnic Relations.* Minneapolis: University of Minnesota Press, 1977.

———. "Political Change in White Settler Societies: The Possibility of Peaceful Democratization." In *Pluralism in Africa,* ed. Leo Kuper and M. G. Smith. Berkeley: University of California Press, 1969.

Kuper, Leo, and M. G. Smith, eds. *Pluralism in Africa.* Berkeley: University of California Press, 1969.

Lawyers Committee for Human Rights. *Liberia: A Promise Betrayed.* New York: Lawyers Committee, 1986.

———. *Zimbabwe: Wages of War.* New York: Lawyers Committee, 1986.

Lemon, Anthony. "Electoral Machinery and Voting Patterns in Rhodesia, 1962–1977." *African Affairs* 77 (October 1978): 511–30.

Leys, Colin. *European Politics in Southern Rhodesia.* Oxford: Clarendon Press, 1959.

Leys, Colin, and Cranford Pratt, eds. *A New Deal in Central Africa.* London: Heinemann, 1960.

Liebenow, J. Gus. *Liberia: The Evolution of Privilege.* Ithaca: Cornell University Press, 1969.

———. *Liberia: The Quest for Democracy.* Bloomington: Indiana University Press, 1987.

Lijphart, Arend. *Democracies.* New Haven: Yale University Press, 1984.

———. *Democracy in Plural Societies.* New Haven: Yale University Press, 1977.

———. "Review Article: The Northern Ireland Problem." *British Journal of Political Science* 5, no. 1 (January 1975): 81–106.

Linden, Ian. *The Catholic Church and the Struggle for Zimbabwe.* London: Longman, 1980.

Linz, Juan. *The Breakdown of Democratic Regimes: Crisis, Breakdown, and Reequilibration.* Baltimore: Johns Hopkins University Press, 1978.

———. "Totalitarian and Authoritarian Regimes." In *Handbook of Political Science,* ed. F. Greenstein and N. Polsby. Vol. 3. Reading, Pa.: Addison-Wesley, 1975.

Lofchie, Michael. "The Plural Society of Zanzibar." In *Pluralism in Africa,* ed. L. Kuper and M. Smith. Berkeley: University of California Press, 1969.

———. *Zanzibar: Background to Revolution.* Princeton: Princeton University Press, 1965.

Lustick, Ian. *Arabs in the Jewish State.* Austin: University of Texas Press, 1980.

———. "Stability in Deeply Divided Societies: Consociationalism versus Control." *World Politics* 31, no. 3 (April 1979): 325–44.

———. *State-Building Failure in British Ireland and French Algeria.* Berkeley: Institute of International Studies, 1985.

MacDonald, Michael. *Children of Wrath: Political Violence in Northern Ireland,* New York: Blackwell, 1986.

McGuffin, John. *Internment.* Tralee, Ireland: Anvil, 1973.

McKeown, Michael. "Chronicles: A Register of Northern Ireland's Casualties, 1969–1980." *The Crane Bag* 4, no. 2 (1980–1981): 1–5.

Mandaza, Ibbo, ed. *Zimbabwe: The Political Economy of Transition.* Dakar: CODESRIA, 1986.

Marchetti, Victor, and John D. Marks. *The CIA and the Cult of Intelligence.* New York: Dell, 1974.

Martin, David, and Phyllis Johnson. *The Struggle for Zimbabwe.* London: Faber and Faber, 1981.

Mathews, Anthony. *Freedom, State Security, and the Rule of Law: Dilemmas of Apartheid Society.* Berkeley: University of California Press, 1986.

Maudling, Reginald. *Memoirs.* London: Sidgwick and Jackson, 1978.

Ministry of Information, Posts, and Telecommunications. *A Chronicle of Dissidency in Zimbabwe.* Harare: Government Printer, August 1984.

Mlambo, Eshmael. *Rhodesia: The Struggle for a Birthright.* London: Hurst, 1972.

Moorcraft, Paul L., and Peter McLaughlin. *Chimurenga: The War in Rhodesia.* Marshalltown, South Africa: Sigma and Collins, 1982.

Moxon-Browne, Edward. *Nation, Class, and Creed in Northern Ireland.* Aldershot: Gower, 1983.

Mutambirwa, James. *The Rise of Settler Power in Southern Rhodesia, 1898–1923.* Cranbury, N.J.: Associated University Presses, 1980.

National Council for Civil Liberties. *Report of a Commission of Inquiry Appointed to Examine the Purpose and Effect of the Civil Authorities (Special Powers) Acts (Northern Ireland) 1922 and 1933.* London: NCCL, 1936.

New Ireland Forum. *The Cost of Violence Arising from the Northern Ireland Crisis Since 1969.* Dublin: Government Stationery Office, 1983.

———. *Report.* Dublin: Government Stationery Office, 1984.

Nonet, Philippe, and Philip Selznick. *Law and Society in Transition.* New York: Harper and Row, 1978.

Nordlinger, Eric. *On the Autonomy of the Democratic State.* Cambridge, Mass.: Harvard University Press, 1981.

Northern Ireland Assembly. *Debates.* Belfast: HMSO.

Northern Ireland House of Commons. *Debates.* Belfast: HMSO.

O'Donnell, Guillermo. *Modernization and Bureaucratic Authoritarianism.* 2d ed. Berkeley: Institute of International Studies Press, 1979.

O'Donnell, Guillermo, and Philippe Schmitter. "Tentative Conclusions about Uncertain Democracies." In *Transitions from Authoritarian Rule,* ed. Guillermo O'Donnell, Philippe Schmitter, and Lawrence Whitehead. Baltimore: Johns Hopkins University Press, 1986.

O'Donnell, Guillermo, Philippe Schmitter, and Lawrence Whitehead, eds. *Transitions from Authoritarian Rule.* Baltimore: Johns Hopkins University Press, 1986.

O'Malley, Padraig. *The Uncivil Wars: Ireland Today.* Boston: Houghton Mifflin, 1983.

O'Meara, Patrick. *Rhodesia: Racial Conflict or Coexistence?* Ithaca: Cornell University Press, 1975.

O'Neill, Terence. *The Autobiography of Terence O'Neill.* London: Rupert Hart-Davis, 1972.

Palley, Claire. *The Constitutional History and Law of Southern Rhodesia.* Oxford: Clarendon Press, 1966.

Palmer, Robin. *Land and Racial Domination in Rhodesia.* Berkeley: University of California Press, 1977.

Parliament of Rhodesia [Southern Rhodesia]. Assembly. *Debates.* Salisbury: Government Printer.

Parliament of Zimbabwe. Assembly. *Debates.* Harare: Government Printer.

Prager, Jeffrey. *Building Democracy in Ireland.* Cambridge: Cambridge University Press, 1986.

Rabushka, Alvin, and Kenneth Shepsle. *Politics in Plural Societies.* Columbia: Merrill, 1972.

Ranger, Terence. *Crisis in Southern Rhodesia.* London: Fabian Commonwealth Bureau, 1960.

————. *Peasant Consciousness and Guerrilla War in Zimbabwe.* Berkeley: University of California Press, 1985.

Reid Daly, Ron. *Selous Scouts: Top Secret War.* Alberton, South Africa: Galago, 1982.

Rich, Tony. "Zimbabwe: Only Teething Troubles?" *World Today* 39, no. 12 (December 1983): 500–507.

Rogers, Cyril, and Charles Frantz. *Racial Themes in Southern Rhodesia.* New Haven: Yale University Press, 1962.

Rose, Richard. *Governing Without Consensus: An Irish Perspective.* Boston: Beacon, 1971.

————. *Northern Ireland: A Time of Choice.* London: Macmillan, 1976.

Rossiter, Clinton. *Constitutional Dictatorship: Crisis Government in the Modern Democracies.* New York: Harcourt, Brace and World, 1948.

Rotberg, Robert. *The Rise of Nationalism in Central Africa.* Cambridge, Mass.: Harvard University Press, 1965.

[Scarman Tribunal]. *Violence and Civil Disorders in 1969: Report of a Tribunal of Inquiry.* Cmnd. 566. Belfast: HMSO, 1972.

Schatzberg, Michael, ed. *The Political Economy of Zimbabwe.* New York: Praeger, 1984.

Schutz, Barry, and Douglas Scott. "Patterns of Political Change in Fragment Regimes: Northern Ireland and Rhodesia." In *The Politics of Race,* ed. I. Crewe. London: Croom Helm, 1975.

[Shackleton Report]. *Review of the Prevention of Terrorism (Temporary Provisions) Acts.* Cmnd. 7324, Lord Shackleton, Chair. London: HMSO, August 1978.

Shils, Edward. "Opposition in the New States of Asia and Africa." In *Center and Periphery: Essay in Macrosociology.* Chicago: University of Chicago Press, 1975.

Shipler, David. *Arab and Jew.* New York: Penguin, 1986.

Simmel, Georg. *Conflict and the Web of Group-Affiliations.* New York: Free Press, 1955.

Sithole, Masipula. "Zimbabwe: In Search of a Stable Democracy." In *Democracy in Developing Countries,* vol. 2, *Africa,* ed. Larry Diamond, Juan Linz, and Seymour Martin Lipset. Boulder, Colo.: Lynne, Rienner, 1988.

Skocpol, Theda. *States and Social Revolutions.* Cambridge: Cambridge University Press, 1979.

Smooha, Sammy. "Control of Minorities in Israel and Northern Ireland." *Comparative Studies in Society and History* 22, no. 2 (April 1980): 256–344.

————. *Israel: Pluralism and Conflict.* Berkeley: University of California Press, 1978.

Soames, Lord. "From Rhodesia to Zimbabwe." *International Affairs* 56, no. 3 (Summer 1980): 405–19.

Standing Advisory Commission on Human Rights. *Annual Report for 1984–1985.* Belfast: HMSO, 1985.

Stepan, Alfred. *Rethinking Military Politics: Brazil and the Southern Cone.* Princeton: Princeton University Press, 1988.

Stoneman, Colin, and Lionel Cliffe. *Zimbabwe: Politics, Economics, and Society.* London: Pinter, 1988.

Sunday Times Insight Team. *Northern Ireland: A Report on the Conflict.* New York: Vintage, 1972.

Tapia-Valdés, J. A. "A Typology of National Security Policies." *Yale Journal of World Public Order* 9, no. 1 (Fall 1982): 10–39.

Taylor, C., and D. Jodice, eds. *World Handbook of Political and Social Indicators.* New Haven: Yale University Press, 1983.

Tilly, Charles. *From Mobilization to Revolution.* Reading, Pa.: Addison-Wesley, 1978.

Tomlinson, Mike. "Reforming Repression." In *Northern Ireland; Between Civil Rights and Civil War,* Liam O'Dowd, Bill Rolston, and Mike Tomlinson. London: CSE Books, 1981.

van den Berghe, Pierre. *Race and Racism.* New York: Wiley, 1967.

van Onselen, Charles. *Chibaro: African Mine Labour in Southern Rhodesia, 1900–1933.* London: Pluto Press, 1976.

Walsh, Dermot. *The Use and Abuse of Emergency Legislation in Northern Ireland.* London: Cobden Trust, 1983.

Weinrich, A. K. H. *Black and White Elites in Rural Rhodesia.* Manchester: Manchester University Press, 1973.

———. "Strategic Resettlement in Rhodesia." *Journal of Southern African Studies* 3, no. 2 (April 1977): 207–29.

Weitzer, Ronald. "Contested Order: The Struggle over British Security Policy in Northern Ireland." *Comparative Politics* 19, no. 3 (April 1987): 281–98.

———. "Continuities in the Politics of State Security in Zimbabwe." In *The Political Economy of Zimbabwe,* ed. Michael Schatzberg. New York: Praeger, 1984.

———. "In Search of Regime Security: Zimbabwe since Independence." *Journal of Modern African Studies* 22, no. 4 (December 1984): 529–57.

———. "Policing a Divided Society: Obstacles to Normalization in Northern Ireland." *Social Problems* 33, no. 1 (October 1985): 41–55.

———. "Policing Northern Ireland Today." *Political Quarterly* 58, no. 1 (January 1987): 88–96.

Wilkinson, Anthony R. "The Impact of the War." *Journal of Commonwealth and Comparative Politics* 18, no. 1 (March 1980): 110–23.

Wilson, Harold. *The Labour Government: 1964–1970.* London: Weidenfeld and Nicolson, and Michael Joseph, 1971.

Winckler, Edwin. "Institutionalization and Participation on Taiwan: From Hard to Soft Authoritarianism." *China Quarterly,* no. 99 (September 1984): 481–99.

Zimbabwe African National Union. "Central Committee Report." Presented by ZANU President Robert Mugabe to the party's Second Congress, 8 August 1984.

Zolberg, Aristide. *Creating Political Order: The Party-States of West Africa.* Chicago: Rand McNally, 1966.

SELECTED PERIODICALS

African Times, Salisbury, Rhodesia.
Belfast Telegraph, Belfast, Northern Ireland.
Bulawayo Chronicle, Bulawayo, Zimbabwe.
Financial Gazette, Harare, Zimbabwe.
The Guardian, London and Manchester.
The Herald, Harare.
Irish News, Belfast.
Irish Times, Dublin.
MOTO, Gweru, Zimbabwe.
Newsletter, Belfast.
The Observer, London.
Rhodesia Herald, Salisbury.
Sunday Mail, Harare.
Sunday Times, London.
The Times, London.

Index

Compositor:	Point West, Inc.
Text:	10/13 Sabon
Display:	Sabon
Printer:	Edwards Brothers, Inc.
Binder:	Edwards Brothers, Inc.